*The Gee Years, 1990–1997*

# The Gee Years, 1990–1997

MALCOLM S. BAROWAY

The Ohio State University Press
Columbus

Copyright © 2002 by The Ohio State University.
All rights reserved.

Paper (ISBN: 978-0-8142-5704-3)

Text design by Sans Serif Inc.
Type set in Minion by Sans Serif Inc.

This book is dedicated to Dr. Israel Baroway (1899–1975), my father, Professor of English at Queens College in the City of New York, a member of the original faculty at its opening in 1939; a scholar of John Milton and the Bible as Literature, teaching 15 hours a week until his retirement in 1965.

# Contents

*Foreword* ix

*Prologue* xi

1 The Search  1
2 Vernal, Utah  8
3 A Lesson in Interviewing  14
4 The Consultants' Review  19
5 Cleaning Up the University Area  28
6 The Hutchinson Years  37
7 War and the Home Front  57
8 Elizabeth  62
9 Rebekah's Fish Bowl  69
10 Flagship Revisited  74
11 Gee and the Governor  82
12 The Huber Years  90
13 Diversity and Divisiveness  106
14 Sisson Begins  118
15 Firestone  124
16 Managing the Future  131
17 "Affirm Thy Friendship"  140
18 Athletics as Pressure Cooker  146
19 More Gee and the Governor  162
20 The Great Communicator  166
21 More on Diversity  176
22 Constance  187
23 Five-Year Evaluations  194
24 Short Subjects  199
25 The Dave and Andy Show  212
26 California  229
27 The NRC  235
28 Health Care  241
29 Research and Research Parks  252
30 The High Street Legacy  266
31 Public Records  271
32 Trustee Retreat 1996  276
33 More Short Subjects  283
34 The Philanthropists  301
35 Crises and Condolences  314
36 Gordon for Governor  318
37 Les Wexner  325
38 Brown  331
39 Over and Out  340

*Appendix*  351
*Chronologies*  358
*About the Author*  395
*Index*  397

# Foreword

> Until the lions have historians, tales of hunting will always glorify the hunter.
> —An African proverb

Unlike others who have written the histories of Ohio State presidencies, I worked for the president. I was Ohio State's chief public relations officer, my title, executive director of University Communications. Gordon Gee believed his communications person should know what's going on. Not all presidents do. This gave me a singular base from which to begin this book, and a cast of characters to approach. My sincere thanks go to the many people quoted or referenced in *The Gee Years* who gave me their time, their memories, and their opinions.

As a boss, Gordon Gee was demanding—but no more so than he was of himself. He laid out the ground rules the first time we met. I had, he told me, six months to prove myself. I must have succeeded, for I was still here when he left. As a boss, when not dealing with tragedy, he was also always light of heart and made working hard on his behalf a privilege as often as a job. As a leader, with a new order of Ohio State trustee, he shared a vision for his university. To help close the gap between reach and grasp is an adventure. This was such a time at Ohio State.

This is the twelfth volume of history of The Ohio State University and, perhaps, the last to benefit from the printed archival document. Gordon Gee and his staff kept virtually and, perhaps, literally every document that entered or left the President's Office. Thanks to Raimund Goerler, University Archivist, and Bertha Ihnat, his associate, I had the opportunity to review them all. But toward the end, came e-mail. Who knows what hard copy the future will bring?

To Barbie Tootle, Gordon Gee's special assistant, now retired, I owe a huge debt of gratitude for the day-by-day, often hour-by-hour file she maintained of agendas, briefings, and reports. To George Paulson, thank you for writing *The Ohio State University College of Medicine*, used liberally in the health care sections. To Mary Fisher and, later, Michelle Compston in President Kirwan's Office, this book could not have been done without their assistance. Nor could it have been completed without the good work of Maureen Sharkey and Lucy Gandert in the Office of the Board of Trustees.

My thanks to my review readers, official and otherwise, particularly Seymour Raiz, Joan Huber, Dick Sisson, Steve Snapp, Manuel Tzagournis, Jerry May, Herb Asher, Dick Stoddard, Barbie Tootle, Thomas Sawyer, "Chip" Elam, and John Rothney. Professor Rothney, who teaches historians how to write history, gave me a copy of Edward Hallett Carr's *What Is History?* which begins with this quote: "I often thought it odd that [history] should be dull, for a great deal of it must be invention." To my knowledge, nothing here is invention and little, I hope, is dull.

Finally, my appreciation to Brit Kirwan and Ginny Trethewey for the opportunity to find a few lions, glorify the hunters, and write this book; to the Johns Hopkins Writing Seminars for teaching me that fine writing sings; and to Dee, my wife and number one fan.

Malcolm S. Baroway

# Prologue

When Ohio State President Edward H. Jennings called his staff into his office on December 1, 1989 to tell them he would be resigning, most were flabbergasted. The man had survived two media disasters that would have destroyed a weaker leader. The first had been the firing in November 1987 of "Old 9 and 3," Earle Bruce, Ohio State's embattled, and sometimes underappreciated, football coach who had proceeded to circle the wagons, inspire his underdog team to victory over the hated Michigan Wolverines, sue both Ohio State and Jennings for $7.4 million, and emerge a hero to any David who had ever dreamed of settling with Goliath behind closed doors.

The second had been a European vacation trip, scheduled innocently enough when both he and the woman who soon would become his wife thought their individual divorces would be safely behind them. Only his was not. Jennings's divorce proceeding had been extended, the trip was not canceled, and, in a less sophisticated time than now, the story fed the jackals for days.

In both cases, a wellspring of goodwill from the faculty and his friends had risen to serve Jennings well. His presidency, to many, had been inspirational, building an institutional pride that had not been there and opening the way for selective admissions and an undergraduate student body that since has been better credentialed every year. Moreover, his rugged persona had cultivated a sense of security. A baseball catcher in high school, he still looked as if he could block the plate to transgressors figurative and literal, and homer with the bases loaded whenever needed.

In the words of the Faculty Council of the University Senate, which had come to Jennings's aid after the Earle Bruce firing, he had done "a superb job ... in furthering and promoting the educational, research, and service missions of Ohio State." He also had raised some $460 million in private money in one of the largest fund-raising campaigns in the history of higher education; had weathered both aforementioned media storms; and, it seemed, continued to draw sustenance from administrative responsibility and the thrill of decision making.

That was why it was such a great surprise to many people who knew him

## PROLOGUE

when Ed Jennings told his staff he would be returning to the full-time faculty, and that the press conference to announce it would be later that day. Jennings would stay on as president until August 31, presiding a day earlier at summer commencement as his final public duty. On September 1, 1990, the E. Gordon Gee administration would begin.

# 1

# *The Search*

If Ed Jennings personified the image of a leader, Gordon Gee not only did not; he made a shtick out of it. "When I get up in the morning," he would say, "I look in the mirror and I'm so disappointed." Then came the kicker. "And so is my wife." And the audience, every audience, loved it.

If Ed Jennings shunned the press after his Goliath and Travelgate episodes, Gordon Gee courted it. He had a remarkable ability to know what the press wanted and provide it. "All he had to do," *Denver Post* editor Gil Spencer wrote the day Gee made his Ohio State announcement, "is get out of bed . . . and media would follow him around like a puppy dog." In Columbus, as it turned out, Gordon did not even have to prop up his pillow.

E. Gordon Gee became the eleventh president of The Ohio State University through a closely held search process. One week after the Jennings announcement, the operation already was under way. It ended on June 26, 1990, at a special meeting of the Board of Trustees in which this forty-six-year-old lawyer with a doctorate in higher education, who had been president of two other universities, and who had spent one year clerking at the U.S. Supreme Court during Watergate and three years as a Mormon missionary in Europe, accepted the appointment.

A few minutes earlier, an Ohio State King Air plane with the Gee family aboard—Gordon, his wife, Elizabeth, and his daughter, Rebekah—had been met at the university's Don Scott Field, where, right off the bat, the new Ohio State president demonstrated an impressive talent. As *Columbus Dispatch* fashion reporter Marshall Hood reported, "in front of God, OSU trustees and the Columbus news media," the new biggest Buckeye accomplished what "64 percent of the American male population cannot . . . or won't even attempt." He

# Chapter 1

tied his own bow tie, and without even looking! Clearly, the new president would make news on more than the education page.

So who was this Gordon Gee, selected to replace the well-liked and respected Ed Jennings? *Dispatch* editor Bob Smith sent higher education writer Tim Doulin to Colorado, where he reported on the uncanny popularity Gee had achieved as president of the University of Colorado. The Ohio State announcement, Doulin wrote, had "sent shock waves through the . . . Rockies, from the Boulder Foothills to Denver and beyond." In Denver, meanwhile, Spencer reminded his *Post* readers that Colorado "had never seen anyone like Gordon Gee before (and) who has?"

Doulin's article, meanwhile, accurately painted a picture of a man to whom both popularity and success had come early. In high school (Uintah High, Vernal, Utah, population 3500), Gee had played drums in the marching band, been a National Merit Scholar, the president of his senior class, and an Eagle Scout. "If that wasn't enough," Doulin added, he "never missed a day at school." If he had known the story, Doulin might have added that, to earn his ultimate merit badge, Gee, never an athlete, had taught himself to swim in the one pool in town—after school, outdoors, and at a motel.

The new president's first name (the E) was Elwood, after his late father, Elwood A. "Gus" Gee. Gordon Gee was married and had one daughter. He was a Mormon and, as such, did not consume alcoholic beverages. But—thank goodness for the future of fund-raising at Ohio State—when entertaining university guests, he served alcohol in his home.

Were the people of Colorado shocked and surprised by Gee's decision? Shocked, undoubtedly. Through five summer tours that had reached virtually every high plains city and mountain town, his was the smile that had greeted most of Colorado, if not personally, at least in the local paper, on the local radio station, or on Denver TV news. In Paonia and Montrose, in Cortez and Durango, Gordon Gee had become synonymous with higher education and comfortable as an old shoe. Gee, in fact, had been so popular that, he would acknowledge later, an unpublished poll projected he could have run for governor and won—on either ticket.

His departure, the *Post*'s Spencer wrote, was "in every sense a tragedy for Colorado."

Were the people who knew him as shocked and surprised as the public? Perhaps even more so. Ohio State had conducted its search so discreetly, none of the names of its fifteen finalists had leaked to the press. But Spencer suggested that Coloradoans might not have been surprised had they taken closer notice of events, when he reprinted Gee's warning that passage of a pending ballot initiative to preclude all tax increases "would destroy Colorado, including the university." Regent chairman Roy Shore also told Doulin he knew Gee was the "pick of the litter" in any presidential search.

How "the pick of the litter" had come to accept the Ohio State presidency was as much his wife's and his daughter's decision as his—and a saga in itself.

## E. Gordon Gee

His favorite book was the Bible. His favorite food was popcorn. His favorite animal was the dog—although small ones. His favorite color was blue; favorite car, "a convertible"; favorite holiday, Christmas; favorite month, October; favorite performer, Luciano Pavarotti; and favorite newspaper, *The New York Times*.

At birth, on February 2, 1944, Gordon Gee had weighed in at 5 pounds, 2 ounces and was 21 inches long. He had one older sister and no brothers. As a child, he found it "easy to grow up without television" and "hard to grow up without access to great music and art." In high school, his favorite class had been history, "learning about both famous and not so famous people." He had thought he would become a physician but changed his mind in college. His first role model was his father, Gus, who taught him about living; his second was his wife, Elizabeth, who taught him to maximize life in the face of death. His success had been achieved, he wrote, through "hard work and luck"; its major lesson had been "to value people much more." His advice to youngsters was his own credo: "Be committed and be yourself."

These seemingly random snippets of information are answers to questions sent to Ohio State University President Gordon Gee by a fourth grader and a fifth grader in 1992, two years after his OSU tenure began. That he answered the students' questionnaires himself—in longhand—exemplified one key to his immense popularity in Colorado and what apparently had set him apart from the competition in his interviews for the Ohio State presidency. Except for the quacks, no one who wrote or called him was ever unimportant. Everyone was answered. By telephone, letter, or the developing medium of e-mail, he would make people feel that they were appreciated, if not friends. In person, as David Adams of the *Akron Beacon Journal* would write on November 4, 1990, he would "share his warm Irish smile generously and genuinely . . . his steely blue eyes (making) . . . strong contact . . . his looks . . . disarming, his manner engaging and his wit dry."

His answers to the children's questions also conveyed the seemingly

## Chapter 1

At a grade school, 1990: They're never too young to be recruited.

paradoxical tastes that would help him relate to people of all ages and experiences. Search committee staffer John W. "Chip" Elam—the one person who talked to all fifteen presidential finalists—would say later that Gee was "by far the most interesting," though most were sitting presidents and many were considered charismatic.

Here was a man who could be sophisticated and unsophisticated at the same time, neither being a put-on. Though he had dined at the finest restaurants and tables throughout the world, his favorite "foods" were the tastes of childhood: popcorn, closely followed by soft pretzels, Big Macs, and M & Ms. But here also was a man who had the self-control to maintain the weight he grew up with, who, when at dinner with donors, alumni, faculty, or students, demonstrated time and again that his desire to greet each guest personally far exceeded his need to eat.

That Gee did not feel deprived growing up in a television era with no television at all, this before cable could reach beyond the Wasatch Mountains to the desert town of Vernal, was because he was fascinated by literature and energized by people and personal accomplishment. Here was a man who would write an inquiring librarian that his favorite childhood book had been *The Secret Garden* by Frances Hodgson Burnett, "the adventure of finding a secret place and sharing it . . . a good story about how to be a friend and how to make friends" (letter to Anne DiSabato, February 28, 1992).

Here had been a young man who, captivated by what he read and read about, understood the dimensions of what Vernal, Utah, could not provide. He had set out to enculturate himself—first at college in Provo, then as a law and graduate student in Manhattan, as a legal clerk in the Bronx, as a judicial fellow in Warren Burger's Supreme Court in Washington. His favorite performer by 1992 was an acclaimed operatic tenor with whom he could discuss arias, and did, and his favorite newspaper was now only one of nine clipped for him each morning.

The person who would supervise the clipping process, and many other daily mechanics of Gee's Ohio State presidency, was to be the thirty-two-year-old Ohio State lawyer-administrator who had staffed the search, Chip Elam. Elam had been plucked by search committee chair Jack Kessler from the office of Madison Scott, vice president for Personnel Services and secretary of the Board of Trustees. Elam had no role in the decision of who would be president and would offer no opinion to the committee members as he prepped the candidates for their interviews, but he would say later that he would have been "greatly disappointed" had Gee not been selected. "He was the right fit for Ohio State."

The firm hired to find the right fit and to supervise the screening of candidates was Heidrick & Struggles; its executive for this search, William Bowen. Bowen himself solicited Gee. The trustees, Kessler recalled, had directed the search committee to come in with two finalists for the full board to interview. The two were Gee and Steve Sample, president of the State University of New York at Buffalo, who later would become president of the University of Southern California. "Blessed with a fabulous search committee," said Kessler later, "to reach that point, the process had played out flawlessly."

## *The Committee*

On that committee were four trustees, Kessler, Shirley Dunlap Bowser, Hamilton "Joel" Teaford, and Alex Shumate; five faculty members, Bunny Clark from Physics, Nathan Fechheimer from Dairy Science, Judith Koroscik from Arts, William Moore, Jr., from Education, and Nancy Rudd from Family Resource and Management; two nonteaching staff, Arts and Sciences' Mona Dove and the Hospitals' Joan Patton; Dean William Kern of Mathematical and Physical Sciences; Alumni Association President Dan Heinlen; and students David Straub and Catita Williams. "Our job," said Kessler, "was to identify the best

## Chapter 1

person. Our commitment to the trustees was that we would bring them two candidates.... They were insistent we keep the names confidential, and I was determined there be no leaks."

There weren't. Preventing the leaks is half the battle in consummating a public university presidential search, where an open-records law can be damaging as a wrecking ball. To help ensure the confidentiality the trustees demanded, Kessler had the committee do all its local work in a room staffed by Heidrick & Struggles at the university-owned Ramada Inn, and west of town at Darby Dan Farms, owned by former trustee Dan Galbreath. Applications were read at the Ramada; initial interviews took place at Darby Dan.

The system was so secure that resumes of applicants were given to all committee members, including trustees, only by a Heidrick & Struggles employee, and could not be taken out of the room at the Ramada. This system was refined even further by Elam and his colleague David Sweasey in the later search for an athletic director, when individually coded materials were made for each committee member so errant copies could be tracked to any culprit. There were, of course, no errant copies.

In the penultimate round, the committee divided into three subcommittees, each chaired by a trustee—Shumate, in his first year; Teaford, in his second; and Bowser, her last. Each group interviewed five semifinalists in a different location—the Gainey Ranch outside Phoenix, the Chicago Ritz Carlton, and the Chicago Fairmont. David Schooler, Ohio State's travel agent, Elam would recall, was sworn to secrecy.

The trustees' concern about confidentiality was legitimate. While provosts, who are so often presidents-in-waiting, might choose to leverage leaks for a higher salary where they were, no sitting president desired to see his or her name in print as a candidate elsewhere. Most if not all sitting presidents, they knew, would pull out if exposed.

The *Cleveland Plain Dealer* and Ohio State *Lantern* each sought a list of candidates through Ohio's Freedom of Information Act, but Kessler refused to respond. The last such committee had recruited Ed Jennings from the University of Wyoming with no one smoked out, and Kessler was determined to be equally successful. "We outlasted the challenges," he said later with understandable pride.

He would recall a conversation with a *Dispatch* reporter toward the end of the search. "I'm only calling you out of courtesy," he remembered being told. "I'm not asking for confirmation. But we've got it. We know who you're going to recommend. We're running with it tomorrow and we've absolutely got it confirmed." Kessler's heart had sunk and he nearly forgot to ask who the candidate was.

"I finally gathered up my wits because I was so startled and I said, 'Well, who is it?' They had the wrong name."

The name was Graham Spanier—soon to become president of Penn State. Kessler called the *Dispatch* management back and told them they definitely had the wrong name. The next day's *Dispatch* ran a story only suggesting Spanier as a prospect.

Had the story been about Gee, he would have pulled out immediately, finalist or not. At his pre-interview with Elam, Gee had said that should his candidacy become public prematurely, he would thank Ohio State for its interest and stay at Colorado. In an interview more than ten years later, he would reiterate the value of such confidentiality. "If the search had not been carried on in the confidential fashion it was, I would not have come. If my name had been leaked to the press, if I had been out there in the public setting, given my relationship to Colorado, I simply would have withdrawn."

And Ohio State would have had a different president.

# 2

# *Vernal, Utah*

Gordon Gee, when reflecting upon his youth, said, "If asked would I want to move back to Vernal, the answer would be 'no.' If asked would I have wanted to grow up in Vernal, the answer is 'yes' because of the community . . . and an American value system I greatly appreciate."

Vernal, Utah, is the largest city on Highway 40 between Salt Lake City and Denver, a distance of about 700 miles. As Gordon Gee remembered it, it was "surrounded by scenery and dominated by the Mormon culture."

Gordon Gee's father, Gus, his mother, Vera, his whole family were devoted Mormons. Gus and Vera had met at Brigham Young University and married in the Salt Lake City Temple on June 7, 1933. Gus's mother's family, the Showalters, were prominent; his grandfather was one of the wealthiest men in the area. Each of the Showalter children or their spouses ran a part of the family business—automobiles, ranching, and oil. Gus and Vera were in oil. Gus, who had been a teacher, became a distributor and sat on a number of company boards. Vera received her master's degree in special education and taught classes in that field as well as third grade. Gus and Vera had two children, daughter Cherie and, nine years later, Gordon.

In the early days of talking movies, a young Mickey Rooney starred in films that idealized small-town family life where he, witty young Andy Hardy, would apply his creativity, charm, and organizational skills to the problem of the day and, by gosh, solve it and then some! And sometimes with a parade! That idyllic life, minus parades—though Gordon played bass drum in the high school marching band—was Gordon Gee's real childhood.

Vernal sure was a great place to raise children! As a teenager, there were sock hops and record hops. "I love to dance. I love to dance to this day." They would be held in one of the church gyms. "I'd go over there and the girls would show

# VERNAL, UTAH

Gordon resurrects the Sock Hop, revisiting his youth, 1991.

up and the boys would show up and then we'd just dance." And there was rock and roll and Elvis. "I can remember my cousin describing in graphic detail Elvis Presley and how awful it was, swiveling his hips." And dating. "Sort of community dating, not individual dating. Sometimes we would pair up and go off.... It was a wonderful life."

"We were a relatively wealthy family in the community. My mother and father were enormously supportive of me, had high expectations of my performance and, in turn, were always there for me, always my greatest cheerleaders." By "always," he meant just that. "I was one of the few people whose parents came to all my events—the Junior Prom, everything! If you can imagine! The kids today would just be totally embarrassed. I thought it was wonderful to have my parents come. They would come and be there and take great joy out of it."

Undoubtedly, Gus and Vera would take great joy out of Gordon's academic successes, as well, for he was a young man as bright as he was popular—who not only bridged the gap that often exists between academic excellence and social popularity, but was able to close it completely.

"Real smart, always a good student, and the people always liked him," his mother would recall in a *Cleveland Plain Dealer* story in 1996 (December 22).

CHAPTER 2

"They wanted to put him a grade ahead in first grade, but we wouldn't let them. And he was always at the top of his class no matter where he was."

When he graduated from high school, Gordon was definitely at the top of his game. He was student body president, an Eagle Scout, National Merit Scholar, and class valedictorian. Along the way, he had been class president a number of times and, whether chairing a school committee or organizing a church youth event, had found that people looked to him to organize. "I was always well organized and could get the job done."

He also was happy to be in charge. And he discovered that people enjoyed having him in charge! He learned early that, if he were not a born leader, he certainly was a natural. No one would outwork him or outthink him. He could inspire loyalty, motivate others, and lead by example. Nothing would change all through the career that led him to the eleventh presidency of Ohio State.

Years later, he would acknowledge that he took with him from the small town of Vernal "an established value system prevalent in almost everything I am today." But, in her moving diary, published as *The Light Around the Dark* by the National League for Nursing Press, Elizabeth would note that, in the state tours Gordon loved to make, the small towns of Colorado would take him back to this essence.

"I can tell," she wrote, "by the sound of his voice when he phones me late at night that he likes to travel to small towns similar to the one where he was born and where there is the chance to visit down-to-earth, practical folk."

He would find plenty of small towns and down-to-earth practical folk in Ohio.

## *Preparing for a Presidency*

"The Ohio State University seeks a President who can lead it toward its goal of enhancing its position as a pre-eminent public university. . . . The president must be able to provide innovative and creative leadership in the development and implementation of a strategic plan for the university and to communicate this persuasively to the university community, government leaders, and the people of Ohio and the nation.

"The president . . . must hold an earned doctorate or its equivalent, be respected by the academic community as a nationally recognized leader, and have an outstanding record of scholarly achievement. The successful candidate must be cognizant of and sensitive to the aspirations and interests of all members of a multicultural university community and be dedicated to, and preferably have a record of achievement in an effective program for affirmative action.

"The president must be able to delegate responsibility and to work effectively in a strong vital system of shared government. She or he should foster an environment in which students, scholars, staff, and administrators of distinction can be attracted to the university. In addition, the president must be able to establish and promote favorable relationships with other constituencies including alumni, business, industry, and government. Above all, the president must exhibit high standards of intellectual, personal, and professional integrity.... In sum, the university will select a decisive and vigorous individual to lead The Ohio State University into the era of global interdependence."

This was the job description Gordon Gee and the other applicants read from the resolution adopted on February 2, 1990, by The Ohio State University Board of Trustees. For a man who, as a youth, "had never seen a non-Mormon or a Democrat," Gordon Gee had come a long way experientially to satisfy some of those credentials.

After Uintah High School, from which his mother also graduated, he had gone on to the University of Utah, where he graduated with honors in 1968 as a history major. There he had met Elizabeth, also a history major and in the same class. She was very bright, very beautiful, and very engaged to be married.

"I saw her at a fraternity-sorority party... a wonderful looking woman. I still remember her standing by a fireplace talking to a number of people. I thought, now there is a very striking person I would like to get to know. So I found out who she was. I was introduced to her by a mutual friend, then I started asking her out. Yes, I took her away from somebody else. And, yes, I take great pride in that."

They dated during their senior year at Utah and married on August 26, 1968, two weeks before leaving Salt Lake for New York and their basic training in urbanity. As Elizabeth Gee was to write in *The Light Around the Dark*, before moving to New York, "we were both naive—not only about education, but the social, political, and cultural issues as well. Everyone we met in New York City seemed articulate, informed, and urbane."

As newlyweds, they lived in a damp and cramped basement apartment in Yonkers sharing a white Volkswagen Beetle that sometimes had to be rolled out of the driveway until it pointed down a steep street. With Gordon on his way to Columbia and Elizabeth to her job as registrar of the American Express Language School, "Gordon would get a good push and jump in next to me while I tried to pop the clutch. Finally, it would sputter into motion and we

CHAPTER 2

would begin our drive through the back roads in Yonkers to avoid the first 50 cents toll on the Sawmill River Parkway."

When Gordon was not studying and Elizabeth was not working, they might find time to explore the shops and museums and, when they could afford it, taste-test the cornucopia of Manhattan's ethnic restaurants—Elizabeth favored fondue. Occasionally they would get together with another small-town boy, young Rob Walton of Bentonville, Arkansas, and would become good friends. Rob had been working in his dad's store, Walton's market, now called Wal-Mart.

Meanwhile, Gordon had discovered it was possible at Columbia to create a program that blended law and higher education and that the university would grant the J.D. degree in three years and the Ed.D. in four. "I did so with the expectation I probably did not want to practice law per se, but would go into academe and possibly academic administration. I was, and remain, a great fan of law degrees because they are renaissance degrees with which one can do almost anything, including practicing law." And so he did.

By the time he and Elizabeth left New York, Gordon had earned both the law degree and the education doctorate, specializing in legal and administrative problems in institutions of higher education, and had been both a legal intern in the Bronx County District Attorney's Office and a special assistant to the Honorable Herbert Brownell, chairman of the Committee on Criminal Justice of the Bar of the City of New York. He also had coordinated a study by the Council on Legal Education, *The Costs and Resources of Legal Education,* while finishing the doctorate and spent a year clerking under Chief Judge David T. Lewis of the United States 10th Circuit Court of Appeals.

And so in 1973, Dr. E. Gordon Gee, Esquire, and his wife Elizabeth—who later would receive her own doctorate and become a scholar of medical ethics—returned to Salt Lake City. He had accepted the post of assistant dean for administration at the University of Utah College of Law, where he would manage admissions, student recruitment, the budget, continuing legal education, and state bar relations.

A year later—the year of the Watergate tapes—they were back on the East Coast, this time learning Washington and living two doors from Watergate figure and Nixon lawyer John Dean in suburban Virginia. Gordon had been named a judicial fellow and staff assistant to the United States Supreme Court. He would work directly for and with Chief Justice Warren Burger on administrative and legal problems confronting the Court and the federal judiciary.

In negotiating with members of Congress, as well as the judiciary and the bar, he began to hone his skills in the essential art of lobbying. It was not so hard for a man who, Elizabeth would write later, is "as invigorated by public contact as I am by geese in a storm."

They would return to Utah again after only one year in Washington, now to the J. Reuben Clark Law School at Brigham Young University in Provo. There, Gordon would be both a tenured associate professor and assistant dean. By 1976, he had been promoted to associate dean, sharpening his solicitation techniques by heading alumni relations and fund-raising. For the first time Elizabeth would see in practice that her husband's "idea of a good time ... is a reception for four hundred people." There he also would forsake long ties forever and adopt what would become his sartorial signature, the bow tie.

Two years later, he would be promoted to full professor, and, a year after that, in 1979, the West Virginia University law school in Morgantown would hire him as dean. Meanwhile, as *Ohio Lawyer* noted in its January/February 1991 issue, during his research he had been writing extensively about running a university, "as well as advising others on how to do it successfully. Finally, someone challenged him to practice what he had been teaching." In November 1981, he became president of the University of West Virginia, where he would stay four and a half years before becoming president of the University of Colorado on July 1, 1985.

By this time, Gordon and Elizabeth Gee were an academic team. Elizabeth had completed her bachelor's degree while in Utah with Gordon, a master's degree in American history at Brigham Young while he was there, and a doctorate in interdisciplinary studies and higher education administration at West Virginia. At Colorado, she became a faculty member in the School of Nursing, special assistant to the president of the University of Colorado Foundation, and senior research associate in health, ethics, and policy in the Department of Women's Studies.

One of her goals at Ohio State, she later told the Ohio State *Lantern* (March 15, 1991), would be to "do something to make the institution more conscious" of women's issues. "I'm very concerned about women and the handicaps they endure in society." It was therefore symbolic, but only coincidental, that Gordon Gee's preliminary interview for the job of president of Ohio State would take place on Mother's Day.

# 3

# *A Lesson in Interviewing*

"We tried to get balance. We tried to get minorities. We tried to get women. We had trouble getting women. We couldn't find any women" who were truly qualified, Jack Kessler recalled. There were only two women among the fifteen semifinalists and none among the final five—all but one were sitting presidents of large universities who had dealt with the classic trouble spots, football teams and medical schools. The woman they did find was Elizabeth Gee, who had joined Gordon both on the interview trip to Chicago and the final visit to Columbus.

Chip Elam and Kessler believed that Elizabeth's pleasure at what she found in Columbus was the key to her husband's acceptance of the offer. Kessler credited his daughter, Jane, who had shown Elizabeth the Columbus School for Girls, where Rebekah would go, and suggested how wonderful it would be if the university could find a new presidential residence in the same neighborhood. Elam said the pressure Kessler put on Gordon to make a decision that weekend made it happen. Les Wexner, then only in his second year as a trustee, knows that but for a behind-the-scenes agreement he made with Gee in private at Gordon's instigation, they would have been choosing another candidate the next day.

## *Behind the Scenes*

Gee already knew a great deal about Les Wexner. As founder of the Limited and CEO of it, its derivatives, and its acquisitions, "he was considered to be one of the most powerful merchants in the country. He had built a remarkable retail chain in a very short period and had made some very, very savvy acquisitions. He was viewed as a very smart and capable man."

Gee did not know when he asked to speak privately to Wexner at the final interview that Wexner had been considering leaving the Board. In leading one of retail's most complex organizations, which included Victoria's Secret, Bath and Body Works, and Abercrombie and Fitch, Wexner was used to thinking out of the box. Expecting his appointment by Governor Richard Celeste to involve significant stewardship over perhaps the nation's most complex university, he had found instead a Board, too often for his disposition, rubber stamping the administration.

He felt he was wasting his time at monthly meetings in which little advice was requested and the trustees' hardest decision might be *should they have dinner at the Jai alai (restaurant) or eat on campus, and should they have steak with red wine?* But he would wait to see what the next presidency would bring.

What Gee asked Wexner in private at the Wexner home was, if the presidency were offered, would Wexner agree to complete the nearly eight years left on his nine-year term? This was the first time Wexner and Gee had met. Wexner had been on the trustee subcommittee that had interviewed the other finalist. Impressed by Gee and stimulated by the question, Wexner said he would, and then turned the tables. "I said 'Turnabout is fair play and I need your assurance that you will stay as long as I am on the Board.'" And Gee responded, "If that's the case, then that's fine. But if you had answered otherwise, I would have withdrawn today." The deal would be consummated as a private understanding, and both would return to the living room to continue the give-and-take of the presidential interview.

That agreement not only would open the door wide to Gee's acceptance of the offer to come, but also would influence the length of time he would stay on as president of Ohio State. In time, Wexner would be the impetus to change the character of the Board of Trustees into a policymaking body that would become a model for emulation, and Gee would decline a number of offers to become president elsewhere.

## *Kessler*

Jack Kessler was one of the best-known and well-liked power brokers in Columbus. He was a tremendously active volunteer and civic leader, a major figure in the university's just completed $460 million capital campaign, on its foundation board, an Ohio State trustee, and now chair of the presidential search committee. Suspected at first by some of the committee's faculty members as being too busy, too smooth, or both, he had proved masterful at running the search—beginning with his selection of Elam, highlighted by his control of the information and the interview arrangements and, finally, the manner in which he pressured a Gee commitment.

The trustees had first met that day at the Wexner home, interviewing Gordon and Elizabeth there. By evening, Kessler was confident the top candidate was Gee. Dinner with Gee and his family was scheduled with the Kesslers that night. Would Gee accept if formally offered? "It was set up that we would have dinner together at my house on Park Drive—Gordon, Elizabeth, my wife Charlotte, my daughter Jane, and me." Over dinner, pending the June 26 trustee vote, Kessler said he believed Gee was the top candidate, and he would like to know the president's interest before the Gees went home.

"Jack was very clever and a very good negotiator," Elam remembered. "He had picked up that Gordon was a spur-of-the-moment kind of person and that there was a moment of opportunity here; that if the Gees were allowed just to return to Boulder, the eventual answer might be 'no.'" In retrospect, Gee agreed. "Elizabeth might well have changed my mind if we had gone home first." They also had told fourteen-year-old Rebekah they did not want to make a commitment without consulting her, and had discussed having her come to Columbus to see for herself where she might live and where she might go to school.

Kessler's strategy worked. "After this pleasant but long dinner, I drove him back and we decided we would have breakfast the next morning." That night, at the downtown Hyatt on Capitol Square, the Gees discussed the situation and talked by phone to their daughter. Elizabeth had been pleased with what she had heard about the neighborhood and the Columbus School for Girls (CSG) from Jane Kessler and had been impressed in a visit with Head of School Pat Hayot. Rebekah had been in public schools in Boulder. She was not happy being treated by her classmates, for better or worse, as the daughter of the man who signed most of their parents' paychecks. The Gees believed she needed more order than she was getting and wanted her in an environment where Gordon, Elizabeth, and Rebekah were just another family. They had been considering sending her to a private boarding school, but the thought of sending their only child away—and an adopted child at that—had been very hard on them both. So, Columbus School for Girls might be just right.

And so might Bexley. Elizabeth had found the suburb due east of downtown very pleasing. Living on campus, as they had done in both Boulder and Morgantown, afforded little privacy and no community. She might be happy to live in Bexley, in a real neighborhood where her daughter could walk to school. And, as had already been discussed, there could be a position for her at Ohio State as there had been at Colorado.

"I'll never forget as long as I live," Kessler recalled for this book, "when breakfast finally came, only Gordon appeared. Gordon said, 'Elizabeth thinks this should be between the two of us.'" After the two talked, Kessler believed he had just left the next president of Ohio State.

## *A Few Details*

The probable next president of Ohio State and the apparently successful chair of the presidential search committee did discuss a few details, including presidential housing. The last university residence had been monstrous for entertaining and personal fund-raising. It had been purchased in 1972 in a rush at the last trustee meeting of the Novice Fawcett administration, following public and *Cleveland Plain Dealer* criticism of plans to build a "Taj Mahal" on campus. Jennings had urged the trustees to sell it before a new president was hired and had to live in it, which had been done. But no new home had been purchased.

Kessler had expected a new president to want a housing allowance and buy his or her own home. "I had an excellent package prepared." So he was surprised when Gee said he and Elizabeth would prefer a home owned and maintained by Ohio State. They would like private quarters upstairs, and, for Rebekah, they wanted to be near CSG. Gordon also said he would be ready to take over at Ohio State as soon as possible—a decision he regretted in retrospect as being unfair to Colorado.

Later, Kessler found them a house to look at. "I didn't like it, but they did." Elizabeth picked it out and Kessler negotiated the purchase. A corporate executive was renting it from the owners and did not want to move. Kessler did more negotiating and the executive left. Kessler also negotiated a contract with Gee's attorney, who flew in from Colorado. "It was easy negotiating. It took an hour." Following that hour, the Gees had two salary packages, two cars, and the house, and Gordon Gee had seats on the Limited and Bank One boards. In that one month, they said farewell to Colorado and Colorado said farewell to the Gees. They also flew Rebekah in to see Bexley and the Columbus School for Girls, and she loved them both.

One of the major reasons Gordon Gee accepted Ohio State's offer was singular and, in the end, sorrowful. The Arthur G. James Cancer Hospital and

CHAPTER 3

Wearing "Gee Whiz" T-shirts, Dick Stoddard and the Bricker Hall staff greet Gee his first workday.

Research Institute just had opened that month. Elizabeth had been diagnosed with breast cancer in 1987 and had had surgery and chemotherapy at the University of Colorado Medical Center in Denver, as well as surgery for a ruptured disc. Living with a mother so ill was, of course, hard on Rebekah; it was good to have the prep school up the block. And it was good to have a major medical center with a hospital dedicated to cancer research and treatment close at hand.

On September 15, 1990, Elizabeth Gee celebrated her forty-fifth birthday. She was in her new home in Bexley. Her daughter was in school at CSG. Her husband was running Ohio State. And she had had no recurrence or surgery for cancer for three years to the day.

# 4

# *The Consultants' Review*

As had become standard operating procedure for new university presidents, Gordon Gee put assessment of the carryover administration atop his right-now agenda. He had learned from experience as president of West Virginia University, when he had asked for resignation letters from the entire central administration, that being "presidential" did not mandate entering with guns blazing. He acknowledged later that he had lost some good people at WVU by preempting his own opportunity to make longer-term judgments. At Ohio State, on July 12 he would commission what became known as the Auburn Report. "Recommendations for President-elect E. Gordon Gee—The Administrative Structure and Related Matters" was in his hands in five weeks.

Three of the four review-team members were retired university presidents, each with singular presidential experiences. Chair Norman Auburn had been president of the University of Akron and thus knew the nuances of Ohio and its state legislature. William E. Friday of the University of North Carolina had led a multicampus system with a flagship at Chapel Hill. John E. Corbally of the University of Illinois knew Ohio State as few others did. Hired as an administrator in Ohio State's education college in 1955, Jack Corbally had risen to become Novice Fawcett's personnel director and, in the volatile years surrounding 1970, academic vice president and provost.

Gee knew all three and considered Bill Friday one of his mentors. But the fourth he knew especially well: his good friend Peter Magrath, president of the University of Missouri, an institution Gee had competed against for faculty and football victories when at Colorado. Magrath also had been president of The University of Minnesota and, as did Corbally, knew the singularities of the Big Ten Conference and its academic counterpart, the Committee on Institutional Cooperation.

## Chapter 4

In 1992, as president of the National Association of State Universities and Land-Grant Colleges (NASULGC), Magrath would appoint Gee to chair its national lobbying committee, thereby giving him unique visibility in the halls of Congress. And in 1995, Magrath would again be retained by Ohio State, this time by its trustees, to conduct Gee's own five-year review.

The Auburn team swooped onto campus on July 29 and, in two days, interviewed Vice President and Provost Fred Hutchinson, trustees Shirley Dunlap Bowser and Jack Kessler, outgoing President Ed Jennings and most of his executive officers and deans, and the University Senate Steering Committee, chaired by Professor Judy Genshaft—thirty-seven people in all.

Two of the interviewed were "acting" deans, as were four vice presidents, providing Gee exquisite room to adjust his administration without, so to speak, firing a shot.

The acting deans were Astrid Merget, Business, appointed at the retirement of Justin Davidson, and James R. "Bob" Warmbrod, Agriculture, appointed when A. Max Lennon went to Clemson as its president. The acting vice presidents were Thomas L. Sweeney, Research, appointed at the retirement of Jack Hollander; William J. Shkurti, Finance, appointed at Weldon Ihrig's departure for the Oregon system; Treasurer James L. Nichols, Business and Administration, appointed at the retirement of the late Richard Jackson; and Donald E. Glower, Sr., Communications and Development, successor to Thomas Tobin, who had joined the University of South Florida.

Of the six, only Shkurti and Nichols would be in the Gee administration at its end. Shkurti, once Governor Richard Celeste's state budget director, became Finance vice president. Nichols, a jack of all trades who would also do the spadework for what became Campus Partners, would remain treasurer.

The other deans interviewed were Roy Koenigsknecht, Graduate School; William R. Wallace, Dentistry; Ronald A. Wright, Veterinary Medicine; G. Micheal Riley, Humanities; Donald P. Anderson, Education; C. William Kern, Mathematical and Physical Sciences; Francis X. "Frank" Beytagh, Law; Manuel Tzagournis, Medicine, also vice president for Health Services; and Joan Huber, Social and Behavioral Sciences.

Over the course of the Gee administration, sociologist Huber would become a strong senior vice president and provost with a reputation for straight talk and high standards and would retire in 1993. Tzagournis would retain both his vice presidency and deanship for another half-decade, until Bernadine Healy would become medical dean in 1995 and Tzagournis would continue as vice president through the Gee administration.

The rest would retire, return to the faculty, or leave Ohio State. Fred

Hutchinson, after recovering from a heart attack and near-fatal bike crash, moved to the presidency of his alma mater, the University of Maine.

## *Private Investigation*

From the first, Gee was also doing his own investigative work. He would schedule interviews with those who might report to him or work closely with him on his staff. In those sessions, he would ask about both the interviewee and his or her colleagues. "Tell me about so and so." He was particularly interested in the so-and-sos from the Jennings administration who, if they stayed, would be advising him, scheduling him, representing him, raising money, and managing presidential events.

The principal figures here were Herb Asher, political science professor, counselor to the president, and university lobbyist in the Ohio State House; Madison Scott, vice president for Personnel Services and secretary of the Board of Trustees; Sue Blanshan, executive officer for Human Relations administration; Russell Spillman, vice provost for Student Affairs, to whom the athletic director and the intercollegiate athletic program reported; Malcolm Baroway, executive director of University Communications; Carol Ries, director of Special Events; Richard Stoddard, in charge of Federal Relations; Barbie Tootle and Leah Weaver, executive speech writers; and Mary Basinger, secretary to the president.

Before the summer was over, most either would travel to the University of Colorado or meet their counterparts in Columbus.

As president of a system that had a chancellor at each of four campuses—Boulder, Colorado Springs, Denver, and its Denver medical school—Gee had had few direct reports compared with what he might inherit from Jennings. Each chancellor had an administration, and Gee's central staff was small.

Though seven vice presidents and a staff had reported to him, Jennings had run his meetings as more of a listener than a facilitator and used a small inner circle of confidants to help make decisions. Gee's preference, his staff would soon learn, was going to be wide inclusion. He invited opinions. The idea of a complex organization reporting to him was more off-putting to the review committee than it was to him.

The overall tone of the Auburn Report was anything but negative. "There is much good news for Gordon Gee as he is about to assume the presidency of the Ohio State University," it began. "University administrators and faculty members whom we met are very enthusiastic about Gordon Gee; morale is good, the environment in short is positive. Happily, the new president does not inherit an array of pervasive, longtime internal difficulties; rather, his is the energizing assignment of redefining the mission of the University for the 21st century." The sole but strong caution issued in the report's introduction was that Gee move neither "too fast" nor "too soon, without adequate conferral time." Evidently, his reputation for action, intensity, and some impatience had preceded him. "Haste in every business brings failures," the report quoted an interviewee quoting Herodotus. A "long and strong history of faculty involvement in educational policymaking," it reminded if not warned, should be "treated seriously."

## *Red Flags Waving*

There were, however, enough warnings in the body of the report to give even a calm person pause. Jennings was much admired and given credit for great strides by the university, the report said, but it questioned some of the institution's current big budget priorities. First was the Arizona telescope consortium, "budgeted for $15 million but said by one dean to carry a price tag of $50 million." Then there was reform of the undergraduate curriculum and the "concomitant infusion of dollars into Arts and Sciences, the Cancer Hospital and the Wexner Center." In the few years when state funding had been adequate, major financial decisions had been made with "no priority framework." One faculty member had likened Ohio State to a "giant clad in a threadbare Brooks Brothers suit whose pockets are filled with IOUs."

Major reallocations would be needed if the new president were to follow through on these projects. The new president had better establish a task force to scrutinize the next budget cycle—coming up fast, the report warned. And first he had better review all financial commitments made for the next five years for, while overcommitment was at the one hand, undercommitment was at the other.

One undercommitment was underinvestment to attract federal research funds. Creating whatever infrastructure might be required to do this was the committee's recommendation. Another problem was underinvestment in the quality of the student body, manifested in minimal student recruitment and too little no-need aid. Ohio State, the review team noted, was not even the institution of choice for the best and brightest in Ohio. "Miami University is the envied institution when this idea is discussed. Miami even has higher tuition.... A sure sign to many that Miami is of higher quality."

While Ed Jennings had dealt with faculty morale "with remarkable success," the report countered that Ohio State had not yet lost "its inferiority complex." Ohio State has "this self-image problem." And why was that? The report did not need to remind the incoming president that Ohio State had been an open admissions institution until 1987. But it did cite "inadequate attention" to student recruitment since then. It had found, for instance, the admissions and financial aid offices to be "almost completely devoid of the use of new technology. Indeed, the system used to process [financial] aids materials seems to date from the 1940s." The Jennings administration had seen drastic budget cuts in the early 1980s in which "student services had suffered," and the suffering was continuing.

Addressing these problems—institutional self-image, student recruitment, attracting more research money—should be the new president's highest priorities, the report concluded.

How to begin? Motivate the faculty in your first speech, President Gee. You will have a new governor, and you have a new chancellor, Elaine Hairston, an Ohio State alumna. Lobby them hard. Meet with everyone, "trustees, administrative groups and faculty within the university, with alumni, and with friends in cities, large and small, across the state. . . . Listen to the hopes and dreams they hold for the future" and make similar contacts with editorial boards, "to improve the image several have about OSU." And, as for your central administration, "streamline"—for both efficiency and effect.

## *Administrative Restructuring*

"If the president can implement administrative reorganization and reduction in the senior echelons of the university, he will then be in a strong position—*after* this has been done—to insist on cutbacks." The report urged Gee to restructure his leadership team so that only two senior administrators—a senior vice president for Academic Affairs and another in administration—would report to him. His inner circle, it said, should be only nine people: the two senior vice presidents; the Student Affairs vice provost; a vice president each for Research and for Communications and Development; a Government Relations special assistant; a general counsel; a combined secretary to the university and to the trustees; and a Human Relations executive assistant, for whom the report also recommended a monitoring role on minority issues.

The Human Relations assistant, it said, "should be given the immediate task of straightening out the confusion about who is doing what in this critical

## Chapter 4

Madison Scott hoods Ohio Senate President Stanley Aronoff, 1990.

area." Given the perception there is "an affirmative action officer behind every tree" and anyone with a grievance can "wander" until they find an administrator "to press their case," the team urged this position be acted upon "immediately... despite our earlier warning of haste."

Left out of the circle would be all the other vice presidents, who would report either to the provost or to the recommended administrative counterpart. In particular, the report referred to the vice president and dean of Agriculture, who, "regardless of title," should do most of his or her "business with the provost."

Not only should the Health Services vice president, it recommended, report to the provost rather than the president, but eventually this office should be separated from the deanship in Medicine. An obstacle to recruiting a separate dean, it acknowledged, was the respect enjoyed by the incumbent, Dr. Manuel Tzagournis, "highly regarded ... doing an excellent job" with "fine people in place in hospital administrative positions." Dr. Tzagournis also had as patients the leadership of the state of Ohio, including the governor, speaker of the House, president of the Senate, and ranking members of the majority in the U.S. Senate. Although the report suggested the disconnect await the doctor's retirement, Dr. Bernadine Healy would become dean well before that.

## THE CONSULTANTS' REVIEW

Although Ohio State had a history of strong agricultural leaders who could wield influence in rural legislative districts, the report recommended that this vice presidency no longer report to the president, this in a state whose number one industry remained agriculture. Gee did not accept this recommendation and soon would have another politically perceptive academic, Bobby Moser, as vice president and dean. He also would never create a senior vice presidency in administration.

As well as the Auburn team might have known Gordon, its members did not understand how much he thrived on information. He was an uncanny listener, who could absorb what he was hearing even if he appeared to be paying attention elsewhere, and he wanted both information and feedback. When immediate decisions had to be made, he certainly would make them. But he preferred to have all potential points of view at the staff conference table every week rather than squeeze them in at the last minute into his packed breakfast-through-dinner daily schedules.

One of the people he definitely wanted to hear from would be his athletic director, Jim Jones. Consistent with a recommendation about to be made by the prestigious Knight Commission on Intercollegiate Athletics, Gee had told the Auburn group he would have the AD report to him. The committee, although Bill Friday was cochairing the Knight Commission, thought this a bad idea for Ohio State.

It reminded him that both Ohio State and the Big Ten had a history of faculty control over intercollegiate athletics. It had been the University Senate that had voted against sending the Buckeyes to the Rose Bowl in 1961, prevailing despite "intense pressure from the Board of Trustees and the press." Under Jennings, ADs Rick Bay and Jones had reported to Student Affairs vice provost Russ Spillman, who had been an education professor. Jennings, however, had monitored the athletic department closely, and it had been Jennings himself who had hired Bay from Oregon in 1984, fired Coach Earle Bruce the week of the 1988 Michigan game, and then accepted Bay's resignation, made in protest.

Gee knew he would exercise his presidential prerogative over hirings and firings of high-profile coaches regardless of the organizational chart. He loved the panorama of big-time athletics, considered it a catalyst for the promotion of academics, and never would be far from it. He had been the one at Colorado to give head football coach Bill McCartney a legendary, and at first incendiary, fifteen-year contract; whereupon McCartney's team won the national football title in 1990. At Ohio State, he would decide to accept the Auburn Report's cautious approach and let the dual reporting relationship remain on paper, if not in spirit.

CHAPTER 4

In time, he would also grow to recognize the value of an upper management buffer between the president and the athletic director. If controversy should surround athletics, as it often did, should he choose to, the president always could defer to the vice provost as well as his AD. Thus in July 1993, when David Williams became President Gee's newly appointed Student Affairs vice president, Williams, who said he would not have taken the job without it, had athletics in his portfolio. By this time, the position no longer reported to the provost. Williams was vice president, not vice provost, and reported directly to Gee.

President Gee's first reorganizational decision was not to return Chip Elam, who had managed the presidential search, to Madison Scott's office. He asked Elam to stay on and coordinate the transition and, in September, would appoint him special assistant to the president.

By October 15, Gee was conducting five searches for his new administration: vice presidencies in Student Affairs, Business and Administration, Finance, Agricultural Affairs, and Research. In addition, he had appointed Hutchinson *senior* vice president and provost, as recommended. In following two other recommendations, he had Madison Scott continue as secretary too the trustees and become his executive assistant, moving the personnel office into Business and Administration, and planned to add the monitoring of minority issues to the human relations job as a "complement (to the) existing offices and organization for minorities."

While the report made it clear Ohio State would need "some radical surgery," it hardly could have been more positive about the reception awaiting the new president. "President-elect Gee is entering friendly territory." "The natives are enthusiastic about his arrival." "It is time to get ready to change the reins and begin Geeing up the team."

By October 18, however, the team had cantered into its first mudhole. In adding the minority affairs aspect to the job held by incumbent Human Relations officer Sue Blanshan, a Caucasian, President Gee had sought to illustrate his commitment to issues of equal opportunity and affirmative action. Leaders of a campus organization named "JustUs" had read just the opposite into it: a diminution, if not elimination of the Office of Minority Affairs and perhaps its director, Joe Russell, who was African American and reported to the provost. The change was even thought to be leading to, perhaps, the removal of Vice *Provost* Russ Spillman, another African American, as part of that search for a vice *president*.

Certainly, this was not Gee's intent. Quoted in the *Lantern* as being "damn mad," he gave the Ohio State community the first inclination that this Mormon from Utah not only had a temper but even used the "D" word. However, he did recant the recommendation he was unsure of in the first place and, in due time, clearly demonstrated his commitment to diversity in his own hiring practices.

It would take eighteen more months for the Auburn Report's "young and vital leader, qualified by outstanding experience, proven intelligence, fresh ideas, and abounding energy" to put his initial full administrative team in place. By February 1992, following the search, Russ Spillman would become the Student Affairs vice president. Distinguished jurist Robert Duncan would become Gee's special assistant for Legal Affairs and, later, vice president and secretary of the Board of Trustees. A new position, special assistant for Business and Community Relations, would be filled by corporate executive Sarah Austin, who once headed the Cleveland Round Table and knew many of the country's African American leaders. All three administrators were African American.

Three other women also would join his executive team: Linda Tom, from Rhone-Poulenc Rhorer Pharmaceutical, as vice president for Human Resources and Relations; and Janet Pichette, from banking and Eastern Michigan University, as vice president for Business Administration. And Joan Huber would become senior vice president and provost.

In addition, the word "acting" would be removed from Shkurti's title; and the Office of Development and Communications would be separated—with a search committee announced to seek a new vice president for Development, and Communications head Baroway now reporting to the president.

Throughout that period, and all through his presidency, Gee paid considerable attention to one other Auburn Report recommendation—attending to and listening to the University Senate. With more than a century of academic experience combined in its four members, the Auburn Committee wrote that it knew of no system that duplicated Ohio State's "shared governance structure," with its cornerstone, the University Senate. "No Ohio State president can ignore the senate," it had cautioned, and told the new president that, as had his predecessors, he "would have to pay . . . the toll of delay and frustration in order to build consensus."

That, it said, was the only way Gee would get his "ticket stamped at Ohio State."

# 5
## *Cleaning Up the University Area*

> My son was stabbed on N. High St. He is not the first nor will he be the last person to be attacked in the university area. Something must be done to make OSU a safe place for our children to attend college. The police tell me the south campus area is the most dangerous part of the city. Many parents I've spoken with want their children to transfer to another university. The violence has become rampant and no one seems to be able to do anything about it. I beg you please keep the promise you made in the fall. Get involved in this serious situation and help rid the university area of this violence. Thank you for listening to another mother's plea."
>
> —From a letter to the president

On his first drive through the neighborhood on his first day at work, the new president of Ohio State recognized that something would have to be done about the "university area." Compared with the gemstone bordering his Colorado campus in Boulder, this section of stores, bars, restaurants, pizza parlors, laundromats, and student housing was a handful of grit.

To the west of campus was the affluent bedroom community of Upper Arlington, to the north modest well-kept Clintonville, to the far south gentrified old-brick Victorian Village. Then to the east, and a bit to the south, there was this—at best an eyesore, at worst a dangerous place. Within weeks, Gee brought in for a conversation about his concerns Donald Lenz, an alumnus then in charge of urban redevelopment for greater Cincinnati.

Gee and Columbus's activist Mayor Dana Rinehart began to communicate confidentially about the problem immediately, and, on September 7, 1990, Rinehart wrote Gee that in two weeks he and his staff would have an initial plan for partnering with the university. "This could be fun!" Rinehart wrote, and Gee, a man for whom most challenges also were "fun," wrote back, "I like your style." The plan was *Proposals for Change,* a comprehensive set of twelve data-driven recommendations published the next month by the University Community Business Association (UCBA), much of it done by a senior team of Ohio State planners and business administrators: Jim Nichols, John Kleberg, Ben Brace, Gus Van Buren, and Jean Hansford.

This was not the first such set of recommendations for what is known officially as the University District: 2.83 square miles bordered clockwise by the Glen Echo Ravine, Conrail tracks, 5th Avenue, and the Olentangy River. Nor would it be the last. The first had been written in 1973, a second in 1985. Both had led to some capital improvements and safety initiatives, but little else. This time, however, certain situations had reached crisis proportions. As the report stated, "a host of social, economic, and infrastructure problems" all were "contributing to a declining quality of life" in the district.

Soon university administrators were in serious conversation with the Columbus sanitation division, which led to increased trash pickup, and were meeting about general area safety and attacks on students with the 4th Precinct Columbus police. Within three months, Columbus, Franklin County, and the university together funded the new Community Crime Patrol, a cadre of volunteers, mostly students, paid to walk the area streets and alleys. A new Ohio State escort service began providing van rides home to students working or studying on campus nights and weekends. On campus, lighting was increased, bus service hours extended, and new emergency telephones added.

## A Hectic Few Months

However, other issues rapidly dominated the president's agenda. The 2400 members of the Communications Workers of America threatened a walkout, then settled at an eleventh-hour agreement. A white female student falsely reported being raped by an African American man, creating a campus uproar and a presidential call for civility when the lie and its stereotyping were revealed. Nationally, Assistant U.S. Secretary of Education Michael Williams warned that race-exclusive scholarships would become illegal, and Gee and fellow presidents fired off a response.

A portion of his first address to the University Senate was met with

CHAPTER 5

Gee and Mayor Greg Lashutka announce city-university initiatives, 1994.

accusations of racism by the protest group JustUs in a misinterpretation of his commitment to the concerns of minorities. A new alcohol and drug policy was drafted in response to the federal Drug-Free Schools and Communities Act, which threatened to curtail federal support of any college that did not act on the policy by October. A shooting incident shut down student dances at the Ohio Union, particularly unfortunate because sponsors were African American fraternities, which had no houses for social functions.

Provost Fred Hutchinson passed out while steaming along on his racing bike. Though wearing a helmet, he struck his head so hard his heart stopped. He did live to return as provost, but beloved Business Vice President Richard Jackson, who had recently retired, died of a heart attack at 56. Another driver at a red light on Kenny Road killed distinguished cancer surgeon and anti-smoking firebrand John Minton, also just 56. Husband and wife Dominic Mandalfino and Lisa Gunyula, Ohio State doctors, and Hospitals Board member Linda Thomas all died in the Los Angeles crash of a Boeing 737.

The James Cancer Hospital lost $8 million in its first five months of operation. A $262 million deficit for Ohio's government translated into a 4 percent $12 million budget cut for Ohio State, requiring a freeze by Gee on nonessential hiring. Some 100 Ohio State military reservists were activated against the armies of Saddam Hussein in the Gulf War. All this was within Gee's first six months.

Of course, the president also had been developing his own agenda: building his new leadership team; hiring Joseph Alutto from SUNY Buffalo as dean of the Business College; designing a partnership with Bernadine Healy and the Cleveland Clinic; fostering interdisciplinary programs; creating one commission to address women's issues and another to review and redress salary inequities; and finding scholarship money to strengthen future freshman classes. Ohio State was then ranked by *U.S. News* an abysmal 143rd among 204 national universities in "student selectivity."

The president's most comprehensive goal became known idiomatically as "the student experience." Though some of that experience depended upon what did or did not happen in the University District, it would take until January 1994 for the president and new Mayor Greg Lashutka to begin rolling the big ball up High Street, in the form of the University Area Improvement Task Force.

## *The University Area Improvement Task Force*

Chaired by Ohio State Treasurer Jim Nichols, with vice presidents David Williams and Janet Pichette on the team, the UAI task force included Columbus Safety Director Ron Poole and representatives of the faculty, students, staff, and four area associations and commissions. Its charge was basic: to define the salient issues, learn what other university communities had done in similar situations, and recommend both short-term and long-term repair for a part of the city that had been sliding downhill for decades. In a speech to the University Community Business Association (UCBA), as reported by the *Lantern* (February 10, 1994), Gee warned the absentee landlords, "We had some people come in and build structures that you would not want to have your son or daughter moving to, and it is those people we are going to put out of business. If they are coming in here to be sharks and leeches on the community . . . they are no longer welcome . . . and we're going to kick their rear ends right out of here." He also said Ohio State was going to "put millions of dollars" into the project.

In their reconnaissance, UAI task force members visited Temple and the University of Pennsylvania in Philadelphia, Columbia in Manhattan, Marquette in Milwaukee, and Washington University in St. Louis, all urban campuses, all with urban problems. All, concluded Williams, had denied reality too

## Chapter 5

long. In a sense, so had Ohio State; it had shelved the report of 1985 and done too little with the *Proposals for Change* of 1990. "We remember when we were where you are," Williams characterized comments from interviewees at the four universities visited. "We had a choice and did nothing. And that's how we ended up where we are."

When this task force published its report, its first conclusion was undeviating. Things were even worse than before. There is a "dire need," it said, for "dramatic intervention and long term changes. In short, people need to be safe." There were thirteen recommendations, including the creation of a not-for-profit improvement/redevelopment corporation. What the report failed to mention was the murder of an Ohio State coed two months after the task force had been formed and four months before it reported.

The student's name was Stephanie Hummer, and her murder was the tragic impetus that finally moved Ohio State and Columbus into real action.

## *Stephanie Hummer*

Stephanie Hummer, a nineteen-year-old freshman honor student from Finneytown near Cincinnati, lived in the Evans Scholars House on 14th Avenue. She had gone out very late on a Saturday night, as many students do. At 3:30 a.m. she was last seen a half-block from High Street in Pearl Alley on her way to the house of a friend. Her body was discovered thirteen hours later near a railroad track far from campus. It was the first "campus" homicide of an Ohio State student in twenty-five years. Trustees David Brennan and Les Wexner each put up a $5000 reward for information leading to capture of the murderer, and the *Dispatch* made it "Crime of the Week."

"Until now," Mark Tatge wrote in the *Cleveland Plain Dealer* (March 9, 1994), "students had assumed they were immune to some of the more violent crimes that occur four to five blocks east of the older student housing area bordering the campus." While "four or five blocks east" was not as far as Europe, for many students the psychological distance was wide as the sea.

Soon, the *Columbus Dispatch* (April 4) would report on crime in the larger University District, as had television stations that had sent in crews from Cincinnati and Dayton. According to police, the *Dispatch* reported worsened conditions since crack cocaine had arrived in Columbus in the mid-1980s. "Within blocks of where many students live, drug dealing and prostitution are commonplace," parents read, and "police are regularly dispatched to shootings in the area." The district had one of the highest crime rates in Columbus. On a per capita basis in 1994, violent crime was 14 percent higher than in greater Columbus. Property crime was 22 percent higher (*Redevelopment Plan for the University Neighborhoods,* October 1995).

Over time, a number of factors had coalesced to reduce the quality of life in what once had been a mixed residential and student neighborhood. Too many area landlords were inadequately maintaining their properties. Recent gentrification of the Short North, with its art galleries, restaurants, and condominiums, had pushed a transient population north into the traditional campus area. Alumni who in the 1970s had lived on 8th or 9th Avenues east of High Street and never locked their doors would simply no longer live there.

Specifically, home ownership had plummeted from 50 percent in the 1950s to 11 percent. More than 2,000 low income "Section 8" government housing units had been built, which was the highest concentration in the city. While the student population had dropped by 2000, the University District still had 7 percent of the city's population on less than 2 percent of the land. The consequent fear of schoolmates, families, potential students, and their parents jerked Ohio State upright about what had to be done.

## *Getting Started*

Though they were helpful, the Community Crime Patrol and the University Escort Service that were begun four years before did nothing to affect root causes. To quote one letter from a 1959 graduate written to President Gee in 1994, "The avarice of many developers and landlords . . . bootleg apartments, short cuts in building construction and downright thievery from students have conspired to make the area . . . less than desirable to live in. Why not live on Bethel Road where there is a parking place waiting each evening and a whole car . . . ready for the trip to OSU in the morning and the landlord isn't waiting to rip off your security deposit?"

A later article in the magazine *Urban Land* (April 1996) commented that "a concentration of ill-kept bars" was seen as the source of many problems, "primarily illegal underage drinking . . . drunkenness . . . and resultant aggressive and sometimes dangerous activities." One of the singular problems successfully handled was what appeared to be gang-related dares to start fights with Ohio State's football players by insulting them or their dates; the bigger the player, the more the prestige. In one particular bar off High Street, provocations had ended in bloodshed and gunfire. As evidence of the effective relationship the

CHAPTER 5

university's Nichols had developed with the city as UAI task force chair, he made a phone call. Within days, the bar was closed.

Then there were the muggings. The personal files of letters to Gee included a number of pleas by parents of students robbed and beaten or stabbed near campus. It did not take the subsequent verification of Professor Ron Huff, Ohio State's national expert in gang behavior, to acknowledge that roaming groups of youths were knocking heads to fulfill initiation rites or just have a good time. And it did not take Student Affairs VP-in-waiting David Williams witnessing drug transactions while driving to work to know what was going on.

What it did take was an understanding among representatives of the president and the mayor; the U.S. Justice Department; the U.S. Bureau of Alcohol, Tobacco and Firearms; and the City Attorney's Office that it was time to do something about the drug problem near Ohio State. It also took the formation of Campus Partners for Community Urban Development, Inc. Funded with $28 million from the university, Campus Partners soon would begin a lengthy process of buying property and building consensus for a makeover of the university area.

## *Corralling the Short North Posse*

The first time most Columbus residents heard of the Short North Posse was on the evening news of May 27, 1994, after Rostamon Wilson and Raylynn Diamond had talked trash on the main escalator of Columbus City Center. Diamond was shot to death and Wilson was accused of aggravated murder. Wilson was a member of the Bloods. Diamond was a leader of the Short North Posse.

Some ten months later, Robert Ruth, the *Dispatch*'s celebrated investigative writer, reported on a raid conducted on "Northside bars, houses, and street corners." Forty-six alleged members of "a violent, cocaine-dealing gang that terrorized a 42-block neighborhood . . . for six years" had been charged. Thirty-two were being held without bail. U.S. Attorney Edmund Sargas characterized the bunch as the "largest and most violent gang" in the Columbus area. They were the Short North Posse.

By December, more had been rounded up and forty-three were convicted of federal drug charges. The following May, four more and three major suppliers went to prison. The letters complaining about student muggings stopped arriving at the president's office. A cooperative effort that few people ever traced to the healthy relationship between the city, the university, and local and federal policing agencies had paid off for Ohio State and the residents of the University District.

On May 16, 1997, a recreation park for children was dedicated in the name and honor of Stephanie Hummer. It is at 143 E. Patterson Avenue, a few blocks north of campus on the grounds of the Catholic Social Services Center. Dan and Sue Hummer said they believed their daughter was there in spirit, and they continued to hope her murderer would be caught.

## *Campus Partners: Phase 1*

In October 1994, with President Gee and Mayor Lashutka leading the cleaning brigade, Ohio State held its first "High on Pride" day. Hundreds of students, staff, and faculty removed 60 tons of trash from a square mile of the University District. A few months earlier, Gee had recommended to his trustees a $1 million first-year start-up investment for what would become Campus Partners. "It is worth noting," he wrote, "that conditions east of High Street undercut student recruitment."

This he had known since his first conversation with Director of Admissions Jim Mager. In 1990, Mager told him stories about parents bringing their youngsters in for interviews from the east off I-71. Sometimes they turned around and went home before they ever reached campus. The aesthetics of the area were so distasteful, he told Gee, his office staff now directed all visitors in from the west.

With a background as a systems analyst and a Ph.D. in statistics, Mager paid even more attention to data. By 1990, "crime" was one of the five main reasons accepted students chose other colleges. Right after the death of young Stephanie Hummer, it spiked to number one.

In March 1995, twenty area and university leaders developed a vision statement for the university community. "University neighborhoods," it read, "shall become a high quality city within a city, characterized by diverse, enriched, safe, livable and commercially viable neighborhoods with community features and programs that create a district-wide framework of transportation, open space, amenities and human services." Idealized as it was, the vision statement established the framework for the next step. It had been facilitated by developer and planner Barry Humphries, hired by the university to start Campus Partners. Humphries had headed redevelopment of the gentrified Victorian Village, south of campus off Neal Avenue, in the 1970s.

The next fall, Humphries presented the *Redevelopment Plan for the University*

# Chapter 5

*Neighborhoods* to the Ohio State trustees. Consultants had been called in and had built a master plan. Eleventh and High would be a mixed-use center. Fifteenth and High would be the arts district. Lane and High would emphasize international goods and restaurants. There would be new housing, new parks, neighborhood centers, street improvements, and traffic directional changes.

Humphries asked the trustees for $28 million over the next five years and got it. The money would come from interest on endowment and designated private gifts, not from the general fund. Using all but $3 million, Campus Partners was to buy properties and then find developers to improve them. The rest would pay for programs coordinated by Campus Partners, including an academic outreach and research component, the Campus Collaborative.

By this time, all trustees understood the need to act, but there were different levels of enthusiasm. Vice President Williams, to whom Campus Partners reported, later said Wexner, Skestos, and Shumate were "most instrumental in backing Gordon." Wexner, ever the large-scale thinker, felt $28 million was not nearly enough, that, reported Williams, "to change the neighborhood and make it what it should be, you should be willing to put $100 million in it."

Skestos, a developer himself, saw the need early and worked closely with Lashutka; then he and Dan Slane, the two trustees appointed to Campus Partners, steered the process. Throughout his tenure on the board, Shumate supported it and continued to support it even as he left the board in 1998 and later became president of the Columbus Area Chamber of Commerce.

Humphries would resign at the end of March 1996 to return to private business, and an experienced city administrator from burgeoning Dublin, Ohio, would take over. With a master's in urban planning, $225 million under his belt in development agreements in Dublin, and a daughter at Ohio State and living in the High Street area, there was no question Terry Foegler had both the experience and the incentive.

# 6

## *The Hutchinson Years*

> We were not considered to be the school of choice. The overall profile of the students we were attracting was a distant last in the Big Ten. The best students who could afford it definitely were going on to other places they perceived to be more prestigious.
>
> —Director of Admissions Jim Mager, on the
> undergraduate student body before the 1990s

When Provost Fred Hutchinson fielded complaints about international teaching assistants whose accents made them hard to understand, he loved to tell about the "foreign" TA who turned out to be from Maine. A "Mainer" himself, Hutchinson carried the accent and epitomized the steadiness of the stereotype, but dour he was not. While quick of wit and sharp as a razor, Hutchinson preferred reasoning to skewering and made virtually no enemies.

A realist as well, when Ed Jennings suggested he become acting provost at the departure of Provost Myles Brand in late 1989, Hutchinson had replied, "My god, that won't work. I don't see any way that the (other) deans would accept that." "That" was the fact he headed the College of Agriculture, to which, he recalled later, "hostility was quite high." Though he was not about to take it personally, he knew some deans believed "Aggies" belonged in a tech school, and others had had problems with his predecessor, Dean Roy Kottman.

Jennings then called a meeting with Hutchinson and the other deans, which developed into a blunt discussion led by Humanities Dean Micheal Riley, whose reputation for frankness preceded him. At the end, Hutchinson was

CHAPTER 6

asked to leave the room and the deans voted. "They think you should do it," Jennings told him. The support was unanimous. "So that was how I became acting provost."

On December 1, 1989, following a national search, the "acting" was dropped and Fred Hutchinson was named a provost in full. Soon he would find himself the chief official of Ohio State—in reality, if not title—when Jennings would tell him privately about his pending full-time return to the Business faculty and trigger the search for a new president.

It was Hutchinson, then, to whom the trustees looked to manage the store during the transition to a new president—Fred Hutchinson, who had been recruited from the University of Maine to head Ohio State's agricultural experiment station in 1985 and who had succeeded Max Lennon as Agriculture dean after Lennon became president of Clemson University. Fred would have a very strong ally and friend in trustee Shirley Dunlap Bowser, a farm girl from southern Ohio who had graduated in a class of twelve from a rural high school, gone on to excel at Ohio State, and "rejoiced" at "having an agriculturist in the provost's office."

As Bowser, who became the trustees' chair that May, would recall, "until Gordon Gee's arrival Fred Hutchinson pretty well ran the place and guided us very skillfully."

A scientist by education, Hutchinson was a particularly excellent selection as provost at a time when some major academic decisions were to involve research and there was no research vice president yet in place. Ohio State would collaborate with the Cleveland Clinic, an Office of Technology Transfer would be established, the James Cancer Hospital would go on line, and Ohio State would have to reconsider whether it could be a full partner in the controversial and expensive "Columbus Project" telescope.

## *The Transition*

During the nine-month transition—between December 1, 1989, and September 1, 1990—key departures included Associate Provost Joan Leitzel, for the National Science Foundation; Business Vice President Richard Jackson, to retirement; and Finance Vice President Weldon Ihrig, who had wielded tremendous influence with his finance professor president, for the Oregon system.

Key hires were Joseph Russell of Indiana University as vice provost for Minority Affairs and two new Ohio Eminent Scholars: the University of Illinois' Hamish Fraser, in high-temperature structural materials, and Wisconsin's

Muttaiya Sundaralingam, in biological macromolecular chemistry. Funding of the Eminent Scholar Program, created by the Ohio Board of Regents in 1983, was curtailed in 1990 with the crash of the state's tax base. Fraser and Sundaralingam were Ohio State's eighth and ninth filled Eminent Scholar positions. Of the thirty-six $500,000 grants awarded statewide through 1990, seventeen were to Ohio State.

Early in January 1990, the university's AIDS Education and Research Committee issued a new white paper on a disease that only then was being recognized as a killer in the U.S. heterosexual population. Also during this period, Elaine Hairston became the fifth chancellor of the Board of Regents; and realtor and interactive video entrepreneur Ted Celeste, brother of the governor, became Richard Celeste's final trustee appointment, following prominent attorney Alex Shumate in 1989. The two would be the only trustees to serve the Gee administration from beginning to end, although Les Wexner would complete his term only fourteen days before Gee would accept the presidency of Brown.

As the interim presidential period went on, selective admissions for freshmen were extended to summer and winter quarters by the trustees; trustee John Barone stimulated Board approval, allowing a student finance class to invest $5 million of the university's $302 million endowment; the university's first capital campaign closed with more than $460 million in gifts and pledges; and a master plan was approved for the future of Don Scott Field, as was a master's degree in women's studies.

## *Floating the Semester System*

By the end of his first week as president, Gordon Gee already had memoed Hutchinson to conduct a "formal and comprehensive review of the quarter vs. the semester system." The new president wanted his academic agenda to begin, if possible, by shifting the university calendar from quarters to semesters, and doing it quickly so as "not to plague" other academic planning.

Hutchinson appointed a calendar committee, which found support for semesters among both graduate students and faculty. The Graduate Council resolved to adopt an early semester calendar of two fifteen-week terms and an abbreviated summer term. A poll of 315 faculty indicated 54 percent for semester or early semester, 20 percent for the quarter, and about the same percentage not answering. Most had worked or studied elsewhere in the semester system.

## Chapter 6

While a follow-up note to Gee from the calendar committee chair indicated a discussion could begin on teaching load and "timing for the conversion," nothing would happen. Judged too expensive and too time consuming, if not too contentious among students who knew no other system, semester conversionitis disappeared as a precondition for change—although Gee would continue to seek the shift throughout his presidency. One "conversion" that did happen, however—and arguably the most transforming policy change of the Gee era—began with Hutchinson: strengthening the academic quality of the undergraduate student body.

The point of departure was a plan to recruit National Merit and National Achievement Scholarship semifinalists, the crème de la crème of high school seniors. It was the base camp, so to speak, for the peak to be scaled if Ohio State were to become a highly competitive, if not world-class, undergraduate institution. While Hutchinson thanked Gee with a personal note for approving "this exciting new dimension for OSU" that he had recommended, Gee would have done it himself if his provost had not. The Auburn Report already had signaled the need.

## *The Competitive Environment*

It was no secret within the faculty that the academic quality of the Columbus undergraduate student body of some 40,000 students did not approach that of the graduate student body of some 10,000. As admissions director, Jim Mager remembered that through the late 1980s faculty would query him "almost daily. They would say, 'Do you realize,' and I would say, 'I very much realize.'" "They would say, 'Don't you know.'" And he would say, "I very much know."

Those who didn't know or didn't care were the ones who really counted—call them "the voting public." Ohio thought Ohio State was just fine as it was. A poll done by the communications office verified that Ohioans equated very big with very good. And how was the public to know whether Ohio State was better than Michigan, worse than Wisconsin, as good as Illinois? Academic departments were not ranked like football and basketball teams. There was no rating system, at least none to which the public or the media yet paid attention, and the university itself had not yet established and publicized its own benchmarks and comparatives.

More than enough students, then, were enrolling at Ohio State in autumn 1990 as Gordon Gee became president with Fred Hutchinson as his provost: 60,165 total on the six Ohio State campuses and 54,094 in Columbus—the highest total since 1980. Minority enrollment in Columbus, at more than 5,000, was the highest in ten years. A new General Education Curriculum (GEC) was inaugurated, adding both "foundation" and some "capstone" courses to the curriculum. And the selective admissions policy instituted for the autumn quarter only in 1987 had just been extended to include summer and winter.

But Ohio State still had more than a perception problem among the brightest high school seniors in Ohio. Most who could afford to avoid Ohio State still were avoiding it. The best in Columbus might even be embarrassed to say they were considering it. While autumn selective admissions had increased undergraduate academic quality somewhat, the dent had been small.

Then, if parents of potential freshmen looked at recent graduation rates, they even might be more disheartened. In great part because of the new GEC requirements, which were adding a quarter to the curriculum in many colleges, four- and five-year graduation rates were falling. The five-year rate for the class entering autumn 1989, for instance, was 51.3 percent. For the next class it would be 46.8 percent (Source: Office of Enrollment Management). The finest selective admissions universities graduated nine of ten entering freshmen, and most of them in four years.

## *Getting Started*

For three years, since the inauguration of autumn quarter selective admissions, Admissions Director Mager had made his annual budget requests to upgrade freshman recruiting. And for three years, his office had been turned down. More than enough students were applying above the lowest acceptance denominator. And virtually no top administrators had come from the private university sector, and thus seen the impact an effective student recruiting program can have. "I would try to make the most compelling argument that the potential of the university is not being reached because we were not investing in admissions outreach." Mager had an assistant director, two counselors, and virtually no travel budget. "To this day, I still tell people our admissions staff was smaller than Otterbein College's."

The situation was an embarrassment to Gee and, even more importantly, to the new breed of trustee. "Let's face it," trustee Shumate recalled later, "there were a number of trustees who went to Ohio State during that open admissions time and very strongly believed in it. There was significant debate." Nor had it been good enough for Hutchinson. Early in the transition period, Hutchinson had appointed a task force on undergraduate recruitment and chaired it with an enthusiastic new dean, psychologist Robert Arkin. As associate dean for undergraduate studies for the Colleges of the Arts and Sciences, Arkin, with degrees from UCLA and USC, had himself been disappointed in the freshman classes he had seen since arriving from the University of Missouri in 1988.

He soon was to learn that, in 1988, with Mager's input, Communications Director Baroway had written a university marketing plan that had stressed how a noncompetitive freshman class was hurting the national reputation of Ohio State. In particular, because they were published annually in the most reputable guides to colleges and universities, parents and prospective students compared national test scores: the ACT, taken primarily in the Midwest, and the SAT, predominant in the rest of the country.

As comparatives, the plan had pointed to the median ACT scores at Michigan (27.5), Illinois (27), and Ohio State (22), with SAT comparables. A follow-up plan a year later had found Ohio State's scores tied for last not only in the Big Ten, but among the eleven Ohio public and private universities listed in the influential *Yale Daily News*'s *Insider's Guide to the Colleges:* Antioch, Case Western Reserve, Cincinnati, Denison, Kenyon, Miami, Oberlin, Ohio State, Ohio, Wittenberg, and Wooster.

If reading that guide would not puncture faculty egos, the old standby *Barron's Profiles of Colleges and Universities* could. *Barron's* scale (most competitive, highly competitive, very competitive, competitive plus, competitive, etc.), which considered freshman class selectivity and high school class rank as well as test scores, had rated both Ohio University and Ohio Northern University "very competitive." Embarrassingly, Ohio State—with all of its program breadth and diversity—was two ranks below.

In addition—embarrassment of embarrassments—recent publicity had the University of Toledo, by offering full no-need academic scholarships, burying the Buckeyes in attracting National Merit Scholar semifinalists.

None of this information was lost on Arkin's task force, nor was a report from the previous year by a Jennings-appointed Committee on Student Recruitment. It had verified Ohio State losing ground with the top high school graduates even as selective admissions was supposed to be gaining it. True or not, myths, half-myths, or no myths, Mager's research had found Ohio State still rebuffed as "too big, too impersonal, and non-academic." Its residence towers were "large, overcrowded and rowdy." Its campus safety was "poor." Its classes were taught by "too many foreign TAs who speak English poorly." Such were the perceptions of the top students Ohio State wanted but did not get.

Given these negatives to fix and misinformation to dispel, Arkin's group

Investing in 100+ National Merit Scholars moves Ohio State atop the Big Ten, 1991.

concluded the obvious: Ohio State was "far behind virtually all private and public universities and colleges in off-campus efforts—including staffing, media, publications and public relations." It recommended a strategy to make Ohio State competitive in student recruiting, institutional marketing, and financing no-need academic scholarships. It was approved by Gee and Hutchinson found the funds.

For the short term, by offering both full and partial scholarship packages through competitive testing of National Merit and Achievement semifinalists, Ohio State would build a critical mass of young scholars with which to strengthen the academic reputation. It also would make its modest honors program, begun in 1985, into a significant recruiting tool that, by the mid-1990s, would be serving a third of the undergraduate population.

For the long term, student recruitment would be intensified; this included hiring more counselors, attending more "college days," involving alumni clubs in a coherent recruitment and scholarship program, and producing a direct mail and video campaign that would carry a prospective student from inquiry through acceptance and enrollment.

The committee also recommended the customization of campus tours to the special interests of visiting students and personal telephone follow-ups by students and faculty. The site of the admissions office, Lincoln Tower, was such an abomination that had the administration sought the worst environment on campus it could do no better. Location, location, location! Move it to a classic collegiate site, urged the committee—which would finally be found with the renovation of Enarson Hall on the South Oval in 1996.

Given the history of administrative inaction, though Hutchinson had commissioned the task force, his go-ahead with $500,000 in immediate money shocked Arkin. In the last year before Ohio and Ohio State budgets skidded into the red, the provost's office had carried a surplus. Thus, Arkin came out of the meeting with nearly everything in the start-up plan approved and funded. "It was the highest experience I ever had as an administrator, maybe the most memorable hour I have ever had as an academic."

The first year, ten applicants selected from the top 3 percent in ACT scores would be awarded full-ride $8,100 scholarships as Presidential Scholars, and 40 Medalist Scholars would receive full in-state tuition worth $2,300 the first year. Development Vice President Don Glower looked forward to raising the funds from private sources to support the additional three years for each student. The long-time engineering dean himself had illustrated the need by telling Gee of a small high school he had visited where the average SAT score was an extraordinary 1290. Every student there took physics and calculus. And every student accepted by his engineering college had enrolled somewhere else.

Though it would be playing a half-century of catch-up with its private university competitors, Ohio State finally would begin marketing itself and granting no-need academic scholarships.

Gee would pick up the ball and run with it, as increasing Ohio State's academic stature had been one of his highest agenda items to begin with. Then along came *U.S. News and World Report*, with, said Mager, "the biggest wake-up call this university has ever had." Now Gee had just the data on internal reallocations, lobbying, and fund-raising that he needed to justify the drive to put more Ohio State money into academic recruiting, academic scholarships, and its honors program.

## *The Impact of* U.S. News

How good, really, was Ohio State academically? Although Ed Jennings's "excellence" drumbeat through the 1980s had helped build faculty morale, as a platitude it had cut both ways. In his commencement speech in August 1990,

English professor John Gable had praised Jennings for it, saying Jennings's "Excellence, excellence, excellence" was so incessant "we have begun to believe it." As Trustee Les Wexner commented later, however, believing and being are two different things. An excellence myth could become a problem, in particular by perpetuating complacency.

Good students who read the college guides certainly knew Ohio State's low admissions standards and poor level of state support were lead weights on its quality ratings, and so did their parents. But the Ohio citizenry, the alumni body, and the Ohio General Assembly, who did not read such guides, had no reason to distrust what Wexner recalled hearing at Board meetings: "That everything was excellent and everything was terrific." That was not exactly what Gordon Gee had read in the Auburn Report.

"Certain kinds of coaches tell the team when they're winning and tell the team when they're losing," Wexner said later in an analogy to football. "And they tell them when they're not very good, and they tell them what they have to do to get better." He was sure Ohio State's new president was prepared to be that kind of coach.

As Shumate would recall, Wexner himself soon became "the driving force in the development of benchmarking, peer groups, and national standards, in having the Board be more scrutinizing, more critical in our analysis of information we were provided." Early in the Gee administration, Wexner started prying open the door to comparative analysis when, at one trustee meeting, he very deliberately began to ask of the administration, "How do you know?" and "By what measure?" Then *U.S. News* came along and blew the excellence door off its hinges.

Though *U.S. News* had been publishing a college ranking since 1987, with the smallest circulation of the "big three" news magazines (*Time, Newsweek, U.S. News*), little attention was paid to its "college edition" until 1990, when the confluence of rapidly increasing tuitions, a declining economy, the public's fascination for rankings, and better self-promotion began to make it a "must read" for many people.

Whereas most readers of college guidebooks had been college-bound high schoolers and their parents, a broader college-educated cohort was picking up *U.S. News*, where an embarrassed Ohio State was ranked not in the top 10 among "national universities," nor in the top 25, nor in the top 50, but somewhere in the second quartile.

By taking the wraps off comparative data, *U.S. News* gave those at Ohio State who wanted a truly selective student body the ammunition they needed to move forward. As Shumate recalled about the trustees after reading the

## Chapter 6

ranking, "We had to get serious. We weren't where we wanted to be and nobody else was going to lie down and rest" as Ohio State "just kept going incrementally and evolutionarily."

Soon *America's Best Colleges,* published both in the magazine and as a separate periodical, eclipsed all other guides in influence and sent disenchanted alumni of many American colleges and universities into administration-bashing and letter-writing frenzies. By the mid-1990s, imperfect as accusers might allege, its annual rankings were the oracle comparing undergraduate schools, graduate and professional programs, and America's hospitals. By then, both University Hospitals and the James also were paying attention, for they were also being ranked.

On May 14, 1991, Ohio State announced that 103 National Merit and National Achievement semifinalists had accepted admission, up from twenty-two from the year before. By fall, more than 400 students with ACT scores of 29 or above also had accepted University Scholarships, up from 250 the year before. In one year, Ohio State leapfrogged into the top 10 nationally for National Merit Scholars enrolled as new freshmen, as well as to the top of the Big Ten.

On November 9, 1991, President Gee, who himself had been a National Merit Scholar, met with sixty-five National Merit semifinalists and some 130 family members in the West Ballroom of the Ohio Union. He touted the university's comprehensiveness, its size as an asset, its spirit, and its traditions and promised to work tirelessly to assure them their Ohio State education would be outstanding. Each left campus with a poster from the Honors Center illustrating Albert Einstein wearing his "Block 'O'" varsity sweater. It was titled an "Ohio State of Mind. . . . Where Great Minds Go," and it began a poster series using the theme.

The following March, 435 teenagers at the top of their classes vied for the fifty new scholarships. Each already had been offered one of 600 University Scholarships guaranteed at $1,000. Each already had been mailed a recruiting poster starring Gee himself. John Hoffmeister, the staff writer who created it, could hardly believe Gee had posed for it. Running horizontally beneath the headline "Find Your Place at Ohio State" were ten little Gees, running, jumping, dribbling a basketball, hamming, each dramatizing the line below it:

> Some here find their star on stage.
> Some find the stars beyond.
> Some find their place on football fields.
> And others cheer them on.
> Some Bucks are big on basketball.

And some for business bound.
Some here have a bookish bent.
And some in labs are found.
So find your way to Ohio State.
And take a look around.

The poster became an instant classic, pinned to high school guidance counselors' bulletin boards and students' bedroom walls, and replicated as a television public service announcement seen statewide and nationally on football broadcasts. Gordon Gee was an approachable guy, it said. What a character! While some faculty must have hid their heads in their hands, what it said to students, parents, and guidance counselors was, "You might want to take another look at a place with a president like that."

The response to the invitation to compete, said Arkin, "was beyond our wildest dreams," and Mabel Freeman, the indispensable associate director of the growing honors program, hit the nail on the head: "Scholarship opportunities begin to make us competitive. High school counselors are saying, 'Yes! Ohio State is finally on target.'" They also were being charmed by Gee. And no one at Ohio State was worrying any longer about Toledo.

## *AIDS on Campus*

"Since it emerged in 1981 as an isolated problem among the gay population, AIDS has become the nation's leading health concern. More Americans have since died from the disease than were lost during the entire Vietnam War. And the illness has shifted from threatening a few high-risk groups to endangering the general population. No one is immune." So read the cover copy on the autumn 1989 issue of *Quest,* the university's now extinct external tabloid for alumni, the same issue announcing that Jennings would step down.

The University Health Service had diagnosed its first case of Acquired Immune Deficiency Disease in 1983. The patient lived for one year. At that time, it was not yet known that nearly all people who tested positive for the HIV virus eventually would contract AIDS, which then was a death warrant.

An Ohio State information task force had been created. It was first chaired by Infectious Diseases Department Chair Robert Perkins, then by Professor of Internal Medicine Michael Para, with significant leadership also from Professor of Law Rhonda Rivera and Business's Robert Haverkamp. It had developed university guidelines for cases in the student body, faculty, and staff. Ohio State

## Chapter 6

was bound by the Vocational Rehabilitation Act of 1973, the university community was told. The act prohibited discrimination based upon a handicap, and PWAs (people with AIDS) *were* handicapped.

Despite the committee's introduction of seminars, information mailings, and the addition of an AIDS unit to freshman orientation, in 1990 AIDS on campus was still the "It could never happen to me" disease. Nationally there was concern that college campuses would become sites of the next spike in the epidemic. Though condom machines had been installed in residence halls at Ohio State and across the country, "safe sex" was only slowly entering heterosexual terminology.

In January 1990, the university committee issued a new question-and-answer document that spelled out the latest information on AIDS and its spread beyond the gay population. No, it could not be caused by "casual contact." No, it would not be contracted by giving blood. But, gay or straight, college students should "know the sexual background and habits of partners" and should "use contraceptive measures (condoms and spermicides) that could prevent entry of a virus into the bloodstream and kill it." And no, "There is no vaccine or cure for AIDS."

When AIDS first entered the United States, because the only known cases were among gay men, AIDS was not believed to be transmitted through vaginal intercourse. That, of course, proved very wrong. Many African nations soon came under siege by AIDS in the heterosexual population. It was being transmitted from infected mothers to unborn children. A generation of infected children was being born.

By late 1989, heterosexual transmission in the United States was up to 5 percent and growing. In total, more than 100,000 cases had been reported nationally, 1485 in Ohio and 302 in Franklin County. Experts were predicting 500,000 cases nationally by 1993 and an annual death toll of 100,000.

Ten years earlier, Mike Para had been an infectious disease specialist at Ohio State who had entered the field with the happy prospect of helping nearly all his patients recover. By 1990, he was heading a federally funded trial at University Hospitals that enrolled 180 HIV positive people; all had been expected to die. He and his team were testing AZT, the only drug that was at all effective in slowing the disease at that time, and they had begun to collaborate with the Department of Family Medicine, linking family doctors around the state with experts at OSU.

Afraid the stigma would scare away other patients, hospitals in general had not wanted to be known as AIDS centers. In 1990, University Hospitals (later the "Medical Center") "came out of the closet." Over all, the work of the AIDS education and research committee helped the campus avoid hysteria, overreaction, and misbehavior as college students gay and straight began to ask potential partners if "they had been tested." It was hoped that they also waited to decide about sex until each had and knew the other's answer.

Later in the decade, Para and his colleagues tested and administered the multiprescription "cocktails" that seemed to hold back the disease and ward off the killer opportunistic infections for a number of years, if not longer. By this time, Para himself had become one of the nation's leading researchers in the field, as well as a friend and champion to many of the men and women who had come to the Ohio State Medical Center for treatment.

## The Cleveland Clinic

The Ohio State University had one of the nation's finest and largest—perhaps too large—medical schools. It also had the newly opened "James," dedicated to researching, treating, and curing cancer; one of the great rehabilitation centers in Dodd Hall; and a fine reputation overall. The Cleveland Clinic was one of the celebrated hospitals of the world, ranked among the best five or six in the country in the new *U.S. News* rankings, and at the very top in cardiology, cardiac surgery, and gastroenterology. However, the clinic granted no degrees and had no medical school.

Surely, thought Dr. Bernadine Healy, chair of the Research Institute at the Cleveland Clinic Foundation, the new president of Ohio State will be interested in combining their complementary strengths, so "I just called him up as soon as I heard he was on the scene." By the end of Gee's first month in the saddle, they already had met in Cleveland, and Hutchinson had advised his deans that the dialogue was beginning. He had appointed Ronald St. Pierre, associate vice president for Health Services, to chair Ohio State's half of the exploratory task force.

On February 28, 1991, Ohio State and the Cleveland Clinic signed an academic partnership agreement involving the biomedical sciences, medical bioengineering, biotechnology, the health care professions, and the allied health professions. Under the agreement, the Cleveland Clinic Foundation Health Sciences Center–The Ohio State University would be established at Ohio State.

Along the way, the Ohio Board of Regents wanted a look, because at least one member from the Cleveland area preferred the clinic affiliate with Case Western Reserve. As Hutchinson recalled it, newly appointed Chancellor Elaine Hairston, "always helpful, never an obstructionist, helped me through that," and the regents endorsed the program that June. By autumn, the first significant joint R&D project, development of a motorized heart pump for patients with weakened hearts, was announced.

From 1993 on, several dozen Ohio State medical students a year went to the clinic for training. In exchange, clinic faculty received Ohio State appointments (George Paulson, *The Ohio State University College of Medicine* 1998, 173).

In 1995, Healy, who by now had also directed the National Institutes of Health in the George Bush administration from 1991 to 1993, became dean of The Ohio State University College of Medicine. Gee had called her as soon as the search was initiated and urged her to apply. After that, he called her every month. When he got off the phone, she would tell herself, "That man knows how to recruit." As did she. Her international contacts and reputation would attract a coterie of distinguished new faculty to the Medical Center. As the on-air medical expert for CBS television, she also became a splendid symbol of the academic ascendancy of Ohio State during the Gee administration.

Energized by an offer she "fell in love with" where she felt she could make even more of a difference than at Ohio State, Healy would leave to head the National Red Cross in 1999. Upbeat as ever, she had worked from home for awhile following brain tumor surgery, flying secretaries up to Cleveland to keep up with her, and, vital as ever, had spoken only days after surgery at a Columbus event honoring the university. Whether or not it was Dean Healy's presence that held the Ohio State–Cleveland Clinic relationship together, in 2001 the two separated when the clinic announced it would open its own, albeit small, medical school.

## *Mt. Graham and the LBT "Columbus Project"*

There had never been a telescope like it. "It would be sensitive enough to detect the light from a burning candle at twice the distance to the moon—500,000 miles—or see a penny more than 500 miles away," wrote Ohio State's premier science writer Earle Holland. The Large Binocular Telescope, or LBT, at the Mount Graham International Observatory was to be the largest in the world. First known also as "the Columbus Project," it would house two eight-meter spin-cast mirrors. Used together, these two creations of new technology would have the range of an 11.3-meter single lens (38 feet), which was impossible to build.

In 1985, Ohio State's president and astronomy department had agreed to collaborate with the University of Arizona. The Columbus Project would, of course, be completed in 1992, the 500th anniversary of Christopher Columbus's discovery of the New World. Its site would be near the summit of the 10,720-foot Mount Graham in Arizona. Though it would cost a lot of money, what it would do for the reputation of the Ohio State astronomy department and Ohio State's place in the competition for "big science" would be worth the investment. And surely, most of the funds could be raised privately.

That was 1985, under a president comfortable with big decisions and a Board of Trustees, as Wexner said later, often comfortable leaving decisions to the president. The prestigious University of Chicago also had joined the team, as would the Arcetri Astrophysical Observatory of Florence, Italy, a year later. One often is known indeed by the company one keeps, and this was very good company.

The trustees, in fact, had approved a "Phase 1" resolution to spend what trustee Hamilton "Joel" Teaford recalls as "a teeny little bit of money" to explore the telescope's potential. Compared with the $60 million that became the final estimate of Ohio State's long-term cost, $300,000 was, in fact, a drop in the bucket. That a decision to form a multiparty corporation and authorize bonding had never come before the Board mattered little until 1990, when Teaford became its vice chair, knowing that a fund-raising feasibility study had discovered the bucket had a hole in it. So had the University of Chicago, which already had backed out.

While more than $460 million was raised or pledged privately to Ohio State between 1985 and 1990, no big donors had anted up for the telescope, none were on the horizon, and money was not the only problem. There were also the resident San Carlos Apaches, split between the quiet progressives who wanted the jobs and revenue the telescope could bring, and the vocal traditionalists who saw only desecration of sacred land. Though the lower reaches of the mountain long had been given over to vacation cabins, logging, and even squirrel hunting, the top still was mostly undisturbed.

Then came the environmental activists, championing the Mt. Graham red squirrel, a subspecies whose fate, they said, would be endangered by such construction on the mountain. As *Science* magazine explained (June 1990), they viewed the astronomers "suspiciously like developers trying to lock up the last high mountain in Southern Arizona." Led by the Sierra Club Defense Fund, they had filed a federal suit to force the U.S. Fish and Wildlife Service to redo its opinion that a particular land-use plan would protect the Mt. Graham squirrel.

Which is where Gordon Gee, the new president of Ohio State, came in, as,

## Chapter 6

from the periphery, did Ohio Governor Richard Celeste. For the university had become aware that Ohio's tax revenue was plummeting again and that Celeste soon would announce huge budget cuts. Was this any time to invest millions in a telescope?

Hutchinson thought not and confidentially recommended that Gee terminate it. Although construction would cost Ohio State "only" $15–20 million, when operating expenses and the cost of new faculty hires were added in, the Columbus Project would cost the university $4.6 million a year for fifteen years. This would exceed the average new program funding available to all colleges for each of the last eight years. And that was in good times!

On the Board of Trustees, Teaford had opposed it from the beginning. An astronomy buff, he was related by marriage to George Ellery Hale, after whom the huge Mt. Palomar scope was named. Teaford thought Ohio State's department too weak and such large out-of-state expenditures bad policy at any time. He had visited the Mt. Graham site with Hutchinson and Ed Hayes, the new Research vice president just hired away from a similar position at Rice. Hayes knew both his science and his economics. A respected quantum chemist, he not only had once headed the areas of chemistry and dynamics for the National Science Foundation, he also had been the foundation's controller. Teaford, Hutchinson, and Hayes all came away concerned about the project's cost relative to its academic and reputational value.

Meanwhile, University of Arizona President Henry Koffler would write Gee, urging him to proceed expeditiously, and Gee would continue to support the project—but only, he said, *if* the federal court approved it and *if* the money could be raised.

The final decision would not be made for another year. In the interim, the Mathematical and Physical Sciences Dean, Bill Kern, hired his own public relations firm, Paul Werth and Associates, to support the cause and promote the project, while the Arizona team continued to ignore Ohio's state budget crisis and President Gee's "ifs."

"If it weren't for me the telescope project would be gone by now," the *Lantern* (March 9, 1991) quoted Gee, who added that he would not build it *if* he couldn't afford it. And Ohio State couldn't.

Neither, it turned out, could Johns Hopkins afford to join the same University of Arizona and the Carnegie Foundation on another scope, the Magellan Project, and for the same reason: no big donors. Hopkins's announcement in April to drop Magellan paved the way for Ohio State's announcement five months later.

On September 7, 1991, Ohio State played Arizona in a football game in

Ohio Stadium. The game brought the new president of the University of Arizona, Manuel Pacheco, back to Columbus. A distinguished Ohio State alumnus, he just had delivered his alma mater's summer commencement address and was returning now to sign an agreement to build the telescope and then watch the game. As the home team, Ohio State had the rights to produce the national television public service announcement for the game, but Ohio State's Baroway, with Gee's OK, would not do the piece on the telescope partnership the Arizona administration wanted. Even that refusal apparently sent no signal to Pacheco's administration that it would have an unhappy meeting at Ohio State.

In the end, there was no agreement and two casualties. Dean Kern, the *Dispatch* announced (September 11, 1991) "will leave his position Oct. 31, in part, due to OSU's decision to drop out of the project. Kern will return to teaching and research in the OSU chemistry department." Also, "Eugene Capriotti said he planned to step down as chairman of the astronomy department to protest the university's decision."

"When you are canceling math classes to build a telescope," Gee told the *Dispatch* afterward, "you have a problem." Hutchinson reported Ohio State had raised all of $450 for it "as of last week." And Teaford said the most important reason for lack of support was that "Mount Graham is not in Ohio."

In 1992, the year the Columbus Project was to have been completed, the trustees did approve plans to build a $2.4 million astronomical instrumentation facility on campus to design and build instruments in exchange for observing time on large telescopes. One of them would be the Large Binocular Telescope. Hayes and Dean Jim Garland had helped mend fences between the administration and the faculty, and neither the squirrel lobby nor the sacred ground lobby had won the day on campus.

"There is a feeling of putting things back together and moving forward again," Acting Astronomy Chair Gerald Newsom told Tim Doulin of the *Dispatch*. This certainly was verified in 1995, when the National Research Council announced its once-per-decade rating of doctoral programs. Astronomy was ranked 23rd, with the 10th best improvement rating in the nation. Soon that improvement would be rewarded with a $2.5 million gift from the nonprofit Research Corporation, specifically for additional time on the yet to be completed LBT. Meanwhile, the "endangered" Mt. Graham squirrel population had nearly doubled.

In retrospect, through three provosts—Fred Hutchinson, Joan Huber, and Richard Sisson—Ohio State appeared to have made the right academic and financial decisions all along. Arizona President Manuel Pacheco, Hutchinson

CHAPTER 6

said some years later, had been ever the gentleman. In 1991, "he could have quietly badmouthed us. And we were vulnerable, frankly. But that is not what happened." Ohio State also won the football game, 38–14. And, for a while, still had "the Big Ear."

## The "Big Ear" and Perkins

The second largest radio telescope of its kind in the nation had run the world's longest continuous search for extraterrestrial intelligence (SETI) and had conducted the largest all-sky astronomical survey of natural radio sources ever made. This was The Ohio State University's "Big Ear," which was not in Columbus but in nearby Delaware, on twenty-four acres originally leased from Ohio Wesleyan University.

Like a giant erector set, it consisted of two flat steel beam reflectors, was 105 feet high and 100 yards long, and weighed 150 tons. Professor John D. Kraus and his students had built it in the early 1960s with $250,000 and a $50 war surplus crane. When Ohio Wesleyan sold the property, because it abutted the nine-hole Delaware Country Club, mashie bashers salivated at the prospect of nine more holes. But, responding to SETI advocates around the world, Ed Jennings, an excellent golfer himself, had negotiated a new lease with the new owners. Robert Dixon, director of the university's academic computing center, was staffing the scope now as the volunteer "assistant director."

Hutchinson would explain all this to Gee following Dixon's invitation to the new president to come up to Delaware and see him sometime. The lease would be over in five years, but could be renegotiated for another ten. Gee already knew of the Big Ear's fifteen minutes of fame. In 1977, Jerry Ehman, a volunteer, had recorded a seventy-second signal from space so strong he wrote "Wow!" on the printout. Could this have been the first verification of extraterrestrial intelligence?

Over another twenty years, the legendary "Wow!" signal never was heard from again. But the SETI advocates were. In 1997, despite a torrent of letters in print and in the new medium of e-mail, Gee chose not to renew the lease. It was not that he liked golf. He was a dancer, not a golfer. But the Big Ear needed a $100,000 paint job and its capabilities had been replicated elsewhere by much smaller receivers. Dave Lore of the *Dispatch* would write (December 21, 1997), "the pulsars gave way to the putters," as he announced that the Big Ear would sign off forever on midnight December 31, 1997. Coincidentally, so would Gordon Gee, who, the next day, New Year's Day 1998, would be on the payroll of Brown University.

Six months earlier, a termination notice for an allied telescope agreement had been handled much more quietly. Since 1930, Ohio State had shared Ohio Wesleyan's Perkins Observatory, a domed unit near the Big Ear. Since 1961, when its large mirror was moved to the clearer skies of Arizona, Ohio State had maintained support of a smaller Perkins scope. That, too, Gee would end effective July 31, 1998.

## *Maine*

Meanwhile, in April 1992, Hutchinson had left Columbus to become president of the flagship university in his beloved state of Maine after three years as provost, including his six-month recovery from his bicycle accident in 1990. During that period, much credit was due Associate Provost David Boyne, who worked masterfully in the background as a shadow provost until Hutchinson recovered well enough to be briefed by Boyne daily at the Hutchinson home. On April 7, Gee wrote to "all" of Maine's larger newspapers about Hutchinson. From Augusta to Bangor, from Biddeford to Brunswick, from Portland to Waterville, he congratulated the state for attracting "a man of uncompromising integrity . . . the treasure [it] had just stolen from Ohio."

Hutchinson had been the administrator to facilitate the first academic budget cuts and the earliest elimination of a program—the Department of Photography and Cinema. He had worked with the Pew Foundation, which did an institutional scan of Ohio State as one of twenty universities selected. His administration, through commissions and committees, had moved further toward equity for women and minorities in salaries and promotions. And unknown to most people, he had been the colleague to pick up administrative slack during the last months of Elizabeth Gee's life and a good and close friend to his president following her death.

It was the intervention of Ohio State's newest trustee, Mike Colley, he said later, that gave him the tools to "be there" for Gordon Gee. A trust and estates lawyer, through his work Colley knew more than most people about the process of grieving.

"Gordon is going to need you to understand what he's going through. And he'll never ask you," Colley told Hutchinson. "People don't." He explained the stages of grief—denial and isolation, anger, bargaining, depression, acceptance—and their predictability as processes and the variations in their

CHAPTER 6

duration. In addition, the head of a large organization was burdened with the added isolation of leadership. One day, when the president entered Hutchinson's office and hesitated as he got ready to leave, Hutchinson asked him how he was doing.

It would not be the only time they talked.

# 7

# *War and the Home Front*

> For the past several years I have been working with [an] Amvets Post . . . composed primarily of university employees who are Vietnam veterans. There remains a lot of hard feelings and emotions from that war. . . . [Also], many others are being forced out or leaving voluntarily. . . . We already have 1,600 such students on campus. They ended the Cold War and served because they wanted to. That puts them in the category of patriots and they deserve our special attention.
>
> —From a letter to the president

On January 18, 1991, President George Bush announced to the world that the United States and a coalition of thirty-two allies, including Canada, Britain, and France, would be fighting a war in the Persian Gulf. In the next two weeks, as military reserve units were activated and Ohio State people were called up, demonstrations involving thousands of students were held on and off campus, both to support and to oppose the war. In a "From the President's Desk" mailing, used periodically to reach the campus on short notice, Gee urged the community to join him in encouraging "vigorous discourse" but to show "tolerance and respect."

Iraq was supposed to have a fearsome defense in Kuwait and a battle-hardened army. "A long war or a short one?" writer Tom Spring asked in *onCampus* the next week (January 24, 1991). Professor Richard Hermann's answer was that, if it were primarily an air war, it would not "last terribly long" but that a ground war "could be a messy affair." Hermann, associate professor of political science,

CHAPTER 7

had worked on Persian Gulf policy for Secretary of State James Baker just the year before.

Ohio State military historian Alan Millet, a retired Marine colonel who had written the definitive history of the Marine Corps, drew a parallel between the dug-in Iraqi defenses and the island bunkers of the Japanese during World War II. There would have to be some kind of ground campaign to throw the Iraqis out of Kuwait.

Defense specialist Joe Kruzel was more specific. He outlined a three-phase coalition strategy. Air superiority had just been gained. It would be followed by massive saturation bombing, followed in turn by an air and land battle. Within the next two weeks, he said, Iraq's half-million troops would be subjected to the "most massive and sustained bombardment in the history of warfare." "Battle weary" as well as battle hardened, they would be without "a wink of sleep" and would not even know "whether Baghdad still exists. It seems to me a possible outcome would be that the Iraqi army will be unable to mount any coordinated, sustained resistance to Allied ground forces."

Kruzel was right on the money. Following the saturation bombing, in 100 hours the coalition forces liberated Kuwait and defeated Saddam Hussein's army. After rejecting Iraqi peace offers, under international pressure to stop the bloodshed, on February 27 President Bush called a cease-fire to Operation Desert Shield/Desert Storm.

Four years later, Kruzel would go on leave from the university to become U.S. Deputy Assistant Secretary of Defense for European and NATO Affairs. On August 20, 1995, called in to help negotiate a peace in Bosnia, he was killed when a land mine exploded under his vehicle on a dangerous road near Sarajevo.

## *The Vietnam Veteran*

Soon most of the Gulf War veterans of Ohio State were on their way home and the country would begin to hear about a new medical problem, Gulf War syndrome. Coincidentally, the university administration was now under fire itself for perpetuating a syndrome from the last war, the Vietnam War: the benign neglect of America's own veterans. While for twenty years following the pullout of troops from Vietnam, Ohio State's veterans on the faculty and staff had been silent, national enthusiasm over the Gulf War had given them the environment to speak out and be heard.

Ohio State, many Vietnam veterans felt, was not complying with the little known Vietnam Era Veterans Readjustment Act of 1974—the equivalent of the Civil Rights Act of 1964, which brought federal legal protection against discrimination based on race, sex, religious beliefs, or national origin. They had formed the Vietnam Era Veterans' Issues Committee, which met with Gee assistant Chip Elam and Human Relations officer Sue Blanshan. "Gee," Blanshan wrote after the meeting, "should consider conducting a thorough review of the state of veterans' issues on campus, the creation of an office for veterans' affairs and the development of an appropriate affirmative action plan."

In a letter to Gee, Evyln Skurow of the Engineering Research Center, who had served with the Agency for International Development during the Tet Offensive, spoke for the committee when she wrote, "Having survived a terrible war which they were not allowed to win, the Vietnam veterans knew what was most important for their healing upon their return. And they know in their very souls how devastating it was not to receive it." They had waited for the light at the end of the tunnel, "but were never allowed to reach it. I think the establishment of a Veterans' Affairs Office would [be] a giant step forward, finally reaching the end of that long, difficult tunnel."

Within a few days, Gee appointed John Guilmartin, Jr., associate professor of history, to chair an eleven-member veterans task force. All were veterans. Guilmartin himself had been an Air Force rescue helicopter pilot, had served two tours and won the Silver Star with oak leaf cluster, the Air Medal with five oak leaf clusters, and the Legion of Honor. His colleagues included Phoebe Spinrad, associate professor of English, who had been an Air Force captain with a Medivac unit in the Philippines. Representing the president's office *ex officio* was Madison Scott, executive assistant to Gee and secretary of the Board of Trustees, who had retired from the Army with the highest rank a noncommissioned officer can gain—command sergeant major.

"The faculty of today," Guilmartin explained in *Quest* (winter 1992), had come of age intellectually, politically, and socially during the antiwar movement and still saw the war through its eyes. Said Spinrad, "They took their academic deferments. They finished up. They got tenured and administrative positions. But they have the same feelings about us as they did then."

Some veterans wanted no special advocacy but kept quiet about it. Most faculty and staff had been unaware there was a problem. Some were surprised, if not stupefied, by the bitterness of some colleagues, as was Gee, who had lost a good friend in the Tet Offensive in 1968 and empathized with anyone who had been in the war or was touched personally by it.

One who was not surprised was the author of the article itself. *Quest* editor Earle Holland had been a Special Forces paratrooper and a National

## Chapter 7

Guardsman on active duty for eleven months, but had not been sent to Vietnam. In 1971, Holland the guardsman had been attacked by twenty "regular Army" in retaliation for the Kent State killings, which he had had nothing to do with. Another who wasn't surprised was Bill Wahl, a veteran who ran Ohio State's campus tour program and later established Gee's Parents Association. Wahl had returned from a Vietnam tour as a military policeman, with the ghastly duty of placing the dog tags between the teeth of dead GIs, only to be teargassed in his new civilian clothes while walking by a student demonstration.

By the fall of 1991, the task force had reported that the university was not giving veterans preferential treatment and was not in compliance. Gee would establish the veterans' office, he said, and work to improve the environment on campus.

But he did not concur that the university had been out of compliance. The former Law School dean, Jim Meeks, then Gee's special assistant for Legal Affairs, had concluded that two different compliance regulations affected veteran employment. For "classified" employees, normally understood to hold staff jobs and not the higher paying administrative ones, yes, the university gave veterans a twenty-point testing advantage under Ohio law. But state law did not apply to "unclassified" jobs, which were most of the true administrative positions. Federal law did and demanded equal, not preferential, treatment.

Gee would recommend to the trustees the establishment of the new veterans' office as part of the newly titled Office of Human Resources, soon to get its new vice president, Linda Tom. What it would also get was a two-month investigation by the U.S. Department of Labor and a review by the Ohio Office of Veterans' Affairs.

Within the same time frame that Ohio State gained another new vice president, Jerry May of Michigan in Development, and deans Jose Cruz of the University of California–Irvine in Engineering and its own Jim Garland in Mathematical and Physical Sciences, it also got the Labor Department report. Ohio State, it said, had in fact already formed the Veterans' Affairs Office and hired former Ohio National Guard Inspector General and twenty-eight-year veteran Bill Hospodar to head it. It had distributed employee forms urging all veterans and disabled veterans to identify themselves. It had agreed to update affirmative action programs for disabled veterans and improve communication of job opening information to the Ohio Bureau of Employment Services.

It had failed, however, to maintain an environment free from the harassment, intimidation, and coercion of veterans. "The university has a strong policy under which we will not tolerate any acts of discrimination against any member of the university community," the new vice president for Human Resources said in response. "We will enforce that policy vigorously."

Case closed.

In the interim, by the fall of 1992, Bobby Moser had been named dean of Agriculture, and Mac Stewart, dean of University College. Bob Duncan had been appointed to head the new Office of Legal Affairs while Jim Meeks returned to the Law School faculty. Computer graphics pioneer Chuck Csuri had retired. Revered oncologist Arthur James had passed his eightieth birthday.

The trustees had lifted the mandatory retirement age of seventy, following the new federal mandate. Lena Charles Bailey, who would live only four years longer, and have a lecture series established in her name, retired as dean of Human Ecology. Violet Meek had been named dean of the Lima campus following a contentious firing of James Countryman, who stayed on as president of Lima Technical College. Joe Russell had been reassigned to study influences on minority retention, and David Williams was named vice provost for Minority Affairs pending a national search.

Joan Huber had taken over as senior vice president and provost for Maine-bound Fred Hutchinson, with a national search to begin in which she did not wish to participate. And Edward Hayes had arrived from Rice as vice president for Research. Columbus's international flower show, AmeriFlora, in which Ohio State displayed its International Garden of Knowledge, had come and gone; film and theatre director Peter Brook had received the first Wexner Prize, $50,000 and a commemorative sculpture designed by Jim Dine.

And, sadly, Elizabeth Gee, the first lady of Ohio State, had passed away.

# 8
## *Elizabeth*

> There is no greater anguish than confronting mortal illness, but for some, like Elizabeth Gee, a deeply spiritual and highly courageous woman, her confrontation became an affirmation of life.
>
> —BERNADINE HEALY, M.D., Director,
> National Institutes of Health,
> from the back cover of Elizabeth
> Gee's *The Light around the Dark*

Molly Davis has a small prism hanging in the west window of her Beechwold kitchen. "Every evening there's a sun to see, we have a rainbow where we're sitting." Molly Davis did research work and wrote speech drafts for Elizabeth Gee. The prism was a last gift from her boss and friend. "Elizabeth wanted to leave a tangible thing so that people would know she was thinking about them." Toward the end, she sent out many personal notes, often with a prism.

Elizabeth Dutson Gee was from a new generation of first ladies. "It would have been absolutely impossible," she told *Columbus Monthly* (June 1991), for her husband to have accepted the Ohio State presidency if the offer had not included a salaried position for her. She held three appointments at Ohio State: senior research associate at the Center for Women's Studies, adjunct assistant professor in the College of Education, and senior associate in the Office of Development. The last acknowledged her significant role in the carousel of breakfasts, brunches, dinners and receptions—fund-raising, friend-raising, faculty schmoozing, and student-rewarding—that she would organize and host at her home in Bexley.

Elizabeth and Gordon Gee at the new Bexley residence, 1990.

"It's your whole self-identity," she said of her career, which, not coincidentally, had been dedicated to women's issues and medical and legal ethics. Her doctoral dissertation had been on ethics education in the legal profession. An example of what should change, she had told a *Lantern* reporter that spring (March 15, 1991), was divorce law because, as a rule, it exempted women's work at home from compensation formulas. As a medical ethicist, she was on the board of the Hastings Center for Ethics and Life Sciences in Briarcliff, New York. At Colorado, she had helped found the Center for Health, Ethics, and Policy at the university and the Center for Human Caring at its nursing college.

At Ohio State, she had helped propose to Richard and Annette Bloch what would become the Bloch Cancer Survivors Plaza at Lane Avenue and Olentangy River Road. She had rekindled the Critical Difference for Women Program, which helped women returning to school as students, and would later honor her with a research fund in her name. Her testimony clinched passage in the Ohio House Bill 642, which proposed insurance coverage for mammography screenings. It would pass the Senate after her death. She hoped at Ohio State to help staff of the James Cancer Hospital work through the issues of extending life through radical measures, of palliative care, of "pulling the plug." It was not in the *Lantern* story, but, at that moment, she herself was awaiting the results of a biopsy.

## Chapter 8

On one of his first "state tours"—the outreach trips across Ohio that would eventually take him to all eighty-eight counties—her husband was less than an hour from campus. The day before, he had charmed the Springfield Rotary and the Montgomery Alumni Club and met with the editorial board of The *Springfield Sun*, State Representative Joe Haines, and the central administration of Central State University. When he called Elizabeth and heard the biopsy results, he left immediately to be by her side. It was March 19, 1991.

Greg Brown of the university's communications office and a minister's son, was coordinating the tour. "When the president left to be with his wife, we had to reconfigure the next three days," he wrote in his notes. "Faculty and staff stood in for the president in fine fashion.... We all became ambassadors for Ohio State and the vision of Dr. Gee.... We all were concerned for Elizabeth and we remain thoughtful of her, Gordon, and Rebekah. Many individuals and groups prayed for her recovery and comfort."

Eight months later, in the November 1991 issue, editor Linda Crossley wrote the *Ohio State Alumni Magazine* cover story, "The Ninth Woman"—the one in every nine who some day would develop breast cancer. On the cover and again on the facing page were color portraits of this "ninth woman"—a beautiful lady with an engaging smile and a sparkle in her eyes—Elizabeth Gee. "This spring," the story read, "there was a major recurrence. The disease reached an even more serious stage this fall, and as Gee was making preparations to undergo an experimental treatment, she took time to talk about her illness and what it has meant to her life."

"I would hope," she told Crossley, "that there would be a message for other people in what I am sharing."

Elizabeth would die in her home in Ohio on December 17 at the age of forty-six. In her last year, she had completed the exquisitely written chronicle of courage, *The Light around the Dark*, an affirmation of her life that she had begun on September 4, 1987. "Surgery will be in 10 days," it had started. "We haven't told Rebekah about the surgery, but will tonight. She will be relieved to know what's wrong."

Rebekah Elizabeth Gee would know what was wrong from that next day when she was nearly twelve until she was sixteen. At her sixteenth birthday party on December 11, 1991, Rebekah saw her mother walk for the last time. "She got all dressed up, put on makeup," Rebekah would recall. "I don't know how she did it, because I hadn't seen her walk in two weeks. [She] walked down the stairs and shook everybody's hand. And came to the party. And walked back upstairs. She had, I think, lived to see me have my sixteenth birthday."

There is "A Daughter's Tribute" at the end of Elizabeth's book, published a year later. "My mother is with us today and will be forever," it begins. "She had three roles in my life—my mother, my sister, and my best friend. I always said we grew up together."

## *The Mormon Faith*

Elizabeth and Gordon were Mormons. Raised primarily by her mother, who was left a widow at thirty-three after her husband's death in a plane crash, Elizabeth had called upon her faith early. "How can I speak about my involvement in prayer?" she wrote in her book. "Let me simply say that my spirit engages in heartfelt conversation with God." With the help of her religion, wrote Rebekah, Elizabeth remained able to "love life and its small joys" throughout her illness. Elizabeth often read from the *Book of Mormon*. She was a member of the editorial board of the *Journal of Mormon History*.

She wrote of entering the Mormon Temple in Denver and feeling "a peace that seemed held in a reassuring, transcendent spirit"; her beliefs were not a "mere coping mechanism, but . . . a gift of truth in which I am enlightened by a wondrous story about what it means to be human." If she was distressed by the male domination of her church, she did not make it public.

Her husband, the Ohio State president, was "not your typical Mormon, but I don't mean that in a bad way." In fact, continued Keith Smith, he was "a great ambassador of the religion." As the highest official of the Church of Jesus Christ of Latter-day Saints in the Columbus area "stake," Smith was religious counselor to both Gees. As the director of Ohio State Extension, with agricultural agents throughout the state, he was also a senior official in the Gee administration. The president loved to embarrass him by announcing, "My religious leader is here so I know we can start the meeting."

Smith also would blanche at Gee's vocabulary, as when quoted by the *Lantern* as calling Governor Voinovich a "damn dummy" for drastically cutting the higher education budget—or his oft-used laugh line at VIP football brunches about seeing his "damn budget running up and down the field."

"I would remind him that the young deacons listen in on the half-time programs [that Gee would do with WBNS's Skip Mosic on statewide radio each football game].

They might think that is OK, and that is not. I would mention those kinds of things to him and he would laugh and say he would try harder and then he would forget." Whether he would forget, or whether he knew such bits of

CHAPTER 8

Selling academics on half-time radio, Gee and Skip Mosic, 1996.

irreverence defused questions of church and state, at no time in his Ohio State presidency did any tenet of his religion become an issue. If anything, his religion's focus on the family as the basic unit and its teachings that marriage and family relationships can continue in the next life were a bulwark through the dark days of 1991 and 1992.

At his final interview with the presidential search committee in 1990, he had been asked directly by trustee Alex Shumate to "talk for a moment about the fact you are a Mormon and how that relates to your leadership." The history of the Mormon church, he answered, had made him particularly sensitive to concerns of women and minorities. Questions about his faith, he told the *Alumni Magazine* (September 1990) very early in his tenure, were welcomed because he wanted people to feel at ease with him. Its teaching had given him "a high level of expectations of integrity and morality," he said, "and it's very much a part of the way I operate. At the same time, a lot of people know that Mormons don't drink, et cetera [smoke, consume caffeine], and sometimes people feel a little uncomfortable about that. They shouldn't . . . we entertain properly. We want to make people comfortable."

He tried to live up to the Mormon standard "spiritually," he told journalist Ben Marrison (*Plain Dealer*, December 22, 1996). Then, when asked about an empty can of (caffeinated) Dr. Pepper on his desk, he threw up his arms in mock despair and shouted, "I admit it. I'm a sinner, damn it." And, of course, laughed.

What exactly is a Mormon? Gee's first executive secretary Mary Basinger remembered that, when the name of the new president was announced in 1990, "You heard 'Gordon Gee' and, in the second breath, you heard, 'He's a Mormon.'" She and others in the president's office went right to the Internet to try to find out. "We expected this pious, very rigid person. And here comes Gordon bouncing in."

Many people believed incorrectly that Blacks remained second-class citizens in the church hierarchy and wondered about Gee's commitment to diversity. Few outside the Mormon faith seemed to know that Africans and African Americans had been admitted into the priesthood since 1978, and that mixed and predominantly Black Mormon congregations were now thriving. To the rightly or wrongly informed, his commitment to diversity showed quickly with his appointment of African Americans high up in his central administration. While some people also may have wondered about his attitude toward gays and lesbians, his consistent support of their university housing and health insurance rights as couples—with which the majority of his trustees disagreed—answered that. Though he never publicly criticized the secondary role given women in the church hierarchy, they certainly were not treated that way in his home or his administration.

Mormon Kenneth Anderson of the American University law school has written about "contemporary intellectuals who also happen to be Mormon." Though they have, "broadly speaking, the political and social views of the National Public Radio Constituency, on abortion, feminism, gay rights, the environment, race and ethnicity in America... they desire deeply to... stay within the church" (*Los Angeles Times Mirror,* November 28, 1999). Perhaps this described Ohio State President Gordon Gee, who considered himself a social liberal and a fiscal conservative. If it is not exactly right, the description comes close. He was certainly not the same Mormon who had left Vernal at eighteen never knowing a non-Mormon or a Democrat.

But in his heart was still some of the child, who extension chief Smith finally found the opportunity to embarrass back at a banquet in 1993. He introduced Gee, the honoree, with stories purportedly from Gordon's mother. Included were two poems "Gordy" had written as a child:

>I love to smell the dusty ground
>And taste the buttercup,

# Chapter 8

But most of all I love the sound
Of water drying up.

O little blade of grass so tall,
That wakes in spring and sleeps in fall
Adorned with necklaces of dew,
I hope somebody steps on you.

Following the friendly jab, Smith, the Mormon leader, reflected on being with Gordon and Elizabeth during one of the final days of her life. "Instead of selfishness, I saw selflessness and charity as Elizabeth expressed concern for you and Rebekah, not for herself," he said. "I also saw courage in her eyes, not fear. As I saw your hand clutch hers and tears well in your eyes, I saw love, eternal love, not hate. It was a special moment. Thanks, Gordon, for letting me see a little heaven on earth. God bless you."

# 9

## *Rebekah's Fish Bowl*

Children just don't like change. "I'd rather move to Hell than Colorado," Rebekah Gee had told her father at age nine on their first trip to Boulder. Evidently, in 1990 at age fourteen, she felt the same way about Columbus. So in the plane circling Ohio State's Don Scott Field the day of his introduction as Ohio State's president, daddy bribed her into silence with the promise of a new BMW when she turned sixteen.

Or did he? "No, it was all very much a joke," part of the father-daughter game, she explained by the time it needed no explaining. When the story reached the media, however, which was very early in her first term at Columbus School for Girls, many people believed it and formed their opinions about her and her father from it. A few weeks later, the *Dispatch* (October 12, 1990) reported the public's concern about the "new president of the largest public institution in the state" sending his daughter to private school. Of course, CSG's presence had been a significant factor in his accepting the presidency. These were the first two examples at Ohio State of what Rebekah would call "growing up in the fishbowl," the mixed blessing that would be hers until she left for college in the fall of 1993.

In that time, her mother would become ill again and father and daughter would connect in extraordinary ways, forming an even stronger bond in her mother's passing. She would, she would recall, lead a dichotomized life—"protected" by a devoted father "who really tried to ensure I had fun in high school"—while, at the same time, being "the first lady of the university" for nearly two years.

She would be the youngster with the uncomfortable yet amused sensation of knowing women were "hitting on my father . . . lots of women," with "Mormon women sending him scrapbooks with pictures of themselves." All of which she would understand because he was "obviously a wonderful man and a very eligible" widower. "And I was a very serious kid."

While she would feel the normal loss and jealousy when her father did remarry on November 26, 1994, at the same time she also "thought it was great." With the help of a Buddhist monk, she would develop a healthy relationship with Constance Bumgarner Gee, the new woman in her father's life and "one of the most honest and straightforward people I know."

"Right after he got married, we went to Asia." Rebekah, now a sophomore in college, and Constance were in Bangkok at the Temple of the Emerald Buddha. A monk was guiding their tour. "'Hold out your hand,' he said to me. I held out my hand. He started pushing my arm. 'Why are you doing that,' I asked? 'I can tell there is tension between the two of you,' he said. 'When there is tension in the heart, it is like the heaviness I put on your hand. It gives an unbearable weight to life that is insupportable to life and it weighs your days with an anger and hatred. If you let it go, you live so much more of a loving, light life.'"

Rebekah and Constance looked at each other "and just started to cry and knew it was going to be OK."

## *And the Glass House*

To some extent during her years in Columbus, Rebekah Gee not only lived in a fishbowl, she lived in a "glass house." As early as mid-July 1990, the Columbus press was publicizing the $600,000 price of the new residence Jack Kessler was negotiating for The Ohio State University Foundation, comparing it to the old president's home valued at only $285,000. Built in 1912, the home at 2416 Commonwealth Park North had 4,779 square feet, five bedrooms, three bathrooms, two fireplaces and a three-car garage. It also needed a lot of work to convert its top floor into a space for family living and prepare the first floor for university entertaining; and another $100,000 was spent, and publicized, before the Gees—Gordon, Elizabeth, and Rebekah—moved in in mid-September.

Though only private money was being used both for purchase and renovation, Gee knew expenditures for presidents' homes were often magnets for negative press. Better to get it all done in the honeymoon. And it was. And scads of money were raised in it. And many friends were made. By the time he left for Brown, the $850 million capital campaign Gee had initiated and led for the university was past its midpoint, well on its way to the $1.2 billion record it eventually reached in the year 2000.

## *Accepting a Legacy*

Rebekah Gee "has not taken a day for granted" since her mother died. She was taught by her mother "to sit and notice the details of life." To "notice the designs and the patterns and the beauty you have in the moment, because that may be all you have." Rebekah knows that, in those last months of Elizabeth's life, she "went from being a girl into being a woman." Taking the role of caregiver and parent to a mother is an unusual role for a sixteen-year-old. "It gave me the sense of life as a very serious thing and something precious that I have to live fully. My mother was an ethicist . . . and my father had dedicated his life to public service. They gave wonderful examples to me and I have no choice but to go the same way."

Before she died, Elizabeth Gee wrote her daughter letters for each birthday from sixteen to thirty. The nature of each letter changes every year, depending upon how she perceived Rebekah would be at that age. "Last year," Rebekah said in her interview for this book, she was the same age her mother was at her marriage, and "she wrote about marriage and men and how I might live my life." For nineteen, Elizabeth had written about choosing a career and having confidence in oneself as a person and a student. Rebekah's father has the sealed letters and turns another one over to his daughter each year.

Elizabeth also left four friends, "the Steel Magnolias": Mary Ann Shea, Maxine Green, Christina Johnson, and Phyllis Updike, women who supported and encouraged each other and began doing the same for Rebekah, now the fifth Steel Magnolia. And she left her mother, Rebekah's grandmother. "I call her twice a week just to talk to her. She and I have the connection of my mother across generations."

Rebekah had chosen to be a doctor, probably an obstetrician-gynecologist, and was completing medical school as this book was being written. She was also very interested in public health, motivated by a 1996 trip to Uganda with her father, Constance, Agriculture Dean Bobby Moser, and a team of faculty. There she met many Ohio State Ph.D.s who teach at Kampala's Makerere University and work with local communities, and are helping develop a self-sustaining agricultural economy.

The same trip incorporated a week in South Africa, in which the Ohio State men's basketball team was the first to play in that country since the end of apartheid. She met Nelson Mandela. He held her hand and she felt "incredible energy coming from him."

"To see President Mandela, in prison for thirty-six years, with no spite or hatred for his captors; to see there are real struggles in the world . . . to know there is a lot to be done in the world. There is not enough time for me to waste," she affirmed. "I want to be somebody who is making the world better. My mother was."

## *Gordon and Rebekah*

After the passing of his wife, the president of the university met with his staff and told them he knew his method of dealing with the grief would be to work all the harder. How he performed his dawn to deep into the night daily routine, living off junk food, hardly sleeping, was an amazement to most of the people who worked for him. Driven to be the best father for his daughter as he was to be the best president for his university, he kept an astounding schedule. The comfort he developed quickly as the single parent of a teenager, which "made our days easier and our life happier," he credited greatly to the good advice and strong assurances of his friend Ann Wolfe.

Each morning the father would be sure he and the daughter shared breakfast and had time to talk about the day to come. If Rebekah called at the office, she said, "He would pick up the phone no matter who he was in a meeting with—no matter how important—and talk to me about whatever problem, no matter how small." On trips away from campus, he would check in after her school day to see how she was doing. When on business in New York, he would buy her favorite cookies from her favorite cookie store and bring them home. She was on the junior varsity basketball team; "not the best shot but I loved to play." He made her games.

And he was asked to give her high school graduation speech. "I remember him sitting up late at night. He worked harder at that than any speech I ever saw him write. There were literally tears in all our eyes and in the eyes of my classmates when he gave it. . . . It was only a high school talk and I've seen him talk in front of thousands of people, but I've never seen him so nervous."

"It was his special gift," Rebekah knew. Her father had helped her pick out her graduation dress. He took her to her college interviews. "He was both a dad and a mom . . . filling in for her and doing everything he knew she would want him to do."

As the day of her leaving for Columbia approached, the president of The

Ohio State University wrote a column for high school newspapers titled, "Chance to Grow Means Letting Go." It was one in a series done for teens and distributed by his office. This column asked parents and students to acknowledge the emotions of breaking away and ended with a specific request to seniors. "Like all parents," he wrote, "I still see the toddler wobbling toward me, the child with a shiny new bike, the teenager in her prom dress. But I look forward to knowing the confident young woman she is becoming. So if your parents get a little teary, cut them some slack.

"Remember that we are all adjusting to a new balance in the parent-child relationship. And above all don't forget to call."

# 10

## *Flagship Revisited*

> He who wishes to keep thoroughly posted in Agriculture as a science, or with the constant progress in the Mechanical Arts, Chemistry and other sciences will need to read as many books in the French and German as he will in English. . . . The mere fact that agriculture or mechanics are to be taught in our school will not secure its success, which will depend more upon its being a good school. . . . And the manner in which things are taught will be as important as what is taught.
>
> —From the second annual report of
> The Ohio State University Board
> of Trustees, March 1, 1873

Ohio State was not an open admissions university in its infancy. It had substantial entrance requirements when it opened as the Ohio Agricultural and Mechanical College. When examinations in arithmetic, geography, English grammar, and elementary algebra were challenged as too severe, President Edward Orton countered that the trouble lay with the lower schools: "The standard of teaching and scholarship in many of them is deplorably low."

High school graduates who found the university's entrance exams too difficult, Orton said, should attend Miami and Ohio Universities, the "free schools of the state." It was not long, however, before budget realities first struck: Too many applicants were failing the algebra test.

James E. Pollard's *History of the Ohio State University, The Story of its First 75 Years* explains that, against the wishes of the faculty and the president, the trustees ruled that the algebra exam be dropped, allowing twenty students, or some 10 percent of the student body, to enter the following fall. Arguing that the trustees had chosen to "prefer the interests of those who are not fitted for college work," Orton offered his resignation—which was declined by the Board.

Unlike Cornell and the University of Illinois, which were Orton's examples of well-supported land-grant institutions, *Ohio State had not been singled out for flagship funding by its state legislature.* So by 1880, nearly all entrance requirements beyond earning a high school diploma had to be dropped. The university needed all the tuition income it could get. Graduates of Ohio high schools in cities with a population of at least 5,000 were admitted with no examination at all, as were graduates of other schools whose programs were considered "sufficiently standard and thorough."

Thus, within ten years after its founding, primarily for lack of special state support, a selective admissions university had become an open admissions university, which it remained until the presidency of Ed Jennings more than 100 years later.

## *The Land-Grant Movement*

Despite the Civil War, in 1862 Abraham Lincoln signed Vermont Representative Justin Morrill's Land Grant College Act, which offered scrip for all states in the Union to buy land for a "land-grant" university. In the U.S. Senate, a companion measure was offered by Ohio's Benjamin Wade. Along with free land for homesteading and grants to build railroads, the Act opened what then was considered "the West."

Not unlike a century later, Ohio's agricultural productivity and manufacturing productivity were about equal then; thus, whereas city-dwellers wanted their land-grant universities to aid industrial development, farmers wanted them to further agriculture. So, explains William Kinnison's *Building Sullivant's Pyramid*, it was no surprise when Ohio's land-grant university embraced both equally when chartered in 1870. Thanks to President Orton, however, Ohio State did so in the framework of a liberal education, rather than as what Orton explained "transforms its possessors into narrow and conceited specialists." Nevertheless, by 1880, Ohio State had dropped its entrance exams, and, in 1881, there being some cause and effect, Orton resigned the presidency and returned to teaching.

More than a quarter-century later, in a 1907 review for foundation funding

## Chapter 10

(as reported by Kinnison), the Ohio legislature was chastised by the Carnegie Foundation for creating three major public institutions—Miami University, Ohio University, and Ohio State. To the benefit of none, the review said, all three had been reduced to a common standard by the "sheer competition for survival."

All three, wrote Carnegie's Henry Pritchett, were burdened with students who should have been required to stay in high school. Ohio State, in particular, had "not received commensurate [state] support to become a Wisconsin or a Michigan." Nor had Ohio State excelled with a more limited curriculum, as had Purdue. Particularly, Pritchett wrote, for those founders and leaders who had expected Ohio State to be "a great university patterned after Cornell, was the disappointment hard to bear."

## A "Great" University

What would it take for Ohio State to become "a great university"? In 1997, E. Gordon Gee could have written the same conditions for success as Pritchett did in 1907. First, Pritchett said, the state universities that had grown strong had "upheld fair standards." In other words, they were selective admissions institutions. Second, they had leaders who "have appealed unequivocally to the state for their support." In other words, their presidents and trustees were good lobbyists. Given such effective advocacy and high admissions standards, these universities, he wrote, had become the "real heads of [their] state systems." Ohio State President William Oxley Thompson later added one more criterion: A great university required a group of powerful friends. Ohio State, he said, never enjoyed all three at one time.

Such a legacy was what President Ed Jennings began to turn around in 1984 when, to be admitted unconditionally as freshmen, he required high school students to complete a college preparatory program. Two years later, he was able to leverage the combination of a state-mandated capped enrollment and a crush of applicants into a selective admissions policy for first-quarter freshmen. He also established excellent relations with many of Ohio's political leaders and led the university's first major private fund-raising campaign.

The legacy Jennings left became the nucleus of the "high morale" Gee's 1990 review committee found at Ohio State, which Gee was able to build upon even as U.S. higher education was being assaulted by critics and Ohio higher education was being assaulted by cuts.

## *The Mission Statement*

Question: How many faculty, department chairs, deans, and administrators does it take to write a mission statement? Answer: Lots.

Question: How long does it take to write a mission statement? Answer: More than a year.

Question: Is a mission statement all there is? Answer: No, a vision statement provides appropriate support.

Question: When did Ohio State finally adopt a mission statement and a vision statement? Answer: December 4, 1992.

Question: How often will Ohio State's mission statement be reviewed? Answer: Every ten years.

It took more than a year of writing, commenting, and editing to craft the mission statement. The process began when Gee got up in the middle of an executive committee meeting and, as Associate Provost Ed Ray recalled later, with "an apparition-like quality, suddenly appeared in my doorway. I sensed a presence and looked up. Gee simply asked, 'Can you write a mission statement for me?' I said I could produce one by next Monday and he left."

In late September 1992, the suggestions and criticisms about that draft arrived back on Ray's desk from many quarters. Paul Beck, chair of Political Science, thought it was fine but made three suggestions. Judith Koroscik, associate dean in the College of the Arts, suggested the insertion of two additional phrases. Steve Loebs, professor of Public Health and Public Policy Management, thought the draft should be more a statement of intent. Gerald Newsom, vice chair of Astronomy, questioned the meaning of some of the definitional phrases. Mark Roche, chair of German, suggested avoiding stringing prepositional phrases.

Amy Riemenschneider, associate professor of Social Work, took issue with some phrasing and supported changes and inclusions urged by the Women's Grass Roots Network. The network had met with Associate Provost Howard Gauthier ten months before and later endorsed language developed by Andrea Lunsford, professor of English. Bradley Peterson, professor of Astronomy, argued that to be both "the leading comprehensive teaching and research university in the state" was an oxymoron, and Stan Thompson, chair of Agricultural Economics and Rural Sociology, said any agreement with the same definitive phrase depended upon "who you talk to!" Steve Buser, associate dean in the College of Business, supported the document with no new suggestions, then jokingly congratulated Ray for his neat printing and "the way you stayed within the lines."

## Chapter 10

A more serious George Smith, chair of Industrial and Systems Engineering, suggested the university needed a three-part document: "mission statement (who we are), the statement (who we aspire to be), statement of guiding principles (how we want to behave)." In fact, he was right, for in March 1994 the trustees approved a "functional mission statement" that expanded upon the goals of the following:

Approved by the Board of Trustees, December 4, 1992.

Mission Statement
"The Ohio State University has as its mission the attainment of international distinction in education, scholarship, and public service. As the state's leading comprehensive teaching and research university, Ohio State combines a responsibility for the advancement and dissemination of knowledge with a land grant heritage of public service. It offers an extensive range of academic programs in the liberal arts, the sciences, and professions.

"Ohio State provides accessible, high-quality undergraduate and graduate education for qualified students who are able to benefit from a scholarly environment in which research inspires and informs teaching.

"At Ohio State, we celebrate and learn from diversity and we value individual differences. Academic freedom is defended within an environment of civility, tolerance, and mutual respect.

Vision Statement
"The Ohio State University is a community of scholars in which:

"Teaching and research are recognized as part of the same process: learning.

"Academic units and curricula are structured to foster learning and nurture creativity.

"Administrative services, facilities, and technology enrich the academic experience.

"Academic programs and research opportunities are extensive and excellent, but not exhaustive.

"Human resources complement our promise: High ability students, and faculty and staff from diverse backgrounds participate in leading programs and enrich an environment that sustains learning and growth.

"Ideas, intentions, and creative work are made accessible to practitioners throughout the state of Ohio and the world in keeping with our land grant mission."

Three good friends: House Speaker Verne Riffe, Gee, and Ed Jennings, 1994.

After more than a year of self-examination and discussion, the university community finally had defined itself and its aspirations well enough to guide its long-range planning. It had ratcheted up the recruitment of top students significantly. It had responded to Governor George Voinovich's Managing for the Future Task Force. It had lifted the mandatory retirement age for faculty. And it was now ready to respond to its own Managing for the Future report.

By corporate standards, Ohio State's mission and vision statements were somewhat mushy and overlapping. Business and marketing consultant Myron Leff, now president of a firm that bore his name, later simply explained, "The vision is where your organization will ultimately peak and the mission is what you are going to do to get there." Leff had been president of the agency of record for both University Hospitals and the James during Gee's presidency and, in particular, had helped steer such thinking at the cancer hospital. Ohio State, the university, had gone well over a century without redefining itself beyond being a land-grant university.

Gee's "passion about what he did," Leff believed, was the instrument that finally drove the internal process while, externally, Gee's personality made him "the living logo" of Ohio State.

CHAPTER 10

## *Managing for the State's Future*

Some two months before the Ohio State trustees approved the "statement of mission and vision," the twenty-one-member state Managing for the Future Task Force, appointed by the regents at the request of the governor, issued its report. Enacting its entire set of recommendations would have been a mixed blessing for Ohio State.

The crux of the report was more emphasis on Ohio higher education as a statewide system, giving the regents more authority and a greater role in establishing an overall educational mission for higher education, public and private. Although the various boards of trustees still would set policy for each institution, institutional control unquestionably would have been diluted.

The task force also recommended that faculty workloads be established for each institution, accompanied by a system of performance evaluations. It also urged the redefinition of tenure as a commitment to academic freedom but not a lifetime guarantee of employment. Time-limited contracts would be established for faculty who were nonproductive and ineffective.

In addition, it recommended the merger of Ohio's "colocated" university branch campuses and two-year technical colleges. There were only seven such situations in the state, and four were Ohio State's: Lima and Lima Technical College, Marion and Marion Technical College, Mansfield and North Central Technical College, and Newark and Central Ohio Technical College. In no way did the Ohio State faculty, at what now were being termed "extended" campuses, want their stature reduced by merging with tech school faculty. Nor did their students want the prestige of their degrees diminished.

Had every recommendation been enacted, the quid pro quo for Ohio State could have been a version of what William Oxley Thompson longed for back in 1912. Ohio State and the University of Cincinnati would officially be designated the state's only two "comprehensive research institutions." Other state universities would be funded for individual centers of research.

In effect, the task force was recommending a two-tiered public university system; the top tier would consist of two "comprehensive research institutions" with, as Tim Doulin explained in the August 4, 1992 *Dispatch,* "graduate programs competitive at national and international levels."

In the same story, Bill Napier—then vice chancellor of the regents, four years later Gee's executive assistant—explained that, where preeminent research programs already existed in the other universities, "they would be the center for teaching and research in that subject in Ohio." Kent State's excellence in liquid crystal R&D and Akron with its polymer center were good examples. Neither would be lost to either Ohio State or Cincinnati, and both would be supported as state centers of excellence.

A reality check would have told anyone at Ohio State who believed the two-tier system would be accepted that water could as easily run uphill. Even Governor Voinovich, who supported the concept, when interviewed years later, acknowledged that the politics of the state gave it no chance. In his story, Doulin quoted University of Toledo President Frank Horton as having "a great deal of a problem with the notion" and another "official" as whining about "a feeling the two institutions get everything anyway."

Although the two-tier recommendation was supported by the regents themselves, as Napier recalled later, it was "a lightning rod" outside of Columbus and Cincinnati and among the other universities.

On October 11, 1992, the Ohio University trustees formally voted to oppose the designation of Ohio State and Cincinnati as "comprehensive research universities," resolving that the other schools then would be handicapped in responding to regional needs and in attracting funding, students, and faculty. A week later, Task Force Chair N. Victor Goodman wrote an op-ed piece that specifically cited three major recommendations: system coordination, mergers of technical schools and branch campuses into community colleges, and tenure reform.

The two-tier system never had a chance. Ohio State would write its mission and vision statements without it. It also would argue against combining its campuses and the technical schools into community colleges and win.

In March 1994, under the stewardship of Provost Richard Sisson, Ohio State published a soup-to-nuts thirty-six-page functional mission statement, its eighteen objectives a blueprint for "preeminence in higher education."

# 11

## *Gee and the Governor*

> Here are some buckeyes. . . . In times of great stress, the buckeyes can be the equivalent of worry beads. One just sort of rattles them in one's hand as one contemplates a complaining dean, irate parent, or angry legislator. Some solace should be forthcoming.
>
> —From a 1990 letter to Gordon Gee,
> Ohio State's eleventh president,
> from Harold Enarson, Ohio State's
> ninth president

In February 1992, Harold Enarson wrote a second letter to Gordon Gee, this in commiseration. For Gee's "amusement," Enarson attached his University Senate speech of 1980. It had addressed state budget cuts "unprecedented except for the Great Depression." Enarson had warned he might have to sell one or both university golf courses—the sensible Gray and the championship Scarlet—shut down WOSU radio or WOSU television or both, and even disband the Best Damn Band in the Land. In 1980, overseas competition was just beginning to ravage the Midwest manufacturing economy, and Ohio higher education was absorbing nearly half the state cuts while being told "to do with less." Enarson chose to retire and leave the problem to his successor, Ed Jennings.

In 1992, then, after a decade in which rejuvenation had followed recession, it was "déjà vu all over again." But this time the governor was George Voinovich, not Jim Rhodes, the president was Gordon Gee, not Harold Enarson, and the charge was not just to "do with less," but work "harder and smarter" and do *more* with less.

In his State of the State address in March 1991, the new governor reported that soaring Medicaid costs, the Gulf War, and low tax revenues were creating a financial crisis comparable to 1981. He had ordered a $127 million budget cut for the remainder of the fiscal year and more would come. Gee counselor Herb Asher recalled later that, when Gee arrived at Ohio State from Colorado in 1990, he was prepared for cuts under Governor Dick Celeste, but not for what he considered the "disproportionate amount" the new governor would slap on higher education.

Part of the problem was Voinovich's pledge to be "the education governor." Gee considered the "education" budget seamless from kindergarten through college. The governor didn't. He increased the state's portion of primary and secondary education support by 5 percent, protecting or expanding nearly everything affecting children. Gee knew that arguing against children is impolitic if not just wrong.

By December 30, 1991, Voinovich had announced another series of spending cuts. Of the total $196 million, higher education would be dunned $57.3 million (*Dispatch*, January 16, 1992). In a letter to the Ohio State community, Gee said the university could expect a $14 million hit immediately and a repeat of it the next fiscal year. Making up about 13 percent of the state budget, higher education had absorbed 29 percent of the December 1991 cut, then 39 percent of another cut in February 1991.

By June 1992, the governor was projecting another set of cuts, $224 million for higher education or some 61 percent of a total $370 million (*Dispatch*, June 19, 1992). Although the Ohio constitution required a balanced budget, Gee continued to argue it did not have "to be balanced on the back of higher education." Was the governor going after higher education?

Asher, who otherwise considered Voinovich "a wonderful governor, who would not allow the right wing of his party to push some very mean-spirited proposals," did see a residual distrust from the 1970s, when then Representative Voinovich cosponsored two Ohio House bills targeted against campus protestors. One would have authorized trustees to dismiss faculty and students summarily without a hearing; the other would have banned sound amplification equipment used without administrative permission. But certainly, the governor had only no-win choices, regardless of Gee's insistence that an investment in higher education would help the state more than an investment in "sewers, roads, and prisons."

CHAPTER 11

Meanwhile, behind the scenes, Gee and Voinovich were working together toward an eventual tax increase.

## *"The Damn Dummy"*

On July 22, 1997, not long after Gordon and Constance Gee announced they would leave Ohio State for Brown, Gee received a letter from Governor Voinovich. "I cannot tell you how disappointed I am that you are leaving the university," the governor wrote, and added that one of his regrets over the past several years had been his perception that the media had gone out of their way to depict bad blood between them. "I think you know that I respect and admire you not only as an outstanding educator," he said, "but also as an outstanding human being."

"Our admiration for you and Janet is really boundless," Gee wrote back. "Even though in the public arena, people will depict, on occasion, potential conflict—fortunately all four of us are well groomed in that school. We appreciate all that both of you have done for the state and for us."

That Gee and the governor had come to like and admire each other might be a surprise to people who remembered only Gee's "damn dummy" comment in the heat of the budget battle six years before. The response that the governor was a "damn dummy," to a question from students while he was visiting Papa Joe's Bar on one of his mingling nights, had stuck like glue. Run first in the April 27, 1992 *Lantern*, repeated in the state media, and reported again when a denial turned into an apology, it never was taken seriously by the governor. In laughing off the incident, Voinovich got off one of his own best lines when three days later the *Plain Dealer* reported he was certain the teetotaling Gee would now "stay out of bars after 11:30."

But the comment did intrude upon a confidential correspondence initiated by Gee in a seven-page letter that followed a meeting between the two. In his letter, Gee first demonstrated Ohio State's accountability, detailing what the university already had cut and consolidated, citing its national leadership in energy conservation, speaking to Gee's program to eliminate red tape and his promise to "reduce university bureaucracy by another ten percent." It then reinforced faculty responsibility, debunking the "unholy myth that university faculty do not teach." That myth had been intrinsic to the creation of the governor's Managing for the Future Task Force, which would be making its recommendations that summer.

A recent comprehensive survey, Gee continued, had determined that "this

A "Go Bucks" from Governor George Voinovich; a big grin from Gordon Gee, 1991.

year only 46 of our 3,000 full-time faculty members are not fully engaged in teaching" and "the average faculty member at The Ohio State University works between 50 and 60 hours a week . . . far in excess of any hourly average, either in the public, government or private sectors."

"Frankly," an agitated Gee wrote on, "I am more than tired of hearing about the lack of work habits of our faculty. . . . Anecdotes provided to you and others make good reading and political rhetoric. However, they do not make reality. . . . Quite candidly, I believe you need good information to make your case and are receiving very little regarding higher education. I hope this is a beginning."

Perhaps surprisingly, not only was what the governor sent back only five days later an extremely supportive response, it led to the two men working together against unfunded federal mandates and in support of a state tax increase. "We may need your help and the help of your national organization," Voinovich wrote of the antifederal mandate program he was leading among his fellow governors. He also urged Gee to charge ahead in informing Ohioans about the accomplishments of their colleges and universities, and to prompt his presidential colleagues and the Board of Regents to do the same.

# Chapter 11

"Your point on how well our higher education system is doing compared with our global competition is very well taken and one which should be underscored over and over again. It certainly would be part of a foundation to go to the voters for additional support."

In essence, the governor was telling the president that higher education needed a higher profile and a more vocal constituency, and that Gee was the person to make it happen. His fiscal strategy, the governor said, was to get through the next year "with the resources we have." Then, when "all the facts are out on the table," he hoped "the legislature will see fit to provide me with an additional $200 million worth of permanent revenue."

"Delighted" by Voinovich's response, but believing that $200 million would "not be sufficient to meet the budget problems," Gee wrote back that he was already making the case. He was writing opinion pieces for the print media and would be traveling the state extensively starting that week "to tell the story for higher education. I will do that in every corner and on every occasion." He also suggested "we convene some of our best thinkers" to attack the overall problem. He ended his letter with, "I await your charge."

That charge did not come. But one and perhaps two Gee slip-ups did. The first was the "dummy" comment; the second, floating his think tank idea to the editorial board of the *Plain Dealer,* which elicited a supportive editorial and perhaps put the governor in a spot he did not appreciate. At least the *Plain Dealer* thought so when editorial page editor Mary Ann Sharkey wrote (February 14, 1993) that Gee's idea had caused the governor to suspect "Gee wanted to justify paying big salaries to people who think great thoughts for a living but fail to share their knowledge in the classroom" and "basically told Gee to buzz off."

Ironically, Sharkey, who had once been the *Plain Dealer* Statehouse bureau chief, would become the communications director for Voinovich's successor, Governor Robert Taft.

## *Barnstorming*

"In the state of the university address this year, Cornell President Frank Rhodes took on the high cost of education through an equation I like. The estimated full cost (room, board, tuition, books, and services) of a year at Cornell, he said is $103 a day, 'only slightly higher than what you might expect to pay for the room alone at a modestly appointed hotel. . . .' By comparison, Ohio residents who are undergraduate students at Ohio State who live on

A band shell ice cream social: Gee on a state tour, 1991.

campus pay $32.57 per day, only slightly higher than what you might expect to pay for one of those motels without the swimming pool and the mint on your pillow." So noted President Gee in one of his periodic letters to the faculty and staff, which then was reproduced and mailed to opinion leaders throughout Ohio.

At Rotary meetings and ice cream socials in small towns, in the press and in his own *onCampus* columns to his faculty, throughout the spring and summer of 1992, Gee took the case for value and quality throughout Ohio and, most particularly, to the leadership of the Ohio Senate and House.

On June 30, Senate President Stanley Aronoff, a Republican, as was Voinovich, urged his governor to modify a new proposed executive cut to higher education and to freeze it at the existing level. To make up for another shortfall, Voinovich had just recommended another $370 million cut, with $224 million hitting higher education. He first had proposed a new tax on alcohol and tobacco, expected to offset up to $120 million in cuts, but it was being opposed strongly, primarily by Democrats.

"More than 10,000 jobs will be lost and the education of our young people will be dealt a severe blow," Aronoff wrote the governor. He would even support increased sin taxes, "if that is what it would take to soften the impact."

CHAPTER 11

A day earlier, House Speaker Verne Riffe, the legendary Democratic leader, had written Gee. He did not, he wrote, support the governor's proposal to "burden higher education with disproportionate funding reductions." He would continue to review alternatives to address the state's fiscal dilemma "without compromising higher education." He had already informed the *Dispatch* he would consider whatever tax increases were necessary—after the November 3 election.

A few days before, Gee had called a press conference in which he had outlined the damage the governor's pending cuts could inflict just on Ohio State. They included closing the University Press, eliminating support for WOSU radio and television, eliminating all university-subsidized activities offered free to the public, a "drastic reduction in our teaching, research and service capabilities," and the "elimination of 1000 positions."

They also included "the sale or lease of university assets," particularly land on or near the campus and "in Upper Arlington and Northwest Columbus"— translated golf course and airfield. As Enarson had done twelve years before, Gee was pulling out all the stops.

In the end, the statewide higher education cut was $170 million, $74 million less than originally predicted. Ohio State would reduce its work force by those 1,000 positions, mostly through attrition, and Gee would wait to see if a sin tax was passed *after the election.*

In November 1992, Bill Clinton won the U.S. presidency and, in Ohio, a backlash against incumbents placed term limits on its legislators. A few days after the election, Gordon Gee spoke in a closed session to more than 170 public university presidents at the annual meeting of the National Association of State Universities and Land-Grant Colleges (NASULGC). As cochair of the group's presidential Council on Government Affairs, he said the first item on its first agenda would be to "help see that unfunded mandates are ended or, if not ended, severely circumscribed. While their motives are worthy—including health care for the poor, protection for the environment, and policies that advanced educational opportunity—federal mandates should be federally funded."

Also, he added, he would be working with the National Governors Association and the National Council for State Legislatures. And they should, too.

Five weeks later (December 18, 1992), the *Dispatch*'s Lee Leonard wrote that "with surprising ease," twenty-four Republicans joined forty-four Democrats in the House and four Democrats joined seventeen Republicans in the Senate to pass a "$195 million smorgasbord of taxes nestled in a $1 billion capital improvements appropriation and went home for Christmas. While disappointed lobbyists encircled the chamber and looked on helplessly," new taxes were placed on soda pop, alcohol and tobacco, and certain services and retail sales.

One lobbyist disappointed only that the smorgasbord was not larger was Gordon Gee, who publicly thanked the "governor and the legislative leadership" the next day. He particularly cited "Stan Aronoff and Verne Riffe; Bob Boggs; Jo Ann Davidson and Corwin Nixon. . . . Senator Ben Espy and Representatives Otto Beatty and Mike Stinziano—and our other Franklin County friends—Senators Ted Gray and Gene Watts and Representatives Dean Conley, Richard Cordray, Ray Miller and E. J. Thomas."

The president certainly had gotten around. His signed op-ed pieces had appeared in most of Ohio's major and many of its smaller papers, and editorials supporting higher education had sprouted like Ohio corn. He, Asher, his trustees, the regents, and the other higher education presidents had made their case. But there was no question who had been the leader of the pack. And there was no question in Gee's mind that the new tax bill could not have passed without the quiet support of the governor, who had already made more than $600 million in budget cuts since taking office (*Plain Dealer*, December 27, 1992).

"You were surrounded," Gee wrote Voinovich, using his standard blue felt-tipped pen, "so I did not have the opportunity to thank you for your magnificent efforts over the past week. They are appreciated by all. Best wishes for the holidays and the New Year."

In November 1994, at least $60 million per year of that tax increase would vaporize when the soft drink and food lobbies would engineer the repeal of what had become known as the "pop tax." A penny a can would prove too much for the taxpayers to stand. Or was it the public's confusion over what constituted "food"? The pop people convinced the taxpayers that soft drinks were in fact a "food" and that the next tax just might be on their Fruit Loops, bread, or bacon.

# 12

## *The Huber Years*

> I am the first to tell you that Joan has a style of her own. But I can tell you, I have worked with a number of provosts over my 12 years as a president . . . and there are none better in terms of values, absolute commitment to quality, and an ability to make decisions. . . . Change, particularly at Ohio State, is not always welcome.
>
> —A response letter from the president

As a preschooler, fifth-generation Ohioan Joan Huber was reared on "Fight the Team" and Ohio State's place in the general scheme of things. She probably had strong convictions by then, as well. If she were designing higher education today, "there would be only intramural sports, because people need a lot more exercise and they don't need to be spectators." As provost, "it's not that I liked to do housecleaning, but I was willing to do it. When it has to be done, it has to be done. It's like being in the army: You may not like being shot at, but it goes with the territory. The financial situation forced us into it. We didn't have any choice. Or at least not much."

Joan Huber grew up in Wooster, Ohio, twin daughter of a former fifth-grade teacher and a father who believed in hellfire and damnation until he learned about Darwin at Ohio State, which changed his life forever, and hers. He had hoped to be a county agent, but was terribly allergic to horses. So he ran the gamut instead through to a Ph.D. in entomology. Later he joined the Penn State faculty, moving the family to State College the year Joan graduated from high school. She went to her new hometown university and graduated in two years because she wanted to go to graduate school.

Instead she got married and temporarily gave up becoming an academic, until her husband moved them from Coshocton, Ohio, to Muskegon, Michigan—where she taught herself French and six years later got a Ph.D. from Michigan State, a 200-mile drive roundtrip. She also got a divorce.

It was a remarried Joan Huber, with her husband Bill Form, both sociologists at the University of Illinois, who "heard the drums beating" at Ohio State under Ed Jennings and Provost Diether Haenicke and came to Columbus in 1984 as dean of Social and Behavioral Sciences. At first, she had not been interested. Psychology Professor Nancy Betz, chair of the search committee, had sought her out if only to have another application from a qualified woman. But the interview changed all that.

Huber came to Ohio State because finally, she said, "they were going to try to turn this behemoth around. In the state of Ohio, there was nothing equivalent to the University of Michigan for bright, poor kids. Way back, my father had been all in favor of open admissions. He thought it was a noble thing and maybe it was then. But, by the time I came back here, there were so many other state institutions there was no reason for Ohio State to maintain it."

As dean, there was no question her standards were high and her expectations exacting. When in 1989 Provost Myles Brand asked her to address the trustees on the relative quality of Ohio State among the nation's universities, she had been her direct, well-informed self. We are near or at the bottom of the Big Ten, she told them. She explained about the National Research Council's once per decade graduate departmental rankings and Ohio State's relatively poor performance in 1982 on the last one. She showed by the high dropout rates how open admissions could be a disservice to students ill prepared for the rigors of Ohio State.

She had come to Ohio State in the hope it eventually would compete academically with the University of Michigan. For trustees who believed that being a "land-grant" college mandated open admissions, she pointed to Wisconsin and Illinois, two of the most selective public universities in the country. At which time, "after I shut up, Les Wexner asked what the trustees could do to help."

Once Gee arrived a few months later, Wexner went into action, asking such questions as, "You say we're good, how do you know?" This resulted in comparative academic data being brought before the Board, in the deans making trustee presentations about their colleges, and eventually the establishment of benchmarks by which Ohio State could measure its aspirations and its

## Chapter 12

progress. "You just can't proclaim yourself superior. If we're not good, then let's get better and let's recognize it," Wexner said later in recalling the meeting. "Let's start looking at rankings."

By January 1992, Joan Huber was the coordinating dean of all of the Colleges of the Arts and Sciences and was being asked by Gordon Gee to be his new senior vice president and provost. She answered that she would think about it. "I just don't say 'yes' or 'no' on the hoof, so to speak. It's something you learn as a dean." She liked being a dean. She was most interested in scholarship, did not like the "kind of things that provosts have to oversee," and was not interested in being provost for the long haul. Reluctantly, she said yes to the president, but only until the university could find her successor.

To emphasize the president's and trustees' unswerving support, though her appointment was temporary, no "acting" was attached to Huber's title. She was *the* senior vice president and provost, with full authority to make the decisions or the recommendations to the president that budget cuts and retrenchment required.

Haenicke and Jennings, she said later, had "roused Ohio State from its self-satisfied slumbers." But by 1992, the state economy had made the game, strictly speaking, not even zero sum. "Everyone had to lose something. But some units would need to lose more than others."

Soon, 170 faculty and 330 staff were taking an early buyout to ease some institutional financial pain. The Labor Education and Research Service would go, right after Photography and Cinema. The Wexner Center, Minority Affairs, and Student Aid directors and the deans of Humanities and Veterinary Medicine all would be doing something else by the time Dick Sisson took over as provost a year and a half later in August 1993.

In a reorganized office, Edward Ray, Don Dell, and Nancy Rudd would become associate provosts, along with incumbent Robert Arnold, and David Boyne, Charles Corbato, and Howard Gauthier would retire and Barbara Newman would return to the faculty. Nancy Zimpher would become dean of Education; Randall Ripley, Social and Behavioral Sciences; Jim Garland, Mathematical and Physical Sciences; and Violet Meek, dean at Lima.

From beyond the university, Jerelyn Schultz would come from the University of Arizona as dean of Human Ecology; Jose Cruz from Cal-Irvine as dean of Engineering; and Dominic Dottavio from the National Park Service as dean at Marion. Sherri Geldin would leave the Museum of Contemporary Art in Los Angeles to direct the Wexner Center, and Jerry May would depart the University of Michigan to head development and the University Foundation.

But appointments and resignations were just tides rising and falling in a sea of economic and, sometimes, cultural travail. Economically, between 1988 and 1993, state support per student in Ohio had fallen from $5204 to $4040, which, multiplied by more than 55,000 Ohio State students, was more than $23 million a year.

In March 1992, President Gee announced the university had already cut costs by $45 million in eighteen months. But a year later to the month, the university community would discover that eleven colleges and academic units had overspent their budgets by $44 million as well. Some of it would be forgiven, which did not sit well with those who hadn't overspent and, specifically, sent the well-liked Dean of Humanities G. Micheal Riley back to the professoriate.

Culturally, in both the customary practice of probing a new president and the context of sometimes incendiary events, issues and advocacy groups were very active. The Women's Grass Roots Network was everywhere there were hirings, promotions, or equity studies. Gays were lobbying for health care coverage for partners and the right to cohabit in university housing. The Right to Life organization wanted, and got, its events on a women's calendar. Faculty seniors wanted and received the early lifting of what had been a federally mandated retirement age of seventy. Racial minorities in general wanted more support systems, and the African American organization ACTION in particular faced off against the president.

Meanwhile, President Gee was trying to get a new capital campaign started, was taking the governor on publicly about his budget decisions, and was deep into the process of planning what could be controlled in the next era of Ohio State history.

## *Streamlining—and a Glitch from Boulder*

In March 1991, with Fred Hutchinson still his provost, President Gee had opened the dialogue on the university's future, suggesting his vision as only a starting point on the road to thoughtful planning. Already, the university had gone through its first round of cuts and a job freeze, and he had testified in the Ohio House that, consistent with Governor Voinovich's bromide, Ohio State was "doing more with less."

At a town meeting on his first round of visits to regional campuses, Gee told the Newark faculty and staff that without a streamlined bureaucracy, program consolidation, and the possible elimination of departments, Ohio State "will simply be the biggest mediocre place in the country. We don't have enough money to invest in ourselves" (*Dispatch*, May 8, 1991). That same day,

## Chapter 12

a story broke back in Colorado that at first caused concern in Ohio about just how Gee might choose to make his investments. In this case, they had been in four vice presidents at Boulder.

In a public meeting, Judith Albino, about to be promoted to Colorado's presidency, had advised her regents (equivalent to Ohio State's trustees) she was making more money as vice president and provost than they had offered her as president. She had, she said, a contract agreed to by Gee the year before that included $12,000 a year in deferred compensation. Three other vice presidents had similar contracts, with deferred payments up to $13,000 a year, none approved by the full Board of Regents of the University of Colorado.

For those who were watching closely, how Gee answered the compensation criticism illuminated his style, priorities, and skills in reading public opinion. He invested in recruiting and retaining outstanding people, he told the *Lantern* on May 9. He had added deferred compensation at Colorado because salaries were not competitive. It was within his purview as president to do it. Yes, his Board chair had known about it. No, he had not told the entire Board, but, yes, if he had it to do over again, he would have and he would use this as a learning experience.

Don't do it at Ohio State, the "learning experience" told him, even as Board Secretary Madison Scott explained that, in competing with the private sector, "We can't offer stock options, dividends or yachts," and new Board Chairman Joel Teaford said Gee could offer deferred compensation in the four ongoing vice presidential searches, if he wished.

He wouldn't wish, Gee said. Ohio State's salary structure was good enough. With that, the Ohio State community had little further interest in what the papers were printing in Colorado. And Gee's mind could return to the matters at hand . . . streamlining, consolidating, and eliminating, which would be the business of Joan Huber in another year.

## *Gordon to Joan*

> June 17, 1992—"I just read that the University of Maryland dropped seven academic departments. They have already eliminated several other programs. We should review the process Maryland has undertaken, as we look at our own planning efforts. I would appreciate your doing so."

Provost Huber was one jump ahead. She knew most units terminated there were "the ones we were worried about," already having asked Maryland's provost for advice. The advice: "Wide consultation is needed. Be sure to bring the University Senate into the process." Huber created the University Priorities Committee, appointing faculty who were very active and highly regarded by the Senate. "A heavy-duty committee," it met every week that summer. "In general, we tried to follow Maryland's procedures."

> June 25, 1992—"In light of lifting of the cap on mandatory retirement and the continuing need to evaluate faculty after tenure, I urge you to undertake a review of how we can best develop a post-tenure review process... one not unduly threatening... [but] allowing us to make decisions regarding faculty who no longer meet the levels of competence and commitment required."

At that time, Ohio State required no evaluation for tenured faculty and only oral reviews for nontenured faculty. "We, therefore, tried to develop processes that would usefully address all nonperformance issues." Associate Provost Nancy Rudd developed Office of Academic Affairs-mandated guidelines for written annual reviews for all faculty members and then took them to the Faculty Council for discussion, making revisions based upon its recommendations. Those guidelines, along with department workload policies, were approved and put in place.

> January 29, 1993—"I recently had lunch with several women from the faculty who wanted to talk to me about salary and salary equity issues, percentage raises for promotion and tenure (i.e., halved to 6 percent because of budget cuts), and that no one in a given rank earn less than someone in a lower rank. Please advise me as to any discussions you are having on these issues."

For many years there had been no issue, as promotion raises of 6 percent were added to the general increase. Only in 1992, when the general increase fell to zero, did the question come up. Huber's counsel was that salary shouldn't necessarily follow rank for a number of reasons. Very productive associate professors may earn more than unproductive long-term full professors. Also, when starting salaries rise sharply, some assistant professors can earn more than some associate professors. Where there were genuine explainable inequities, efforts would be made to address them, if funds were available. "But there probably will never be enough money to address every salary difference perceived as inequitable."

CHAPTER 12

In the first round of budget cuts in the Huber administration in July 1992, academic units took an average 5 percent hit and academic support units, 7 percent, including 24 percent to the Center for Teaching Excellence; 21 percent to Continuing Education, with elimination of its noncredit programs; 15 percent to Graduate School administration; and 12 percent to development. There were no raises for the faculty or nonunion staff, and there were staff layoffs where attrition was not enough. Cleaning, planting, maintenance, and even mowing were all either cut back drastically or eliminated.

And then there would be "Phase 2." The Board of Regents had just announced another cut of more than 10 percent in instructional subsidies and nearly 20 percent in most line items, such as the James Cancer Hospital and Wooster's Ohio Agricultural Research and Development Center (OARDC). It wouldn't get better; it would get worse. And clearly, as President Gee worked to maintain morale, Joan Huber was being asked to play bad cop to Gordon Gee's good cop.

## *Good Cop, Bad Cop*

"Ohio State is a treasure, an institution of learning without equal. It is a place where dreams are realized, lives are molded, truths are found," Gee rhapsodized in a statement for the media, repeated in *onCampus* (July 16, 1992). "A place to which the citizens of Ohio can look with pride because their support for more than 120 years has helped create a model of learning envied around the globe." And, to the faculty and staff, he added he was confident the university would "emerge . . . enjoying even greater good will than in the past."

"We will continue to spread the good news of Ohio State, and, working together, we will face the future with confidence, determination, and enthusiasm." Which he did, shifting into attack mode against the governor's priorities, and for the university's. He gave speeches to civic groups, chambers of commerce, and alumni clubs. He released an economic study, which showed that Ohio State's annual economic impact was seven times greater than the state's investment.

He met with editorial boards at papers small as the *Salem News*, the *Dover-New Philadelphia Times-Reporter*, the *Xenia Gazette*, and *Ironton Tribune* and large as the dailies in the state's seven large markets—the *Akron Beacon Journal*, *Dayton Daily News*, both the *Cincinnati Post* and *Enquirer*, *Youngstown*

*Vindicator* and *Canton Repository*, and, of course, the *Dispatch*, and even the obstreperous *Toledo Blade*.

Meanwhile his provost aimed, fired, and certainly was "shot at," which, as she said, went with the territory. One of the provost's duties, as set by university rules, was to review principal academic administrative officials at regular intervals and to submit recommendations to the president for or against reappointment. At this time, nine persons were coming under review, including five deans, an assistant provost, and two directors.

Once a week, as she was making the tough decisions, she would seek the opinions of Human Resources Vice President Linda Tom, Minority Affairs head David Williams, and Bob Duncan, vice president and general counsel and head of the new Office of Legal Affairs. Sometimes "warm and funny" while "a no-nonsense provost," she had, Duncan later recalled, the ability to listen and the wisdom "not to take herself too seriously."

One of the most public, if not contentious, situations involved the College of Humanities and its dean, Mike Riley. As another dean wrote to the president following the barring of certain information in the *Lantern* (January 21, 1993), "the aftershocks are amazing, and the entire campus is talking about the issue." The College of Humanities had accumulated a deficit of $7.8 million, and Huber and Finance Vice President Bill Shkurti had agreed to a payback of just 25 percent, $1.8 million, and over five years.

The reason for the concession was that much, if not most, of the deficit had accrued because the college had had to hire new faculty and graduate assistants to teach the expanded General Education Curriculum (GEC) and had not been funded sufficiently for it. (No one had.) As an example, after a presidential visit to his department, History Chair Michael Hogan let Gee know that the GEC had poured thousands of new students into his department. His faculty would be teaching 18,000 students that year, most in GEC courses, some having ballooned to 700 students. When, as he left, Gee asked what Hogan needed, it may have seemed too blunt to answer "money."

In addition to the GEC increase, there was also enormous pressure on all departments to become more "student friendly" by adding sections to closed classes. While deficit spending was most egregious in Humanities, it was spread among the colleges like bad butter. Mathematical and Physical Sciences Dean Jim Garland was not alone in taking flack from his own faculty for not driving a harder bargain in settling his college's deficit. He was carrying red ink in astronomy, physics, geology, chemistry, mathematics, and statistics.

With Humanities remaining the only college exempted from repaying 100 cents on the dollar, letters arrived on Gee's and Huber's desks demanding accountability, Riley needed no crystal ball to know he was out and chose to resign and return to the faculty at the end of his current term. David Frantz, professor of English and associate dean, would become acting dean and, in May 1994, historian Kermit Hall, dean of the Kendall College of Arts and Sciences at the University of Tulsa, would become the dean.

## Joe Alutto

Dean Joe Alutto was another story. He had come from the State University of New York at Buffalo in early 1991, where he had been a chaired professor and former dean of its management school. The week his appointment was announced he had been jolted to find Gee putting hiring controls on the university. Dick Celeste still was governor and had projected the first in the series of state deficits.

Alutto's charge was to make the Business School a major national player. Huber's charge was to save "the academic core," and Business was not part of it. Gee the marketer knew, however, that excellent professional colleges were lodestones for overall institutional prestige, and that Business alumni would lead his yet to be announced capital campaign. So, clearly there was discord between promise and formula when Business was required to take the second largest percentage cut of any college.

After only eighteen months into his tenure, Gee knew Alutto was an institutional loyalist and Alutto knew no one could build a first-class college under current circumstances. Salaries generally were noncompetitive and the funds to supplement them were heading south. By January 1993, when it appeared the university could not even come up with a subsidy to fill two new endowed chairs at market level, Alutto may well have been wondering whether he had come to the wrong place.

Much to the chagrin of Shkurti, who knew she would be drawing on an empty straw for long-term, or "annual rate," money, Huber was told by Gee to make the chair offers competitive. Gee had hired Jerry May away from the University of Michigan, where he had been its top major gifts officer, to run his development program and was sure May soon would be able to handle this kind of problem. He also had penned Alutto a personal note back in 1991, assuring him that reallocating money to the academic core was not "some singular shift away from supporting our professional schools. I simply will not allow that to happen." And he didn't.

By October 1993, the newly activated University Foundation Board was told

Max Fisher announces his $20 million gift that names the Fisher College of Business, 1993.

that the deans and heads of major programs all had been asked to identify their objectives and components for the next big Ohio State capital campaign. And that they, the board members, should get ready to give. The administration and campaign leadership would set a goal and get on with it. Serendipitously, but after many talks with Gee, Alutto, Wexner, and others, within two weeks Max M. Fisher—who had arrived at Ohio State in 1906 with "an old mackinaw, one pair of pants, a pair of boots, and $150"—would donate $20 million to the College of Business, which thereafter would bear his name.

By the end of the Gee administration, Alutto could take much of the credit for strengthening the academic reputation of his college. Stimulated by a redesigned MBA program; restructured Ph.D. curricula in finance, marketing, accounting, and labor and human resources; and a complex of state-of-the art facilities taking shape at the northern edge of central campus, the new Max M. Fisher College of Business was already moving up in the ratings. In 1999, Alutto would be named to a chair of his own, the John W. Berry, Sr. Chair in Business, in memory of the late trustee whose gifts to Ohio State totaled nearly $5 million.

CHAPTER 12

## *Beytagh to Williams*

In October 1992, Dean Francis Xavier "Frank" Beytagh of the College of Law memoed President Gee of his plans to work on his new book on the Irish constitution and, following a research sabbatical in Dublin, return to full-time teaching. A few days later, Provost Huber received a note from Gee urging a search committee for a new dean. That same month, *Ebony* magazine ran a five-page article on an administrator and law professor at the University of Iowa. His name was Gregory Williams. Williams directed his law school's "Opportunity Program," which had helped raise African American enrollment to nearly 12 percent in a state where minorities were fewer than 3 percent of the population.

Once a deputy sheriff, Williams had written two scholarly books on criminal law and criminal procedure, particularly as they related to police restraint. And he was writing another book, a memoir at only age forty-eight, *Life on the Color Line: The True Story of a White Boy Who Discovered He Was Black*. "I'm sure I'll write other books in my life," he had told *Ebony*. "But I hope this one is the one that endures, the one that tells America that it cannot be so consumed by race that it discards people."

In June, the *Ohio State Law Journal* was dedicated to Beytagh, in which a tribute by Gee, a former law dean himself, cited Beytagh, "the intellectual iconoclast, the Ohio State basketball fan wearing the Notre Dame cap in St. John Arena," as "the man who changed the College of Law at The Ohio State University." During his tenure, the college had become a national leader in mediation and arbitration and had established with Oxford the Center for Socio-Legal Studies. Beytagh had proved a consummate fund-raiser, having just dedicated a $20 million building addition that later would be named after its major benefactor, John Drinko. And he had "been a friend [to Gee] in the most important way—he has not hesitated to disagree."

As Beytagh was doing his research in Ireland, Ohio State's new Law dean was coming aboard. Joan Huber had recommended the appointment of Gregory H. Williams at the May trustees meeting. She had thanked the eleven-member search committee, chaired by Law Professor Albert Clovis. Williams's memoir would be published the following spring, make *The New York Times* best-seller list, and win the *Los Angeles Times* Book Prize.

In 1996, Law Professor Frank Beytagh left Ohio State for the presidency of Jacksonville's new Florida Coastal School of Law.

Dedication of the Law College's John Drinko Hall, 1993.

## *Social Forces in Social Work*

At 7:30 A.M. on July 1, 1992, Charles Ross, associate professor of Social Work, walked into the Stillman Hall office of former Dean Richard Boettcher, who was returning to teaching, and allegedly declared himself the "elected acting dean." The university had said the acting dean was Beverly Toomey. Provost Huber had recommended Bev Toomey, although the trustees would not meet to approve the appointment formally for another week.

Toomey had been with the school since receiving her Ohio State Ph.D. in 1977; she was a full professor and a 1988 recipient of the Alumni Association's Distinguished Teaching Award. Ross had been with Ohio State since 1970, had been a leading civil rights activist when named to head the newly established Black Studies Division, and had been with the College of Social Work since 1971.

Ross said he was elected acting dean by the faculty (*Dispatch*, July 2, 1993). He said he would fight a plan to downgrade the small college into a unit within a larger one. He said the students in his college could learn from his occupation of the office. "Nurses aren't afraid of blood. Social workers shouldn't be

## Chapter 12

afraid of social action." While Ross had declared election by the faculty, others reported "the faculty" had included adjuncts and that, at a later meeting of only full-time faculty, a motion not to support Toomey had died for lack of a second. Toomey said she would perform the duties of the dean from her old office in Lord Hall. Approved on the condition a subcommittee of the Board would review her qualifications and the appointment process, on July 9, the trustees appointed Bev Toomey acting dean.

The review was immediate. Board Chair Deborah Casto called the subcommittee together right after the regular trustee meeting. Because of the small size of the college, Huber explained to the committee that she had invited all twenty-seven members of the regular faculty to voice their opinions. Faculty input had been received in two forms: the vote that had included adjunct faculty and resulted in the recommendation of Ross, and individual meetings between regular faculty and Huber in which the overwhelming support was for Toomey. In several meetings with the faculty, and again in letters, Huber stressed that deans were appointed by the president following the *Rules of the University Faculty,* who were authorized to delegate to the provost with no faculty vote needed, required, or binding.

The subcommittee found no reason to change the appointment. Following the decision, Ross vacated the office peacefully. A permanent dean would be named after the new provost, Richard Sisson, began work in August.

## *Sexual Harassment*

Although more than one faculty member at Ohio State surely had married one of his or her former students or staff, keeping personal and professional lives separate was always a good idea. In 1992, fueled by the Clarence Thomas confirmation hearings in the U.S. Supreme Court, sexual harassment flared as a principal issue on the nation's campuses. At Ohio State, "Sexual Harassment 101," a session for faculty, staff, and students was first conducted by a volunteer speakers' group.

In 1993, the Human Resources office revised the university policies and ran nearly 3,000 people through longer workshops. In part, the new policies prohibited direct reporting in romantic relationships, defined sexually harassing behavior in the academic setting, and provided procedures to address complaints. In the first year of the new guidelines, there were thirty complaints, and, in thirteen cases, sanctions appropriate to the severity of the conduct were imposed.

## Back to the Cuts

Meanwhile, for fiscal year 1994, all vice presidents and college deans had prepared general fund budgets at 3, 6, and 10 percent reductions from the current year. Though the state was finally projecting a funding increase, probably 3 percent, there still would be a $25 million gap between revenue and expenses. The average cut, Huber announced, would be 5 percent. Some of the state's 3 percent would go to a salary increase. Its average would be a whopping 2 percent, $300 across the board, the rest merit based. The year before there had been no raises except under union contract.

In September, the figures came out. Colleges were cut an average 3.5 percent, academic support units an average 6 percent. The biggest losers were the Graduate School administration, Legal Affairs, Continuing Education, International Affairs, and, showing the proverbial "flag," the president's office, all down 15 percent or more.

On October 1, 1993, the office of the new provost, Dick Sisson, would distribute volume I, number 1 of a document titled *Progress and Priorities*. This edition was a report to the community on highlights of improvements made "to enhance academic excellence" in the Huber administration.

The newly combined Admissions and Financial Aid offices had cut the turnaround time for student loan applications from thirteen weeks to one to two weeks, benefiting more than 30,000 students on financial aid.

The closed course problem was being "brought under control," with 80 percent of all students receiving all requested classes, and a computerized memory system installed to give closed-out students future priority.

Nearly $3 million in new continuing funds had been designated to expand programs to attract and retain minority students and faculty.

An additional $8 million had been made available for scholarships of all kinds. For the third year in a row, more than 100 National Merit and National Achievement Scholars were in the freshman class.

Campus bus service, which had been cut drastically the year before, had been reinstated, but on a pay-for-service basis.

For the first time, the funding of computer needs was based upon university-wide priorities. The year before, a new era of communication had begun when a university e-mail system was instituted for students.

All of this had been accomplished with Huber as provost, a provost trustee Alex Shumate lauded as consequential in moving the university forward, who worked effectively with the president, "loved the university," and was "good, strong and as tough as nails." Cutting back had been so much her business

# Chapter 12

that, at a farewell dinner at his residence when she stepped down, Gee joked that she knew only four words: "'Yes, no,' and 'you're fired.'"

## Along Came Sisson

Meanwhile, a new phrase had entered the administrative vocabulary: "reaching financial equilibrium." This meant that, if the Ohio economy really had stabilized and if all went well in the next year, institutional priorities alone could guide the next stage of restructuring. Those priorities would emerge from the mission and vision statements, recommendations of Ohio and Ohio State Managing for the Future task forces, and a consultation process guided by Gee and his new provost, political scientist Richard Sisson.

Sisson had spent "a wonderful afternoon" interviewing with Gee in Chicago, "talking about a whole range of things, not simply the future of the university or higher education, but outlooks on life, human relationships, books, music. He was very impressive, Gordon was—sharp, clever, funny, but serious, with a quick grasp of complex things." The two had clicked, as had Gee and Sisson's wife, Willa, who never had lived anywhere but California, but who was struck by Gee's acknowledgement of her individual identity—a professional who happened to be a woman.

And so when the offer came, the two Sissons agreed that this Ohio State alumnus from a farm in Gallia County—who had been president of the Men's Glee Club and once considered a career in music—would become the senior vice president and provost of The Ohio State University. And Willa would give up her position as director of personnel of the College of Letters and Science at UCLA.

While Sisson would see Gordon Gee through the rest of his presidency, one issue that had begun on Huber's watch would extend even beyond Sisson's vice presidency. It was the academic misconduct case against Ohio State's most renowned chemist, Leo Paquette. Paquette and Nobel Prize physicist Ken Wilson were Ohio State's only two members of the National Academy of Sciences. In 1992, Paquette published an article that prompted the National Science Foundation to ask Ohio State to investigate. In 1991, he had been barred from serving as a grant reviewer by the National Institutes of Health for taking material from another researcher's grant application, though probably inadvertently, and NSF suspicions were similar.

"His crime, according to OSU," wrote Dave Lore years later (*Dispatch,* June 21, 1998), "is that he plagiarized some introductory sentences and footnotes in the 1992 article, abused his position as a grants reviewer for the National Science Foundation and then tried to cover it up." In May 1993, a faculty committee of investigation had found Paquette "grossly negligent" in committing "relatively minor" acts of plagiarism followed by an attempt to cover up his mistake—whereupon letters of support, disbelief, and indignation arrived on Gee's desk from chemists around the world.

The case would extend five more years. Not until January 1998—in Sisson's first month as Ohio State's interim president following Gee's departure—would Professor Paquette finally settle with the National Science Foundation. With no finding of academic misconduct, he would voluntarily abstain from federal research funding and grant reviewing for two years. Not until a few days before the presidency of William English "Brit" Kirwan would he finally settle with Ohio State. If there were to be any discipline it would be only departmental. "Chemistry Chairman [Matthew] Platz says it's time for closure," wrote Lore on June 21, 1998. "Who can disagree?"

# 13

## *Diversity and Divisiveness*

> It is simply unacceptable that individuals on our campuses suffer the consequences of racism, sexism, and other discriminatory and harassing practices and behaviors. I want the university community—faculty, students, and staff—to know we will be very proactive in our efforts.
>
> —Presidential memo establishing a
> Committee on Diversity in
> November 1992

In 1954, in *Brown v. Board of Education*, the Supreme Court of the United States held the societal need for racial integration of public schools to be compelling. Ten years later, Congress passed the Civil Rights Act. Title VI forbade discrimination in education programs. It authorized voluntary affirmative action by public and private schools and colleges and universities to overcome conditions limiting participation by persons of a particular race, color, or national origin. Title VII prohibited employment discrimination.

In 1972, Congress passed Title IX, prohibiting gender discrimination in education programs with a few exceptions, including contact sports. A year later, it passed the Rehabilitation Act, which prohibited discrimination on the basis of disability in all education programs and activities, including employment and admissions. In 1990, the Americans with Disabilities Act provided equal employment opportunities and reasonable accommodations for the disabled.

However, in 1978, although it did allow colleges and universities to consider race a "plus" factor in admissions, in the watershed Bakke case the U.S.

Supreme Court struck down a California admissions program that had set aside a specific number of places for "disadvantaged" minority students. In 1989, it also invalidated a local government's minority contracting set-aside program, declaring it unrelated to any proven harm to minorities.

In 1991, a federal district court ruled against the affirmative action program of the City University of New York, saying it had failed to articulate well enough its reasons for promoting diversity. Three years later, a circuit court of appeals ruled a minority scholarship program at the University of Maryland impermissible as a remedy to the effects of past discrimination. And in 1995, a Texas appeals court struck down the University of Texas law school admissions process that targeted certain percentages for Blacks and Mexican Americans, and the University of California regents voted to end affirmative action.

These were the major legal decisions that most affected affirmative action in higher education during the seven and a half years of the Gee administration.

## *Affirmative Action, Phase 1*

One document awaiting new president Gordon Gee in late summer 1990 was from Nancy Zimpher, who in 1993 would become dean of the College of Education and, eight years later, president of the University of Wisconsin–Milwaukee. In an early demonstration of her administrative skills, Zimpher had chaired Ed Jennings's task force on spousal equivalency. As "an issue of fairness and equity among employees," the task force had overwhelmingly recommended extending the benefits of married partners to domestic partners of faculty and staff. In a personal cover note to Madison Scott, Gee called the recommendation "worthy of positive consideration" but wanted more information on its "substantive and political implications."

In particular, as secretary to the trustees, Scott might know how its members would vote if the issue were to come to them. One question was, did it have to?

Unmarried heterosexual partners might benefit from a new policy, but they had no unified lobby. Gays and lesbians did. Columbus had become one of the most welcoming cities in North America to its gay community, and Ohio State had just opened a gay, lesbian, and bisexual student services office.

Not surprisingly, while Gee was lobbied inside the university to extend benefits, the religious right was generating an equally predictable campaign against the office itself. "As a Christian," a typical letter began, "I am convinced, and am sure you are aware, that the Bible, God's written revelation to man, clearly speaks against this sexual and social practice." Others called for his resignation "if you continue this immoral support of sodomy and do not return to morality." In addition, one legislator, State Senator Gary Suhadolnik, was making the office closing a personal cause, one he would not win.

Meanwhile, Gee had met with the Gay and Lesbian Alliance (GALA) and generally supported its three major issues: domestic partner equivalency in health care coverage; family and medical leave benefits; and university housing, particularly in the university's married students' community, Buckeye Village. Ohio State's nondiscrimination/equal opportunity statement prohibited discrimination against any individual for "sexual orientation" as well as race, color, creed, religion, national origin, sex, age, disability, or veteran status.

Were any of the GALA issues truly "discrimination"? As his note to Madison Scott suggested, Gee knew that between his druthers and institutional action ran a deep, wide, and rushing river of very great concern.

On another front, Gee found himself at odds with the U.S. military and the FBI. After the FBI's legal counsel testified in a D.C. circuit court that the agency not only would not interview or hire gays but would discharge agents found to be gay, Law Dean Frank Beytagh banned the bureau from interviewing in the Law building. Based upon the pre–"don't ask, don't tell" policy of the U.S. Armed Forces, adopted during the Clinton administration, the dean had stopped the military from recruiting there as well.

When Gee joined other university presidents in writing their congressional delegations about the disparity between university and military policies, which created particular conflict in ROTC units, the congressional office of the Department of Defense answered that the military services "do not discriminate" and that "nonaccessing homosexuals" was based only upon "the incompatibility of homosexuals with military service."

Legislation soon passed in Ohio prohibiting public colleges and universities from eliminating ROTC and from banning any state or federal recruiters on their campuses. It had been initiated by Ohio State history professor, military veteran, and Ohio legislator Gene Watts.

## *JustUs*

The "imminent de-Afrikanization" of his Jennings-inherited leadership team was what JustUs read into three recommendations Gee made in his first address to the University Senate. JustUs was the 1990s embodiment of African American student advocacy on campus, its lead spokesperson a dazzling law student named Greg Carr, who would prove as effective a negotiator as he was a writer and speaker.

Recommendations in Gee's address that involved African American administrators Madison Scott, Russ Spillman, and Joe Russell had raised the organization's ire and suspicion.

Scott, vice president for Personnel Services, would become secretary of the university and executive assistant to the president, as well as continuing as secretary of the Board of Trustees.

The Office of Student Affairs, then under the provost, would be elevated to a vice presidency, thus reporting to the president, with Spillman, currently vice provost, serving as acting vice president during a national search.

A national search also would identify a person to hold the expanded position of executive officer for Human Relations and Minority Affairs, with Sue Blanshan continuing as executive officer for Human Relations during the search. Gee explained he wanted to bring greater coordination to the university's work in Human Relations and Minority Affairs and bring focus to them within his office.

In a printed broadside posted on kiosks throughout campus, JustUs asked, "How many times have Afrikan administrators been loyally patted on the head with flighty adjectives . . . as they have been stripped of what little influence their tenacity, talent and perseverance have been able to attain for them?" In a few days, it held its first rally against "Gee-o-centrism," below the windows of the president's office in Bricker Hall.

When Gee was then invited to meet with African American faculty and staff in the main ballroom of the Faculty Club, he did, joined by trustee Alex Shumate. In a brief talk, Gee said "the issue of minority affairs" was one of his highest priorities; that he wanted that agenda to be "ours" and not "his"; that his motives had been misunderstood; that he would maintain under Joe Russell the autonomy of the Office of Minority Affairs; and that he would withhold acting on or changing his recommendations until he heard from them.

Then, as he stepped away from the podium, he was blindsided when the members of JustUs formed behind him in the hallway and were given the floor. He was accused of planning, "under the façade of commitment to excellence," to reduce the influence of African Americans in his administration by dismantling "the few programs African people have fought for, been expelled for, lost jobs for, and otherwise struggled for to eke out the barest political landscape at The Ohio State University." Reproached by three speakers for, among other things, being condescending and insulting, the president learned quickly how united his critics were when JustUs left to loud applause.

Following the meeting, he received a letter signed by a dozen of the staff and faculty, which included a set of recommendations.

No, he would respond later, he found it imprudent to extend Joe Russell's reporting line to the president's office as well as to the provost's office.

But, yes, he now would not add a minority affairs responsibility to the human relations position in his office.

No, he could not summarily promote Russ Spillman from a vice provost to a vice president. A national search was on, and the search committee would make its recommendations.

And, no, it was inconsistent with his moral and legal responsibility to guarantee minorities or women half of Ohio State's current and future job openings for chairs, deans, directors, and vice presidents.

## *Hale*

He also met with Dr. Frank Hale, Jr. The former faculty member and vice provost for Minority Affairs had retired from Ohio State and was in the administration of Kenyon College. Hale had developed Ohio State's bellwether graduate recruitment program with traditionally Black colleges and for years had been principal advocate, facilitator, and healer for African Americans on campus. When he retired, he had left a vacuum, and Gee hoped to get him back.

"Thank you for your wisdom and support," he wrote Hale after their talk. "I will need both as we work together on behalf of this great university." But Gee would discover that he and Hale could not work together or in any other way at Ohio State then; as a recipient of the early retirement buyout, under current rules, Hale was prevented from returning to the campus.

Meanwhile, the national tempest created by Michael Williams, the U.S. assistant education secretary for civil rights, had passed. In December 1990, Williams had declared that colleges would be prohibited from awarding scholarships based on race, unless under court order. Met with organized resistance from higher education, President George Bush called for a review, followed by a fact-finding inquiry by his new education secretary, Lamar Alexander. By December 1991, Alexander had ruled as permissible scholarships designed to create diversity or as a race-exclusive aid to remedy discrimination.

On April 27, 1992, Frank Hale and Gordon Gee ran into each other in the Ohio Union. University policy had been revised to allow rehiring early retirees on a 50 percent appointment. Hale told Gee his duties at Kenyon would be over after graduation in mid-May, and he could now take Gee up on his offer. Gee said he, too, was ready, and they agreed to meet again soon. Two days later, south central Los Angeles exploded in looting, rioting, and twenty-four deaths following the acquittal of four white police officers in the beating of African American motorist Rodney King.

Two days after that, Afrikans Committed to Improve Our Nation (AC-TION), the next generation of JustUs, made demands on the Ohio State administration and its president, E. Gordon Gee.

## *Hispanic/Latino*

In 1990, Hispanics at Ohio State were waiting for the university's "Action Plan." In 1987, there had been a proposal; in 1988, a task force; in 1989, a report. But not until May 1991 would there finally be a document titled *The Hispanic Action Plan*. Meanwhile, in 1990, a letter from a Hispanic had put Gee on alert about factionalism in that community. "A handful of Hispanics has been dominated by power groups that fight for their own trivial interests," the note said. The most recent incident had been a challenge to the selection of Victor Mora, a Mexican American, as the director of a new office for Hispanics.

As would be made clear by Associate Provost Barbara Newman, the principal author of the action plan, factionalism was explainable and understandable. Some Ohio State students were first-generation Mexican American, some Cuban American, some Puerto Rican. In all, there were some twenty Spanish-speaking nations represented at Ohio State. Some students preferred to be known as "Hispanic," others "Latino," others by their nationality alone. One melting pot this population was not. And neither were the Asian or Asian American populations, no more so than earlier generations of European immigrants and visitors with their varied customs, characteristics, languages, and religions.

Many, if not most Hispanic students here, she wrote, had strong feelings of isolation and social alienation. There was no academic department in Hispanic studies, no minor, no graduate program, not even one Hispanic department chair, dean, or top-level administrator. Only 1 percent of Ohio State's undergraduates were Hispanic. If even 2 percent were to be achieved, recruitment and financial aid would have to be increased substantially. "The two greatest challenges" in Ohio, the action plan said, "were the low high school graduation rate and the high proportion of families who live in poverty." At least, finally, there was an office in Student Affairs for Hispanics.

CHAPTER 13

# *ADA*

Her purpose in writing was "to create an awareness of a need on campus," a graduate student wrote President Gee in November 1990. "I am mobility impaired, visually impaired, and hearing impaired." While she functioned "very well," the student cited problems presented by her university environment that she hoped the president would fix. While some would be as obvious to the nondisabled as pulling a heavy door, others were as singular as lifting bound journals in the library. The Americans with Disabilities Act (ADA) had become law in July. Compliance was another area Gee would be investigating immediately.

## *Women's Issues*

Annually since the 1970s, when it was organized, The Council on Academic Excellence for Women (CAEW) had issued a statistical report. In November 1990, Gee's first autumn at Ohio State, 24 percent of the faculty were women but only 8 percent were full professors and 22 percent associate professors. Chair Joan Krauskopf wrote Gee that the council "wholeheartedly" supported his call for a commission on women and all similar initiatives, which then included a faculty salary equity review, an athletics salary equity review, and a dependent care task force.

Chaired by Andrea Lunsford of the English department, the twenty-four members of the President's Commission on Women published its report in July 1992. It was dedicated to its late member, Dr. Elizabeth D. Gee. Its members had invited women to share their views in open forums, and more than 350 had responded. It had received more than 100 written submissions from other women and conducted in-depth interviews with selected women through the university.

"The campus climate for women . . . is little changed" from that described in a 1977 report, it began, "and for women of color may well have worsened." Women, it said, still confronted an environment that ignored "critical gender differences," placed impediments in the way of women striving to reach their full potential, and failed to recognize and respect women's professional abilities and achievements. "The data we have gathered strongly suggests that the university itself must change."

Although the climate may not have changed since the 1977 report, most numbers and percentages had. The percentage of women in undergraduate school had risen from 41 to 47 percent, though this was a result of institutional downsizing, as raw numbers actually were down. Numbers were way up, however, for women pursuing master's degrees (2,743 vs. 1,897) and doctoral students (2,222 vs. 1,522).

In 1976, women composed 15 percent of the faculty (332 of 2,161); in 1991, 25 percent (831 of 3,393), which also was up a full percentage point from the year before. In the administration, 10 percent of the department chairs were women (13 of 121), where there had been 2 percent (two of 98) in 1976. Twelve percent of the deans were women (3 of 25), where there had been none (of 15) in 1976. Two of nine vice presidents were women, where there had been none in 1977. And women now held a higher percentage of positions in every professional rank. While numbers were up everywhere, the report concluded that "the opportunities for women to participate in upper level administration remain few... women are not moving up in the ranks as steadily and systematically as men... and the number of women holding the rank of professor (102) is deplorably low."

Many actions were recommended, and some were readily doable, such as making the official language of the university gender-neutral and hiring a board-certified gynecologist at the Student Health Center. Others, as did the base recommendation itself, required education, cooperation, and even transformation: "Attitudes and environment must be transformed to create a campus climate that allows women full participation, productivity, and realization of potential."

By March 1993, a presidential report to the community showed that many of the recommendations had already been executed or were being carried out. As examples, a new and more detailed sexual harassment policy was being developed. In the Student Health Center, the women's care unit now was staffed adequately with doctors, all of whom were women; and date rape education was being given to student groups.

In University Hospitals, allegations of insensitivity to a student rape victim—"The way they treated me was almost like I was being victimized again" (*Lantern*, November 2, 1992)—had led to a better support system in the emergency room. The university police had also created and distributed a 12-point "Sexual Assault Guarantee," committing themselves not to prejudge, to arrange for treatment, to investigate fully, and to keep victims informed during any investigation and prosecution. In the business office, ramping up the exterior lighting program, adding safety and security standards to both interior and exterior construction and renovation plans, and auditing existing buildings were making the campus safer.

Academically, the General Education Curriculum, which required a social diversity component, now offered courses on gender, including "History of Women in the United States" and "Sociology of Women." Based on principles agreed to with the faculty's salary equity review committee, which had just released its report, a salary grievance procedure was being created in the provost's office. Human Resources was updating its staff grievance procedures and developing new family leave policy recommendations and had authorized flexible work schedules. Seeking women and minorities was a focus of a new handbook, *A Guide to Effective Searches.*

Academic and support units had begun developing new three-year affirmative action plans, to be reviewed annually for accountability by the central administration. A university-wide program of diversity workshops was being developed, with the president and his directly reporting staff the first group to get training. At the end of his report to the community was the president's signed statement of recommitment to equity for women at Ohio State.

## *ACTION*

On May 14, 1992, Frank Hale, Jr., released a statement that began: "I've had to make a tough decision today in response to the reaction I have received from a number of telephone calls with respect to my appointment as special counselor to the president. Rather than be misunderstood and to blur the situation, I am not accepting the position. I think all of us are aware that the Rodney King episode and its aftermath has reminded us once again that all is not well in this country and all is not well on this campus."

Two days earlier, on May 12, in a morning meeting with the president, Hale had agreed to become Gee's senior counselor, to work, he said later, "on global issues" and to help facilitate the university's dormant Action Plan for the Recruitment and Retention of Black Students. One day after that, on the steps of Bricker, ACTION (Afrikans Committed to Improve Our Nation), the new generation of JustUs, held its second rally protesting racism at Ohio State. Its members were waiting, but not patiently, for a response to twenty-two demands they had made upon President Gee the week before. That same day the announcement of Hale's appointment went out to the media.

ACTION's first demonstration had been on May 1, stimulated by the acquittal of the Los Angeles police captured on videotape beating Rodney King. Locally, as well, an African American Ohio State student had accused Columbus police of brutality in an incident on High Street, a case he would win.

Loud but dignified, ACTION's first rally had called for more campus diversity, for justice, and for Black unity. But it had been tainted when, after the rally formally ended, the American flag atop the Bricker flagpole was lowered and burned. Later, the Ohio chapter of AMVETS honored an African American student who stamped out the fire and gave the university a flag of her own.

Gee had released a statement the next day applauding the peaceful nature of the demonstration, deploring both racism and the flag burning, and saying he soon would be inviting African American leaders to meet with him. A meeting at his place, however, was neither the locale nor the symbolism ACTION wanted. It would be on its turf. And its turf, incongruously, given what happened next, was the building soon to be named the Frank Hale Jr. Black Cultural Center. ACTION was prepared, the *Columbus Call and Post* had told its readers (May 7, 1992), "to begin the destruction" of Ohio State's "racist system" on May 19 if the demands were not met. May 19 was the birthday of Malcolm X.

On May 13, as the press carried news of both Gee's response to the demands and Hale's appointment, Hale called his own press conference. In so many words, he said he had been accused of being a pawn of the administration. "The last thing I want to do is to compromise [ACTION's] goals, their strategies and whatever is necessary to move forward on this campus." He had, he said, "been misunderstood" but was "prepared to let the agenda roll on." He would not be working for President Gee.

## *Grass Roots*

The Women's Grass Roots Network was formed in 1990 and, by October 1991, had become a campus force. Its 1991 petition, urging Gee to consider hiring women for his four open vice presidencies, had gained 656 signatures. In Gee, the network had an advocate, not an adversary. "I find it helpful to know that there are such strong women in this group who are going to help me," Gee told the *Lantern* (October 8, 1991), while one of its leaders, Associate Professor of Finance Deborah Ballam, announced that this new organization was going to continue to be heard from. If empowerment was one of its goals, it was succeeding. Certainly, both Gee and the network wanted an Ohio State environment in which women did not fear that signing such a petition would jeopardize their jobs.

Chapter 13

# *Hate Speech*

Does the First Amendment of the Constitution, which guarantees freedom of speech and of the press, provide a student newspaper the responsibility or even the right to publish "hate speech"?

In the summer of 1991, Pamela Shoemaker left the School of Journalism at the University of Texas to direct the Ohio State School of Journalism, following the retirement of Walter Bunge. While in time, her main task would be to deal with an undersupply of faculty and an oversupply of prospective majors, it was not long before she learned of the dangers of "laboratory journalism." In October, the editors of the *Lantern*, students whose leadership often changed each quarter, were taking the position that faculty adviser Mary Carran Webster—herself a one-time *Lantern* editor—had no right to pull material she deemed libelous or inciting illegal behavior. Whose newspaper was it, anyway?

When the editors quit to begin their own paper, the issue disappeared until, in early 1992, another set of editors decided an advertisement denying the Holocaust should run as editorial material. On January 22, the school's publications committee, which included faculty and students, in a 5–4 vote, had rejected the advertisement for "violating normal standards of morality and taste" and attacking "an individual, race, nationality, ethnic group, religion, or sex." The advertisement claimed the Holocaust was a hoax and argued that the cruelties suffered in concentration camps were unfounded exaggerations. The committee had met at the urging of Gee after the *Lantern* had given notice to leaders of the Columbus Jewish community that the advertisement would run.

Two days after the vote, the editors printed the text anyway, as editorial material on the opinion page. Beside it was a column by Gee written when he believed the revisionist piece would not run. Defining the issue and expressing his opinion, he had written that, "On a university campus, we hold sacred the opportunity for all points of view to be debated. But a pernicious lie is not a point of view, regardless of the cloak of legitimate scholarship it attempts to wear."

In a meeting with the newspaper's editors, staff, and advisers on January 27, he made it clear that his position applied to both paid advertising and editorial material. The editors, he said, had been "irresponsible" and "hurtful to the Jewish people." Yet, he said he also defended the *Lantern*'s right to publish the piece (*Lantern*, January 28, 1992). The story made national news, including coverage on CBS's *48 Hours*.

While the controversy was uncomfortable for the participants, it did have social value. As Gee pointed out in his column, less than one-third of the U.S.

population was alive during World War II. "The Holocaust revisionists know this," he wrote. Their goal is to rewrite history "for a 21st century population in which there will be no one left who remembers the truth." Certainly, many Ohio State students, Ohioans, and Americans had become aware of the truth because of the *Lantern*.

On and around campus itself, it became an opportunity for further education about the Holocaust. Mel Mermelstein, a survivor who had sued the author of the ad and had won, spoke. WOSU-TV aired a Holocaust documentary. For use as case studies, the Hillel Society gave information to all of its chapters nationally, and the university provided Midwest Anti-Defamation League executive Alan Katchen videotape of the campus events. Graphic Holocaust-related art by Ohio State's Sidney Chafetz, titled "The Perpetrators," was exhibited, and Bea Klarsfeldt, who, with her husband, had been a leader in locating and prosecuting Holocaust perpetrators themselves, spoke.

In general, the Columbus Jewish community applauded Gee's handling of the situation. While it was reported in the *Lantern* that Gee had told its staff that, if the trustees had met they would have shut the *Lantern* down, this was one issue most trustees must have felt fortunate to evade. They had escaped without having to accept that the Board of Trustees was, in fact, the ultimate publisher of the student laboratory newspaper, something no university board would wish upon itself.

# 14

## *Sisson Begins*

The late Walter Seifert rarely held his tongue or his pen. Retired as a professor of public relations in the Journalism School, and reportedly the Guinness champion of published letters to the editor, he also held the unofficial record for conservative opinions noted on paper to Gordon Gee. This particular note was neither critical nor conservative. It was about the newly appointed Ohio State provost, John Richard "Dick" Sisson of the University of California at Los Angeles.

"Our daughter has been employed at UCLA for many years," he wrote. "She called this week to say we were stealing 'one of the most talented administrators UCLA has had.'" Given Seifert's reputation as an antagonist to liberal causes, had the Women's Grass Roots Network known of his even second-hand support, some members might have fought harder yet to continue the search.

A letter signed "the women's grass roots network" and dated March 13, 1993, already had arrived on Gee's desk. "Outraged by the lack of diversity in the final pool of [seven] candidates," which had included two women and one veteran, but no minorities, the letter "strongly" urged that the search continue. "Our community," it said, "cannot tolerate such failures."

This was the second letter from the network. When the search had been announced the prior May, the network had congratulated Gee on filling two of his four open vice presidencies with women—Janet Pichette in Business and Linda Tom in Human Resources. While Tom was Asian American, and Gee's new corporate relations director Sarah Austin was African American, it reminded him of "the lack of women of color in administrative positions."

The search committee of nineteen, chaired by Paul Beck, chair of Political Science, had included seven women. To convert names to candidates, it had hired Bill Bowen of Heidrick & Struggles, the same person and same firm that had recruited Gee. The committee did a mailing to 1,200 women in higher education and advertised as an equal opportunity employer in the appropriate publications, while Bowen's firm worked to convert names into candidates.

Meanwhile, in the same September 1992 issue that held an advertisement for the provost position, *Women in Higher Education* ran an article about the grassroots network that was unflattering to the university. "Outraged by a hostile climate for women on campus," it read, "a grassroots network of women at Ohio State University is rattling cages." It then listed thirteen network "concerns," including a glass ceiling in both the faculty and administration and retaliation against women who spoke up about gender inequities. Had such publicity helped the search, hurt it, or been neutral?

Gee's newly appointed diversity committee, which would be part of the final interview process, also wrote to the president. Its members were "profoundly disappointed" there were no minorities in the final six (one of the women had dropped out) and would ascertain each candidate's commitment to diversity and affirmative action in the interviews.

Another area of pressure on Gee and the committee was being generated about scholarly qualifications. Reflecting what they termed "the will of our faculties," a letter to Gee from two deans, Jose Cruz of Engineering and Jim Garland of Mathematical and Physical Sciences, spoke of a growing apprehension that the search might not produce "a serious scholar," one who had accumulated a significant record of scholarly publications, had supervised doctoral candidates, had a respected international reputation, and would come from a major research university "whose academic aspirations are as high or higher than those at Ohio State."

"The provost is the senior intellectual leader of the campus community, and as such is a symbol for who we are and what we wish to become."

One serious scholar and, for some, the preferred insider was economist Edward J. "Ed" Ray, who had spent his career at Ohio State. A Stanford Ph.D. and Queens College Phi Beta Kappa, Ed Ray's research expertise included U.S. foreign trade and investment policies and their varied effects on economic development; he had published *U.S. Protectionism and the World Debt Crisis* in 1989. He had moved up from assistant to full professor in just seven years and, with sixteen years' experience as his department chair, was respected as an academic administrator. But his experience atop the hierarchy was lean: he had become associate provost only the year before.

The person who got the job, "Dick" Sisson of UCLA, did appear to fulfill the criteria Cruz and Garland had expressed as concerns of the university faculty. Whatever its true value, in the *U.S. News* annual ranking, UCLA consistently

## Chapter 14

could be found among the top five public universities while, given a few multi-way ties in any given year, Ohio State fluctuated between the high teens and midtwenties.

Sisson himself was a well-regarded political scientist with a Berkeley Ph.D. whose scholarly interests were the multicultural societies of South Asia, including Pakistan, India, and Bangladesh. His most recent scholarly works had been on the complexities of the politics and culture of India, and on Pakistan, India, and the Bangladesh war.

He had taught at UCLA since 1968 and chaired his department for six years. Though he then had served as acting Social Sciences dean, he had planned to return full-time to the faculty and finish the book on the Bangladesh war. Instead, he completed it while moving up in the administration as UCLA's academic vice chancellor, and then its senior vice chancellor, equivalent to Ohio State's provost.

He also was a Vietnam-era veteran and a native son of rural southern Ohio, with his B.A. and M.A. from Ohio State. What more could the Ohio State faculty want in its "senior intellectual leader"? As a former Men's Glee Club president, he even knew the school songs by heart!

Could Sisson really be enticed to return to Ohio, as provost and, if so, would he stay for the long haul? Every provost in memory at Ohio State except Huber had gone on to become a university president, and Sisson already was becoming recognized as presidential timber.

The new provost addressed this question in his first public presentation, at an Alumni Association reception in his honor at the Regency Club in West Los Angeles on June 26. "Many have wondered and no fewer have asked," he observed, "why I would consider going back to Ohio State as provost." The answer may seem elusive and complex; but it is deceptively simple. Roots, love of a place; an institution and the idea that inspires it; and adventure and exceptional challenge . . .

"It was there I grew to intellectual manhood; it was there I decided upon the direction I wanted to take. . . . What moves me is simple: Ohio State gave much to me at that most critical time in a young person's life; and I want to give something back. . . ." In closing, he indicated he was indeed returning for the long haul.

Dick Sisson's appointment had been approved by the trustees on May 7, 1993. He would begin work officially on August 1. By a margin of $528, though he would have no university-owned home, he would be paid more than the president: $161,004 to $160,476. And he knew one of his first public addresses should be to the Women's Grass Roots Network.

While he and Willa were driving across country from Los Angeles to Columbus, Sisson was elected president of the Council on Academic Affairs (the council of provosts) of the 214-institution National Association of State Universities and Land-Grant Colleges, an organization in which he continued to be an active leader, his election serving as national affirmation of the decision of President Gee and the Board of Trustees to entice a native son home.

## *Vet Medicine*

Who the new dean of the College of Veterinary Medicine should be was one of the first issues on the plate of the new provost, coincidentally a distant cousin of Septimus Sisson, the veterinary surgeon after whom the college's Sisson Hall had been named. This college, sometimes considered the best in the nation, embarrassingly, had received only conditional accreditation in its last peer review. It needed severe renovation of facilities, including Sisson Hall, as well as academic restructuring. The person Sisson selected, first as interim dean and later as dean, was Glen Hoffsis, the veterinary hospital director.

The discussion of this first appointment and the changes that would be required in the college would be Sisson's real introduction into the agonizing process that would be the signature of his four and a half year tenure as the university's chief academic officer: change. Since February 1991, as Gordon Gee explained in a letter to an inquiring donor, the university had "been asked to absorb $78.74 million in state funding reductions from what the state originally promised and what was included in our budget planning."

The instructional subsidy alone had dropped from $270 million to $255 million to $240 million from fiscal 1991 to 1993. In fiscal 1994, the subsidy was up a bit, but $15 million had been cut internally to fund priorities, including the first raise plan in two years. The raise was a meager $300 base and an average 2 percent for faculty and unclassified staff; 1.5 percent for classified staff and students; and zero for the president and his staff, deans, and vice presidents.

As the new provost was to point out in his first major address to the University Senate, on December 4, 1993, since 1991 most academic support units had totaled permanent budget hits of 20 percent and academic units half that. "The institution," Sisson recalled later, "could no longer think just in terms of cutting. It had to decide its long-term priorities."

CHAPTER 14

## *Reinvestment*

After a series of discussions with deans, the Council on Academic Affairs, committees of the Senate and others, the new provost directed the deans to develop two new budgets by February 1994. Targeted reallocations, now termed "reinvestments," would be at the center of the task. The first budget would show a 7 percent internal reallocation within each college for the following academic year; the second, another 7 percent over several years. Proposals to combine colleges, transfer departments from one college to another, or reconstitute existing programs in clusters, Sisson said, would require greater time.

Realizing that successive budget cuts without a long-term vision and set of guidelines could result in unintended but irreparable harm to the university, the provost sent a memorandum to the university community on November 3, 1993, outlining his plans. In it he stated, "It is essential that we move forward to set academic priorities for the long term. We must explore ways to provide the greatest range at the highest quality of what we do, but with greater efficiency. We must also provide for renewal within the university. It is essential that we seed and nurture new growth in areas of excellence and in new areas where Ohio State has a comparative advantage to take the lead among the nation's universities."

The process of setting priorities and reallocating resources would have to be an open one. "Because our history provides limited guidance for this task," the provost stated, "we must proceed with great care to avoid unnecessary disruption and to safeguard academic strengths and traditions. Two principles are crucial. The process will be governed by existing university rules, and it must involve advice and counsel from the faculty, students, and staff. Because the larger good may not serve individual preferences, all members of the university community may not agree with all proposals. But all must have an appropriate forum to voice concerns. . . . While the process must be broadly based," he indicated, "it will be initiated in the colleges and in the Office of Academic Affairs." After review of proposals, the provost and president would recommend action to the Board of Trustees.

In time, program and budget proposals would emerge from departments, colleges, and academic support units. Where appropriate, they would be submitted to faculty and student groups and then to the administration for review and action. At the same time, the administration and trustees were considering another faculty buyout, or Early Retirement Incentive (ERI) program, as a way to both reallocate resources and stimulate the hiring of younger faculty.

"Colleagues," the new provost said in concluding that first address to the

Senate in December 1993, "the challenges ahead will test our resources, our creativity, and probably our patience. But this academy has a strong and proud tradition of facing challenge and overcoming obstacles in the pursuit of excellence. Let us agree to accept change for what it is—namely, a great opportunity for progress, and embrace debate as the vehicle to move to a better tomorrow. I pledge my unending energy and good will to this task."

By June 30, 1995, as recorded in *The Ohio State University Report to the North Central Association of Colleges and Schools,* the task had included buying out nearly 10 percent of the faculty with each college having a plan approved by the provost for reallocating resources.

Part of Sisson's plan involved allocating central resources to seed new academic growth areas, and to invest matching funds where Ohio State might advance to the forefront nationally. He would launch two university-wide reinvestment initiatives. The first, "Academic Enrichment," would seed interdisciplinary and multidepartmental programs that would create something new and strengthen participating academic units. The other, "Selective Investment," would provide permanent matching funds to particular academic units that had the potential to move to the top tier. These would become the core of the provost's "20/10 in 2010" initiative advanced at the trustees' retreat in the fall of 1997. The objective was to have at least ten major academic units securely placed among the top ten nationally and another twenty in the top twenty nationally in 2010.

# 15

## *Firestone*

> I do not want you to build a lot of houses in my neighborhood. How would you feel if we put houses on your campus! How would you feel? What would you do? Where would the animals go? Do you know what would happen? All of the animals would leave. Some animals would die. Please think again about what you are going to do to that land.
>
> —A letter to Gordon Gee from a
> Bath, Ohio, 8-year-old, signed
> by 21 other children

On August 27, 1992, Gordon Gee flew north to Akron on what would become nearly a five-year undertaking. He and three staff—Business VP Janet Pichette and her real estate operations chief, Robert Haverkamp, and Development Director Art Brodeur—left Don Scott Field at 7:45 A.M. and arrived 45 minutes later at Akron Fulton Airport, original home base of the celebrated Goodyear blimp. They were about to drive to the township of Bath to visit the retired chairman of another tire dynasty, Raymond Firestone, and his wife, Jane, whose 1,503-acre Lauray Farms had been appraised at $8 million in 1987.

Earlier, the Firestones had made a "bargain sale" agreement with President Ed Jennings. After their deaths, Ohio State could buy the estate for $5 million and then sell it. The profit would be their posthumous gift to the university. Gee and his staff were visiting to thank Ray and Jane Firestone and to inspect the property.

Later that morning, the university plane deposited the president at Cleveland's Burke Lakefront Airport before flying back to Columbus and returning to Cleveland that evening. There, Gee made his first fund-raising call with his new young vice president for Development, Jerry May, driving in from Ann Arbor. May was completing his last days directing the University of Michigan's principal gifts program and would not start at Ohio State officially until September 8. They lunched with John Drinko, one of Ohio State's most successful law alumni, now senior adviser to the policy committee of the Baker & Hostetler firm. Drinko wanted to discuss revitalization of The Ohio State University Foundation Board, the major gift organization essential to another capital campaign.

In fund-raising vernacular, this call was about both "cultivation" and "stewardship." Cultivation because there was a major Law building addition going up, with opportunity remaining for a naming gift. Stewardship because Drinko already was the largest donor to the College of Law, and Gee wanted to thank him for it. People like to be thanked. May would discover when he came on board that, because the development office had cut staff after the last campaign, stewardship in general had suffered. It would be one of his first administrative fixes.

This meeting had been arranged by Jim Chapman, also of Baker & Hostetler. The university owed much to Chapman. He had been the catalyst in the resurgence of Buckeye alumni activity in Cleveland in the 1980s and had chaired that city's portion of the Jennings administration's capital campaign. A recurrence of cancer would end his life in only a few weeks. "Thank you for letting me share Jim for the last time," Gee would write his widow, Anita. "It was a wonderfully uplifting memorial service, as was his wont."

As death so often births philanthropy, for Raymond Firestone the end would come in September 1994. Jane would die only two months later. The university was ready, so to speak, to buy the farm. It included the family home, stables, barns, a dozen or so houses leased to employees, and much undeveloped land, including prime wetland. The Board gave its formal approval on December 2.

To investigate selling options, trustee David Brennan of Akron was appointed to head a committee that included fellow trustee Milt Wolf and alumnus John W. Ong, president of B. F. Goodrich, the third tire company in what had been Ohio's Big Three. Other members were trustee Jack Kessler; Jacqueline Woods, then president of Ameritech; and Harvard University's Gerald McCue, trustee Les Wexner's land planning adviser, behind the scenes in other projects, including Campus Partners.

CHAPTER 15

For reasons other than price, it would prove much simpler to buy Lauray Farms then to sell it.

After the meeting with Drinko, Gee dictated a note to greet May on his first day on the job. It was about the foundation board. "Only a reminder that you will move this high on your agenda." Which May certainly did. The foundation board would be reorganized and ready when the $850 million "Affirm Thy Friendship" campaign was announced in September 1995. In October, at Homecoming, John Deaver Drinko Hall of the College of Law was dedicated. Of the $15 million raised in the law school campaign, Drinko had been responsible for $6 million.

## *The Man in the White Hat*

By April 1993, as chair of Governor Voinovich's Commission on Educational Choice, David Brennan had helped develop a plan to give parents a state-funded option to public and private schools. Legislation to test a voucher system, which Brennan called the "GI Bill for Kids," was being prepared for the Ohio legislature as he was being appointed a trustee of Ohio State, where he had earned an accounting degree forty years earlier. The legislation would lead to the Cleveland voucher program, which, nine years later, would be found constitutional by the U.S. Supreme Court.

Because of an affectation he enjoyed, to many people Brennan was "the man in the white hat." When his Akron-based holding company, the Brenlin Group, purchased an Alabama steel mill in the mid-1980s, he was portrayed in Gadsden as a B-western villain, "the man in the black hat" ready to pillage the company. Instead he transformed the former Republic Steel division into a moneymaker and was given a white hat for saving the city's largest employer; it was a "10-gallon" Stetson that would become his trademark.

Education was central to Brennan's philosophies of life and management. He was also a trustee of Case Western Reserve University's law school, where he had earned the degree, and board chair of the Akron Catholic high school where he had earned his diploma. In his businesses, he created learning centers for his employees, given time off each week to upgrade their skills and their education. An early advocate and user of computer-aided instruction in his own companies, Brennan would become the trustee to prod the university to stop lagging in the educational revolution of "distance learning."

But first things first. Gee was receiving inquiries already "about our intentions" with the Firestone land. On September 21, 1994, Gee memoed May,

Pichette, Haverkamp, and Finance VP Bill Shkurti. They, plus General Counsel Ginny Trethewey, Treasurer Jim Nichols, and News Director Ruth Gerstner, would be the internal subcommittee that would help determine the direction to pursue. Would the university sell it all? Would it keep some as university property? Would it sell to the highest bidder regardless of land use? Would it establish parameters for residential development? Where, if anywhere, did profit give way to values? "I have asked Mr. Brennan," the president wrote, to serve as chair of the larger committee.

## *Two More Hats*

"David Brennan wore his trademark white cowboy hat when he squared off with his adversaries yesterday" at the Summit County Metro Parks Board meeting, the *Cleveland Plain Dealer* stated on December 17, 1994. He wore another hat, it said, as a developer, and another as a member of the County Metro Parks Board—from which he soon would resign to avoid a suggestion of conflict of interest. "To many people hoping to preserve the estate of the late Raymond C. Firestone, Brennan is not one of the good guys. . . . Many fear he will be predisposed to push for new homes on the Firestone land," including, perhaps, it suggested, some of his own. The man in the white hat was suspect again.

It was exactly because Brennan was an experienced developer and knew the locale better than any other trustee that Gee had asked him to chair the committee. The trustees, Brennan explained to the Metro Parks board, would be open to suggestions as to how the land should be used and definitely would consider community concerns. However, as directed by the Ohio State Board, he had to add that the university was obligated legally to seek a maximum return on its investment.

Did the university not have an obligation to act, as one man wrote to Gee, "responsibly to the Bath community and to the land . . . undisturbed for hundreds of years, from the founding of our country, through the signing of the Declaration of Independence, the Civil War, World Wars I and II and, in particular, through the decades of growth and prosperity of the '50s, '60s, '70s, and '80s. Through it all, this land has remained unspoiled."

This was, of course, the same Ohio State president who some conservationists had accused in 1991 of being willing to endanger the Mt. Graham squirrel population just to build a telescope. The Firestone estate included a watershed and wetlands. Could this Gee fellow and his trustees be trusted to heed

## Chapter 15

environmental issues? When Brennan told the *Plain Dealer* (November 21, 1994) that, while the trustees had to maximize the value of the sale, "they are not going to do it with disregard for the community," the head of the main advocacy group for Bath residents personalized his response: "We're afraid [he] and his pals will get rich from it."

David Brennan, at nearly six foot six and more than 250 pounds, with his hearty laugh, strong opinions, Stetson hat, and earned wealth, struck many people as larger than life and made for the media. Sometimes, it seemed, Brennan himself could become the issue. But so could Gee, who understood that at times his persona, more than an issue itself, could become the lightning rod for vocal opposition. Gee was sure that, though the phenomenon might be happening with Brennan, the right trustee was in the right place at the right time and would do the right thing for Bath and for Ohio State.

On November 16, 1994, representatives of eleven Bath community groups met and, on the letterhead of the Revere Land Conservancy, wrote David Brennan, urging Ohio State to do four things. Do not sell the land until all options are explored. Consider selling part or all to a public authority as a park. If the land had to be developed, consider only the plans that preserved open space. Communicate regularly with the people of Bath. Brennan wrote back, "pleased" that their requests conformed so closely to the goals of the university.

Meanwhile, residents were devising a plan to rezone the land from "residential" to "agriculture," which virtually would have eliminated housing. It also would have halved the land's value, scotched the university's interest, and defeated the intent of Ray Firestone's bequest. And it could be done by township trustee vote, without landlord consent.

Knowing this, at trustee Milt Wolf's suggestion, Brennan brought in property litigator Tim Grendell, an expert in zoning law. Soon Ohio State filed a plat detailing a plan for enough acreage to "grandfather" the university's rights if the community tried rezoning. The man in the white hat had cut them off at the pass. Residents dropped the rezoning plan and Ohio State withdrew the plat.

By November 1995, however, the property still was unsold and was costing the university $500,000 a year to maintain. It was time, the trustees agreed, to seek an outside real estate company, not to buy the estate, but to market it and facilitate the sale. The winning bidder, the specs said, must "take into account the land's unique characteristics" while giving community groups "ample opportunity" to provide input.

FIRESTONE

## *The Galbreath Connection*

At that same November Board meeting, the trustees named the College of Veterinary Medicine's new $7 million equine care and trauma center in honor of the late Daniel M. Galbreath, former trustee, developer, and breeder of great racehorses. Few recalled it, but Dan Galbreath had introduced Ray Firestone to Ed Jennings in the first place. Purely by coincidence, the Galbreath Company, with offices in Akron and Cleveland, would win the bid the next month to facilitate the sale.

Nearly another year went by before Brennan and his fellow trustees thought they had a winner. In September 1996, they approved a contract with the Biskind Realty Company of North Omstead for sale of the total estate for $13 million, a gain after all expenses of more than $4 million. Biskind's proposal would create an ecologically sensitive "exurban" residential community. More than half the land would remain undeveloped. Biskind would construct wetlands and ponds on the property to filter storm water before it entered the natural wetlands. It also would sell nearly 300 acres of open space to Bath Township, which had passed a levy to purchase environmental areas and create a nature preserve (*onCampus,* March 13, 1997).

And already the university had cleaned up a one-acre farm dump at a cost of $1.5 million.

Gee was pleased. The trustees were pleased. Brennan, who had abstained from voting because of the Metro Parks issue, was pleased. But one man who owned property bordering the estate was not pleased. He filed a conflict of interest complaint with the Ohio Ethics Commission against David Brennan, and the sale again was held up. The commission, noting Brennan had resigned his Metro Parks seat and had abstained from the Ohio State vote, said there was nothing to investigate. Everyone thought the Firestone sale was done.

But it wasn't. The Biskind arrangement collapsed. Nine more months of negotiations finally generated a contract with a resident of Bath Township itself, John Cheblina, who bought the property for $12 million, $1 million less than the Biskind deal. The net profit to Ohio State was down to $2.9 million, even less than expected in 1987, but still not bad for an albatross. Brennan himself and his wife Ann would also donate nearly $1.3 million themselves to the Affirm Thy Friendship campaign, for presidential scholarships.

"Without your tenacity and creativity," Gee penned in a note to Brennan in mid-1997, "none of this ultimately would have happened." Brennan, who had given an immense amount of time to the project since the fall of 1994, was now more than ready to push Ohio State further ahead in distance learning.

## Chapter 15

The Board was studying technological advances at the university, and Brennan urged Gee to make distance learning a priority. They had been talking about it for four years. "Excellence costs money," he wrote Gee. "Revenues restricted by state funds, and tuition caps will never get us there. Distance learning with unlimited revenue will."

"Time," he wrote, "is wasting."

The week that Biskind announced its plans, Ohio State signed another agreement. It concerned the former "Columbus Project," now called the Large Binocular Telescope (LBT). The $60 million arrangement from which Gee had withdrawn in 1991 was back in play with the University of Arizona, but at a much lower cost. For $9 million in cash, past payments, and new instrumentation, Ohio State would buy one-eighth of the time on the yet to be completed Mt. Graham telescope. An external scientific committee had reviewed the astronomy program and reported lack of access to a major telescope as the single greatest handicap Ohio State astronomers and their students faced. The LBT now was scheduled to be finished by 2004. And the squirrels were thriving.

# 16

## *Managing the Future*

> How can the university most effectively address the myriad social and economic forces acting on it? How best, in an era of declining support, can the university strengthen its academic programs, improve its quality, and serve the needs of an increasingly diversified student body? This report seeks to address those fundamental questions.
>
> —From the Executive Summary,
> The Final Report of The Ohio State University
> Managing for the Future Task Force,
> November 6, 1992

If ever there were a time in the second half of the twentieth century in which faculty were maligned, it was the early to mid-1990s. And 1992 was the worst of it, when a number of new books capitalizing on public discontent added to it by trashing academe. Two of the most popular were Martin Anderson's *Impostors in the Temple* and Richard Huber's *How Professors Play the Cat Guarding the Cream.*

"American intellectuals are destroying our universities and cheating our students of their future," blared the cover of the Anderson book, while inside, certain buzzwords sent shivers up the spines of faculty who remembered the McCarthy era. On page 4, for instance, "academic intellectuals" were accused of enjoying the dreams of "any socialist," such as "a guaranteed job for life [tenure]," "subsidized housing," and a review system "in which they essentially judge themselves."

Huber's cover copy read, "Why we're paying more and getting less in higher

## Chapter 16

education." The flyleaf told the browser that "undergraduate teaching is often terrible"; that for tenure and promotion reviews, research could be "goofing off masquerading for productive work"; and, perhaps, most egregiously, "tuition rises faster than the rate of inflation in part because universities enhance their academic reputations by hiring high salary scholars with low teaching loads."

Within this highly critical and often hostile environment, Governor Voinovich's statewide Managing for the Future Task Force had developed its recommendations, Ohio State and thirty-nine other institutions had written their own future planning documents, and now the Ohio Board of Regents was responding.

In December 1992, the regents released *Securing the Future of Higher Education in Ohio,* its own set of recommendations. To some faculty, regents are hardheaded business leaders focused only on the bottom line, a stereotype as overgeneralized as any other. But what would these people, also appointed by the governor, recommend? The end of tenure? Onerous teaching loads? Centralization of power with diminution of each institution's board of trustees?

It was nothing like that. "The Ohio Board of Regents yesterday unveiled a management plan designed to soothe nervous university and college presidents across the state," reporter John Funk wrote in the *Cleveland Plain Dealer* (December 10). They had "wisely," he commented, "sidestepped the hot potato of centralized control from Columbus," choosing to use their coordinating power instead. "In short, the regents voted unanimously to ... keep the present decentralized system, but ... set tough new standards for efficiency and accountability."

The regents, their report said, already had the authority to enact most of their recommendations, including assessing the quality of graduate programs and, after drawing up standards, deciding which to keep to avoid duplication. And it already had the power to redefine faculty workloads based upon degree levels offered and to establish standards for all two-year institutions. The governor said he was satisfied, and so, largely, was Ohio State.

While Ohio State had not been declared and funded as a "comprehensive research institution" as the governor's task force had recommended, unquestionably it would not lose graduate programs. Across the board, most were acknowledged the best in the state. This would be corroborated in 1995 when, in its first peer rating of the nation's doctoral programs since 1982, the National Research Council ranked 36 of 38 Ohio State doctoral programs no. 1 in Ohio.

Following a furious outcry from Gee, his regional campus deans, and regional community leaders, the university had prevailed against the state task force's recommendation to merge regional campuses with colocated technical colleges or otherwise create "community colleges."

A faculty workload policy would impose nothing on Ohio State not imposed elsewhere, and tenure, which some people feared would be challenged, had been championed as "absolutely necessary."

But just how much could Ohioans' futures be secured just through efficiencies urged in *Securing the Future of Higher Education in Ohio*? Not much, the report confessed. Higher education in Ohio already had absorbed $270 million in cuts that year, with more projected. Effectiveness would come, the report concluded, only if "accompanied by additional public financial support."

That support, the $195 million tax increase proposed by the governor, lobbied for by Gee and the other university presidents, and championed by both House Speaker Riffe and Senate President Aronoff, would be authorized a week later as a rider to a $1 billion capital bill. And higher education finally would be spared another round of cuts.

## *The University's Own Report*

Six months after the statewide Managing for the Future Task Force issued its report, the Ohio State task force appointed by Gee issued its own (November 6, 1992). As titled in the document's preface, the "for" was left out. Although this was an editor's error, the hypothesis that Ohio State already was managing its future was not lost on some readers; for, under this activist president, it was the absolute truth.

By November 1992, Gee already had opened institutional dialogue on the future of Ohio State and brought alumni and civic leaders into the discussion that led to the university's mission and vision statements, now only weeks away from publication.

Quite significantly, he already was changing a culture that all too often had taken students for granted. He had opened the institutional dialogue on the relationship between students and faculty and students and staff, and on the need for more academic counseling. And he had appointed a "Red Tape Task Force" to eliminate administrative impediments to student success. Rolling applause would greet him as, at each commencement, he announced "the last line you will ever stand in at Ohio State."

As trustee Tami Longaberger, a 1984 graduate then active in the Alumni Association, later recalled, Gee "was in the dorms, he would walk with students across campus, he would bring students with him to alumni meetings. He

## Chapter 16

Members of the first Academy of Teaching: (Front row, l-r) Nancy Zimpher, Gerald Reagan, Susan Sears, Anna Soter; (Back row, l-r) James Altschuld, Ralph Gardner III, William Heward, John Cooper.

knew what he was doing symbolically." Longaberger had experienced "four-hour waits in Lincoln Tower" herself, "four-hour lines to register at the Ohio Union." She had only "seen a counselor twice" as an undergraduate. "You could have lived in University College forever (Ed. Note: and never declare a major) as long as your bills were paid. Gordon knew that needed to change."

He also knew matters related to gender needed examination that would lead to change; he had established commissions on women and on dependent care and a faculty salary equity review committee. To honor great teaching and to create mentors, from approximately 100 winners of the Alumni Teaching Award he had created the Academy of Teaching. To attract more top students, he had created a task force on undergraduate recruitment. His administration had issued its Hispanic Action Plan, updated an Action Plan for the Recruitment and Retention of Black Students, and opened an African American living-learning center in Lincoln Tower.

The academic partnership with the Cleveland Clinic had been approved and the university had withdrawn from the Mt. Graham telescope program. And he had reorganized his administration.

Gerald E. Mayo, chairman and CEO of the Midland Mutual Life Insurance

Company, chaired Ohio State's Managing for the Future Task Force. Its members from beyond campus were Ross Bridgman of the Vorys, Sater, Seymour and Pease law firm; C. A. Peterson of the Ohio Company; Patrick O'Reilly of Deloitte and Touche; Stephen Cheek of the I-670 Development Corporation; former Ohio University trustee Jody Phillips; and W. Lee Hoskins, president of the Huntington National Bank. The faculty and administration were represented by emeritus provost Albert Kuhn; Lee Walker of the School of Public Policy and Management, once the state's budget director; Associate Provost Nancy Rudd; Robert Arkin, associate dean in Arts and Sciences; and Dean James Garland of Mathematical and Physical Sciences.

For the perspective of those who had experienced the university as policymakers and also knew it as outside observers, Gee had called upon trustee Michael Colley; former trustees Shirley Dunlap Bowser and James Hilliker; and John Kramer, former chair of the University Hospitals Board.

A month before the report came out, the president set the stage in his annual address to the University Senate, this year titled "A Call for Change." He noted that, even as the university budget had been cut drastically, most of the shortfall was being handled through unfilled positions and a year with no raises. Through it all, he pledged, "the academic core" would continue to be protected.

He read the final draft of the mission statement—"this university's defining characteristics, its boundaries and its aspirations"—soon to be approved by the trustees, and reviewed its major points. The statement, he said, would guide a new "competitive and timely" university-wide planning process that would link short-term and long-term budget allocating and "change the face of the university." Institutional priorities and quality of work would distinguish the haves from the have-somes, the have-lesses, and the have-nots.

The good news: "We are bettering the institution." The other news: "The excellent ultimately will edge out the very good." By working together, Gee concluded, "we can achieve great things." To date, he had been Ohio State's president two years and three months.

## *After Sisson's First Year*

What had Ohio State's own Managing for the Future Task Force urged? Essentially, five institutional changes and three by the State of Ohio. By the winter of 1994, two years after the report and one year under the academic leadership of Provost Dick Sisson, here is where things stood:

## Chapter 16

Recommendation 1: *Refine the institutional mission.* Under Dick Sisson, the university was restructuring, as guided by the mission and vision statements and detailed in a functional mission statement that had since been approved.

Recommendation 2: *Review and, if necessary, revise the university's entire organization and governance structure.* The provost's office (Academic Affairs) had been reorganized and three clusters of colleges created: Arts and Sciences, Health Sciences, and Professional Colleges. Reorganizations were under way university-wide and had been approved in the colleges of Engineering; Food, Agricultural, and Environmental Sciences; and Veterinary Medicine.

Recommendation 3: *Undertake a comprehensive plan to implement new information systems for finances, enrollments, personnel appointments, and expenditures.* The university now had its first chief information officer (CIO). In what was expected to be a three-year process to develop new Human Resource and ledger systems, the Administrative Resource Management System (ARMS) was under way.

Recommendation 4: *Create an academic quality measurement system and, in that context, form faculty workload policies for academic departments.* All departments and colleges now had written faculty workload policies, including teaching, research, and the often underappreciated area, "service." All had been approved by the Ohio Board of Regents. The university was preparing for an accreditation review by the North Central Association of Colleges and Schools, and each department was gathering data to evaluate and support its qualitative position among its peers.

Recommendation 5: *Improve academic support services while improving efficiency, increasing quality, and lowering the costs.* A university-wide "continuous quality improvement (CQI)" committee had been created, with training taking place in many units, including University Hospitals, among 1,500 employees in the Office of Business and Administration, and with 200 staff in Human Resources. Staff, in general, had responded well to the urgings of Gee and his administration to eliminate administrative roadblocks.

The task force also had recommended three changes in State of Ohio policies handicapping the university.

Recommendation 6: *Change the subsidy formula so that it did not continue to penalize Ohio State for not continuing to increase total enrollment.* Passionately lobbied against by Gee as unfair to Ohio State, the pure enrollment growth formula was about to be dropped by the Board of Regents. It had announced a new policy, to go into effect in fiscal 1996, that would reduce funding based upon enrollment growth to 50 percent of the formula after one year and 25 percent after two.

Recommendation 7: *Allow Ohio State to manage its own capital construction projects*. Projects budgeted at $1.5 million or less now were authorized for local administration, while the appropriate administrative offices at Ohio State had been reorganized to manage all projects more efficiently.

Recommendation 8: *Allow Ohio State to develop and manage its own personnel system.* The university had hired a consultant to review the existing system and was embarking upon its recommendations, which would simplify job categories and expand pay ranges.

More than three years later, in January 1997, the university would issue another report, which would show a further leap in fulfilling the task force's recommendations. One aspiration not fulfilled, however, and one that probably never would be, was one Gee had written about back in 1992 following the state's Managing for the Future report which had recommended special funding for Cincinnati and Ohio State. In a *Dispatch* op-ed column the day before the 1992 Ohio State–Michigan game, he had contrasted academic support of the two flagship universities in the contest of "The Game."

"What do you think would happen if, every time Michigan's 11-member offensive unit snapped the ball, Ohio State had only six players on defense? And what do you think the score would be if Ohio State had to travel 186 yards for a touchdown while Michigan only had to march the normal 100 yards? Or if the Buckeyes were penalized nine yards for an offside infraction and 28 yards for a personal foul? And what do you think the game's outcome would be if Ohio State got only four points for every touchdown and extra point, while Michigan received the normal seven?"

This was the huge financial disadvantage Ohio State's task force had pointed out: that higher tuition and higher levels of state support allow the University of Michigan to spend 86 percent more per student than Ohio State. "Imagine what we would accomplish," Gee concluded, "if we were able to compete on a level funding field."

That Saturday, the Ohio Stadium field was so level Michigan and Ohio State tied 13–13. When stopped postgame by a phalanx of media, Gee was quoted as having said it was one of Ohio State's "greatest victories." Well, did he or didn't he? Not exactly.

He had prepared comments for both victory or defeat, but never a tie. So, when asked, he drew on his victory statement: that a team expected to lose by a large margin had fought its heart out. And, he added extemporaneously, in the context of being such a huge underdog, this tie might be considered one of the team's "greatest victories." The comment went into history as another Gee unforgettable while, sadly, 86 percent less funding was rarely remembered, if ever read at all.

CHAPTER 16

# *TQM + OSU = CQI*

In the mid-1960s, the motivational management program known as "Zero Defects" so improved quality and on-time performance of U.S. space and defense program contractors that "ZD" became required throughout the U.S. Armed Forces. Some 40 years later, "Total Quality Management" became so important to the revitalized American manufacturing economy that "TQM" became an obligation for many of America's larger universities.

In 1994, TQM became an element of managing for the future when a partnership was announced between Ohio State and the Ford Motor Company. By that time, thirty-five other such pairings had taken place between corporations and universities. Ford had chosen to work with Ohio State because the university was one of its major suppliers of engineering and business talent, and Ford had a dozen manufacturing and assembly facilities in Ohio. Nearly 500 Buckeye alumni were employed by Ford, including Edward Hagenlocker, president of Ford Automotive Operations. Later, Ford also would collaborate with Michigan State, Wayne State, Texas, and Howard University.

"Maximize productivity while minimizing costs" is how TQM often is explained in its simplest form. "Talk to each other" is one of its credos, working in teams its fundamental decision-making process. When busloads of Ohio State vice presidents, deans, and faculty leaders traveled to the "Total Quality Symposium for Ohio State" in Dearborn, Michigan, paradoxically they found themselves talked "to" as much as talked with. Your curricula, particularly in Business, Engineering, and Agriculture, they were told in no uncertain terms, needed to get with it. Young graduates were coming to management ready to be the boss but not the facilitator, talking but not listening.

Gordon Gee listened particularly closely when he heard that, should universities not teach TQM principles, Ford would. Ford already was spending more than $200 million a year training its work force. The press release that announced the partnership had said Ford would "encourage the development and inclusion of Total Quality concepts and processes in various college curricula." But who needed more encouragement? Ford also would "assist Ohio State in implementing a Total Quality system in the university environment."

The staff environment in which TQM, which the university reworked as CQI or "Continuous Quality Improvement," worked best could have been predicted. It was in the Office of Business and Administration, which approached TQM most thoroughly. Vice President Janet Pichette, who had come to the university with a business background, developed a five-day training program taught in small groups mixing her 1,500 employees at every level—the same program for the grass cutter, plumber, electrician, manager, and director.

"If there's a better way of doing it, regardless of whose idea it is," one of the leaders said, "that's what we want to do. Some people think their jobs depend upon their people doing exactly what they did yesterday. But we keep working on it."

Also working on it were Human Resources, Finance, and departments within University Hospitals. Student Affairs borrowed from it the "Things Done Right" award, acknowledging exemplary performance of university employees at trustee meetings.

Where TQM could not have been expected to work well, if at all, was within the faculties. As Engineering Dean Jose Cruz stated, "these concepts do not readily transfer to an academic setting," and Jim Garland, then dean of Mathematical and Physical Sciences (later president of Miami University), wrote to Provost Sisson about a national conference he had attended.

"The university speakers," wrote Garland, "seemed to agree that faculty members tend to be skeptical . . . seeing it as another management fad . . . and that advocates would be wise to avoid the jargon in selling the concepts in their campuses. . . . The truth, I suspect, is that [TQM] really does have something to teach us. [But] I personally think the 'culture' of American research universities is the source of their great strengths, and that one should be extremely wary tampering with it."

Among faculty everywhere, that sentiment would generate a generous "Amen."

# 17

# "Affirm Thy Friendship"

Between 1985 and 1990, the capital campaign of Ed Jennings's administration proved that Ohio State could raise private money. A fund-raising ne'er-do-well until that campaign, Ohio State climbed to just one notch short of America's Top 20 by its close. With more than $74 million raised the year after the campaign's end, by 1991 the university also ranked 21st in annual philanthropic support among all universities, public and private. And with more than $27 million banked just from business, it was nudging the Top 10 in corporate giving, ranking eleventh.

In carrying out what was named simply "The Ohio State University Campaign," Jennings's development vice president, Tom Tobin, had followed the formula originated in the private sector. It begins with a feasibility study by an outside consultant, with whom potentially large donors should feel free to be candid. The study assesses total giving potential and the specific interests of the probable donors. Meanwhile, a list of institutional needs is put together by the administration and the deans. Experienced professional fund-raisers are hired. A volunteer leadership organization is built. Annual fund drives for individual colleges crank up. A public relations campaign builds excitement and acknowledges gifts and givers through press coverage and the university's own materials. And the donors are thanked, thanked, thanked, and thanked again.

The Jennings campaign closed with more than $460 million raised, then a record for a public university. What also may have been a record, however, was the amount of money raised for things *not* on the university's needs list. More often than not, donors wanted to do something else.

Of the 290 identified projects, only 27 were funded fully and 111 received no funding at all. Of the $460 million raised, $294 million was for nonpriorities. In a note to Finance Vice President Bill Shkurti on November 6, 1990, the university's chief budget planner, Eric Kunz, expressed the institutional position. "These data are not intended to detract from the success of the campaign, but to indicate there remains a significant gap between resources and needs." Shkurti forwarded the data and the sentiment to Gee.

That gap, the new president wanted to be sure, would not appear again.

Just four nights earlier, Gee had presided over the gala formally ending The Ohio State University Campaign. He had congratulated everyone on a job well done, particularly Bernie Gerlach, chair of the National Campaign Steering Committee, and his two predecessors, Dick Leet and Fred Ruffner. Then he had presented Jennings the university's consummate fund-raising solicitation award, the Everett D. Reese Medal. Former Engineering Dean Don Glower, who had become the development vice president after Tobin, also spoke. He planned to retire in two years.

A philanthropist himself who gave more than $2 million to his university, banker Everett Reese was even better known as its best fund-raiser. Often describing himself as "the chief wheedler," in the 1960s he convinced President Novice Fawcett that Ohio State needed a major donors' organization, which became the Presidents Club. Established in 1984 to recognize good work for Ohio State, the Reese Medal first was presented to Ev Reese himself. He died at ninety-seven on May 24, 1995. One of his four children, Thekla (Teckie) Shackelford, continued his fund-raising legacy by cochairing the Gee-era "Affirm Thy Friendship" Campaign.

Well before the search began for Glower's successor, Gee was readying for his own campaign. Chaired by Dick Hill, dean of Optometry and one of the university's most effective fund-raisers, Gee's "Task Force for the Next Campaign" was charged to identify the steps to prepare for it and begin to define its principles and parameters.

In September 1992, it recommended first that all deans and key administrators take fund-raising "basic training." Second, it stressed that the university mission and vision statements, still being written, should guide the campaign goals. The feasibility study should compare donor potential with campaign institutional priorities as driven by the mission and vision statements and would take about a year.

One priority, Gee knew, certainly would be raising academic scholarship money to support what he and the trustees hoped would be an increasingly selective undergraduate student body. Another would be to multiply the university's endowed professorships and chairs. Every professorship would require an investment gift of at least $.5 million; every chair, $1.25 million. Compared with bricks-and-mortar projects, both scholarships and professorships historically

CHAPTER 17

Gordon and the Men's Glee Club kick off the Affirm Thy Friendship Capital Campaign, 1995.

had been hard sells for Ohio State. That was one of the reasons that in 1992, only eleven Ohio State faculty were members of the prestigious National Academies, whereas, for instance, the University of Wisconsin had 104 members; Michigan, 84; Illinois, 78; and Harvard, 573 (Source: National Academy of Science, National Academy of Engineering, Institute of Medicine, American Academy of Arts and Sciences).

Gee also knew the development staff, heavily reduced between campaigns by attrition, retirements, and a 25 percent budget cut, would have to be reconstituted. That would wait until the next vice president was hired, as would the feasibility study.

## *Jerry May*

Though perhaps the youngest in a long list of candidates, Michigan's Jerry May impressed both the search committee, chaired by Marketing Professor Roger Blackwell, and the development staff. Since 1990, May had been director of principal gifts—$2.5 million and above—in Michigan's $750 million campaign and, essentially, was the campaign's second in command. He had not begun his career as a fund-raiser, but as an associate dean of students at little New England College in New Hampshire, then becoming the dean while also teaching courses in humanities.

He had been at Michigan since 1978 and had moved up through the development office ranks. First he had directed foundation relations, then a successful capital campaign for the School of Business, then the university's "major gifts" program—which began at $100,000—and now he was raising its biggest gifts from its most affluent alumni.

Already what he termed later "a Big Ten person" when interviewed for the Ohio State job, May found Ohio State's individual giving tradition "very attractive and very compelling." But he had no plans to leave Michigan. When specifically interviewed by Gee, however, he said later he had felt "a connection." What followed, he would learn later, was a case study in Gee's relentless recruiting skills:

"Calling me at 10 or 11 at night. Calling my wife [Deborah, also a Michigan administrator]. Never turning the screw too hard. I knew he was an incredible fund-raiser in just the way I had been recruited. Because in fund-raising you do the same thing. You sell and develop a long-term relationship. You do not go in immediately for a 'yes' or 'no' on that immediate day. You want to create a dialogue. I knew Gordon was a master." May came to Ohio State in September 1992.

On March 4, 1994, the vice president for Development and president of The Ohio State University Foundation, Jerry May, detailed for his president the reorganization and restructuring of the development office he had been working on for eighteen months. To ready for the next campaign, he had held focus groups with every fund-raiser, every secretary, and every researcher. He had run the feasibility study, employing fund-raising guru Burr Gibson, executive chairman of the Marts and Lundy consulting firm. With the help of Provosts Joan Huber and then Dick Sisson, he had won a buy-in from the deans.

Four senior directors were to run the campaign: Jennings campaign veterans John Meyer and Gary Kitsmiller, constituency and campaign giving and development administration, respectively; newly hired Linda Seitz in major gifts; and a yet-to-be-named person for corporate and foundation giving. Dave Ferguson would continue to direct the development communications office; Scott Mueller, the Presidents Club; and Becki Crowell, donor relations and prospect coordination. Four existing development positions still had to be filled, and eight more would be posted.

"I am confident," May wrote Gee, "that if we work together we will grow

CHAPTER 17

professionally and be successful in our principal mission—securing private resources for The Ohio State University."

Indeed, the campaign plan developed out of close collaboration and constant involvement of deans, development leaders, and the Office of Academic Affairs, and was one of the first occasions of such joint planning in higher education.

## *The Kick-off*

It would be another eighteen months before the Mershon Auditorium house and stage lights would cut to black and the Hollywood-created campaign video would cue up. At four minutes in, live on-stage lighting and audio wove into the video. Then the Men's Glee Club, set on risers behind the scrim, began to join in song the image of itself singing on screen. First, *"Carmen Ohio,"* "How Firm Thy Friendship, Ohio," then *"America, the Beautiful."* "And crown thy good with brotherhood." With many eyes tearing already, the mood changed with "If They Could See Her Now," and on walked the evening's host, alumna and CBS *48 Hours* reporter, Erin Moriarty.

"Good evening and welcome to The Ohio State University's capital campaign kickoff, 'Affirm Thy Friendship.'"

The Gee presidency's capital campaign officially was under way, which, in campaign language, normally means at least a quarter of the money had been raised or pledged and more was in the pipeline. Since May's reorganization report to Gee, the foundation board had been reorganized, the National Campaign Executive Committee had been formed, and the regional and constituent volunteer leadership groups had been organized. Max M. Fisher already had made his gift of $20 million to name the Fisher College of Business.

Austin E. "Dutch" Knowlton had made his gift of $10 million to establish the Knowlton School of Architecture, which would allow the renovation of Ives Hall and eventual construction of a new facility. Nineteen twenty-nine business graduate Dorothy Klotz and her California investment partner, Marion Rowley, had given nearly $10 million to the James. Klotz had lost her father and four of her five siblings to cancer. "I graduated from Ohio State," she said, "and that's where my heart is."

$1.2 million from Elizabeth Ross had established a chair in Business in memory of her late husband, Richard M. Ross, who had earned his degree in fine arts in 1938. The new equine center had been named in honor of its major donor, former trustee Daniel Galbreath, who had passed away less than three weeks before. John Deaver Drinko Hall had been named in honor of the alumnus responsible for more than $6 million in the Law campaign.

More than $281 million had already been raised.

Toward the end of the kickoff event, still on the risers, the Men's Glee Club parted (the stage directions read, "like the Red Sea") to form an aisle through which Gee descended to the stage to give a motivational but brief address.

The campaign goal, he announced, was "where no man or woman has gone before." At least no one had in the public sector. "To raise $850 million to perpetuate the greatness that is, and will continue to be, The Ohio State University." At his closing line, "Let the campaign begin," backstage the OSU Marching Band snare drummers struck up the first rattling beats of "Down the Field." As the cheerleaders emerged from the wings, the crowd came to its feet, began to clap, and started to sing along. Suddenly, the band exploded onto the stage and formed in full, then broke into two files, marching up the aisles and out the doors of Mershon Auditorium.

They were followed by President Gee, five of the eight campaign cochairs, John Berry, Bernie Gerlach, Teckie Shackelford, Milt Wolf, and Larry Barnett; Erin Moriarty; the cheerleaders; the glee club; other show participants, including local TV newscaster Carol Luper; and everyone else.

The show was over. It was Thursday evening, September 28, 1995. Two days later, most of the guests joined the crowd jamming Ohio Stadium for the first Notre Dame–Ohio State football game in sixty years and a victory. Two weeks before, Gordon and Constance Gee had been honored by "the Best Damn Band in the Land" as the first nonmembers since Woody Hayes to "Dot the 'I.'" Less than three months before that, Gordon Gee had been wooed by the University of California system and, at the last minute, turned down its offer to be president after a Gee lovefest in Columbus.

It was certainly time now to get on with the next stage of the Gordon Gee presidency.

# 18
## *Athletics as Pressure Cooker*

On Friday afternoon, November 22, 1991, Gordon Gee, Athletic Director Jim Jones, new General Counsel Bob Duncan, trustee Jack Kessler, and a few other members of the president's staff sat at the president's conference table making a last-minute decision. Tomorrow at noon, Ohio State—with eight wins and two losses—would play its nationally televised football game against Michigan. Though John Cooper was having his best season as head coach, he had not beaten the Wolverines in his first three years. In contrast, his predecessor Earle Bruce had won five of nine over Michigan, the last an emotional 23–20 underdog win six days after his announced dismissal.

While the issue at the president's table this day was not the firing of Coach Cooper, the terrible publicity generated on both sides of the Atlantic by the Bruce sacking would be an undercurrent in any discussion of Cooper's coaching future. In addition, star running back Robert Smith had quit the team that summer because an assistant coach, he said, had put winning above studying.

The subject today was whether to extend the coach's five-year contract—on which a year yet remained—and to do it right now. A year earlier—his first at Ohio State—Gee gladly would have extended it after beating Michigan at the end of the regular season. But the Buckeyes didn't—and he didn't. He had waited for the Liberty Bowl, where Ohio State was expected to destroy an Air Force team of relative lightweights. But it was not to be, again. In a cold rain, Ohio State suffered an embarrassing loss. So the president had deferred to his athletic director and waited until the next year.

Next year was now here and nearly over. Distressed local sports media had been warning all season that no contract extension would signal "no confidence," lose the current recruiting class, and guarantee bad times ahead. Yet, no

## ATHLETICS AS PRESSURE COOKER

announcement had been forthcoming. Coach Cooper had not yet created the dominant team many Buckeyes fans desired, if not required.

While they had been mesmerized by the near perfection of his first game ever at Ohio State, a 26–9 victory over Syracuse in 1988, in which Ohio State had incurred no penalties, it had raised false hope. A 42–10 battering by Pittsburgh the following Saturday had illustrated the up-and-down pattern that recruiting parity had created in big-time athletics, but that many Buckeyes fans never would accept. Through his first three seasons, his record had been 19-14-2, less lustrous, in fact, than Bruce's last three, which had been 25-10-1.

On this day, however, if the stars were not aligned for an extension, they would just have to be realigned. As scenarios were played around the president's table, it had become clear that there was but one choice, and that was to wait no longer.

To lose to Michigan this year—and not to have awarded Cooper an extension yet—would indeed forfeit the next recruiting class. It also would increase the clamor to fire the coach and put more pressure on Gee—and the trustees—to see that it happened. Gee then would have to wait until the bowl game and either extend the contract first or wait it out again. And what if Ohio State lost that one, too? Would he then decide not to extend the contract? Or fire the coach who had won eight games? Although certain alumni might do cartwheels over a Cooper firing or, perhaps, a forced resignation, media worldwide would revisit the Smith and Bruce disasters and deliver a debilitating, if not terminal, blow to the president's academic aspirations for Ohio State.

To win over Michigan—and not to have awarded an extension first—might be a better scenario, but not good enough. Not among the national media. Not after the Bruce firing. And not after the Robert Smith story. Weren't eight wins enough, they would write? What, indeed, did a coach have to do to prove himself at that football factory? Yes, it would play OK in Columbus. But not at Johns Hopkins. Or Harvard. Or Berkeley. Ohio State will never be a first rate place until its values change, they would say—and might add, "That might be never."

Surely, then, to make the announcement in the morning would demonstrate the president's support, which the coach really needed. It would motivate the team to victory—guaranteed! And would once and for all clarify the institutional value system under President Gordon Gee. Coaches did not always have to win at Ohio State, as long as they "showed progress," graduated their players, and ran a clean program. Thus, Jones was dispatched to fly up to

## Chapter 18

Ann Arbor, deliver the message to the coach that his contract would be extended, and, before the noon kickoff, inform the media.

Following the game, *The New York Times* wrote it this way: "When a coach has taken a team to 8-2 against tough competition, it really doesn't seem fair to make his entire career hang on the outcome of a single late-season game. That's the way Ohio State's athletic director, Jim Jones, apparently figured it.... Just before yesterday's game, Jones announced that Cooper had been given a 3-year contract extension ... by announcing the extension before the game, Jones made sure that if the Buckeyes beat Michigan, nobody could say the victory had saved Cooper's job. Alas, the strategy counted for naught. The Buckeyes lost to the Wolverines once again, 31 to 3."

## The Rose Bowl

If this was one of the low points in the Gee administration's love-hate relationship with football, certainly a Rose Bowl victory five years later was its apex. By this time Jones, who had begun his career tutoring players in math, had taken a five-year pension buyout offered to faculty and retired. Promoted by the last administration from associate athletic director after the resignation of Rick Bay, Jones had been a popular and stabilizing force as AD but had been stained toward the end by an NCAA investigation of the basketball and track programs.

Associate AD Phyllis Bailey, who had told Jones the prior summer that she was ready to retire, also took the buyout after thirty-eight years at Ohio State.

Andy Geiger, who had directed a legendary winning athletic program at Stanford, had been hired away from the University of Maryland in 1994 and was completing his third year. The Buckeyes had won ten straight in this 1996 season and been ranked no. 1 in the country, only to lose again to Michigan, 13 to 9. It was the second straight year that Ohio State had gone into the Michigan game undefeated—and lost. Although Cooper had in fact turned the program around, fan aspirations again were for nothing short of a national championship—or at least a Rose Bowl victory. And there still had been none of either since Woody (championship in 1968; Rose Bowl in 1974)!

Gordon Gee would tell the story later that in his box, high atop the Rose Bowl, he could not watch. His Buckeyes had gone ahead of Arizona State, Cooper's former team, only to have its quarterback Jake Plummer squirt into the end zone. The year before, Ohio State had lost its bowl game by one touchdown to Tennessee and, the year before that, by one touchdown to Alabama.

# ATHLETICS AS PRESSURE COOKER

John Cooper hoists the roses as Columbus welcomes the team, Rose Bowl 1997.

Would it happen again? Ohio State was on a do-or-die drive with the clock running out. Gee would duck out the rear of the box into the corridor on each play, then return and ask what happened. His wife, Constance, would tell him and he would return to the corridor.

On the last Buckeye play, David Boston, who later would become a National Football League wide receiver, would catch a pass in the end zone from Joe Germaine, who later would become a National Football League quarterback. And the president could finally look.

Down under the stands, in the hallway outside the Ohio State locker room, Gordon Gee and Andy Geiger would greet each other with a hug and real tears. After nine years, the pressure on Cooper to "win the big one" would be off. Geiger could get on with directing one of the nation's largest intercollegiate athletic programs and replacing its outdated and sometimes crumbling facilities. And Gee could move ahead with his plans for what would become an $850 million fund-raising program, his institutional restructuring program, and lobbying the General Assembly for more support for his university. Neither, they hoped, would need to justify again their support for John Cooper.

But it would be two more years until Ohio State would beat Michigan. By that time Gordon Gee would be at Brown University, where, one season later, his football Bears already would have ascended from the bottom to the top of the Ivy League.

## *Athletics and Institutional Values*

The Cooper contract extension was one of the defining moments for Gordon Gee's presidency and for Ohio State.

"We are not playing for the keys to the Republic," he told the *Dispatch* (November 27, 1991). We are not playing for a Nobel Prize winner. Other values have to be considered.... Win at all costs is not the nature of this university." A few days later (December 1) he would tell *Dispatch* Sports Editor George Strode, "*The New York Times, Los Angeles Times* and *Sports Illustrated* . . . are not running [stories] which say . . . Ohio State . . . is masquerading as a university.... Once and for all, Ohio State had to shed its image as a football school and has to assume what it is—a great university. And, by God," he had emphasized, "that's what's going to happen!"

Whether or not the university truly was "great" was a subjective judgment yet to be benchmarked against other leading universities. But, clearly, Ohio State was the major teaching and research institution in Ohio—perhaps the most comprehensive university in the country—and the undeclared academic flagship of the state system. Much of the Ohio public, however, and many of the state's opinion leaders continued to define the university by its football program. Gee's most enduring legacy as a Buckeye might well be that over his seven and a half years as president he would change that.

As a speaker or in private meetings, he would remind people that powerful academic institutions and powerful athletic institutions were more than compatible; they could be symbiotic. He would use Stanford (perennial winner of the Sears Cup for the best overall intercollegiate program), Duke (perennial men's basketball power), or, yes, Michigan, as examples. And he might explain—or wait for the question—that Ohio State would receive $350 million more per year for its academic programs if funded at Michigan's level of tuition and state support.

Would Ohioans stand for such a disparity, he would ask, between Michigan and Ohio State in football facilities or football grants-in-aid?

Meanwhile, behind the scenes, as he would do to recruit the best high school talents and scholars to Ohio State, he would also recruit athletes, male and female, for any coach who asked. He would amaze students and families when a call from his car phone would announce, "This is Gordon Gee, president of The Ohio State University, and I just wanted to tell you how much we would like" you, your son, your daughter, etc. "to come to our school."

It was far from serendipitous that at both Colorado and West Virginia, when Gee was president, the football teams had played for the national championship. He had helped recruit many of their star athletes. It would not be serendipitous that through the 1995 and 1996 football seasons, Ohio State would go 22-3, and the year following his departure would be 11-1 and ranked second in the polls again.

"What I liked and admired most about him," Cooper would recall later, "is that he worked as hard as I did to try to make us successful. He helped us do anything we asked. He'd call the recruits back and he would come over and talk to them at the ballgames. I never saw anyone with more energy or more enthusiasm to help a coach be successful than Dr. Gee."

Football, in particular, and winning athletic teams in general, were vehicles for showcasing academics for Gordon Gee. "A great university is not built on the record of a winning team," he would write in a letter to his colleagues (*onCampus*, December 5, 1991), "but a winning team can be built on the reputation of a great university." On the other hand, he knew that the egg often became the chicken. A "great" university—or at least the legislation that helped fund one, and the capital campaign support that would be "the margin of excellence"—could indeed be encouraged by victorious teams in high-profile sports.

In inviting lobbyists and legislators, publishers and editors, corporate presidents and entrepreneurial whiz kids to sit at pregame brunches with him, his trustees, and his vice presidents, Gee was only following tradition. But by turning the brunches into academic showcases, he would create an entertaining classroom before each game. Here, he would teach the opinion leaders of Ohio about the academic strengths of their university and deliver the message of a higher objective that, with their help, would be reached.

As his administration would strengthen departments through budget reallocations and what became known as "selective excellence" programs, he would spotlight those departments. Even as the university's state general fund budget was being bled by budget cuts in the early 1990s, funds were being reallocated for new academic scholarships—until the number of National Merit and National Achievement Scholar finalists in a single class was topping 100. At each pregame brunch—as he also would at alumni club visits and fundraising dinners—he would ask such students to appear in the program and have them talk about their experiences at Ohio State and why they chose to study there.

## Chapter 18

"There is no free lunch," he would tell his handpicked pregame audiences. And, while there wasn't, who could resent the message? The 150–200 people in the "room"—be it the Wexner Center "black box" theatre, the second floor of Bricker Hall, the patio of Honors House, or one of many other sites—would have been selected through a system Gee had put in place in the University Communications Office.

Whereas, in the Jennings administration, there had been no public relations unit specific to the presidential agenda, staff now were assigned to build and maintain presidential invitation lists, develop a presidential direct mail program, create a presidential annual report, organize press coverage of presidential priorities, and schedule presidential meetings with individual media. Another unit, Special Events, headed by Carol Ries, was responsible for the brunches and events at the president's home, as well as running Ohio State's four commencements a year. A third, with Barbie Tootle in charge, did his hour-to-hour, day-to-day briefings, and wrote his speeches.

Together on home game Saturdays, these staff would create the "no free lunch" where the food was exquisite, the entertainment—often the cheerleaders (national champions in 1993) and marching band—grand, and the master of ceremonies—"The Geeper" himself—always instructive, always hilarious, and often inspirational. Gee would give an always academically directed but joke-filled talk; Geiger would explain what to expect from the day's opponent and lead the cheers. Yes, as a guest of the president, you might expect a fund-raising call or a visit on a legislative matter—and you might even look forward to it.

Ben Marrison, who later would become editor of the *Columbus Dispatch*, would follow Gee for a full game day for the *Cleveland Plain Dealer* (December 22, 1996). On this particular Saturday, Gee would host his brunch in the new Galbreath veterinary medicine building—appearing "from around a corner riding a horse named Brandy." Later, en route to Ohio Stadium, he would make "a beeline for some Buckeyes fans having a tailgate party . . . instantly recognizable and accessible . . . weaving and waving . . . through the scarlet and gray clad crowd."

During the first half, he would work "the [two-level VIP] box, greeting everyone he encountered by name from memory." And at halftime, he would visit media at the press levels and give interviews.

In the second half, he would make his way down to the field, visit the band, and talk to students. After the game, he would visit the coach and players, then,

## ATHLETICS AS PRESSURE COOKER

"after a few words to potential football recruits," head for postgame events or alumni reunions.

About his brunches and life in the president's box, he would explain to Marrison that to "sit with me . . . they have to listen to me talk about academics. And you know what? It works. I can't get 96,000 people to come to a chemistry lecture. But if I can get them here, I can talk to them about the wonderful things we're doing all over this university."

Of course, Gee could not squeeze 96,000 people into his box. But he could and did talk about those "wonderful things" to many more than that. He did so in an interview on the eighty-station Ohio State Radio Network each halftime, with a president's page in each printed program, and by narrating radio and television public service announcements that ran on game days.

Through Steve Snapp, the university's nationally, respected sports information director, the way would be cleared game upon game for Gee to be interviewed on the field or in the booth before millions of viewers. After Gee had been gone three years, left Brown, and become Chancellor of Vanderbilt University, ABC's Brent Mussberger would mention those visits fondly when calling an Ohio State victory over Penn State; and suggest that, with Gee at the top, Vandy would soon be a football power.

Once every year or two, Gee's office would retain an independent polling firm to assess what Ohioans thought about Ohio State. One of the questions asked was to describe in one word or phrase what *first* came to mind ("top of mind" awareness) "when I say Ohio State." While the fact that Ohio State is very large consistently came to mind first in about one of three answers, as late as 1993 so did things "athletic" (31 percent). By 1996—comments "athletic" had dropped significantly (to only 5 percent), and positive statements about academics had more than tripled (from 12 percent) to 38 percent. There was no question that the academic message was getting across.

Meanwhile, *U.S. News and World Report* had begun to rank colleges and universities academically, and in divisions not unlike the football polls. As a "National University"—somewhat comparable to Division 1—in the company of Harvard, Yale, Princeton, Michigan, Berkeley, UCLA, and Virginia—Ohio State was nowhere to be seen in or near the Top 10, or even in the first quartile. Although its criteria for judgment might be challenged, by this time *U.S. News* was making news with this annual survey, and parents of high school juniors and seniors, in particular, were paying attention. Savvy presidents and boards across the country would use this poll as leverage to increase support for their institutions' academic programs. Probably none were savvier than the leaders of Ohio State.

CHAPTER 18

## *Legacies*

All university presidents inherit athletic as well as academic legacies. Three of Gee's were Title IX and two coaches, John Cooper and Randy Ayers. In 1972, Title IX of the Education Amendments Act declared that no person could be excluded because of gender from participation in any athletic or academic program in an institution receiving federal financial assistance. In 1986, the Arizona State Sun Devils beat Michigan in the Rose Bowl, and Ohio State hired its coach, John Cooper. In 1989, Gary Williams left Ohio State to coach the basketball team of his alma mater, the University of Maryland, and Ohio State promoted his assistant, Randy Ayers, to head coach.

Andy Geiger, the man Maryland had hired as Williams's AD, would be lured by Gee to Ohio State in 1994. Here, among his many successes, he would add a number of new women's intercollegiate sports while other universities were fulfilling Title IX by dropping men's teams. As his first decision, Geiger would promote the legendary Archie Griffin to associate athletic director in charge of half the intercollegiate programs, including football.

Geiger would end the sexism that had divided athletic departments into men's and women's units by appointing Miechelle Willis of Temple University as his other associate AD, putting her in charge of the other half of the program, including men's basketball.

A high school senior named Jim Jackson standing at the back of Ayers's 1989 news conference would become the centerpiece of a men's basketball team that would rekindle memories of John Havlicek, Larry Siegfried, and Jerry Lucas. And that December, the football team would play its first postseason game in three years, but would lose to Auburn in the Hall of Fame Bowl.

A month later, while Gordon Gee, the president of The University of Colorado, first was being screened as a candidate for the presidency of Ohio State, Pennsylvania State University would be admitted to the Big Ten. In May 1990, prep star Robert Smith, planning to be a doctor, would choose to play at Ohio State. And in August, while the Gees were planning their move to Columbus, Anne Hayes would turn more than forty years of her husband Woody's memorabilia over to Ed Jennings just before he would turn his office over to Gordon Gee.

By October 1990, while the Gees were just settling into their home in Bexley, Cooper literally and figuratively was already in the eye of the storm. He sensibly had agreed to end a game with minutes still on the clock when a wild thunderstorm began to shoot lightning toward the metal press box and the iron superstructure of Ohio Stadium. But he had been criticized for it. Ohio

## ATHLETICS AS PRESSURE COOKER

State was losing 35–26 to Southern California, with Gee and his guests watching the bolts move closer in from the west, and members of his staff trying to call down to the bench to stop the game. The word, however, never made it to the playing field and Coach Cooper was forced to make a decision that never should have been his.

The following weekend Ohio State lost to Illinois and, as the *St. Louis Post* observed, this time "Cooper was trashed for not objecting strenuously enough when the officials allowed Quinton Parker of the Illini to run 45 yards with an illegal lateral." The Buckeyes were now 2-2 and Gordon Gee already was being urged to fire the coach. Two weeks later Cooper was in surgery for a ruptured disc but gaining little sympathy after a tie with Indiana.

At the football banquet that followed the regular season, Gee gave the assemblage a huge dose of his humor and a good look at his values. At his first game, a win over Texas Tech, he said he "had goose bumps as big as Buckeyes." And he had. From the absolute top of the stadium, he and Elizabeth had marveled at the spectacle. He had been given the game ball—his "eighth day on the job. The football faithful maintain that on the eighth day, God created football—and in the case of my tenure as president, that is correct." After the tie with Indiana, he said he had been asked about the Buckeyes' execution and had said he "was in favor of it." He had run out on the field after the win over Iowa, which had been Cooper's 100th coaching victory, and had "found I was congratulating a lot of belt buckles." Then he became serious.

On the 16–13 loss to Michigan, he spoke to and about the players. "If you did not seek to be excellent in all that you do, if you did not strive for the best against any adversary, if you did not reach for the top—you would not be Buckeyes." They had played "in the finest tradition of Ohio State athletics. These men wanted to win for us," he addressed to the audience, "and we wanted to win for them." Reflecting upon "three-a-day drills in August heat, 40 hours or more a week in meetings, practices, the training room and travel," he said, "Whoever called a football scholarship a 'free ride' is nuts."

Then he quoted Emerson. "What lies behind us and what lies before us are small matters compared to what lies within us." He thanked the families "for sharing these remarkable young men with us" and told the players "I look forward to presenting each man with his diploma—the true reward for a job well done." A few minutes later, he would award the Iowa game ball to Cooper for that 100th victory. He was "delighted," he said, "with what he stands for and the direction he is taking this football program." While the team would lose a few weeks later in the Liberty Bowl, anyone at the banquet would know that the president of Ohio State would continue to support his coach.

CHAPTER 18

The next August, after running for 1126 yards and breaking Archie Griffin's freshman running record in 1990, Robert Smith would accuse offensive coach Eliot Uzelak of putting practice before studying for summer school, would quit the team, and place The Ohio State University value system once more in the national spotlight.

Coach Cooper would acknowledge for this book that "never have I encouraged a young man not to put his academic responsibilities first. All Robert would have had to do was walk in [to Cooper's office] and say, 'Coach, I have a problem.'" But Smith hadn't, and neither had Uzelak. And it was the university that now had the problem.

Smith would return to the team a year later, welcomed back by both Cooper and Gee and ready to meet with Uzelak where "everything," Cooper would say later, "had been worked out." But Uzelak would pull out a tape recorder, Smith would bolt again, and Cooper would "make the decision to fire Eliot because I wanted Robert Smith back." Smith would come back, have a banner 1992 season and leave for the National Football League with two years of eligibility remaining, where he would become the finest running back in the history of the Minnesota Vikings and continue to work on his Ohio State degree.

## The Ayers Years

In January 1991, while Ohio State faculty, staff, and student military reservists were being called up for the Gulf War—and state budget cuts had forced Ohio State to freeze all but "essential" hiring—such as nurses—one of the few morale boosters on campus was Randy Ayers's men's basketball team. Led by Jim Jackson, it would tie for the Big Ten title and go all the way to the "Sweet 16" of the NCAA tournament before losing to St. John's. (The year before, it had been beaten in the first round, but by the eventual champion University of Nevada at Las Vegas.) The U.S. Basketball Writers Association would name Ayers Coach of the Year, as would the Associated Press and the Atlanta Tip-off Club.

In his two years as head coach, Ayers had won thirty-two games and lost sixteen and, with Jackson back for his junior year, could expect another exceptional season. Ayers had come to Ohio State from the U.S. Military Academy, where he had been in charge of recruiting. He had done the same thing for Gary Williams at Ohio State and done it well. Jackson would write later in an Ohio State press guide that Ayers was "the reason I chose Ohio State." As a player, Ayers had been Ohio Player of the Year in high school and team captain, was twice on the Midwest Athletic Conference first team at Miami University, and had been drafted but cut by the NBA's Chicago Bulls.

As a coach and mentor, to quote Chris Jent from the same press guide, he "was special." Ayers's team, Jent said, "was like an extension of my family."

Ayers was handsome, tall, a family man with two young boys. He had a master's degree, and his wife Carol was on the faculty of Columbus School for Girls. Ayers appeared to have "the world on a string." It would be on that string for only another year. On March 27, 1992, Ayers's team would upset North Carolina in the third round of the NCAA tournament and advance to the quarterfinals to play against Michigan, which it had beaten twice already. While the Wolverines would win in overtime, the Buckeyes would return to campus as feted heroes, and St. John Arena would be opened for an impromptu lovefest.

At the end of the 1991–1992 season, anyone who would have suggested that Gordon Gee would someday have to fire—or bless the firing—of Randy Ayers would have been thought insane. As the *Dispatch* editorialized (April 2, 1992) following the NCAA loss to Michigan: "Losers? Not this bunch. Every one of them is a winner... what you see on the court is just part of the picture. They have proved in game after game, on and off the court as well, that athletic excellence and aggressive play are fully compatible with sportsmanship and mature social conduct... one does not have to look far to see programs rated by scandal, corrupted by deliberate, underhanded violations of NCAA rules. Wouldn't it be great if every sports program... in this land would try to measure up to the standard set by Ayers....?"

"Up, up and up," the editorial concluded, speaking of the past three years, but suggesting the future.

Midway through the season, Ayers already had received an extension on his contract, which would go through the 1998–1999 season. "I'm not only very happy with it, but I'm glad for the vote of confidence from President Gee and Jim Jones," he would say about the new contract (*Dispatch*, December 16, 1992). In addition to increasing his salary to $110,000, the university had added financial incentives for winning NCAA tournament games and left him free to keep all income from shoe contracts, basketball camps, his radio and television shows, and any other endorsements.

There was also a mutual buyout clause, which no one then would have thought the university would have to exercise. No one except, perhaps, AD Jones, who had already spent nine years at Ohio State when Fred Taylor—once the most successful coach in college basketball—was released in 1976. At the height of Ayers's popularity and the nadir of Cooper's, Jones had told a fellow

## Chapter 18

administrator that, in coaching at this level, if you waited long enough, the bubble always burst.

In fact, after that NCAA loss to Michigan, Ayers's program would suffer a long downslide over five years, and, on March 10, 1997, Ayers would be released. So would women's basketball coach Nancy Darsch on the same day. She had started her Ohio State coaching career with successes similar to Ayers's. She had taken the Ohio State women to seven NCAA tournaments, but only one in the last seven seasons. In 1993, after reaching the NCAA championship game with All-American Katie Smith, she had pioneered salary equity for Ohio State women's coaches, asking for and receiving bonuses for herself and her assistants equivalent to those of Ayers and his staff. The next three years, however, had been less than successful, and the state's best high school players more often than not were selecting other schools.

Andy Geiger, now athletic director, had established goals for the 1996–1997 year with both coaches. That they would finish in the upper half of the Big Ten was one of them; neither had. Darsch would leave with a year left on her contract and an agreed-upon buyout that included forfeited radio and television income. And she would be hired within two weeks to coach the New York Liberty of the brand new Women's National Basketball Association, which played in Madison Square Garden. While Ayers's teams had suffered back-to-back 10-17 seasons, he also had concurred that Geiger's Big Ten expectations were reasonable. But the losing records had been only an effect. Where Ayers's ability to bring that "family" feeling to his first teams worked with his own recruits, his supportive coaching style apparently had begun to backfire as early as 1993.

First, in May 1993, prize recruit Damon Flint was declared ineligible to play at Ohio State by the NCAA. He would play instead for the University of Cincinnati. The investigation into the accusation that Flint had been recruited illegally would take eighteen months and result in the team's probation and sanctions on former assistant Paul Brazeau, who had already left to coach the University of Hartford. It would also broaden to include sanctions against the men's and women's track teams and severely criticize the Athletic Department administration for its lack of oversight.

Suddenly, the coach praised by columnist William Rhoden in the January 21, 1991, *New York Times* for attracting "quality players with outstanding attitudes" appeared to have a team with more attitude than quality. In the summer of 1993, the purchase of expensive sport utility vehicles by sophomores Greg Simpson and Charles "Killer" Macon and attempted purchases by two other players had created, as the *Plain Dealer* wrote later (December 25, 1993), "a finger-pointing frenzy." Simpson, who had been Ohio's high school "Mr. Basketball," and Macon, who had been "Mr. Basketball" in Indiana, had been projected as stars of the future in a 1992 recruiting class one analyst rated third in the nation.

Instead, following off-the-court scrapes well covered by the press, they would both be dismissed for "disciplinary reasons" after one year. Simpson would transfer to West Virginia University, declare himself eligible for the NBA draft as a junior, and not make it. Macon would play at Central Michigan University. Classmate Gerald Eaker, the first teammate to be dismissed, would transfer to Kansas State and set a single season rebounding record. Nate Wilburn, unhappy with what was happening to his team, would move on to South Carolina and help win a Southeastern Conference championship.

Finally, Derek Anderson, the finest player since Jackson and "Most Valuable Player" in the 1993 U.S. Olympic Festival, would transfer to the University of Kentucky. There he would key a national championship in 1996 and be drafted in the NBA's first round. When Anderson asked for his release as a Buckeye, Bruce Hooley of the *Plain Dealer* (August 20, 1994) wrote that he had "tossed a bouquet [to Ayers] and another shovel of dirt on the grave of Ohio State's basketball program."

Of his reasons for leaving, Anderson had simply said he had to do it. And the public generally understood. Of his coach, Anderson said, "He's the best person I've ever been around, besides my father." And the public largely agreed. But clearly, Ayers's assistant coaches had recruited some ballplayers in the most recent class who, unlike their predecessors in the Jackson era, needed a disciplinarian. If it were not already too late, forty-eight-year-old Ken Turner, who Ayers had hired from Kansas State University, was to be the man to provide the discipline. But in September, the cruelest blow of all would strike. Turner would suffer a fatal heart attack while jogging in his neighborhood, to be survived by his wife and two children.

Randy Ayers would survive another three years, more because of the respect he had earned from his colleagues and his fans than his record. He had already allowed his recruiting coach, Mark Anderson, to resign in 1994 and in January 1995 let Dave Cecutti go. Cecutti had helped him win the two Big Ten championships in 1991 and 1992. The following year, the potential for a decent team was gutted again when two more players, Jami Bosley and Scott Gradney, were dismissed for "disciplinary reasons" and hemophilia finished the career of freshman center Mark Howard.

When finally released by Geiger, Ayers handled the news with his typical class. He had had a closed-door meeting at noon informing his three relatively new assistant coaches, Jene Davis, former Ohio State forward Jerry Francis,

## Chapter 18

and Randy Roth. That morning he had talked to his wife and that evening he would talk to his two young sons. In a statement released to the press, he had written, "[M]y family and I had been very fortunate for the opportunity to be part of The Ohio State University family, and we wish the University nothing but the best."

Interviewed that day by Mike Sullivan of the *Dispatch*, basketball secretary Debbie Cachio said of Ayers, "He's a good guy, a good person who cares about his players. He's always put them ahead of everything," and Geiger would be quoted as "hoping, very much, that it wouldn't come to this." Of the dual firing of Ayers and Nancy Darsch, Geiger had said the day before, "I just didn't see us getting to where we want to be without making this change."

Years later, when asked to reflect specifically on the release of Coach Ayers, Geiger said, "He knew some of . . . [his players] came from hard places, and was convinced he could change their behavior . . . that education was what this was about." But in the process, Ayers had not proved enough of a disciplinarian to "keep them from acting out" and "had failed to stop the bleeding."

The decision to let Ayers go had been made by Geiger, Gee, and Vice President for Student Affairs David Williams, to whom Geiger reported. "There was a sadness about it among all of us," Geiger recalled for this book, and "a fondness and feeling for Randy that persists to this day. . . . He's a good coach . . . but he lost control here and he couldn't get it back."

On April 3, 1997, Jim O'Brien of Boston College would be announced by Geiger as the new men's basketball coach. A day later, Beth Burns of San Diego State—an Ohio Wesleyan alumna who still "had a cassette tape with 'Hang On Sloopy' on it" (*Dispatch*, April 4), would be introduced as the women's coach. Both had interviewed with Gee and had received his strong support.

Meanwhile, after a review by State Auditor Jim Petro, the university was allowed to grant Ayers and Darsch the buyouts Gee, Williams, and Geiger felt the two departing coaches had earned. Their lost compensation, Ohio State's chief legal counsel, Virginia "Ginny" Trethewey, explained, was not just in salaries. The university only recently had stopped individual coaches from negotiating their own supplemental contracts—including shoe, media, and clinics—and those arrangements, too, should be honored.

"Honorable" might well be the appropriate adjective to define this period in Ohio State sports. It would end on June 11, 1997, with a new beginning for Coach Ayers when Larry Brown of the NBA's Philadelphia 76ers would hire him as strength coach. Ayers and Brown had been introduced by a mutual friend, a basketball broadcaster and analyst who had followed Ayers's coaching career from the beginning. The prior December, Clark Kellogg, who had left Ohio State for the NBA in 1982 without finishing his degree, had been handed his diploma in marketing by another man with whom he had become friends, E. Gordon Gee. Appropriately enough, the commencement ceremony had taken place in St. John Arena.

# 19

## *More Gee and the Governor*

> Gordon's downtown lobbying on behalf of the governor's tax increases and he runs into the governor, who thanks Gordon, saying, "I really appreciate what you're doing." Then there's this instant transformation and he says, "Although I still believe there's fat out there and you could probably handle more cuts." There was really something visceral about what the governor perceived to be the elitism of the universities.
>
> —HERB ASHER, Ohio State political scientist
> and lobbyist, reflecting upon the past

Common Cause Ohio, of all people, was questioning President Gee's ethics (*Lantern*, November 16, 1994). Using university funds, a letter to all students, parents, faculty, and staff had explained the "distortion" of Issue 4 that had most Ohioans believing the recently enacted tax on soda pop presaged taxes on "food" at the supermarket. This was not the first time an Ohio State president had chosen to use the mail to fight a tax repeal that would hurt higher education. Eleven Novembers earlier, Ed Jennings had led a successful statewide campaign that blocked one of monumental proportions.

In this case, the soda pop people were behind the campaign to repeal their part of the tax package enacted in December 1992, the one that had saved higher education from even deeper cuts. They were pouring $7.2 million into advertising to pass Issue 4. Over ten years, the state would lose at least $650 million if it passed, and Gee believed a relatively few dollars spent to explain the truth was a wise use of university resources. Damn the critics who believed public institutions had no right to spend in their own behalf. He would not, of course, use state money.

"Vote as your conscience dictates. But know that voting 'NO' . . . is voting 'yes' . . . for the future of Ohio and for The Ohio State University," the president's letter ended. He also had distributed an opinion piece to Ohio newspapers. And he had stood side by side with the governor at a press conference in which Voinovich called the repeal move a scam and the "great bamboozle of 1994."

"Bamboozle" or not, the state suddenly had a surplus of $500 million and the Issue 4 people made sure Ohioans knew it. Gee's decision to argue the Ohio State case through the mail was supported by the trustees, with chair Jack Kessler telling the *Lantern* Gee had "exercised excellent judgment." Issue 4 did win handily, but Gee and the governor had forged another link.

## *Term Limits*

Two years before, Gee had offered his time and advocacy to the leaders of the Ohio House and Senate. While Ohio's governor had been limited to two consecutive four-year terms since 1954, it was another thirty-eight years before similar constraints caught up to other elected state officials. Term limits were placed on the ballot in Ohio in November 1992.

Believing that wisdom came with a long learning curve, and having worked so well with the incumbents, Gee was dead set against term limits. Knowing the legislators would be hard pressed to defend themselves, he and Asher met with both Speaker Riffe and Senate President Aronoff to offer the president's personal support. He would, Gee said, take a leave from his presidency to argue the value of incumbency. It was that important to him and Ohio State. But not, it was agreed, a very good idea.

Though the majority of Ohio newspapers were against term limits, as was the Council of Churches, the League of Women Voters, and organized labor, limiting the rascals' time in office won the day. Gordon Gee still would be able to work primarily with the legislators he knew. But after December 31, 2000, in Columbus, Ohio's elected officials would be operating under eight-term term limits.

Though his advocacy was limited to airing his opinion when asked, Gee's demonstrated support of the incumbents could not have hurt their decision to develop and pass that $195 million per year tax package two months later, the

# Chapter 19

one the *Dispatch* noted had passed "with surprising ease," the one that would be drained of $65 million in soda pop money two years later.

## Bowled Over

State Representative Greg DiDonato of New Philadelphia sent out a press release saying he was "outraged." The *Cambridge Daily Jeffersonian* had run a story (February 19, 1993) that State Representative Tom Johnson of New Concord and some of his fellow legislators had gone to the Florida Citrus Bowl on Ohio State's tab and had even been allowed to bring a friend, at a total cost of nearly $13,000 for the entire legislative group.

DiDonato said he expected a "full explanation" from President Gee and that if the university "has the money to send legislators to football games, then they have pork they can cut." A few days later, Deborah Winston of the *Plain Dealer*, which had broken the original story, asked whether such trips were not a "transparent way for Ohio State to charm the votes off the legislators who control the budget?"

"It's a good chance to make your case to a captive audience," John Hilbert, president of the undergraduate student government and a member of the Ohio State traveling party, had told the *Dispatch* the same day, and the *Plain Dealer* had pointed out the day before that Ohio law allowed officials to accept "expenses 'in connection with conferences, seminars and similar events' if provision of the benefits is not an attempt to improperly influence the official."

What was proper or improper influence? In Gee's answer to DiDonato, he pointed out that the university had been doing this for twenty years and that "our friends, alumni, and supporters welcome the opportunity to meet and share ideas with elected leaders."

While the legislators did participate in university and alumni events at each game, the legislative-related event Gee most looked forward to was their annual breakfast discussion, where the doors were closed in the president's suite, the Ohio State trustees and often the regents were represented, and a candid conversation with the leaders of both political parties took place. This year, the guests had been Senate President Stan Aronoff; Senate Minority Leader Bob Boggs; newly appointed House Minority Leader Jo Ann Davidson; House Education Committee Chair Dan Troy and its Finance Chair Gene Watts; Senate Leader Neal Zimmers; House Whip Johnson; and State Representative Mike Stinziano from the university area. Four were Democrats; four were Republicans.

Dismiss the fact that the trips were paid for from bowl revenue, not state money, or that the Ohio Ethics Commission ruled that legislators did nothing wrong in attending as the university's guests. The publicity was enough of a smear to stop the practice. From then on, all legislators would be invited, but to pay their own way.

Ironically, the one politician specifically invited to all bowl games by Big Ten regulations, whose guest also specifically would be paid for by the Big Ten, was the state's governor. George Voinovich was asked each year he was in office but always found he had better things to do than spend New Year's Day away from home.

## *Ethics and Expenditures*

A year later, expedited in part by the bowl brouhaha, the 1994 Ohio General Assembly cracked down on gifts to state public officials. Under the old law, they had to report the source of their gifts only if the gifts exceeded $500. Under House Bill 492, all gifts valued over $75 were banned, and any gift of $25 or more had to be reported. Under the old law, elected officials could accept honoraria. Under the new one, they couldn't. Under the old law, lobbyists and their employers reported three times a year, listing legislators on whom they had spent more than $150. Under the new law, the ceiling for meals and drinks for any one elected official was $75 a year collectively from any one institution, and reports were required from each lobbyist, each institution, and each public official.

In a note to them, Herb Asher urged chairs, deans, directors, and vice presidents to report all expenditures to his office, but "not to let this law make you shy away from associations and communications with public officials." Whether or not it did, waiters and waitresses downtown were being told much more often to "split the check."

## 20

## *The Great Communicator*

> Gordon Gee brought the university enthusiasm. He brought the university to life. A personality. That is what I think the most when I think of him. And he had a sense of where he was going.
>
> —DAVID MILENTHAL, Advertising
> and Marketing Executive

Few people who knew Gee would disagree with this assessment by Dave Milenthal, whose Columbus-based agency, then simply named H.M.S., grew significantly on the strength of Milenthal's marketing skills and advertising creativity. Milenthal knew that virtually every communications vehicle Gee or his staff could think of was used and crafted with purpose, that Gee knew "where he was going" with the university.

From Colorado, Gee had brought a system to build a personal invitation and mailing list, which over time grew to more than 2,000 opinion leaders with whom he communicated regularly. He wanted them, he said, to "feel they had a direct link of communication from me."

Similarly, as he wanted to communicate the good things about Ohio State to the small towns as well as the large cities in Ohio, a newspaper column series was created just for the state's smaller dailies. Some ran them all. Some ran a few, on subjects diversified as the university and often derived from Gee's own experiences. Between February 1992 and November 1997, sixty-three "Statewides" ran, the last one titled "Goodbye Columbus."

On campus, believing openness to be the best policy with student journalists, he would meet with the full staff of *The Lantern* each quarter, in its newsroom, open to all questions. The meetings were instituted by him, not the paper. He was open to student journalists' interviews as well, whenever they called.

He set up public affairs advisory committees in Chicago, New York, Washington, Atlanta, Cincinnati, and Cleveland, consisting of alumni old and young who populated the advertising and public relations agencies and media in their respective cities. PR executive Bob Dilenschneider helped him extend his national media contacts in New York. Erin Moriarty of *48 Hours* became a fixture as emcee at the biggest fund-raising events and narrated the law school's campaign video.

When a national or international figure was on campus, his communications office made sure he or she was captured on videotape saying something positive about the university for possible later use in television public service announcements or promotional videos. The idea was Gee's.

A group of Washington-based Ohio bureau writers, led by Jack Torry of the *Blade*, Tom Diemer of the *Plain Dealer*, Bill Hershey of the *Beacon Journal*, and George Embrey of the *Dispatch* were happy to solicit column ideas when he visited. In Chicago, Jim Oates, president of Leo Burnett Advertising, donated huge sums of agency time to projects for the university and the Big Ten. In Cleveland, an on-air interview with former newsman and WJW-TV President and General Manager Virgil Dominic could always be expected.

In 1996, he field-tested his own television show on WOSU-TV, moderating topical panel discussions by distinguished faculty. *An Ohio State of Mind* died, however, after two shows when his stretched budget could not support it and the station could not absorb it. Two years earlier, he had been offered an hour-long talk show of his own by WBNS-AM, but could not commit to an inflexible schedule. But he was on Fred Anderle's WOSU-AM call-in religiously, pretaped game-by-game radio shows with Skip Mosic for the WBNS statewide radio network, and was interviewed live on television many times each basketball and football season.

## *Memos from the President*

"I am led to believe that WOSU is no longer broadcasting graduation on the radio. Am I right? And if so, why not? And what about the television coverage? Please inform me." *It was fixed, fast.*

"As I have indicated to you, we need to think about our holiday greeting

## Chapter 20

Keith Jackson interviews Gee live at a nationally televised football game, 1992.

cards and what we want to do. I want to have something clever and inexpensive." *He got what he wanted.*

"As I have been attending the basketball games, I have been struck by the fact we are not using our halftimes appropriately." *Academic messages became part of television halftimes.*

"I happened to be watching the Indiana-Minnesota basketball game. Indiana had a special [academic] report that went on for five minutes. How can we do that? How do they do that?" *Indiana's president's office preempted half the network time arranged for athletic departments by the Big Ten. Soon Ohio State did the same thing.*

## *Gee the Speaker*

In 1994, as a national leader in the field of reputation management, Bill Patterson was deep into the business of speech and media training. Once an on-air news director notorious for his hard-edged approach, he now taught speech delivery and interview control to executives he once might have victimized. Since he already knew Gee as an exciting, professional speaker equally adept at controlling an interview, he was surprised to receive a call asking about his availability as a speech coach.

When he arrived at Gee's office, Patterson first asked Gee why he wanted such training when he already received standing ovations just about everywhere he spoke. "I can always improve," Gee answered. "I want to be the best communicator I can be." So they went to work.

A few weeks later Patterson was back, this time to advise Gee on delivery, inflection, hand movement, and facial gestures for a public service announcement for nationally televised football broadcasts. What he found in the two sessions was "not work, but a trip inside his personality and the discovery of his needs and desires to be a great communicator. I learned as much about advanced speaking skills as he did."

What he also learned, as did all those who risked it, was that this was one leader eager for criticism he could learn by. In 2000, now president of Reputation Management, his own firm, Patterson still ranked Gee "at the top of my list of communicators I have known, heard, or trained in the past 25 years."

## *Effective Communications*

> I want to have the most effective internal communications strategy in higher education. If we can start from the assumption that if we [I] can communicate my [our] values and expectations internally, that will be the platform for our external strategy. This belief in effective communications must drive our planning.
>
> —Gordon Gee

This memo was not addressed to a colleague at Ohio State. It was sent in late 1997 to the vice president of public relations at Brown, advising her of his planning procedure: Important decisions always included a discussion of the message to be given and the media to use.

# Chapter 20

At the core of his decision-making philosophy was his skill in generating and then processing information—by asking questions, being visible, meeting with students, meeting with faculty, writing suggestions and thank-you notes by the hundreds, and applying a level of personal energy that left some people gasping for air. For Gordon Gee, there was no such thing as information overload and no such thing as decision by indecision. Particularly in Bill Shkurti, his Finance vice president, he had a tremendously clear thinking, decisive, and articulate counselor who was nearly as good with the media as he was. In political scientist Asher, the official "presidential counselor," he had not only an expert in political media and polling, but a man who knew, or knew who knew, virtually everyone even vaguely informed in the State House. Many aides, as well as some legislators, had been Asher's students.

Gee moved his communications director into Bricker Hall, the administration building, and made him a so-called direct report, with staff added to support the president's communications agenda. While he met with all his direct reports frequently, by organizing a second-level advisory group called the President's Council, Gee made sure he also met frequently with the line of authority immediately below each vice president.

In July 1991, as keynote speaker at the National Assembly of the Council for Advancement and Support of Education (CASE), he told the assembled public relations, development, and alumni professionals, "If you do not have access to your president . . . formal and informal . . . you have a problem." He left to a standing ovation and an audience clamoring for more. Many did have a problem and went home wishing they could work for Gordon Gee.

At the core of his media strategy was a personality that thrived in the limelight and a public who enjoyed watching and listening to him. If you were in the media and wanted an interview and he knew you, the president would talk to you. If he didn't know you, he wanted to. If there was a radio or television show to be on and it could fit his schedule, he would do it. And if it didn't, he still wanted to. His credo in working with the press, he said at CASE, was "you cannot hide. Neither can your president. The truth may not set you free, but it is always better than the alternative."

While he also acknowledged "there are times you wish you could put a bag over your president's head," he had an incredible ability to turn his own gaffes into laugh lines for the next occasion. "My advice? Lighten up! Enjoy your work and your opportunities. While ours is serious work, do not take it all too seriously. Be able to laugh about yourself."

## *Lightening Up*

Clearly, he was a nontraditional university president. Even his blood type was nontraditional, explained by the Red Cross as having "a more detailed characteristic" than any of the regular letter types, and represented in only .2 percent of the donor population.

Occasionally what the president thought was fun, others didn't. When a complaint did come, it usually was when he was lightly chafing someone's sacred cow. "Some people," he would say, "have no sense of humor." He was sorry, he wrote one letter writer, that he offended her with his "Top 10 Ways Ohio State Is Different from Notre Dame." He had shared the list, he explained, with Father Malloy, president of Notre Dame, and Regis Philbin, television celebrity and Notre Dame alumnus. Both, he explained, "had enjoyed it in the humorous spirit in which it was intended. Be assured I would never ridicule someone's faith with any malicious intent. Indeed, that would certainly violate my own moral standards."

The president figuratively had brought down the house of invitees to his pregame brunch, held in a huge tent rigged on the east bank of the Olentangy, with Father Malloy and Philbin attending. The five reasons that may have offended the writer most were: "Our university seal does not include Touchdown Jesus. . . . Our idea of a religious icon is Woody Hayes. . . . God is on their side; the odds are on ours. . . . They think a 10-yard penalty is nothing compared to eternal damnation. . . . They have the luck of the Irish, but we have Eddie George [who would win the Heisman trophy]."

From Colorado, if not from childhood, Gee had brought with him to Columbus a self-deprecating style of humor that allowed for a balance of shots across someone's or some other institution's bow.

At his first event in Columbus in 1990, hosted by his friend Peter Coors, he had joked that Nebraska fans were still upset at him for explaining how their team members knew the "N" on their helmets stood for "Nowledge." "Nevertheless, when the game was over," he added with mock naivete, "they waved at me." There was a studied pause. "But not with all their fingers." This was a line, staff soon learned, he would use again.

And he knew how disappointed Columbus must be because he was not the archetypal university president—tall, dark, and handsome. "Every time I look in the mirror, I'm disappointed, too." Again, there was a studied pause. "And so is my wife."

Soon after announcing his plans to remarry, he opened an address to the University Wives Club by telling them about his detailed preparation for every

# Chapter 20

speech. "So, when I found out I was coming to the University Wives Club, I thought I'd better get one."

At the sponsors' luncheon for the 1996 Sugar Bowl, he read his "Top 10 Little Known Facts about the University of Tennessee," which began with, "They give a Slim Jim with every application," and included an Elvis sighting as "an acceptable excuse for missing class"; the popular low-brow movie *Ernest Goes to College* as "its student recruitment video"; and black velvet painting as its "most popular major."

When he wanted to, he could fire one crack after another. "The room is full of lawyers," he told a conference of judges, "which, of course, supports the adage that the only thing better than an attorney who knows the law is an attorney who knows the judge. And you know, I, too, am a lawyer, which gives many of our alumni just another reason to yell at me. The United States is closing in on one million lawyers. Fortunately, only about half of them are practicing law."

At the Wexner Jewish Student Center, he participated in a "Kosher Karaoke," which he thought was "some kind of Hebrew gourmet delicacy. How would I know! I grew up in rural Utah." In "singing" "You Ain't Nothin' But a Hound Dog" he evidenced his willingness to laugh at himself and do whatever it took to be a good sport in a good cause. Thanks to a lesson from OSU Baseball Coach Bob Todd, he threw a first-pitch strike opening Ohio State night at an Indians' game. Whether it was leaping onto a Velcro wall in a Velcro suit at a student health fair, Sumo wrestling in outsized protective clothing at the Lima campus's May Week, or enduring dunk after dunk-tank dunk in a student fund-raiser, Gordon Gee would be there. And no one had a better time.

## *The Personal Touch*

When "Jimmy Jam," a Columbus rock radio station personality, knocked on his front door for a before-dawn interview, Gee laughed and did it in his pajamas. When Bill Cunningham, a Cincinnati talk show curmudgeon, called him "a pencil-necked geek," Gee charmed the lion in his lair and was invited to come back. When John Block, publisher of the *Toledo Blade,* slammed both Columbus and Ohio State for their relative prosperity, Gee went to visit, appeared on Block's interview show, and gathered Ohio State faculty to help develop an economic action plan for Toledo.

In Columbus, Gee made sure that Amos Lynch, then editor of the *Call and Post* newspaper, read primarily by the Black community, was kept well informed on issues most important to his readership and that the struggling paper was supported financially through the communication office's limited advertising budget.

In Atlanta, a special friend was Jay Smith, publisher of the *Atlanta Journal-Constitution* and a commencement speaker the year before Gee arrived at Ohio State. When in Chicago he would visit the *Chicago Tribune*, sometimes meeting with syndicated columnist Bob Greene, a Bexley native. In Washington, he would visit alumni Len Downie, Jr., executive editor of the *Washington Post*, and Barbara Reynolds, then columnist for *USA Today*. All four would be commencement speakers while Gee was president.

Carol Luper. Bob Orr. Penny Moore. Bob Conners. John Corby. Doug Caruso. George Lehner. "Munch" Bishop. Barry Katz. Mark Katz. Troy May. Bruce Hooley. Paul Spohn. Brent Larkin. Jane Ware. Phillip Morris. Mark Tatge. Tom Suddes. Wendy Craver. Al Burcover. Angela Pace. Doug Lessels. Dave Kaylor. Ray Paprocki. Allan Miller. Skip Mosic. Bill Hershey. Trevor Coleman. Chip Visci. Gary Robinson. Bob Singleton. Sally Heinemann. Mark Fisher. Doug Letterman. Carol Hymowitz. David Hall. Max Brown. Vince Doria. Paul Delaney. Herb Cook. Harry Whipple. Ed Johnson. Lenore Brown. Tom Stewart. Mike Fiorelli. Mark Ellis. Gene D'Angelo. Bob Smith. Ben Marrison. Tom Walton. Mike Curtin. John Dodson, Jr. Gary Robinson. John F. Wolfe. Big hitters to little hitters. Reporters. Editors. Publishers. Owners. The list of media who would take his phone calls easily approached three figures.

Like politics, to Gordon Gee all communication was personal. As Asher recalled, on meeting people for the first time, "[H]e would start an interrogation. 'Where are you from? What do you do? What does your family do?' A couple of months later, we ran into the same people and, before I could say anything, he would say, 'Hi John, how you doing? How's your father's farm going?' I'd be stunned."

And, following any meeting, there was always time for a thank you. How did he find it?

"We flew into New York on the King Air," legal counsel Bob Duncan recalled. It was 1995, the day Eddie George won the Heisman Trophy, and Duncan already had been working with Gee for three years. "Flying to New York in a propeller driven aircraft seems like it takes forever, so we went to the dinner. Gordon made a presentation. Eddie got the Heisman. I had been with Gordon all day. He still hadn't eaten. By the time we get over to the airport in Jersey, it's 11:30 at night. I'm about ready to die. David Williams is tired. Constance is ready to go to sleep. Gordon gets on the airplane and starts pulling out work.

CHAPTER 20

Eddie gets the Heisman.

And he is working all the way back to Columbus. And the plane is going up and down and the turbulence is all over."

"How is Gordon able to have such high energy, do all these things, pull out his pen, and start writing notes to people? David and I said, 'This man is crazy.' But he did it all the time."

## *Platforms and Sales*

While "crazy" may not have been exactly the right descriptor for Gee's national leadership agenda, "frenetic" would not be inaccurate. At one time, he held a dozen different leadership roles, a number with bully pulpits, including the NCAA Presidents' Council, the America Reads Steering Committee, the Higher Education Center for Alcohol and Drug Prevention, and the Big Ten. From 1995 until he left for Brown, he cochaired the Kellogg Commission, studying the reformation needs of the 195-member institutions of the National Association of State Universities and Land-Grant Colleges.

His personality and expertise made him a president Washington media sought, just as they had in 1992, when he led higher education's charge against federal mandates and, in 1993, when he testified in support of National Science Foundation funding before a House appropriations subcommittee.

Never one to let up on his own staff, he was even more emphatic about promoting the successes of Ohio State nationally. In January 1995, he wrote a memo to his provost, Dick Sisson, urging more funding and a better developed "strategy for focusing on the academic and research missions of the university."

He also memoed his new athletic director, Andy Geiger: "You and I have spoken on several occasions about the need to totally revamp our marketing efforts and to make a national statement about Ohio State. The only purpose of this note is to remind you that this should remain a very high priority. This is brought about by the fact I continue to see many Michigan sweatshirts and paraphernalia from other institutions, even in our own Columbus stores.

"Isn't it fun having me around?"

In 1989, the year before Gee's presidency began, Ohio State's income from trademarks and licensing was $770,000. In 1994, the year before the memo to Geiger, it was $1.4 million. By 1997, Gee's last year, Trademark and Licensing Director Anne Chasser reported receipts of more than $2.5 million. Most of it went to student scholarships. And, yes, many Ohioans would agree, it was fun having him around.

# 21

## *More on Diversity*

In 1988, Ohio State began a statewide early intervention program to help children from poor Ohio families prepare for college. In addition to the handicap of poverty and the probability of a one-parent household, these children often faced peer pressure to fail academically. Black, Hispanic, Native American, and Appalachian white, they were termed "underrepresented" in higher education by federal law.

Get them early, by the seventh grade, because, by the time they're in high school, any opportunity for motivation might otherwise be gone. Philanthropic individuals and corporations should be eager to donate to such a socially enlightened investment in human capital! Such was the thinking of President Ed Jennings and his administration when they created the program they believed they could afford until embraced by the Ohio Board of Regents and funded throughout the state.

By Gordon Gee's arrival, however, Young Scholars was a runaway train red-flagged for braking. The Ohio economy was diving. The regents had other priorities. Fund-raising had proved difficult for the program, and, in four years, Ohio State would be financing its first Young Scholar freshmen.

Four hundred new seventh-graders a year was down to 300 by the time program director Jim Bishop explained the program to the regents in March 1992. This fifth class of scholars soon would be chosen by teachers, principals, counselors, and parents from Akron, Canton, Cincinnati, Cleveland, Columbus, Dayton, Lorain, Toledo, and Youngstown. Selectees would attend a three-week program each summer on campus, living in the dormitories, and could enroll at Ohio State, or any other university, when they completed the program and the twelfth grade on an academic track with a B average. At Ohio State, there would be no loans to pay back. All would be on scholarships and work-study. "Our greatest concern, as you might expect," Bishop said at the end, was financial.

That did not change. Though the Minority Affairs Office budget (which, in a reorganization, came to include Young Scholars) was always held harmless or increased as other units were cut, there was no way the program could be funded as originally imagined. In 1994, faculty member Charles Hancock, a specialist in bilingual education, became the new program director, and Bishop shifted to full-time fund-raising. That same year some 100 members of the 1988 class entered Ohio State.

By August 1996, according to its own information sheet, the direct cost of the Young Scholars Program was $2.5 million a year; nearly 400 Young Scholar alumni were Ohio State undergraduates receiving nearly $5 million in scholarships, most of it federal grants; another 1,256 students were in the seventh through twelfth grade programs, and a third straight class of 120 new seventh-graders was ready to be enrolled. While the ideal may not have been realized, Ohio State was continuing to do perhaps more than any other American university to motivate bright but disadvantaged children for college and toward their degrees.

Concurrently, a program known as "I Know I Can" had been started in 1987 for the Columbus Public Schools by Ohio State alumna Thekla "Teckie" Shackelford, who later on would also chair Ohio State's "Affirm Thy Friendship" capital campaign. "I Know I Can" would help Columbus students select colleges and find scholarships and provide "last dollar" grants for families who needed them. In 1991, Shackelford received the Ronald Reagan Award from President George Bush as the nation's no. 1 volunteer. By that time, according to its report of its first three years, her organization had served more than 3500 local high school students, more than half from single-parent families, and more than half from families with incomes below $24,000. Most were going to college in Columbus, many attending or planning to transfer to Ohio State.

## *Expunging a Nazi*

In late 1993, the university was notified by the World Jewish Congress (WJC) that the late Dr. Hubertus Strughold, whose image was part of a stained glass mural in the College of Medicine, had been a Luftwaffe colonel under Adolph Hitler and a war criminal. Strughold was known to the university only as the founder of aviation medicine in the United States; his Nazi background had been hidden from the American public.

CHAPTER 21

Although the university arranged to alter the mural as soon as it received notification from the WJC, international press coverage elicited criticism from around the world. At the university's request, the World Jewish Congress then sent out a press release praising Ohio State's decision to remove the mural image, acknowledging the university as another "victim" of Strughold's cover-up.

## *The End of Set-Asides*

In 1994, President Gee answered a letter from Ray Miller, then president of Columbus's National Urban Policy Institute, urging him to "stand strong" in a case Ohio State had hoped to settle, but couldn't, before it got to federal court. The Henry Painting Company of Columbus said it had lost $300,000 in contract work because of Ohio State's minority set-aside policy. Gee wrote back to Miller that Ohio State would "present a vigorous defense."

At issue then was not the policy itself; it was the university's implementation of it. To help reach a state-mandated purchasing goal of 15 percent of supply and service contracts and 5 percent of construction contracts to minority-owned businesses, the university allegedly was setting aside 100 percent in areas where minority contractors could compete best. And that included painting—which ended when Henry sued.

As strong as the university's stand was, it eventually lost. On March 29, 1996, Ohio Attorney General Betty Montgomery cleared the way for a settlement. Ohio State would pay Henry Painting $368,000 in damages and legal fees. Part of the agreement, the *Dispatch* reported the next day, was that "Ohio State backed away from a previous claim that it never set aside all of its painting contracts for minorities." While a spokesman for the attorney general suggested this "very specific remedy" would have "little to no impact on any other set-aside program," a few days earlier (*Dispatch*, March 27) one of Henry's attorneys had suggested it was "only a matter of time before the state's entire system of racial preferences came tumbling down."

Statewide, meanwhile, affirmative action programs in general were under fire. In 1995, when California was dismantling affirmative action programs, to some people's surprise, Governor Voinovich had supported them in Ohio. He told the *Dispatch* (July 27, 1995) that, as the grandson of Serbian and Slovenian immigrants, not only had he been exposed to discrimination, but that his father never could have "shown what he could do ... if not for government opportunities." When, the next May, opposition to set-asides built in Ohio, he proposed basing them on social and economic need rather than race, but found few takers. On one side, many conservatives considered this discriminatory as well; on the other, the Legislative Black Caucus did not endorse his position (*Dispatch,* November 15, 1997).

By the end of the Gee administration at Ohio State, the retention of any state set-aside program was in doubt. When, a year later, a U.S. District judge ruled Ohio's construction set-asides unconstitutional and an Ohio magistrate said public officials who granted set-asides could be liable for damages, the state canceled both the construction and supply and service programs.

## *Domestic Partners*

On May 2, 1997, for the fourth year in a row, the trustees approved a student health insurance plan that did *not* include a family benefit for named domestic partners, gay or straight.

Gordon Gee's last gasp for a policy he supported had been a letter written to a group called Students for Domestic Partners. He would not bring the subject up for a vote, he explained, for fear a "no" would close the issue for good. To a gay activist who addressed the Board, in his first meeting as chair, Alex Shumate said he understood and appreciated what the speaker was saying. "But the issue will not be voted on today."

When the student insurance plan was called for a vote as presented, Vice Chair Ted Celeste, who had supported domestic partner benefits from day one, temporarily left the room, for the bathroom, he said, when asked by the media.

That domestic partner issues had to be approved or rejected by the trustees at all, Gee recalled years later, was at the heart of the problem. Domestic partner insurance coverage was no longer unusual in corporate America. And many major universities (Stanford, Princeton, Columbia, Brown, MIT), many of them public (North Dakota, Stony Brook, Colorado, Iowa, Michigan, Oregon, Wisconsin, Colorado), already authorized insurance or housing benefits, or both.

Four years earlier, Gee had been able to provide family leave benefits to named domestic partners of the faculty and staff by not calling attention to the matter. Gee later remembered assuring the trustees individually and privately that such decisions were administrative, not policymaking, and did not require a trustee vote. He would make the decisions, and, should any become both public and notorious, he alone would take the heat. Even so, the matter did come before the trustees in the form of a redefinition of the term "immediate

## Chapter 21

family" governing sick and bereavement leave benefits and was approved in February 1992. Gee did not comment on it, and the motion was made by Ted Celeste and approved with only one negative vote.

Thus, with no fanfare and with no problem, domestic partners, gay and straight—who lived together, had been in the relationship for at least six months, were at least eighteen years old, and were competent to make a contract—were included in the university's sick and bereavement leave program.

But for what he later called "chortling," he might have finessed both the housing and insurance issues the same way. Unfortunately, before it reached the trustees, some leaders of the gay community did themselves and "me no favor by publicly chortling that they had won" on the housing issue. Picked up and featured on page one by the *Lantern*, from there the story that Ohio State was opening its married housing to gay couples moved to the Associated Press, on to Ohio media large and small, and, finally, across the nation. "I am writing to express my anger, outrage and disgust. Have you lost your mind?" and, "If this plan is carried forth [my daughter] will no longer consider matriculating at Ohio State." These statements typified the letters and phone calls that followed.

In a letter to Phil Martin, director of the university's new Gay, Lesbian, and Bisexual Student Services Office, written on May 11, 1993, Gee reemphasized that he wanted to provide the benefits. But "each time I receive publicity for doing so, I find myself in a serious defensive position. That is not the way it should be, but those are the political realities." And so they were. Knowing well what both the process and the outcome would be, he soon announced the deferral of his decision pending a review by the board.

Of course, there would be no open review bared to the public in what would have been an actively lobbied, media-heavy September meeting. By late August, hoping the Ohio State board "this fall would make this a moot issue," Representative Michael Fox of Hamilton led fourteen legislators in introducing House Bill 442, which would prohibit any state-assisted university board of trustees from approving domestic partnerships in married-student housing or for health insurance benefits (*Dispatch*, August 20, 1993).

On September 13, Gee announced that, after discussions with many people, including individual conversations with his trustees, he had decided to remove from consideration any change in the family housing policy for the 396-unit Buckeye Village.

While the housing question did not come up again, as one undiscouraged faculty member wrote him, "public discussion and struggle is necessary if real change is ever to occur. It may take much longer to bring about the changes we want to see, but when they come (and I am optimistic they will, indeed, come), the victory will be more solid, more thorough, and more final."

In June 1994, the university's Student Health Insurance Committee made its annual recommendation to the fiscal committee of the Board of Trustees. After discussion, the recommendation was approved with one exception. The exception was domestic partner coverage. Later, at the full Board meeting, Trustee Ted Celeste moved to reconsider and include the exception. He did not receive a second.

## *ACTION*

In early August 1991, some ten months after JustUs had opened his eyes to the level of discontent among African American students on campus, President Gee received a long letter from Barbara Newman, the same associate provost who had just honchoed the Hispanic Action Plan. Writing on behalf of the executive committee that had produced the four-year-old *Action Plan for the Recruitment and Retention of Black Students*, she reiterated that the committee had found "ethno-violence and harassment reported on almost a daily basis." Included in her letter were a series of committee recommendations, some practical, some not.

Emphasize raising money for minority programs and scholarships in the next capital campaign. In faculty units that have made no progress in recruiting minorities or women, "insist that no non-minority male can be appointed until a woman or minority is." Commit more resources to freshman retention, which was particularly poor among minority students. Train all employees in basic human relations.

Gordon Gee had a university to run, whose budget was being cut and staff positions eliminated. He had an academic planning process under development, a "Red Tape" task force rolling out, a "Managing for the Future" task force forming, and an intensive student recruiting plan in development. And his wife, Elizabeth, was in the last months of her life. In the fall and winter of the 1991–1992 academic year, the president's best intentions to focus on diversity were overwhelmed by other issues and his own personal life. Elizabeth would pass away on December 17, 1991. Throughout the following months, as a coping mechanism, he would work harder than ever, days, evenings, weekends. On May 5, 1992, the climate for African Americans again became *the* issue at Ohio State.

On that day, ACTION gave the president twenty-two demands "Re: Systematic and institutionalized racism in all aspects of The Ohio State University,

## Chapter 21

Gee responds to concerns of ACTION, 1992.

which creates intolerable conditions for Afrikan students, staff and faculty." As in Newman's letter, in dealing with the localized manifestations of a national problem, the demands ranged from the realizable to the impossible: No disproportional layoffs of African Americans during budget cuts. Reauthorization of the four-year-old Action Plan. Second-stage development of the Hale Black Cultural Center (which never had officially been given that name and still bore the old sign as Bradford Commons). A "College of Pan-African Studies." An All-African American housing unit. That no Ohio State salary exceed $85,000 a year. "A $100,000,000 annual Afrikan development fund to be managed by ACTION."

To one of the demands, hiring and promoting more minorities, Gee said he would determine "why we have not made more progress." It was one of his many statements and responses in a gathering on May 18 (*onCampus*, May 21, 1992) in a packed Hale Center that ran from 8 P.M. until after 1 A.M. and was covered by both electronic and print media.

Some people, one man wrote, were "appalled that you would even address that group in the format you chose." Others felt his handling of the situation was one of Gee's finest moments.

## MORE ON DIVERSITY

Always respectful, often thoughtful, he never lost control in a session that never got out of hand but was fraught with both pleas and accusations. He said he recognized ACTION as a legitimate group but not, as they had demanded, as the single representative for all Black students on campus. He would support an African-centered living-learning center, but not limited to a single race of residents. A fund-raising goal for minority scholarships was worthy, but the amount suggested was impossible. He listened and answered where he could and deferred to the future when he had to. Trustee Alex Shumate attended with him, as did members of the president's executive committee.

ACTION leader Greg Carr said that he would "do everything in my power to shut the university down" if Ohio State failed to respond adequately to the demands. "That doesn't mean tearing anything up. It means we'll tell these students to go home, and they'll go home tomorrow." Scotty Graham, a December graduate soon to play in the National Football League, had expressed frustration at some of his experiences as an African American athlete, and Carr had declared that, if Ohio State did not respond to ACTION's demands, "Folks will be eating their sandwiches in the stands and watching a bunch of white guys losing the Big Ten," whereupon the room had erupted in laughter and applause.

Soon, Gee had rejected an ACTION proposal to establish a board of administrators and have ACTION members set university African American policies. Policies, he reminded the audience, were made by the trustees. But he also charged six vice presidents and his capital campaign director, Arthur Brodeur, to develop timely proposals that related to African American faculty, staff, and students. He invited ACTION members to be involved. And, at their June meeting, the trustees corrected an oversight by formally changing the name of Bradford Commons to Frank Hale Jr. Hall.

Soon, David Williams of the Law faculty became co-president (with Reprographics Director Deborah Gill) of the Sojourner Truth–Frederick Douglass Society, "The Black faculty and staff organization at The Ohio State University," and, in August, was named Gee's new vice provost for minority affairs. The president also widely distributed an interim report on the findings of his seven administrators.

By the following April, however, and again in November 1993 with support from the Nation of Islam, ACTION was back beneath Gee's window rallying on the steps of Bricker. The graduation rate for African Americans of only 26 percent was one of its current, and most legitimate, issues. "Shouldn't that tell President Gee that changes need to be made," said ACTION's new leader, Aya

CHAPTER 21

Fubara. Fubara had entered Ohio State's College of Law, where she had been recommended by Gordon Gee, who (*Lantern*, May 26, 1993) kept "his church and state separate." "Capable, bright, and committed," she had, he said, "great attributes to be a lawyer."

While the problem of racism on campus may have been settled in the Gee administration no more than had the problem of racism in America, Gee's commitment to end it should never have been in doubt. In a personal letter to Gee, one African American faculty member expressed along the way what many were thinking, when he wrote he could sense in the Gee administration "an unparalleled commitment to expanding the role of minorities at the university and improving the racial climate and educational benefits enjoyed by Black students matriculating on our campus."

On the last day in July 1997, Gordon Gee, who had just accepted the presidency of Brown, received an e-mail "from an old friend." The friend was Greg Carr, working on his doctoral dissertation at Temple University. "They don't know the boon they have acquired for themselves in getting you," he wrote. "You always dealt with me with integrity and the conviction of your beliefs."

And he had.

## *Final questions*

In early December 1997, with less than thirty days to go in each of their tenures, Gordon Gee responded to three questions from Chancellor Elaine Hairston of the Ohio Board of Regents. What race-based scholarship programs did Ohio State offer, including scholarships earmarked for Appalachian students? What policies did Ohio State have for considering minority status in professional school admission? What policies did Ohio State have for placement tests and remedial programs for minorities?

To the latter, the president answered that Ohio State's placement tests and remedial programs were offered without regard to race. Of $220 million that year in financial aid, less than $9 million involved some consideration of race. Most of that was in the Freshman Foundation and Minority Scholars programs. The first was need-based; the second was merit-based. Each operated "Bakke-style," with race only one consideration. Professional school admissions programs, like all other admissions programs at the university, had been carefully reviewed.

All admissions programs, he said, were consistent with the legal requirements set forth in the Bakke case, where, in 1978, the U.S. Supreme Court had struck down admissions set-asides, but allowed race to be considered a "plus" factor in admissions to foster the educational benefits that flow from a diverse student body.

## *The Diversity and Duncan Reports*

What about diversity in general at Ohio State? Nearly a year earlier, Provost Dick Sisson had published a report he and Gee had commissioned to assess the status of faculty and student diversity.

In autumn 1996, there were 791 regular full-time female faculty, up from 766 in 1987, representing 27 percent of the total, up from 23 percent in 1987. Three hundred and fifty-five regular full-time faculty identified themselves as minority, up from 295 in 1987, representing 12 percent of the total faculty, up from 9 percent in 1987. There were 96 African American faculty, up from 77 in 1987. There were 45 Hispanic faculty, up from 31 in 1987.

In the mid-1980s, Ohio State started the Faculty Hiring Assistance Program (FHAP), a financial partnership between the provost and academic units to fund faculty positions for minorities and women. By 1997, more than $4.5 million had been reallocated, supplementing $8 million from the units, bringing more than 250 minority and female faculty to the university. The best results were the 1995–96 academic year, when more than half of the new faculty appointments were women and minorities.

In the student body, by 1997 more than 7,074 minority students, making up 13 percent of the total student population, represented a 6 percent increase from 1987. As a proportion of all students, the 3,572 African Americans represented 7 percent of the overall student population, up from 4 percent in 1987. There had been a 67 percent increase in Hispanic students, representing a growth from 546 to 910. The number of American Indian students had nearly doubled in the decade, but the total population remained small—185 students. The total 2,407 Asian American students represented 34 percent of the minority population, up from 29 percent a decade before.

In October 1997, the long-awaited Duncan Report had been published. Gee and Sisson had asked the former federal district judge and Ohio State administrative leader, an African American himself, to chair a committee to review the Office of Minority Affairs. By that time, Bob Duncan, who had had heart surgery, had stepped down both as general counsel and secretary to the trustees. He was acutely aware that Ohio State presidents had had a history of commissioning studies of this sort, which, he later said, "were collecting shelf

## Chapter 21

life" and that their lack of implementation was a "curse upon our house." Gee had commissioned the study the prior October right after his annual fall address to the University Senate, revved up for another active year. But by the time the report was completed, he was ready to pass the torch to the next president.

It would be up to that person to use it or add another curse to the house.

# 22

## *Constance*

At the Top of the Sixes restaurant with her mother and favorite aunt, nursing a Shirley Temple with double cherries, five-year-old Constance Bumgarner of Burlington, North Carolina, looked out over Manhattan and knew she would live there someday. A decade and some later, she went to East Carolina University, which had an excellent program in visual arts, as well as in-state tuition.

In her first year there, Constance would contribute to the university's "party school" ranking in *Playboy* magazine (only "honorable mention"), before settling down to gain the grades and exhibit the talent to be accepted in the master of fine arts program at Brooklyn's rigorous Pratt Institute. There she would major in painting, minor in sculpture, earn her work-study grant as a driver for Pratt President Richardson "Jerry" Pratt, and prepare to conquer Manhattan with her brushwork, her MFA, and her love of adventure. Of course, it didn't turn out that way.

After painting by day and tending bar by night, she became an advertising account executive, with clients including Hitachi and People's Express Airlines, and then did marketing for a software firm. When President Pratt invited her back to her alma mater to organize exhibitions of alumni work, she grabbed it. Before long, she was named to direct Pratt's new National Talent Search, which took her to high schools across America. That experience would stimulate her interest in art education, which she would follow in another five years.

After a first year in the doctoral program at Columbia Teachers' College, Penn State would offer her a teaching assistantship. During her time there, the U.S. Senate approved withholding five years of National Endowment of the Arts (NEA) funding from two arts organizations that had exhibited highly controversial photographs: the work of Robert Mapplethorpe, considered pornographic, and that of Andres Serrano, deemed sacrilegious. Although the funding ban later was dropped, Senator Jesse Helms of Constance's native North Carolina also had brought an amendment to the full Senate that would have barred the NEA from supporting art that was "obscene or indecent" or that denigrated a "religion or non-religion."

While the amendment was defeated, NEA grant recipients now were required to sign an agreement pledging they would not use the money to produce anything "obscene." The intensity of the controversy drew Constance's interest. What should the role of government be in funding the arts? In 1993, she graduated from Penn State with a Ph.D. in art education, with emphases in program evaluation and policy analysis. One day later, "I got into my car and drove over to Ohio State" for a job interview.

One of the interviewers was Judith Koroscik, a rising faculty star who would become the next dean. Koroscik had had a similar experience herself. Also an exhibiting painter before going for her Ph.D., she too had interviewed at Ohio State for her first teaching job. Her research area was allied to Constance's. Koroscik studied the rational and emotional human processes that both create art and respond to it. Coincidentally, in 1990 she not only had been on the presidential search committee, she had been the member to sit with Elizabeth Gee and discuss her professional goals. By 1993, she was a full professor and associate dean. In the interview with Constance, she was taken by the quality of the new Ph.D.'s work and her enthusiasm for it. "She was the first candidate at Ohio State or anywhere else whose dissertation I actually wanted to read."

Constance got the job.

It was a *non*-tenure-track lectureship, but one created with the caveat that a tenure-track assistant professorship would be sought. Once created, the incumbent lecturer could compete for it. Meanwhile, she would teach what she never had taught before. In addition, she was to develop a proposal for a graduate program that would blend arts policy and business, normally, Koroscik said later, what only a senior professor would have undertaken. There was nothing like it in the country, and the university already had a donor to support it.

"No one," Koroscik said later, "doubted she could do it."

## *Making the "Ask"*

The evening of September 28, 1993, Constance Bumgarner, non-tenure-track lecturer, briefly conversed with Gordon Gee, president of the university, as one of sixty guests at his annual new faculty reception at the university residence. As was standard, the president carried a cheat sheet with each new faculty member's name and background. Next to hers, the president's secretary Mary Basinger had written, "Not Connie. Constance."

At the reception, Constance would learn that the president already knew about the new public policy in the arts program, and they would talk about it briefly. Not only would it need approval by the college and the university trustees, as something new to Ohio higher education, it would be reviewed by all other state universities and the Ohio Board of Regents, and this at a time in which the governor had all graduate programs under review for duplication, quality, and potential elimination.

She would send the president a thank-you note, but two weeks later. She was too busy to have made it a priority. He would respond a few days after that.

Six months later, she was invited again, this time to one in a series of smaller faculty dinners. Why, she wondered, would a first-year lecturer be invited to a dinner certain to be overflowing with "brain surgeons and Pulitzer Prize winners?" Did she do something wrong? Yes, but not until she arrived. She was fifteen minutes late, appropriate in New York City but bad form in Columbus, or at least at the president's home. Everyone was waiting. The minute she walked in, the president introduced her around and called for dinner. As he had instructed his planner, Constance Bumgarner was seated to the president's immediate right.

In the small talk that followed, she mentioned she had read in the *Lantern* that the next day, February 2, Groundhog Day, would be his fiftieth birthday, and that she just had turned forty. "You just turned 40!" He was heard throughout the room, which, for a few awkward moments, went silent.

"He thought I was younger, God bless him. We haven't changed his eye glass prescription since." Ten years was an acceptable gap for dating, should he get up the nerve. And dancing. They both loved to dance, they discovered. Not only that—each loved New York's Rainbow Room, where Gordon had just taken his daughter, Rebekah. And in the company of the arts dean, Don Harris, the president himself had made the "ask" for the private gift to fund the graduate program for which she was to write the proposal.

## *Larry and Isabel Barnett*

The donors were Larry Barnett and his wife, Isabel Bigley Barnett. Isabel was an acclaimed stage and television actress. She had starred in *Oklahoma* and *Me and Juliet* and had won the Tony Award for the lead in *Guys and Dolls*. She had

CHAPTER 22

had her own television show in England and had entertained on virtually every American variety show from Ed Sullivan to Abbott and Costello.

Once a young violinist and bandleader from Orrville, Ohio, Larry Barnett had gone on from Ohio State to head both the Music Corporation of America (MCA) and General Artists Corporation, a division of Chris-Craft, where he became executive vice president and vice chairman of United Television. Illness had forced him to leave Ohio State in 1935 with only one quarter to complete, and he had returned to earn his degree fifty-three years later.

In their careers, both had seen many artists and musicians who knew too little about business victimized by opportunists. The Barnetts were eager to support a graduate program at Ohio State that combined courses in business and art. It was the program Constance Bumgarner soon would be discussing further with Gordon Gee.

## Dating

A few days after the dinner, at 10 at night, the president called the lecturer, ostensibly to discuss the proposal. That night, she was grading papers. Would it be too forward, he asked at the end, to ask her out for dinner? No, it would not.

"I was so nervous," he told the *Lantern* later (November 22, 1994). "It took me about four hours to work up enough courage to do it. It was like I was 16 again."

That Gordon Gee and Constance Bumgarner were dating was all but a secret. There were no university events, only quiet dinners for two at Bexley's Monk, rides in the country, or walks in the neighborhood. In neither case did Constance or the president want knowledge of their relationship to affect the process of the decision concerning the permanent appointment or the program proposal. She had achieved well on her own. She had earned a doctorate at an age when most faculty already were advanced in their careers. It was very important that what Constance received, Constance earned.

## Being Seen and Getting Married

It was the last thing those in the know thought they knew about his private life; the widower Gordon Gee had been seen with Kim Perfect, vice president of the Center for Science and Industry and a former executive at the Limited. In the

*This Week* newspapers, celebrated chatterers Fred and Howard even had gossiped, "The perfect couple? How about OSU President Gordon Gee and Kim Perfect." But that had been a while. On May 21, 1994, heads turned when the president entered the packed annual reception and dinner of The Ohio State University Presidents Club, on his arm a redhead who recently had been appointed an assistant professor.

The following September, they announced they would be married in a family ceremony in Salt Lake City on November 26. In her presidential briefing for the trip to Salt Lake City, in addition to such details as airline departure and arrival times, Barbie Tootle, the president's special assistant and speechwriter, wrote, "Remember, you are not the keynote speaker. Do not deliver a speech. I have enclosed a card to prompt you at the right time." The card read, "I do."

## *Retaining Identity*

When the announcement was about to be made that Gordon Gee would be marrying Constance Bumgarner, executive assistant Elam and communications director Baroway met with her independently to help prepare her for the immediate impact the announcement would have on her life. Though media-savvy and "street smart" after a decade in New York City, she said later that nothing could have prepared her adequately for the pressures she would soon experience.

The Columbus media would fall all over her. What she did, what she said, how she looked would be "news." There would be expectations that, as the spouse of the president, she would join him at his many social occasions. Some of her faculty colleagues would become more collegial; others, more evasive; most, at least initially, wary. There were those who would judge the president hasty or worse: widowed three years, should he remarry "so soon?" In general, however, both the Columbus and the university communities rejoiced in his good fortune.

"Will Constance Bumgarner take the Gee name?" was the first question on the Q&A sheet prepared for the media. "No, she will retain her maiden name." In the media, the preferred reference would be "University President E. Gordon Gee and his wife, Dr. Constance Bumgarner." "Will further interviews be available?" "As a member of the teaching university faculty, Dr. Bumgarner has a full teaching, advising, and research work schedule. However, she will accept interviews as arranged through the office of university communications."

"My first commitment to the university is my teaching," she told *Columbus*

CHAPTER 22

Queen Constance and King Gordon rule at Renaissance Festival '95.

*Monthly* (March 1995), "that—and the development of my program." As for the adjunctive support role, she was still "working it out. First, to love Gordon a lot and connect every day. That's primary."

One aspect of their relationship that gained the respect of many people and that some thought extraordinary, was the honor both would pay to Gordon's late wife, Elizabeth, even as he was remarrying. He was very much in love with Constance. He showed it and he would tell the world. It was the happiness of his first marriage, he would say later, that let him know he could be happy again. The Mormon doctrine believes that marriage is eternal, and death only a pause. When asked about that once by a staff member, Constance, a member of the Disciples of Christ, said she would deal with that when it happened. She was happy just being his "earthly fling."

It was not too long after the marriage that the preferred name changed to Dr. Constance Bumgarner Gee. It was not long, either, before the university community appeared to accept the Drs. Gee as the prototype of the new American presidential model: the dual-professional presidential couple, where the presidential spouse might well have other things to do than appear at a fundraiser or a basketball game.

What neither the public nor the Ohio State community knew was the in-

# CONSTANCE

tensity of the pressure she was under, from both self-imposed demands and the expectations of others. Teach the art courses (Koroscik: "She would exhaust herself finding ways to give students advice on how they would improve. I really responded to that.") Grade the papers (Koroscik: "She would spend hours reviewing them and writing comments.") Bring in adjunct faculty for the business courses (Wayne Lawson of the Ohio Arts Council and Donn Vickers of the Thurber House).

Adjust to married life (this independent woman who had expected to remain single). Adjust to being a stepmother (and friend to an only child who had lost her mother prematurely). Adjust to living in a public home, nice as it might be (used so often for formal meals and meetings that, until a catering kitchen was added in the basement, your kitchen might be too busy to stand in; the one place you could grade papers in quiet, your bedroom closet). Be the hostess, as you found time. Develop comfort as a peer with very wealthy people. And, as a junior faculty member, accept the lightning change of status your marriage had conferred.

Years later, she said it took at least eighteen months before she felt totally grounded. But by the time her husband was offered the presidency of Brown University, another year later, she had come to love everything about her life in Columbus and did not want to leave.

Clark Kerr, the late president of the University of California, once had warned Gordon Gee not to fall in love with the university he was president of "because it will never love you back." Neither Gordon nor Constance Gee heeded such a warning about Ohio State. In this one case, at least, Kerr had not been right.

Standing beside Gordon at the news conference on June 28, 1997, to announce his presidency of Brown, long after her husband had taken his off, she kept the baseball cap on that she had been given to symbolize the transition. Watching this on television in Columbus, some people misread what was happening. She had pulled down the brim to hide her tears. She was bawling, she said later. It had been tremendously difficult for her to leave the program she had worked so hard to build. She had personally recruited "thirty wonderful students. We had a warm and supportive relationship and I felt a responsibility to them." And Columbus is where she and her husband had "met, where we courted," she explained to the *Dispatch*'s Doug Caruso. "I feel truly a part of the Columbus community." She would, she added when interviewed for this book, "always be a Buckeye."

## 23

## *Five-Year Evaluations*

Gordon Gee knew how to do five years. He had completed five at Colorado before Ohio State hired him away, was working on his fifth at West Virginia when the Buffaloes had lured him to Boulder, and wound up his fifth at Ohio State in late summer 1995. As was written in his Five-Year Evaluation, commissioned by the trustees the previous spring, when Gordon Gee accepted the Ohio State presidency "the university was underappreciated in Ohio and . . . not seen as a national leader in American higher education." Over five years, the "external appreciation of Ohio State" had been "immeasurably raised," as had its "reputation within its Big Ten peer group and nationally," it said.

So singularly smooth was restructuring going in 1995 at Ohio State that *America's Best Colleges Guide*, produced by *U.S. News and World Report*, carried a five-page feature on the process, and the president, "blessed with the . . . abilities to work a room, schmooze with donors, court reporters, cut deals, read budget documents, build consensus, and stay awake during boring meetings on very little sleep—the skills . . . of a master politician."

For "Downsizing the Mega U," journalist Paul Glastris had spent most of a week on campus trailing Gee and was somewhat stupefied by the intensity of the president's schedule. In the article, Glastris referred to a recently published *New York Times* op-ed piece by Oklahoma Senator David Boren about his decision to become president of the University of Oklahoma. Boren had complained about senatorial fund-raising and a sixteen-hour workday that gave him no time for reflection. "Before he gets ready to relax," Glastris wrote, "Boren should spend a day with E. Gordon Gee."

Glastris also contrasted the Ohio State restructuring process and outcome with what Yale and its President Benno Schmidt had experienced in 1991. To handle a budget deficit, Schmidt had attempted to ram through a university-wide restructuring plan all at one time. The faculty had revolted and ultimately Schmidt had resigned. At Ohio State, the process had been both incremental and collegial. Glastris himself had been present for the first university senate vote—on restructuring the College of Agriculture.

"E. Gordon Gee," he wrote, ". . . leans to the microphone and asks for a show of hands. . . . Now Gee is asking senate members—most of them tenured professors—to put aside their natural aversion to change and vote for a sweeping plan for restructuring the College of Agriculture from eleven departments to eight and shift the focus of the school's research from crop productivity to food processing.

"Everyone in the hall recognizes that the vote is a watershed—the first in a series of . . . restructurings . . . the president is pushing to cut costs at the massive university. Gee . . . sits silently as the votes are counted. Finally, the results are announced: 93 to zero in favor. Gee smirks, leans toward the microphone and quips: 'May I faint?'"

That the College of Agriculture had stepped up to the restructuring plate first had been no accident. As Gee explained to Harvard's Len Schlesinger two and a half years later—at his exit interview upon leaving for Brown—in choosing the internal candidate Bobby Moser to head the college, he had appointed a visionary and a change agent. What better way to accomplish university-wide restructuring than to have "the most conservative element of the university" be his lead dog. With the ag college's work accomplished—even its name changed to Food, Agricultural, and Environmental Sciences—he would say to the other colleges, if "the most entrenched part of the university" can do it, so can you. And he had.

The genesis of the relative calm in which restructuring was occurring in 1995 had been the campus dialogue begun in 1991 at Gee's "Ohio State can no longer be all things to all people" address to the University Senate. It was there he had announced his town meetings and open forums that built the consensus he continued to enjoy. As early as his Senate speech in October 1992, he had warned that, lacking "the courage and the will" to manage their own future, "it will be done for us." Meanwhile, down High Street at the State House, via the many editorial boards he visited, and through mailings six to ten times a year to Ohio's most influential citizens, a sophisticated information campaign was going on that would continue throughout his presidency.

The man with the bow tie, the ready smile, and such ease at a news interview sure could coin a quotable phrase. "Universities must be the architects, not the victims, of change" was one line that resonated well wherever he spoke. "I often feel like I am president of Noah's Ark, with two of everything"

# Chapter 23

appeared in the *Washington Post*, as did, "When looking down the barrel of a gun, the reality of change becomes much more focused."

Repeated many times by others, including other university presidents, was his allusion to a best-selling novel and blockbuster movie: his warning that American's universities could become "the academic equivalent of *Jurassic Park*." *USA Today* ran that one. To survive, universities would have to be "nimble" and "responsive," he said as he was demonstrating that Ohio State was perhaps the nimblest and most responsive of all.

And so by April 5, 1995, when Peter Magrath, president of the National Association of State Universities and Land-Grant Colleges, submitted his written review of Gordon Gee to the Ohio State trustees, the university had, in his words, "started and in some respects accomplished (though hardly completed) one of the most ambitious and well thought out academic and managerial restructurings in American higher education."

In doing the review, Magrath had interviewed trustees, the Dean's Council Steering Committee, the Faculty Council, the University Senate Steering Committee, student leaders, and a number of Columbus's most influential business leaders. The consensus had been that Gordon Gee had "done superbly in the six areas of presidential valuation," while "exhibiting the highest possible standards of personal and professional integrity."

(The six areas were: "Enhancing the university position as a preeminent land-grant university; communicating the university's needs and purposes to various constituencies; responding to the diversity of aspirations and interests inherent in a large public university; delegating responsibility to trusted associates and working within a system of shared governance; fostering an environment in which all who are part . . . can aspire to distinction, and recruiting students, scholars, and staff of distinction; and exhibiting the highest possible standards of personal and professional integrity.")

"He had provided courageous and excellent leadership . . . at a difficult time for American higher education and a university that is one of the largest and most complex in the United States." Most specifically, he had "immeasurably raised the external appreciation of Ohio State." Handed a handful of lemons, "Gordon Gee, backed by the Board of Trustees (something the governing boards do not always do!)," was making . . . "high quality lemonade . . . at OSU."

The challenge to the trustees, the report concluded, was twofold: to keep restructuring going—and "to keep Gordon Gee."

As Glastris had written, Gee was demonstrating "with the zeal of a convert" that downsizing could be the catalyst to increase quality. It could also be the catalyst to enhance a university's academic reputation. And, as Magrath had

# FIVE-YEAR EVALUATIONS

Move-in Day, autumn 1992.

noted in his report, as Ohio State's academic reputation was increasing, so was Gee's "personal profile . . . to perhaps one of the highest in the nation for a state and land-grant presidency."

In Ohio, that profile had become as recognizable as the Mona Lisa. To keep the university's communications office abreast of public perceptions about Ohio State, a survey of Ohio voters was conducted periodically by pollster and alumnus Thomas Sawyer. Included in the questions were ones to assess Gee's name recognition. After his first year, in 1991, 6 percent of Ohioans knew the name of the new president of Ohio State. By 1993, the figure was 21 percent, more than twice that of the Speaker of the House, Verne Riffe. A year later it was 31 percent.

By 1996, the last poll done, Sawyer said an "astounding" 39 percent of Ohio's voters gave an unprompted correct answer to the question, "Who is the president of Ohio State?" The same percentage could answer. "Who is Gordon Gee?"

And so could many of the committees searching to fill open university presidencies. Executive assistant Chip Elam would field telephone calls from executive headhunters fishing for presidents; communications director Baroway would speak to journalists fishing to corroborate rumors or published reports.

## Chapter 23

Over time, queries came in about his being wanted by Michigan, Utah, Michigan State, Johns Hopkins, the State University of New York System, the University of North Carolina System, Brigham Young, and the Kellogg Foundation. It even was rumored that the Museum of Modern Art in New York was interested in this consummate fund-raiser who had recently married an art historian.

The standard answer to the media, after a check with Gee, was that such a well-known academic leader could be expected to appear on any speculative list; that he was very happy doing what he was doing at Ohio State; and that he would not be a candidate, thank you very much. Though staff sometimes speculated that the best Southern private universities—Duke, Emory, Tulane, Vanderbilt—might snatch him because his new wife had been raised in the South, that Gee would *not* be a candidate continued to be the answer until Saturday, June 17, 1995.

That morning, the *San Francisco Chronicle* and *Oakland Tribune* both broke the story that E. Gordon Gee (and who in the world, Californians wondered, was he?) was that state's Board of Regents' choice to become the new president of its nine-campus university system—perhaps the most powerful job and biggest bully pulpit in American public higher education.

Acknowledging the *Tribune,* Columbus's *Dispatch* would note in its own story that, in their April job performance evaluation, "the trustees said their top priority is to make sure Gee stays at Ohio State." Gee is paid $168,500 annually, it said, and Jack Peltason, the incumbent in California, was paid $243,500. It also said the president was en route from Kuala Lumpur, Malaysia, to Manila, the Philippines, and "could not be reached last night."

Were the California papers correct? Baroway answered the *Dispatch,* as he did all such inquiries. "He has been such a visible academic leader during his time at Ohio State that he has been on just about everybody's short list." But this time Gee very much knew he was the choice and had decided to accept the offer. His plane was scheduled to land in California late Thursday night on his return trip. As far as California's regents knew, he would take the job at a news conference yet to be scheduled for the next day.

# 24

## Short Subjects

In the life of a university and its president, things happen that do not necessarily fit well into the structure of a coherent chapter. Many are important. Others are just plain interesting.

### 1991
#### Barbie

"Gee makes doubters eat words," read the *Dispatch* headline. Rarely indeed, if ever, had a standing ovation been given a speech in Ohio Stadium; this for 5300 June graduates and six times as many family and friends.

"What a waste. What a joke . . . bad choice . . . sham . . . scam . . . hogwash," the May 24 *Lantern* had editorialized about Gee as speaker. "The University of Michigan had President Bush . . . Could this be another lame PR stunt?" No, it was the result of General Colin Powell's late declination, Hungary President Arped Goncz's preference for another day, and a tranquil time in American history that made who speaks at commencement the major campus issue. Behind the scene of Gee's resounding speaking success, then and after, was a unique mind meld between the president and his chief speechwriter, Barbie Tootle.

In the language of the field, Tootle, a motivational speaker herself, "caught his voice" immediately. Both were voracious readers. Both enjoyed the sound of well-honed language. Both loved trivia and laughed at the same things. Tootle also was the member of the president's inner circle who, in the darkest days of his wife Elizabeth's illness and then passing, could best lift his spirits. "I

## Chapter 24

worked and work with a lot of good people," the president said years later. "But the chemistry between Barbie and me never can be replicated."

### The Russian Revolution

When Jim Scanlan and Gordon Gee visited Eastern European universities, because he was older and taller, people assumed Scanlan was president. The emeritus professor of philosophy chuckled over this in recalling their visit to Warsaw, Prague, Budapest, and Moscow. He would say, "I'm sorry. Let me introduce you to President Gee." Gee, who enjoyed the mix-ups, was in Europe to discuss cooperative agreements or sign official documents authorizing earlier ones.

Elizabeth was ill again and Gordon called home every day. Arranging for time to return to the hotel room and make the call was part of the scheduling Scanlan handled as he, his wife, Marilyn, and the president moved from place to place. When they reached Moscow and joined an alumni association boat trip up the Volga River, Elizabeth was also able to join them, as was daughter Rebekah. Though Elizabeth was dependent on medication that had to be refrigerated, she wanted to take this trip, and there were little coolers in each stateroom.

Mikhail Gorbachev had been president of the Soviet Union since 1985, but *glasnost* and *perestroika,* his programs of reform and restructuring, were in trouble. On a ship in the middle of Lake Ladega in northern Russia on August 19, 1991, a frantic social director announced to the Ohio State party that there had been a military takeover and Gorbachev had been deposed.

What they would find when they reached shore they didn't know. A country in upheaval? A revolution? Would the airport be closed? Would they be held hostage? The only clear radio transmission was British Broadcasting, which reported that Gorbachev was a prisoner. Nevertheless, Scanlan, a scholar of Russia, was calm. He was certain, he told everyone, no coup would succeed.

When they reached Leningrad, the Gees, Scanlans, and the alumni party were met not by a revolution, but by a Dixieland band playing "When the Saints Go Marching In." In Moscow, Boris Yeltsin, president of the Russian Republic, had denounced the coup attempt and called for a general strike. The next day there was a giant demonstration at the Russian Parliament and one in Leningrad. By August 21, the coup had failed and Gorbachev was restored as president. The day the Ohio State contingent returned to the United States, Gorbachev resigned as leader of the Communist Party and several republics declared independence, including Yeltsin's Russia.

SHORT SUBJECTS

The Soviet Union collapsed on December 26, 1991, and Boris Yeltsin simply continued on as president of Russia. Since December 17, the day of his wife's death, Gordon Gee also had continued on.

## Extension What?

Excepting Ohio gubernatorial candidates in whistle-stop days, until Gordon Gee came along, Keith Smith may have been the only person ever to make it his business to visit all eighty-eight Ohio counties. Smith was an Ohio state employee, director of a huge Ohio state operation, but you wouldn't know it by the signs on the windows and doors of his eighty-eight offices. They read only "Ohio Cooperative Extension," and, on the new president's first major trip into the state, he threw a mock fit at the first such sign he saw.

"All these places are Ohio State. And who knows it? We need to change the name." What Gee had learned from Smith was that, long before, two extensions had been authorized by university bylaw: "Ohio Cooperative Extension," just for agriculture, and, so as not to confuse, an "Ohio State Extension" for outreach in general. Not quick as a wink, but within months and not years, the Ohio Cooperative Extension became the Ohio *State* Extension—and all the signs were changed.

Not long after, the college that would be renamed Food, Agricultural, and Environmental Sciences teamed with the Kellogg Foundation in "Project Reinvent," broadening institutional outreach further as a prototype for American land-grant universities. By the end of the Gee era, there was talk of an institutional vice presidency in "outreach," which, early in the next administration was formalized when Bobby Moser, vice president for Agricultural Administration, also became vice president for "university outreach."

## *1992*
## Chief Legal Counsel

By statute, since 1953, the attorney general of the state of Ohio was also Ohio State's chief legal adviser, with Ohio State having no chief counsel of its own. But in 1953, affirmative action was hardly a concept and there were no laws governing hazardous waste, no Age Discrimination Employment Act, and no Americans with Disabilities Act.

In 1991, with Ohio State dealing with an alphabet of legal issues from "accreditation" to "zoning," Gee brought in a team of legal consultants chaired by

# Chapter 24

lawyer Ira Michael Heyman, the retired president of Cal-Berkeley. It recommended that Ohio change its law or arrange de facto authority with Attorney General Lee Fisher. In time, Gee and Fisher announced that one of the state's most distinguished jurists would become the university's first chief legal officer.

Robert M. Duncan, a former Justice of the Supreme Court of Ohio, of the U.S. Court of Appeals, and the United States District Court—had just retired from private practice and was not one to be idle. In 1995, Virginia "Ginny" Trethewey replaced Duncan, who retained his other roles as secretary to the trustees and counselor to the president. In 1991, Trethewey had left the prestigious Vorys law firm to raise her youngest son, John McCorkle. John now was in prekindergarten, and, she said, was "ready to resume my professional career."

## Ernie

While, as much as anyone in the United States, he had taught institutions about wheelchair access and opportunities for the disabled, victims of the ubiquitous computer knew physiatrist Ernest Johnson best for his diagnoses of carpel tunnel syndrome. Then, in 1991, he was named the Henry Betts Laureate; he was the first M.D. honored with the premier award in the field of rehabilitation.

In his 1998 *The Ohio State University College of Medicine,* George Paulson cited Ernie Johnson as the pioneer in creating adaptive living homes for tetraplegics and the man who made Ohio State the most wheelchair-friendly campus in the nation. In 1994, a new park by Dodd Hall was named in his honor, another recognition, wrote Gordon Gee, of Ernie Johnson's "extraordinary life of service to Ohio State."

## *1992*
### Mass Transit

It seemed like a neat idea. To cut traffic congestion and ease just getting around, Ohio State might link the main, west, and Medical Center campuses by "people mover." Early in the year, a feasibility study was done for a system like the monorail in Walt Disney World or the dual rail loop in downtown Detroit.

The answer came back that this would be feasible but expensive. A line from the West Campus parking lots, with stops on main campus and a spur to the hospitals, would cost $118 million to build and $5 million a year to run. Someday there might be federal, state, or local support, but not today. No government money would be forthcoming. Customer revenue could not cover the cost. The study was shelved.

In the mid-1990s, though first cut back in a controversial cost-saving measure, the campus bus system expanded. In 1997, the Columbus public transportation system, COTA, offered Ohio State students unlimited access from anywhere on its lines for a $9 per quarter fee, subsequently approved by student referendum. COTA also added campus routes to and from German Village, the Brewery District, and the new Bethel-Sawmill and Lennox Town Center shopping and entertainment areas.

## Barnebey

The Barnebey Center was a 1,200-acre outdoor learning laboratory in Fairfield and Hocking Counties owned by the university and managed by the School of Natural Resources. As budgets tightened, when President Gee hinted at selling university property, the airport and golf courses got the most public attention, not land 12 miles south of Lancaster. In September, the trustees authorized selling the entire center for $1.2 million to the Columbus and Franklin County Metropolitan Park District, which, as it turned out, could afford only a third of it. Chunk by chunk Barnebey was sold off, often with mineral and timber rights, to private owners, until the last 345 acres was bought by the Metro Parks in 1996. The money remained with the university natural resources program, creating endowment funds for scholarships.

## *1993*
## No Smoking

An outcry to President Gee went as follows: "Their utterly ridiculous initial recommendation that smoking be prohibited outdoors as well as indoors is an indication of the committee's complete lack of sensitivity to smokers' rights. They view all of us as enemies . . . who deserve no rights."

Initially, faculty and staff could smoke in private offices. However, with Environmental Protection Agency data showing how air flow reached nonsmokers' offices, a review committee chaired by Hospital and Health Services Administration Chair Stephen Loebs ended that. "The freedom of individuals to work in a smoke-free environment," Loebs wrote Gee, superseded anyone's freedom to smoke in individual offices or public places . . . "regardless of time of day or day of week."

Every Ohio State building became smoke-free, and, throughout campus, nicotine-craving employees took their breaks outside, weather be damned. Pedestal ashtrays were erected near all buildings, which smokers now huddled around on even the coldest days and wondered why the world had turned against them.

In Ohio Stadium, smokers no longer could grab a smoke beneath the stands. If they were to light up at halftime outside the gates, the next play they would see in person would be at the next home game. No one, Senior Associate Athletic Director Paul Krebs wrote to a disgruntled smoker-alumnus, would be allowed back in. Krebs's issue was crowd control, not smoking. But the result was the same. If you must smoke, be ready to be a couch potato. No one knows how many fans were cured of their addictions when forced to make the choice.

The issue *had* been smoking for Dr. William Havener, Ohio State's celebrated chair of Ophthalmology, who had retired at sixty-five in 1988 and continued to lecture. A man of strong opinions on many things, Havener had campaigned hard that the entire campus might become smoke free and had lived to see University Hospitals become a smoke-free environment. In a classic tragic irony, however, the doctor himself developed cancer. As George Paulson wrote about Havener in his history of the medical college, giving his last lecture only ten days before his death in 1991 and moving many in the audience to tears, Havener made a final public plea that the entire campus eliminate cigarettes. It did just that on February 4, 1993—including the machines that sold them.

## Community Shares

In the game of Monopoly, it was known as the "Community Chest," a name that remains in some communities. But in most places, charity used to be raised through the "United Fund," which then became "United Way." In 1993 in Columbus, along came "Community Shares," wanting in on the university's payroll deduction program. A new national fund, Community Shares included such local organizations as the Open Housing Coalition, Ohio Coalition for the Homeless, Stonewall Community Agency, and Ohio Coalition on Sexual Assault.

President Gee created a committee, which found not only that many employees wanted to donate to Community Shares, but that many commuters wanted to help their hometown agencies and others to help the United Negro College Fund. In 1997, Ohio State expanded what it now termed its "Community Charitable Drive" to include three United Ways (Franklin, Delaware, and Fairfield counties), Community Shares, the College Fund/United Negro College Fund, and the Black United Fund of Central Ohio.

## Cost Savings

Through the years of state budget cuts, employees were encouraged to find ways to save or earn the university money. One of the most significant came from a suggestion by Catherine Bianco in the Payroll Department, who uncovered a provision in the Ohio pension rules that allowed the university to pay the state quarterly. The university was paying monthly. In the first year alone, the simple change earned Ohio State $500,000 in interest!

## The Wexner, Inside and Out

In June, 50 tons of recycled broken safety glass formed into swirls and mounds by artist-in-residence Maya Linn, creator of the Vietnam War Veterans Memorial, became the first permanent outdoor sculpture at the Wexner Center for the Arts. Later, too much outdoors began to enter indoors, and repairs were made to guarantee the controlled-environment exhibits such as the one the 1995 $100-million Roy Lichtenstein retrospective demanded.

Eventually, the university would announce a $10 million overhaul of ventilation, heating, and lighting for the building, whose bold "deconstructionist" design had been bringing Ohio State and architect Peter Eisenman worldwide accolades since 1989.

## The Electronic Bookshelf

Before historian Martha Garland moved into the provost's office, she and department chair Michael Hogan developed the idea: an on-demand database for their American history courses. Ohio State faculty would produce modules on major topics, each to include original documents, essays by prominent historians, a reading list, and questions to guide the students. The market was national. Teachers anywhere could create their own courses and order printed texts for their classes.

In September, Gin Press announced *The Ohio State University American*

CHAPTER 24

Vietnam War Memorial creator Maya Lin and her "Groundswell," 1993.

*History Bookshelf.* It was, Gin said, "the first time a major U.S. university had sponsored a personalized on-demand electronic data base." In a memo to President Gee, Hogan noted that the faculty not only had contributed their energy and talent to this project, but were surrendering their copyright. All royalties were to return to the department to "further advance . . . great teaching and research."

## Taking a Daughter to Work

Sometimes research data only verify what people already know; sometimes they stimulate action. Here data verified that adolescent girls indeed did receive less attention in school than boys did and indeed did have lower career expectations.

One response to this was made by the Ms. Foundation for Women, which in 1993 started "Take a Daughter to Work Day." It was embraced by Ohio State. By 1996, Ohio State's day included fifty workshops and was being run by the Women's Place. The Women's Place was a new office in Academic Affairs. "Empowered by our differences and our unified voices," its promotional flyer said, "we celebrate women's creativity, strengths, and achievements; promote equity, justice, and dignity; and aim to improve the lives of current and future generations."

## Advanced Practice Nursing

With the United States long on specialists and short on primary-care physicians, advanced practice nursing (nurse practitioners, clinical nurse specialists, and nurse midwives) had become a critical medical resource. The first nurse practitioner program, Dean Carole Anderson reminded her president, was started at Gee's own University of Colorado when she was on its faculty. Not only was there no such program at Ohio State, there were none in any Ohio public university. Her plans this summer, she wrote, included thinking through the resources needed "to move in that direction."

Before the end of the decade, "that direction" included Ohio State master's degrees for practitioners in neonatal, pediatric, family, and school nursing, as well as nurse midwifery, and post-master's programs for certification in advanced practice. And all core courses were available on line. In a few years, proven administrator and professor of psychiatry Carole Anderson would be named vice provost for academic administration under Provost Ed Ray, successor to Provost Richard Sisson in the presidency of William "Brit" Kirwan.

## *1994*
## Regional Trustees

To signify their degrees were the same coin of the realm as those from main campus, Gordon Gee liked to call "regional" campuses "extended," but the appellation rarely stuck. Whether "regional" or "extended," Mansfield, Marion, Newark, and Lima had never had their own trustees—advisory councils, yes, primarily for fund-raising and lobbying, but never a group with clout. That changed in 1994 when the university trustees approved regional boards. Each board was authorized to advise its dean in administering each campus, to participate in strategic planning, and to review operating and capital budgets. On each board were nine local residents, one student, and, for oversight and experience, one Columbus trustee. The first set of appointments was split into three-, two-, and one-year terms. After that, all appointments would be three years.

The first group named was at Newark. It included J. Gilbert "Gib" Reese, major donor and spirited supporter of the campus since its inception, and son

# Chapter 24

Trustee Chair Debbie Casto offers a giant frog to a good sport on his fiftieth birthday, Groundhog Day, 1994. Castro had been marketing director at the Columbus Zoo.

of Ohio State's consummate fund-raiser Everett Reese; and Eugene "Gene" Branstool, former Ohio senator and an assistant secretary of agriculture under President Clinton. Howard LeFevre, another early supporter and major philanthropist, was named Newark's first emeritus trustee.

## Teflon

In 1938, Roy Plunkett was but two years beyond his Ohio State Ph.D. in chemistry when he discovered a resin that wouldn't stick to anything. Three years later, he patented Teflon. In May 1994, the Buckeye who revolutionized cooking and added a descriptor to the English language passed away at eighty-three. Just like Ronald Reagan, Gordon Gee was often termed a "Teflon" president. He so disarmed his critics that nothing seemed to stick.

## Thurber

James Thurber finally earned his Ohio State degree in 1995, a posthumous award as Doctor of Humane Letters. Valuing honorary degrees as tributes to both the honorees and the institution, Gordon Gee had urged his vice presidents and deans to give the process their attention. Recommendations were brought to or by the University Senate and then were considered by its voting members. As the Thurber dossier, Senate Secretary Gerald Reagan distributed "A Not Completely Brief Biographical Sketch... Mostly in His Own Words."

"James Thurber was born in Columbus, Ohio," it began, "where so many awful things happened to him, on December 8, 1894. He was unable to keep anything on his stomach until he was seven years old but grew to be six feet one and 1/4 inches tall and to weigh 154 fully dressed for winter." Thurber was "born in the blowy uplands," the dossier further explained, "... in a district known as 'the Flats' which, for half of the year, was partially underwater and during the rest of the time was an outcropping of live granite, rising in dry weather to a height of 200 ft. This condition led to moroseness, skepticism, [and] jumping when shots were fired ... and, finally, a system of floating pulley-baskets by means of which the Thurber family was raised up to lower down from the second floor of the old family homestead."

James Thurber dropped out of Ohio State in 1918 to fight in World War I, but was rejected because of poor eyesight. Shortly before his death in 1985, he played himself in the Broadway revue of his work *The Thurber Carnival*. Today, the world's richest repository of Thurber manuscripts, drawings, and letters is the Ohio State Libraries.

## Lichtenstein

Ric Wanetik, president of the Wexner Foundation and Gee's dollar-a-year "cultural adviser," wore a polka-dot bow tie to honor the return to campus of alumnus Roy Lichtenstein, the artist who elevated printing's Benday dots to a fine art. Lichtenstein was here for a major retrospective of his work and the dedication of the Hoyt L. Sherman Studio Art Center. He had enrolled at Ohio State in the early 1940s and, after serving three years in World War II, finished both bachelor's and master's degrees here and instructed in the Fine Arts department.

However, as one professor warned President Gee by mail, "Roy was denied tenure at OSU and left the university with some bitterness." Gee wrote back that not only had he and Lichtenstein discussed that at length, they had reflected on what students might have gained and the world might have missed if things had been different. They and Arts Dean Don Harris also had discussed a mighty large gift for a practicing artist. That gift, from Lichtenstein and his wife, Dorothy, was $200,000 in honor of the late professor Sherman, who had taught the painter's first drawing class and remained an influence throughout his career.

## Chapter 24

President Bill Clinton, Rebekah, Gordon, and Constance at the Roy Lichtenstein retrospective, 1995.

While the university had healed whatever wounds there might have been with an honorary Doctor of Fine Arts Degree in 1988, even before that the artist had donated a series of signed and numbered lithographs as gifts for major donors in the first capital campaign. And now the artist was honoring his university and his mentor, Hoyt Sherman. At a dinner at the Wexners' Abigail House, with his usual glass of something other than wine, Gee toasted the artist's "innovative intellect, generous heart, and creative spirit."

Roy Lichtenstein lived only two more years, passing away on September 29, 1997, at the age of seventy-three. Ironically, in Washington that evening, President Bill Clinton was hosting a dinner for patrons and leaders of the humanities and arts. It was the President himself, reported the *Straits Times Press Limited* (October 1, 1997), who announced to the gathering that Roy Lichtenstein, "treasured by us in the White House," was dead.

### Gender Neutrality

When the report of the president's Commission on Women recommended that policies and publications, institutional to departmental, be gender-neutral, the president e-mailed copies of the Association of American Colleges'

# SHORT SUBJECTS

*Guide to Non-Sexist Language* to all vice presidents and deans. The bottom line, the guide said, was two questions: Would you say the same thing about a person of the opposite sex? Would you like it said about you?

In the section recommending "titles that do not stereotype women" one of the words eliminated was the historical college "coed." All students were just "students." "Waitperson" or "waiter" replaced "waitress," "homemaker" replaced "housewife," "unwed mothers" were now "mothers," married or otherwise, and "Lady Luck" lost "lady."

On the male side, "sportsmanship" became "fair play," "Dear sir" disappeared, "male chauvinists" simply were "chauvinists," and "draftsmen," "policemen," and "weathermen" were "drafters," "police officers," and "meteorologists."

The section "repeat a noun or use a synonym" gave this gender-free example: "The professor who gets published frequently will have a better chance when faculty tenure is granted." Gee's cover memo said nothing about reappointment for the dean or vice president who did not use gender-neutral language.

# 25

## *The Dave and Andy Show*

On May 26, 1994—less than thirty days after Elwood Gordon Gee had named Ferdinand "Andy" Geiger Ohio State's seventh athletic director—a cartoon in Columbus's *Other Paper* had a puckish Gee, wearing number 1, dribbling a basketball through the legs of a confounded Mayor Greg Lashutka. The ball read "State Arena Money," referring to $15 million placed in the Capital Improvements Bill by House Speaker Verne Riffe for a campus arena the mayor wanted downtown.

If the *Other Paper* had known about the full court press Gee had used to land Geiger, there might have been a second cartoon. Acknowledged publicly for his aggressiveness in pursuit of his goals—the arena being the latest—he was just as dogged about recruiting his new administration. Janet Pichette (now Ashe) had been one of the first candidates to succumb. Hired as vice president for Business and Administration in February 1992, she had not wanted the job. A certified public accountant with corporate management experience, she was in charge of all business operations for Eastern Michigan University and had interviewed for Ohio State's vice presidency in finance—the university's chief budget officer.

Gee, however, expected the finance search committee to recommend Acting Vice President Bill Shkurti, as it did, and saw Pichette as his fit for the business opening. She was not interested, she had told Gee, in a job that supervised all construction projects and employed 2200 staff, including the university police force and the traffic and parking office. She had two young daughters to prepare for school and wanted to be able to get "some sleep in the middle of the night." She returned to Ypsilanti.

Gee then called her every day for three weeks, often in the evenings, urging her to at least interview with the search committee. To daughter Lindsay, the voice on the phone was "that man from Ohio again." To Lindsay's mother, however, the persistence of that man from Ohio was becoming compelling, and his enthusiasm, catching. She would agree to interview again, accept the offer, and team with Andy Geiger on all athletics construction projects, including the Schottenstein Center, Bill Davis Baseball Stadium, and the renovation of Ohio Stadium.

## *Landing Geiger*

At the time he was sought as a candidate for Ohio State's athletic directorship some two years later, Andy Geiger had been happy and challenged in his three years at the University of Maryland. When called by Chip Elam from Gee's office, he had half-heartedly agreed to fly into Chicago for a search committee interview. Then he changed his mind and withdrew. "I remember it was a Sunday—and the interviews were to be at the O'Hare Hilton [that day]. I was at home in Silver Springs and the phone rang and my wife came into the living room and said, 'There's a Gordon Gee on the phone.'"

Not at all ready to give up on the man he had been told was "the best athletic director in America," Gee had obtained permission from Maryland President William E. 'Brit' Kirwan—who later would become Ohio State's next president—to speak to Geiger. Geiger, his wife, and two children were preparing for a vacation at Disney World. Yes, on the return trip, Geiger would be willing to "at least come and look." He also would talk to the search committee and sit down with Gee for ninety minutes.

What Geiger would find in Gee, he said later, was "a kindred soul." A man "determined to honor the law from the Higher Education Act of 1972 by incrementally building women's athletics, not by dismantling the men's program." Who "encouraged and nurtured entrepreneurial thinking." Who "understood the power of athletics to get people's attention on behalf of the university." And who "dearly liked victory."

Geiger would think seriously about an offer, should one come. In fact, Geiger was hooked. Two weeks later, in a telephone call from the president's home, with Vice President Williams listening and communications head Baroway there to prepare the press release—Gee would make the offer and Geiger would accept.

"The press conference was the day before the spring football game. Gordon and I and Eleanor toured (it), met a lot of people, and in another two weeks (April 29), I was here."

## *And Williams*

David Williams laughed when he answered how he came from the Ohio State law school to first be named Gee's interim vice provost for Minority Affairs and, later, Andy Geiger's boss. He was a teacher, not an administrator. He had taught at Central High in his native Detroit for ten years. Though he had left the system to get both MBA and law degrees and had tried tax consultancy (Coopers and Lybrand), he was teaching again (the University of Detroit Law School) when Ohio State hired him onto its law faculty in 1986. Gee appointed him to the university's athletic council—the faculty body that sets athletic policy—and was impressed with what he heard.

From Robert Duncan, the former federal judge who was now the university's legal counsel, Gee also knew that Williams had become the College of Law's unofficial advocate for students and, in particular, for minority students. This associate professor who had just received tenure, Gee decided, would fit well in his administration.

"I didn't want to be vice provost. I said I have to think about this. I'm headed off to England [to direct a summer abroad program] and I'm not sure I want to do that." Gee's response was to call Williams every day in England. "He would either talk to me or call and ask 'Could you call me back.'" Which Williams would do.

"On the fourth or fifth day, he finally wore me down. I told him 'I'll help you out for one year and then I'm going back to the faculty.' That was 1992." In July 1993, Williams would succeed Russell Spillman as vice president for Student Affairs, overseeing the offices of Counseling and Consultation Services, Disability Services, Student Life, Student Affairs, Recreation and Intramural Sports, the residences and dining halls, the Ohio and Drake unions—and the Department of Athletics.

To signal the integration of the athletic department into the mainstream of student life, Gee would include in Geiger's title an assistant vice presidency under Williams. In 1997, when Gee moved to Brown, neither Williams nor Geiger would move with him. But in 2000, when Gee moved to Vanderbilt as its president, he would hire David Williams away from Ohio State. In the meantime, the administration of David Williams, Andy Geiger, and, sometimes, Janet Ashe had changed the face of Ohio State athletics.

# THE DAVE AND ANDY SHOW

Gordon, Andy, David.

## *An Athletic Inheritance*

"A situation rife with problems" was how the *Baltimore Sun* (June 12) defined the program Andy Geiger took over in 1994. Under NCAA investigation for more than a year, the department he inherited, the *Sun* wrote, "was about to hear its fate." The football team, though it had lost only one game the previous year, "had lost the wrong one." Again. "Ohio State athletes' names on police blotters seem to have reached epidemic proportions." And the university and the city were "trying" but had thus far failed "to reach a compromise on a domed arena that would serve both."

"At the time I came here," Geiger recalled later, "Gordon was having the arena discussions, and the decision had been made that Ohio State was going to go its own way. Gordon said, 'Build me the best arena in America.' So we set about doing that. Ohio State had been trying for years to get a new baseball stadium built and the project was stalled. The baseball community was very upset, so I determined we needed to jumpstart that. And when I toured Ohio Stadium for the spring game I realized that, as wonderful as it is and as revered as it is, it was old." How old and how much in need of work, he would discover in a few months.

## Chapter 25

But these were only the capital projects. The new AD had not experienced the recoil from a four-loss football season. He did not yet know that John Cooper was losing some fine coaches every year to lateral positions, sometimes at lesser programs, because Ohio State salaries were not competitive. He had not yet reviewed his thirty-two head coaches, either for quality of their work or parity between men's and women's paychecks. Football star Joey Galloway had not yet been suspended for taking $200 from an agent. Geiger had inherited a "show me" attitude from many strong supporters of the popular Archie Griffin for his job. And NCAA sanctions would not be announced until June 23.

## *And Legacy*

"Andy Geiger without Gordon Gee? It's like the Sundance Kid without Butch Cassidy, Dean Martin without Jerry Lewis, Jim Messina without Kenny Loggins." Acknowledging that he was getting "a little verklempt over all this," on the eve of Gee's announcement to depart for Brown (July 3, 1997), Martin Rosenman of the *Other Paper* continued, "The two were just such a pair. They made things happen at Ohio State, didn't they? They stepped up to the plate, didn't they? They just did it, didn't they? . . . We've got an elite football program again and there's hope on the hardcourt for both men's and women's basketball."

They "had pulled the trigger on more than a few coaching changes" and raised salaries both to be strong in the marketplace of elite programs and to build parity between men and women coaches. They had added men's lacrosse and soccer and women's lacrosse, soccer, and crew to the scholarship programs. They had straightened out the compliance program and vastly increased academic counseling. William C. (Bill) Davis Stadium, one of the finest venues in intercollegiate baseball, had been built.

The football team, ranked number 1 in the polls as the 1997 season began, by 2002 would be playing in a restored and enlarged Ohio Stadium for which $120 million in tax-exempt revenue notes had been authorized. And the Schottenstein Center, which "would revive the fading soul of our white collar town," was "going up like a 20,000-seat stack of pancakes. . . ." That the Schottenstein Center, with an interior Value City Arena, was actually under construction and at a site selected by the university was the end of an epic that, in a sense, had begun on Gee's first day in office.

Schottenstein Center interior, under construction.

## *The Arena Wars*

Way back in September 1990, Ohio Speaker of the House Verne Riffe was in University Hospitals recovering from sinus surgery. Gee's staff counselor and lobbyist Herb Asher had called this to Gee's attention. Before "I could even get out the words, 'Do you think you might have time to go over,'" they were on their way. They had a wonderful conversation, and it was not long before Gee and the Speaker were good friends. It was Riffe who, with the support of Governor Voinovich and Senate President Stanley Aronoff, eventually would set the Ohio State arena process in motion by placing $15 million in the 1994 capital budget.

"There is no doubt about it," Riffe told the *Dispatch* (March 5, 1994), "I favor Ohio State having an arena because (St. John) arena is 40 years old."

One arena or two? Downtown or on campus? A university and city that worked together or were at odds? Asher had warned Gee there was an issue in an advisory memo back in November 1991, immediately following Greg Lashutka's election as Columbus's mayor and after Randy Ayers's teams had reached two consecutive NCAA tournaments. He had suggested to Gee then that "the new multipurpose arena will rise to the top of the agenda." The issue,

# Chapter 25

he told Gee, affected the university because many of Columbus's most powerful leaders believed a new arena would be viable only if the Ohio State men's basketball team played there.

There had been a number of earlier efforts to build an arena in Columbus, he continued, but they were unsuccessful, once because voters defeated the ballot issue. "I suspect that many community leaders believe now is the time to raise the issue again. . . . You are the one likely to be caught in the crossfires. With a state capital budget upcoming, I think we need to be prepared."

Gee, in fact, would be "caught in the crossfires," and the ensuing conflict would become perhaps his most uncomfortable public experience as president of Ohio State. To fund the high-quality new arena he wanted—one large enough and plush enough to attract NCAA regional tournaments—he would need the income from corporate skyboxes. He would even cochair a tax levy initiative for a downtown arena—with the understanding, he believed, that, win or lose, his skyboxes could be built.

Meanwhile, as Asher had suggested he do, Gee had begun talking to Riffe about a capital commitment to an Ohio State arena as early as 1992. Both Gee and Riffe knew they would have to wait for the Ohio economy to improve. An Ohio State faculty whose state general fund budget was being savaged of $80 million never would stand for a gift horse of $15 million to build a playground for tall people.

At about the same time Gee and Riffe first talked arena money, the late *Dispatch* sportswriter Mike Sullivan wrote a column (January 29, 1992) that, if attended to by others, could have saved a lot of people a lot of grief. The city wanted a downtown basketball arena, he pointed out, to raise "the stock of Columbus as a site for the next NBA franchise. . . ." Were that to happen, he wrote, NBA and Big Ten schedules would conflict. "Starting with the theory that NBA and college basketball don't mix, at least in the same building," Sullivan reminded his readers that "a major university's obligations [are] to its student body and the parents who pay the tuition."

"Ohio State is the big dog. And there are times when the big dog has to sit exactly where it has to sit. This is one of those times."

In the long run, the space/time conflict would turn out to be about hockey, not basketball, for Ohio State wisely would add ice to its arena and Columbus would attract the National Hockey League Blue Jackets to its own downtown Nationwide Arena. But it would be another two and a half years before those who could make the decision came to the same conclusions Sullivan did in 1992.

That Ohio State was planning an arena of its own to supplant the 13,276-

seat St. John surfaced again when *Dispatch* sports editor George Strode sat down for an interview with Gee (December 19, 1993) after John Cooper's 9-0-1 football team had been thrashed at Michigan, 28–0. Besides supporting his coach, Gee mentioned a "master plan for athletic facilities" that would include a "new arena-ice complex" that "should be on campus." Two and a half months later, Mayor Lashutka, in a speech to the Columbus Rotary, hammered the need for a civic arena as the keystone of a vital center city.

Former mayoral executive assistant Ronald Rotaru, then in state government, would advise Lashutka that Gee was in the State House talking arena money with Riffe. The city's capital budget request to the state already was loaded with major items, including $32 million to expand and relocate the Columbus Museum of Science and Industry to the Scioto Peninsula, $5.1 million to restore the Southern Theatre, and $8.5 million on Ohio State's campus for the Edison Welding Institute. Lashutka would request only $1 million to help plan a 20,000–25,000-seat Columbus civic center.

Gee, on the other hand, had met with Riffe again that spring. The economy had turned by 1994 and Ohio State would get its $15 million. But not before the city would make enough noise to generate House Bill 790, which would withhold the $15 million unless the city and university reached an agreement by October 15 on a site and a "unified plan of operation."

Enter as negotiators two highly respected local citizens. In this corner, for Gee, developer and Ohio State trustee George Skestos. In the other, for Lashutka, developer Ron Pizzuti. Both were invested in the betterment of downtown, in bringing new sports and cultural opportunities to metropolitan Columbus, and preserving a town–gown alliance. Each had a team of advisers and each wanted a "win, win" scenario. Meanwhile, major league soccer had awarded Columbus a franchise and Gee had authorized its short-term use of Ohio Stadium.

Setting aside the scheduling riddle that college and pro teams would face, Ohio State put on the table a complex joint venture close to downtown and within walking distance of the campus: an arena and soccer stadium in part of the blighted area in the vicinity of High Street and 5th Avenue east toward the Fairgrounds. An independent organization, with university and city representation, could own the arena and the stadium. State and federal funds could be found to level properties, relocate residents, and perhaps even connect I-71 and State Rt. 315. Parking would be in the Fairgrounds lots. Skestos, who had been a major contributor to Lashutka in the mayoral race, met personally with him. The answer was no. It was too complex and it was not downtown. "That," Skestos said later, "was the end of the discussion."

## Chapter 25

Two months later—and a month before the state's deadline—the president and the mayor held a joint press conference to announce the conclusions of the Skestos–Pizzuti discussions. Not only would scheduling conflicts preclude a joint facility, but so did regulations of the Big Ten. Federal tax laws also restricted the use of a university-owned facility by private profit-making entities, such as professional basketball or hockey tenants. The university and the city would shake hands and go their own ways.

But, in a letter signed by Pizzuti and Skestos, two major constraints were placed on Ohio State that day. "The use of the OSU arena will complement, not compete with, a civic arena," and "sky-boxes, club seating or other amenities affiliated with professional sports arenas will not be part of the OSU arena."

Could the university fund a new arena without the income from seat licenses and luxury boxes? State Representative Patrick Sweeney of Cleveland, a member of the State Controlling Board and chair of the House Finance Committee, thought not. Having monitored funding plans for arenas in Dayton and Cleveland, when the controlling board released its first $5 million he told Skestos and the press that Ohio State would "make an enormous mistake if you don't include loges." Skestos said he would take it back to the trustees, and Pizzuti would send him a letter that day that began, "We were all surprised when we read the article in this morning's *Columbus Dispatch:* 'Skyboxes Pushed for OSU Arena.'"

Had Ohio State known in advance that Sweeney would raise the issue? "You're assuming too much," Sweeney told the *Other Paper* (June 8, 1994). "They're not that smart."

In 1998, after Gee had left for Brown, the Value City Arena at the Jerome Schottenstein Center would open. The naming gift of $12.5 million had been donated by the Schottenstein Family and the Value City and Schottenstein stores. They and Verne Riffe had made possible the largest arena in the Big Ten, which now contained an exclusive donor area, the Huntington Club, and had more luxury suites than any other university arena.

The building had claimed one victim, Marvin Kuhn of Columbus, killed in a freak accident when, on July 21, 1997, a crane toppled upon his car from the construction site. In a sense, some said it also had claimed Gordon Gee's presidency—or at least contributed to his decision to leave for Brown.

For in February 1997, Gee had agreed to cochair a campaign for a three-year, 0.5 percent sales tax to pay for a downtown arena and a 30,000-seat soccer stadium. Convinced from the start that Columbus could support two arenas, he saw no conflict in the role. Advertising executive David Milenthal, who ran the promotional part of the campaign, recalls that Gee "did everything he was asked to do." On Sunday, March 16, Gee placed an op-ed piece in the *Dispatch* that argued enthusiastically for a "downtown entertainment district" anchored by "the proposed downtown arena and stadium project." And he was on television, in the first campaign commercial, touting both the need and the tax.

He was convinced by this time, however, that the agreement not to build skyboxes at his own arena had been a mistake. And he had told his closest confidants that, win or lose, a behind-the-scenes agreement now allowed him to announce them once the campaign was over. Though little noticed, the same day that Gee's op-ed ran, in a related story John Christie, chair of the Franklin County Convention Facilities Authority, said that "if the Downtown arena went down, sure, they can go out and aggressively market sky boxes."

And on May 6 the tax proposal did, in fact, go down, by a 56 percent majority. That a civic arena could be built privately was one argument that swung voters against the tax. That tax money might better be used for schools was another. That there was no need for a soccer stadium was a third.

However, three days earlier, the *Dispatch* had carried a letter from Constance Bumgarner Gee. It began, "This letter refers to the Columbus City Council's announcement that up to $12.1 million will be spent to improve Columbus neighborhoods if voters approve a countywide sales tax to help pay for a Downtown stadium and arena. Perhaps I am interpreting this proposal incorrectly; however, I cannot help but think it sounds very much like a bribe." The $12.1 million could have been voted upon independently, she said, and suggested that the "dangling" of "carrots in front of citizens to garner votes" was "unworthy of our esteemed and well-meaning City Council."

Anyone who knew Gordon and Constance Gee would know the letter was hers alone and that, although he would have preferred she not send it, he respected her right to exercise her opinion. However, there were those who thought he should have stopped her or stopped it from running, and others were certain the president had put her up to it. When on the day following the loss of the tax issue, Gee announced Ohio State would now "consider" luxury suites in the Schottenstein Center, they were sure of it.

A week later, a $5 million donation to build the Huntington Club in the Schottenstein Center was announced by Gee and Huntington President Frank Wobst. It would be open, the *Dispatch* said, "to occupants of the suites and others in the more than 4,500 seats for which seat licenses had been purchased." Over $35 million more would be raised privately, primarily through seat licenses and the fifty-two suites.

# Chapter 25

Soon, Dimon R. McFerson, chairman and CEO of Nationwide Insurance, would announce (*Dispatch*, September 9) construction of the Nationwide Arena. Eight months later John H. McConnell, founder of Worthington Industries, and John F. Wolfe of the *Dispatch* and Wolfe Enterprises would win a civil trial against billionaire Lamar Hunt, who claimed partial ownership of the new National Hockey League team to be based in the new arena. The expansion franchise would be named the Columbus Blue Jackets.

By that time, the Gees were in Providence, and there were those who were certain that the astringency of the arena wars had tipped the scales toward their move to Rhode Island. Gee later would discredit that speculation adamantly. Yes, he said, he had grown weary of battling for his budget dollars in a state that continued to place higher education at the bottom of its priorities. But the arena wars? Forget it. Water off a duck's back.

## *The Schott*

Gordon Gee thought big, bigger, and biggest, but would be practical when he had to. When Andy Geiger explained to his president that a right-sized new arena for Ohio State should have fewer than 20,000 seats, that every extra row would be both cost-prohibitive and include bad seats, Geiger recalls that Gee "was crushed. He wanted 25,000. I mean he wanted 125,000 seats for the [to be renovated] stadium. . . . He died hard on that one."

Gordon Gee also thought optimistically and with his heart. Although Syracuse University's Carrier Dome had pioneered corporate identification of university athletic facilities, no other Big Ten arenas yet bore company identities. Some of the faculty, he knew, would self-destruct at the thought of a "Value City Arena," and some of the sports media also would give the university grief. But the Schottenstein family had stepped up when other corporations, as Geiger remembers it, "had pretty well hustled us out the door."

When Geiger told Gee he had a commitment for a $12.5 million naming gift from the family of the late Jerome Schottenstein, Gee was ecstatic. Then Geiger said he had "other news." The news was "Value City." Gee thought for a moment when he heard it. "That's a great family," he told Geiger. "They've done wonderful things for the university. We'll work it out." And they did.

An inside-outside naming plan was fostered by Gee while, says Geiger, the Schottenstein-run Value City Stores did a "complete change in image" consistent with their expectations for the arena. "They changed their advertising style. They changed their logo. They changed their colors." The building would be named the Jerome Schottenstein Center, in honor of the late community leader, philanthropist, and founder of the Schottenstein Stores. The court area itself would be the Value City Arena.

There was an initial flurry of media jokes and local talk show phone calls about the mediocrity implied in one interpretation of "value." But once the building began to go up, the criticism plummeted. The Schott would be grand. A classic. On February 28, 1998, the last men's basketball game was played in St. John Arena. It now would host volleyball, wrestling, fencing, and gymnastics, intercollegiate sports that had previously had no decent home. The Schottenstein Center would seat 17,000 for hockey, 19,500 for basketball, and 21,000 for concerts and would be open for the next season.

Value City, the fans who later filled it would generally agree, was certainly the "Best Damn Arena" in the Big Ten and one of the finest in the country. And it was bringing Ringling Brothers, the WorldWide Wrestling Federation, Bette Midler, and Holiday on Ice and on and on to Columbus. It also helped attract two new head coaches to basketball.

Jerome Schottenstein had given significantly to many charities and institutions but had sought no credit for it. In 1990, Gee's first year, he had begun funding what would become the university's 8,000-item Historic Costume Collection and, in his wife's name, the Geraldine Schottenstein wing of Campbell Hall in which to house it. A year later, he made a major gift to the yet-to-open James Cancer Hospital. A year later, he was gone. At his death, the *Dispatch* wrote that he "seemed almost uncomfortable with praise at what he had done" philanthropically. Only when he no longer could refuse such credit, and after much angst over whether to put his first name on the Jerome Schottenstein Center, could his family so honor him.

## O'Brien and Burns

Andy Geiger already had interviewed Jim O'Brien of Boston College at the Final Four in Indianapolis and, "for reasons that had little to do with basketball and had much to do with him," felt him "a perfect fit for Ohio State." And so would Gordon Gee. If Geiger had found a "kindred soul" in his interview with Gee, Gee would find another in his interview with O'Brien.

"Jim O'Brien—I'm not sure we ever talked about basketball," Gee said later. "We talked about our personal circumstances and families." Gee's Elizabeth had died in December 1991 after battling breast cancer, O'Brien's Christine in March 1991 from heart failure after chemotherapy for Hodgkin's disease. Gee

## Chapter 25

Brutus, new plates, and the new coach Jim O'Brien, 1997.

was raising one daughter; O'Brien, two. "When you go through that refiner's fire," he told the *Plain Dealer*'s Bruce Hooley (April 4, 1997), "you know a person's character. I had looked at all of his information. I don't know a lot about basketball, but I know a lot about character."

O'Brien would sign a five-year contract on April 2, 1997, and, in two years, would have his team, led by Scoonie Penn and Michael Redd—a team of great "character"—playing in the Final Four.

The day O'Brien was announced, Beth Burns, who had played her basketball fifteen miles north of campus at Ohio Wesleyan, also was back in Columbus. She had received her master's degree at Ohio State, was an assistant coach of the Buckeyes in 1980 and 1981, and most recently had coached San Diego State to four NCAA tournaments in five years. Her athletic director was Rick Bay, who had resigned as AD of Ohio State to protest the firing of Earle Bruce. "Probably the highest compliment I can pay her is I hate to lose her," Bay said. And lose her he did, to a five-year contract with salary parity ($150,000) and a similar incentive package as the men's coach.

In an interview with the *Dispatch*'s Bob Baptist (April 4), Burns said, "Once *Carmen Ohio* bites you, it doesn't go away." Neither did Gordon Gee. Gee had interviewed her and supported her appointment. But, in the small world of universities, they already were friends. Burns had been an assistant coach at Colorado when Gee was president there. "A champion of athletes," she called him. Men's and women's basketball was ready for a new day. (The "new day" lasted only through March 2002, when she was not retained after five seasons.)

## *Bill Davis Stadium*

Gordon Gee sent so many thank-you notes to Dorothy Wells Davis that she kept them in a scrapbook. Health Sciences Vice President Manuel Tzagournis was one of her dearest friends, and development officer Linda Bowers was her closest confidant. Davis was a Buckeye and, by all accounts, a remarkable woman. She dressed outrageously and loved making an entrance. Geiger remembered her later as "brilliant in some ways, with a terrific management sense, fun to work with, fun to be with, exciting and enthusiastic."

Few people knew it, but she was a pilot and an expert in celestial navigation, which she was teaching in Brazil when she fell in love with a Navy man and Ohio State graduate, William H. Davis, and married him in 1949. For 35 years they were together and, in 1986, following his death, Dottie Davis funded the William H. Davis Medical Research Center for arthritis and geriatrics.

In 1991, William H. Davis, his son and her stepson, driving home from an Ohio State football game, swerved his car to miss an animal that had darted into the road, and crashed. Although he was able to drive himself to University Hospitals, he still died as a result of the accident. Three years later, Dottie Davis donated $1.6 million to name a new baseball stadium in his honor. She had been visited by Archie Griffin, and had placed the stadium on her list of projects she might support at the university. Then, at her winter home

# Chapter 25

Bernie Gerlach and Dorothy Davis at the Bill Davis Stadium groundbreaking, 1994.

in Florida, Jerry May and Gordon Gee paid a visit. Standing in her kitchen, May said later, as if "it was a huddle at a football game," the president stretched out his arms, one hand gripping her shoulder, the other May's, and leaned in.

"Dottie, we want to put Billy Davis's name on the baseball stadium. What will it take to get it done?"

"I think that's a good idea."

Ohio State had its baseball stadium.

As the stadium was going up, when she was in town, Dottie Davis would visit it weekly, and when she wasn't, her beloved nephew, Bill Wells, would mail her pictures. "In the fall of 1996," Wells recalled for this book, "we got into the discussion of who would throw out the first pitch. She said the responsibility went to her. 'Come to Florida in the spring of the year,' she said, 'and teach me how to throw a fastball.'"

Dottie Davis, who had survived cancer three times, died suddenly—and cancer free—that November, before she had a chance to learn to pitch. Seven months later, Bill Wells, now the head of the Davis Foundation, "on one of the hardest days of my life," threw out the first ball.

## The Horseshoe

"We had an offer to rename Ohio Stadium for some big money that we walked away from," Janet Ashe explained. "You cannot rename Ohio Stadium, and nobody was going to waver on that."

What it would cost to build an arena had been her province in 1992. Though the starting point with Riffe had been $6 million, her analysis of new arena packages at Penn State, Michigan State, and other campuses had established $15 million as the minimum need from the state. What it would cost to restore Ohio Stadium would be an even bigger challenge, and this time help from Ohio was out of the question.

Cracks had appeared in A deck. "We'd been losing a few hundred seats here and there to the fire marshal every year," she recalled. Seat width was down to 17 inches, although Michigan Stadium's was 16." The cost to bring the stadium up to code alone would be $50 million and the stadium would lose 10,000 seats unless expanded. Building a new stadium was estimated at up to $350 million in October 1997. The decision was made to preserve and renovate. It would cost "only" $145–$150 million.

In 1871, the trustees of Ohio State had purchased 11 acres of land because the Whetstone River (now the Olentangy) was washing away a certain portion of what was then the college farm. The riverbed was moved west, a dam was built, and, in 1922, the area became the site of Ohio Stadium.

In the July 19, 1996, *Dispatch,* Andy Geiger would note that the base of New York City's World Trade Center was under the water table of the Hudson River. (On September 11, 2001, 2,801 people would lose their lives in the terrorist attack that would destroy the Center.) "It's a feat. It's doable. They build skyscrapers under the water." What was going to be doable was lowering the field below the Olentangy water table. A concrete "bathtub" would be built 40 feet down to the bedrock around the circumference of the playing field, with a system of pumps to remove any water that entered it. Crews would have to complete the job between football seasons.

This would be the first phase of a monumental renovation that would expand C and A decks, replace B deck and part of A with hospitality suites and club seats, and build permanent stands at the open end of the Horseshoe.

The track would be removed and rebuilt with a soccer/lacrosse field in a small stadium of its own dedicated to Jesse Owens and seating 8,000–10,000. At one point, Williams would give a tour to Lamar Hunt, owner of what would become the Columbus Crew soccer team, exploring the potential of expanding it to 35,000. Hunt would decide to build his own stadium instead.

# Chapter 25

A new façade would be erected around Ohio Stadium that would maintain the integrity of the old design and buttress the new nosebleed seating atop C deck. The stadium would seat at least 98,000 and would have wider aisles and concourses, improved disability seating, and additional elevators and escalators and be topped by a giant press box. And, most important to many patrons, it would have ten times the women's restrooms and four times the men's.

In the 1998 season, just before work would begin on the renovation that his presidency had started, Gordon and Constance Gee returned to Ohio State from Brown. His presidential portrait was unveiled in a luncheon ceremony in the brand new Schottenstein Center. Then he and the Missus visited Ohio Stadium, seated for the first time as guests, not as president and faculty member/spouse.

They reminisced about the honor of Dotting the 'I'—"The #1 Best Thing About College Football" pundit Beano Cook calls it. Together, three years before, on September 16, 1995, Constance had strutted out behind Gordon in her red dress with polka dots and they had bowed to the crowd as one, dotting the 'I.' They recalled playing Notre Dame at home in 1995, the first time in sixty years since the Buckeyes had lost on the last play of "the Game of the Century." And winning. And winning again in 1996.

He would recall his 1992 locker room visit to a freshman back named Eddie George—impossible to console after fumbling twice on the goal line in a 16–18 loss to Illinois—telling George there was a lot of football left to play in his college career. Chip Elam would recall Gee's hospital visit to the former offensive coordinator Eliot Uzelak, criticized for conservative play calling. Uzelak was recovering from coronary bypass surgery and sleeping when Gee arrived. "Throw the ball," the president had stage-whispered as a subliminal suggestion, sending the attending physicians into convulsions.

"There were times when Gordon just couldn't help himself from acting on life's incongruities," explained Elam. "And that was one of them."

On this day, with Gordon and Constance Gee back for the portrait unveiling, Ohio State was undefeated and ranked number 1. This team, which Gee himself had helped recruit, could win the national title that had eluded him by one game as president of both West Virginia and Colorado. But Ohio State would be upset that day by Michigan State, 24–28, then run the table against Iowa, Michigan, and Texas A&M in the Sugar Bowl. The season would end 11–1, the Buckeyes would rank number 2, and President Gordon Gee of Brown still had no national football championship.

# 26

## *California*

On July 1, 1995, a hand-written note from Gordon Gee was delivered to Governor George Voinovich, giving "deep thanks" for his support during "my recent visit with the University of California." A copy of it was filed in the president's office under "Staying." That file was to grow very large before the end of the month.

Two weeks earlier, Rebekah Gee had been awakened at three in the morning by a telephone call from the *Ohio State Lantern*. The reporter had wanted to know if her father was going to accept the presidency of the California system. Rebekah said she didn't know and went back to bed in her room at the Hotel Manila in the Philippines. The *Lantern*, like the *Dispatch*, had picked up the story out of California.

Chip Elam, Gee's executive assistant, had been ready to move to California if it came to that. As the administrator who handled Gee's schedule, he was one of the few people at Ohio State who knew what was going on. While it may be the most prestigious presidency in public higher education, he believed the California job had two big negatives. First, system headquarters was in an office building and in Oakland, not on a campus and not in San Francisco.

Then there was "affirmative action." Gee was an advocate. Governor Pete Wilson was not. Unlike in Ohio, the governor of California is also president of the state board of regents. Wilson had been lobbying hard to end both race-based admissions and affirmative action in hiring and contracting. Jesse Jackson was in town leading the opposition. A vote probably would take place at the new president's first meeting. Gee told Elam he would deal with that when he got there. That is, if he took the job.

Getting him there, logistically, also had been Elam's job. He and presidential secretary Kate Wolford had worked out the itinerary for the trip that Gee,

## Chapter 26

accompanied by his wife and daughter, was taking as president of the Big Ten's Midwest University Consortium for International Affairs (MUCIA). They had landed in Seoul, Korea, on June 12 and then gone to Kuala Lumpur and Manila, where Rebekah had taken that phone call. Hong Kong and Bangkok lay ahead.

On the way home on June 22, United Flight 806 was scheduled to stop in San Francisco on route to Chicago. The California regents expected the Gees to deplane in San Francisco and to appoint him their president at a special meeting of the full board the next day. They knew nothing of Jack Kessler and the full court press.

"We knew he was interviewing," Kessler recalled later. "And we knew he was serious." So he spoke with Les Wexner and *Dispatch* publisher John Wolfe, "who were very much committed to keeping him here. And we put our heads together with Chip [Elam] and Kate [Wolford]," and with trustees Alex Shumate, George Skestos, and Milt Wolf and others who could be persuasive and could be reached.

Wexner both talked to Gee while Gee was in Hong Kong and wrote him a long letter telling him how valued he was, reminding him of the friends he had made, and citing the university's progress under his leadership. He urged Gee to consider whether he was "just tantalized by curiosity" and to "think twice before he made the leap." And he reminded Gee that he had made commitments not yet filled.

"You're a restless guy," he said, and suggested, "the devil you don't know" may be worse than the one you do.

Milton Wolf, chairman of the OSU Board that year and on a philanthropic trip of his own, also reached Gee, by telephone from Israel. And in a *Dispatch* article on the 20th, Skestos and Shumate both acknowledged they had talked to Gee and would fight to keep him at Ohio State. The always expressive Skestos said Gee would "have to climb over me" to leave.

On the 21st, the *Dispatch* ran a piece so supportive its writer still thinks of it as the "Gordon we love you, please stay here" editorial. Headlined "Ohio State should do its best to keep him," it had been written personally by Mike Curtin, by then the paper's editor in chief. "We had to make an all-out effort and marshal the troops and get out the cavalry," he said later. The editorial did just that. After lauding Gee's work at Ohio State, it urged the trustees to do "all they can" to persuade him to stay. And it explained that the California pay was 45 percent higher than Ohio State's, noting that "the trustees have indicated an intent to address this issue" and recommending "they should."

Kessler also contacted Peter Magrath of NASULGC, he who had just done

## CALIFORNIA

Gee's five-year review, which warned the trustees their principal job could be keeping Gee at Ohio State. Magrath did call and did discuss the affirmative action issue, reminding Gee, he said later, that he would have to "come in there and position himself against the governor. . . . I had this agonizing talk where we went through all the pros and cons. I mean I was drained. And I said, 'Gordon, don't ever do this to me again.'"

To the press, meanwhile, Gee did acknowledge through communications director Baroway that he understood he was the first choice of the California search committee. Baroway now was apprising Gee, sometimes more than once a day, of the media coverage in California and Ohio, including the *Dispatch* editorial. In California, a spokesman for the regents also acknowledged that the recommendation indeed would be Gee, and it would be by unanimous vote of the eight-member committee.

In the end, Gee said later the people of Ohio "and particularly Les [Wexner] and Jack [Kessler] and John [Wolfe] did a remarkable job of re-recruiting me. I still remember the general manager of the Regency Hotel in Hong Kong coming up to the room with a basket full of faxes and telling me he didn't know what was going on but I was burning up the fax machine. Being offered the presidency of the University of California, which may be the most important job in higher education in this country, was something no one would be expected to turn down. There was an expectation in California I was going to accept it and there was an expectation here I was going to accept it. But Les and Jack and John simply made me feel this was not the time."

Gee said he woke up the morning of the flight and began to pack his bag. "I was going to leave early and fly to California to have a press conference as the president of the University of California, and I looked at all those notes. Several new ones had come in overnight and I read them, too. I simply woke Constance up and I said, 'I cannot do this. I do not have the ability to turn my face away from Ohio State.'" And so he stayed.

To subvert any California attempt to change Gee's mind again, an ever-vigilant Kessler sent Kate Wolford to San Francisco in a private plane to pick the Gees up on the tarmac. She and the Gees then returned home together. In his journal, which the president had maintained for years as part of his Mormon heritage, he wrote, "This has been a wrenching decision for Constance and me. My heart tells me that we have done the right thing."

On Sunday, June 25, both the *Plain Dealer* and *Dispatch* rejoiced in Gee's decision with heartfelt editorials. Headlined "A good man to have around," the *Plain Dealer,* whose editorial staff Gee had visited many times, wrote that the expectation of his leaving had "evoked a sadness," that he had "met every

CHAPTER 26

The Board that kept him: (front row) Alex Shumate, Les Wexner, Gee, Jack Kessler, Milt Wolf, Ted Celeste; (back row) Board Secretary Bob Duncan, Tom Smith, Mike Colley, George Skestos, Jim Patterson, David Brennan, Amira Ailabouni, 1995.

critical standard used to judge a highly successful university president"; and that, "better than any academician or politician in recent memory," he had enunciated the link between higher education and the Ohio economy.

The *Dispatch* piece began, "Ohio State won big last week." It cited the "tremendous outpouring of support, seemingly unprecedented in Ohio or elsewhere," and concluded the "university and Columbus community are fortunate." It did not, of course, cite the significant role that, in his typically unobtrusive way, its publisher had played in the drama.

On the next day, his first back at work, the Ohio State pep band serenaded Gee as he entered Bricker Hall. On the steps were some seventy-five employees and student leaders all wearing scarlet T-shirts reminiscent of those worn on his first day as Ohio State president five years before. Those shirts had read, "Gee whiz, he's here." A carat sign had been inserted between "he's" and "here" and above the line was the word "still." In his office he found stacks of letters and e-mails from faculty and staff, students and parents, alumni and other citizens asking him not to leave or thanking him for staying.

Back in California, at its next meeting, that state's board of regents voted 14–10 to end race-based admissions and 15–10 to halt affirmative action in

CALIFORNIA

Gee said no to California, so "Gee whiz, he's still here," 1995.

campus hiring and contracting. In Ohio, meanwhile, at their next meeting, Ohio State's trustees unanimously voted to raise the president's pay by 31 percent to $220,000. A major raise, in fact, already was pending in the context of Gee's five-year review and the new fiscal year that began July 1. Gee now would be making $220,000, still not the highest salary in the state system but more than that paid to Harold Nestor, the much-admired president of the local community college, Columbus State.

Years later, Gee said he had come to believe upon reflection he "would have been caught in a very difficult position" in California. "I'm a Mormon. The issue of affirmative action was coming up. I might have been a hamburger between Jesse Jackson and Pete Wilson." And Chip Elam was right. Without a campus, working from a high rise in Oakland, "It would have felt like a corporate job." But that was upon reflection. In an interview for this book, Magrath substantiated that Gee's decision to stay in Ohio had everything to do with Ohio and nothing to do with California.

"Gordon's got confidence in himself," Magrath said. About conflict over affirmative action he said, "He figured he'd be able to handle it." Magrath also noted the Gees were in a new marriage and there was an appeal in starting over together in a new place. This they eventually did by leaving for Brown two

## Chapter 26

years later. Ironically, by that time Constance Gee had fallen in love with Ohio State and preferred to stay. Even after Gee left Brown for the presidency of Vanderbilt in 2000, Magrath still said, "the love of his life professionally was Ohio State." As for Brown, Magrath's own alma mater, "It was too small a sandbox." When Gee left for Vanderbilt, "I have to tell you, my surprise level was about zero. It was also about zero when he chose to stay at Ohio State."

# 27

## *The NRC*

> The idea of visiting departments and giving them a barrel of apples for their final [National Research Council] rankings is a great one. Let's try to do it in a two-day period, have fun, and get good recognition for this. I will ask you to work together.
>
> —Memo from Gordon Gee to
> Dick Sisson, Barbie Tootle,
> and Kate Wolford

Gordon Gee had been presenting apples symbolic and real to the annual winners of faculty teaching and research awards. Individual award winners, covered by print media and TV, enjoyed the publicity, as did their proud families, colleagues, and students. Everyone did have fun, especially Gordon. So why not give a whole barrel of apples to each department that had achieved in the most important measurement of faculty quality since 1982? It was autumn 1995, and the man who recently had said "no" to the California system was already in high gear in this, his first sixth year of any of his three presidencies.

The apples came from the 116-acre fruit farm of the university's one current trustee in the business of agriculture and the newest trustee, James F. Patterson of Chesterland. His pick-your-own apples and strawberries were a fabled crop in northeast Ohio. A fifth-generation business on the same land, Patterson's family market had been visited many times over many years by the Voinovich family of nearby Cleveland.

Jim had been surprised early that summer by a call from the Voinovich who

CHAPTER 27

On the podium Gee surprises Music Professor Michael Davis with a 1995 Distinguished Teaching "Apple."

now was governor. Although trustee Ted Celeste had great interest in it, Ohio agriculture had had no alumni advocate on the Ohio State board since Shirley Bowser rotated off in 1991. "Would you," George Voinovich had asked Patterson, "be willing to serve? Accept only if you can commit the time and dedication to do this hard job well." Yes, Patterson would, and yes, Patterson could. On June 14, 1995, while Gordon Gee was in the Far East fielding "don't go to California" telegrams, Jim Patterson, College of Agriculture 1964, became the university's newest trustee.

Though the National Research Council (NRC) was seventy-eight years old in 1995, few people knew of it outside academe. An agency of both the National Academy of Sciences and the National Academy of Engineering, its once-per-decade nationwide survey of graduate faculty was awaited that September with considerable interest by the Gee administration. The first had been done in 1970. The second, and most recent, in 1982.

In 1982, Ohio State had fared splendidly compared with other universities in Ohio. But when compared with what its faculty considered its national peers, it had come out average at best, as dean of Social and Behavioral Sciences and provost-to-be Huber had explained to the trustees back in 1989. And there was no disrespecting this survey, as some were wont to do with U.S. News. This poll was of peerage: faculty assessing the scholarly quality of faculty and the effectiveness of each program in educating research scholars and scientists.

The report would measure more than 3,600 programs in 270 institutions in forty-one fields of study (arts and humanities, biological sciences, engineering, physical sciences and mathematics, and social and behavioral sciences) from 1982 to 1993. Ohio State had ninety-nine doctoral programs, thirty-eight in the new study. Though the survey had been conducted only three years into the Gee administration, its results would be an early barometer of progress in this, Gee's fifth year. Though the university leadership regretted the survey had not been conducted further along in restructuring, 1993 still would be a reasonable monitor of direction and early achievement.

Acknowledgment of achievement is, of course, what Gee, Sisson, and the deans hoped to see; as did department chairs, who now knew reallocation budgets would be driven by just such data.

And so did the trustees, who, by this time, were paying close attention to quality comparisons. As Peter Magrath had written in Gee's five-year evaluation just six months earlier, among the accomplishments of the Gee presidency had been "a decent burial of the notion that being 'good enough' is really acceptable."

## More Tough Decisions

While the university was awaiting the NRC report in the fall of 1995, tough administrative decisions were being made across campus. Perhaps the most grieved loss would be the esteemed publisher of specialty books, the Logan Elm Press. Given a grace period in which to raise funds privately, its advocates had not been able to keep it afloat. It would be shut down. Another small gem to disappear, the Robert Shaw Institute in the College of the Arts, would be closed reluctantly by Dean Don Harris, its namesake and his wife, both ill. Its profitability was in question. Restructuring in the College of Education eliminated the individual identity of the School of Health, Physical Education, and Recreation, despite opposition from many of its alumni.

The same could be said for the eventual merger of the School of Journalism and the Department of Communication, a process that raised havoc among many Journalism School alumni, who also felt a loss of identity, if not a

# Chapter 27

dissolution of the curriculum. Social and Behavioral Sciences Dean Randall "Rip" Ripley also lost Journalism School Director Pamela Shoemaker to Syracuse University, where she could wave goodbye to administration and concentrate on scholarship.

In Provost Sisson's office, a discrete academic Office of International Affairs would be closed, eliminating any duplication of the International Studies centers and the International Students Office. The Mershon Center, Ohio State's multidisciplinary resource for the study of war and peace, was restructured under Ripley's social and behavioral sciences college. A disagreement arose about the center's obligations and purpose as its long-time director Chuck Hermann retired and then went to Texas A&M to direct its George Bush School of Government. Ned Lebow became Mershon's new director in 1996.

Roy Koenigsknecht stepped down as dean of the Graduate School at the end of his second term to return to the faculty, succeeded by art history professor Susan Huntington, a distinguished scholar and teacher also recognized for her administrative skills. And the proposal to merge the small College of Social Work into the large College of Education created such a ruckus, it was withdrawn.

Centrally, meanwhile, as much to facilitate two-way communication as to coordinate colleges, Gee and Sisson created three new umbrella roles among the academic deans. All would meet weekly with Gee on his executive committee. The medical dean and "Health Services" vice president, Manuel Tzagournis, was now vice president for "Health Sciences," combining Medicine, Dentistry, Nursing, Optometry, Pharmacy, Veterinary Medicine, and the Hospitals. Nancy Zimpher, now executive dean of the professional colleges, coordinated her home College of Education plus Agriculture, Engineering, Human Ecology, Law, and Business. Jim Garland, now executive dean of Arts and Sciences, was responsible for his home College of Mathematical and Physical Sciences as well as the Arts, Biological Sciences, Humanities, and Social and Behavioral Sciences. Garland also had the Honors Program and even ROTC.

Then there was the president's ad hoc Committee on University Outreach, chaired by his do-it-all dean and vice president, Bobby Moser of Agriculture, which had reported out in April. Gee had formed this group to promote on campus the value of service done off campus. More than that, he hoped that, through the committee's work, in making tenure and promotion decisions faculty would gain new respect for the service element of the land-grant credo: "teaching, research, and service."

As Sisson had written to Gee that August in his annual report, the trustees and administration had "staked their course" and "secured much" in the

1994–1995 academic year. This included "financial equilibrium," which allowed him to report to the University Senate in December that the year coming up would be the first since 1990–1991 with competitive pay raises given and academic priorities sustained without university-wide budget cuts.

Yes, the worst days of state budget cuts finally were over. In the process of getting there, Sisson reiterated for Gee that the college deficits Gee had inherited when assuming the presidency had been wiped out completely. Disparate information systems units had been merged into University Technology Services. Promotion and tenure principles and procedures were under review, and the report of Moser's Outreach Committee was being factored into it. The administration had developed an Academic Enrichment program to fund long-term interdisciplinary and intercollegiate activities, thus creating collaborations among more members of what Gee often termed traditional "academic silos." And preparation was under way for Ohio State's decennial accreditation review, to be conducted in 1996 by the North Central Association of Colleges and Schools.

Now the administration would begin to explore something called "incentive-based budgeting," later termed "responsibility-centered management" or "RCM." This was a reward-oriented budgeting system that guaranteed that the academic unit could keep, rather than return centrally, some portion of increased revenue it attracted. It had been carried to the extreme at Harvard, where "every tub stood on its own bottom," and reportedly was the reason a Johns Hopkins president retired when Medicine so outstripped the rest of the university the humanists revolted. But it was being tested at Michigan and Indiana in more moderate forms, and Sisson had an expectation Ohio State would have its own version by July 1, 1997.

In doing all this, Sisson had written Gee, "We have moved forward with a shared vision and in a structured manner." Now they would find out whether faculty across the nation recognized that something important was happening in the departments at Ohio State, as reflected in the report of the National Research Council. The analysis was to be done by the new dean of the Graduate School, Susan Huntington.

## *The Report*

The answer was, yes, they had! Sixteen of the 38 programs evaluated ranked in the top 25 nationwide (aerospace engineering, astrophysics/astronomy, chemistry, classics, electrical engineering, geography, German language and literature, industrial engineering, linguistics, materials science, mechanical engineering, philosophy, physics, political science, psychology, sociology). Thirty of the 38 were above the national average.

Twenty-six of the 29 (90 percent) programs ranked both in 1982 and 1995 had higher ratings in 1995. In particular, geography had moved from 6 to 5 of 49 programs. Linguistics had moved from 11 to 8 of 35 programs and was the number one program in the Big Ten. Physics jumped 15 places, from 39 to 24 of 121; and psychology, 11 places, from 32 to 21 of 150. Of the 38, Ohio State ranked number one among Ohio public universities in 36 (95 percent) and in the top half of the Big Ten in 26 of them (68 percent).

In terms of score for program quality, the national average being 50, psychology ranked highest (63), followed by chemistry and geography (both 62), political science (61), and physics and electrical engineering (both 60).

In a letter to his 2,000-plus "friends" following the study's release, the president wrote that the results demonstrated "both high-quality and significant progress." He reminded them that in his last speech he had urged faculty and staff to "raise the bar—increase expectations of yourselves and your colleagues—set high standards and to reach for excellence." Now, he wrote, he was committed to raising the bar even higher.

He and Sisson expected even more significant progress by the next study, expected perhaps in the year 2007.

# 28

# *Health Care*

> As the national debate roars to a congressional climax over who pays for medical care and who is entitled to it, the American public is hardly aware that the future of medical education, medical research, and advanced techniques and technologies is at stake here, as well. . . . Because of the complexity of their missions, academic health centers will be the institutions most vulnerable to health plans based strictly upon the lowest common denominator of cost.
>
> —GORDON GEE, the *Columbus Dispatch*,
> August 23, 1994

Managed care? Before the term entered the average twelfth-grade vocabulary, Steve Loebs was writing about it. Ohio State's Loebs had led a task force studying why health care costs were skyrocketing in Ohio—as everywhere else in the country—and recommending how to control them. The team of twenty-eight Ohio State scholars in eight different disciplines—economics, finance, public health, public policy, management, nursing, medicine, and Loebs's own hospital and health services administration—reported out in August 1992.

Among other things, as *onCampus* (October 8, 1993) reported, Loebs's team had counted 13,000 excess acute care hospital beds in Ohio alone. "They're still open and we're paying for them." Just taking those beds off line would save Ohioans between $380 million and $530 million a year (and, of course, reduce income to Ohio hospitals, including those at Ohio State).

Everyone knew that new tests and technologies were expensive, and, said

CHAPTER 28

Loebs, experts predicted health care costs would double again before 2000. The answer was basic insurance reform, replacing conventional commercial insurance with *managed care*, saving huge sums of money by enabling businesses, health-care providers, or large companies to form networks of hospitals and physicians who would negotiate budgets for all services.

The state of Ohio, with 55,000 employees, had saved $10 million by switching to managed care in 1991. That approach was similar to what was being discussed in President Clinton's National Task Force on Health Care Reform, chaired by First Lady Hillary Rodham Clinton. While the proposed American Health Security Act of 1993, which would have provided universal health care, would be lobbied into oblivion, managed care itself was here to stay, despite some resistance from both doctors and patients.

## *Patient Choice*

For the individual, what would happen to patient choice in selecting doctors under managed care? And for the hospitals, where in the quest for cost containment might "efficiency" cross the line into irresponsibility? Or worse? And what of these academic medical centers like Ohio State, burdened with the added costs of training residents, with their difficult mix of the most acute cases and preponderance of the indigent?

The DRG (Diagnostic Related Groups) system of Medicare payments, which establishes rates based upon diagnosis, was not sufficiently sensitive to the added cost of patient care at teaching hospitals like Ohio State's. Though at the time of the report of the Loebs task force, 1991 data showed Ohio State to be less costly per case than other top academic medical centers, including Duke, Stanford, Yale, and Michigan, Ohio State was the most expensive per case of nine hospitals in Franklin County. And that would have to change.

## *Closing the Vise*

Of some 5,500 hospitals in the United States, fewer than 400 are teaching hospitals or "academic medical centers" (members of the American Association of Medical Colleges), which educate our doctors, perform the most specialized surgeries and procedures, conduct medical research at the cutting edge, and serve the neediest patients.

Even more complex are the country's 125 academic health centers such as

Ohio State, which combine a teaching hospital and medical school with allied schools in public health, nursing, optometry, dentistry, and pharmacy, all with research programs and most with clinics.

In September 1995, Bill Napier, then acting chancellor of the Board of Regents, reported to Governor Voinovich the regents' concern for the future of Ohio's public teaching hospitals—Ohio State, the University of Cincinnati, and the Medical College of Ohio. Managed-care programs, he explained, were affiliating with hospitals "solely on the basis of price, ignoring the fact that teaching hospitals face costs other hospitals need not incur." The regents were "worried that the pace of change can be more than they can handle. It is not an exaggeration to say that teaching hospitals across the country are in or very near a state of crisis."

Congress, meanwhile, was tightening the financial vise by threatening to cut funds for biomedical research. "Caught between the nation's relentless search for cheaper medical care and budget-cutting fervor among politicians," biomedical research, wrote Elizabeth Rosenthal in *The New York Times* (May 30, 1995), "threatens to become a silent casualty of the reorganization of the country's health care system."

Ohio State, however, would refuse to be a casualty, silent or otherwise. By spring 1995, under Research Vice President Ed Hayes, Ohio State was increasing, not losing, federal research support. Under Hospitals Board Chairman Don Shackelford and Vice Chairman Bill Bennett, led by an administrative first team of Manuel Tzagournis, Hagop Mekhjian, and Reed Fraley, it also was more than two years deep into "reengineering" and cutting costs in its hospitals.

## *The First Team*

Manuel Tzagournis entered undergraduate school at Ohio State in 1952 and medical school at Ohio State in 1956, graduated, interned at Philadelphia General Hospital, and then returned to Ohio State. Except for two years in the Army, he had been at Ohio State ever since, as resident, faculty member, and administrator. Tzagournis started in administration when Henry Cramblett became dean of Medicine in 1974, subsequently became medical director of the hospitals, associate dean, dean, and then also vice president.

Throughout his years of administration, he maintained his practice in internal medicine and endocrinology. He had been the physician to Ohio State presidents Harold Enarson and Ed Jennings; to presidents of the Ohio Senate

Oliver Ocasek, Paul Gillmor, and Harry Meshel; to former governors James Rhodes and Dick Celeste; to current Senate President Stan Aronoff; to House Speaker Verne Riffe; to Governor George Voinovich; to U.S. Representative Chalmers Wylie; and to Wendy's chairman Dave Thomas, among others, when he accepted as new patients the Gordon Gee family in 1990.

Hagop Mekhjian received his M.D. from the American University in Beirut, where he also completed his internship and residency, became a resident in gastroenterology at Boston's Lahey Clinic, served in the Mayo Clinic, and arrived at Ohio State in 1969. As a scientist, he was a principal investigator on more than twenty national studies, many federally supported. Since 1985, he had been associate dean for clinical affairs, then medical director, as well as professor of medicine and a practicing gastroenterologist.

R. Reed Fraley, a West Point graduate and Vietnam veteran, entered hospital administration at Ohio State in 1974. He earned his master's in the field a year later, went on as head operating officer at the Medical Center of Virginia, then as CEO of a major health care system in Dallas, and returned to Ohio State to run University Hospitals the year before Gordon Gee arrived from Colorado. He would quickly gain a reputation as an administrator of impeccable integrity and credibility.

As George Paulson, former Kurtz Chair in Neurology, cited in *The Ohio State University College of Medicine,* the ability of Fraley, Tzagournis, and Mekhjian to work so well together allowed most of the major decisions about patient care and medical education to be made smoothly during the conversion to managed care.

A fourth key figure all the while was otolaryngologist David Schuller, the first and only director of the James, steering it from anonymity in 1990 into a leader in oncological treatment and research and, in 1995, one of only thirteen founding institutions of the National Comprehensive Cancer Network. As Paulson would write, Schuller's joint appointment acknowledged both his skills as a surgeon and "his apparent limitless ability to work and to tolerate stress." Some of that administrative stress had been relieved since the beginning by the James's one and only administrative director, Dennis Smith, hired in 1988 to set up a hospital two years before it even opened.

## *What's in a Name?*

The University of Colorado had its Colorado Health Sciences Center; the University of Texas its Texas Health Sciences Center; the University of Oregon its

HEALTH CARE

Bernadine Healy dedicates a Jamescare Mammography Center in downtown Columbus.

Oregon Health Sciences Center; and the University of Alabama its Alabama–Birmingham Health Sciences Center. Then there were the Johns Hopkins Medical Institutions, the Cornell University Medical Center, and the Duke Medical Center.

And what about Ohio State? It had University Hospitals, with its individually named specialty centers, the James Cancer Hospital and Research Center, the College of Medicine, plus nursing, public health, optometry, and dentistry.

A 1993 memo to President Gee counseled him that, by not unifying the elements under one umbrella title, Ohio State was projecting a less than dominant image.

And what about advertising? The James, with a regional/national patient base, advertised from the time it opened. But University Hospitals still did not. As many lawyers felt about their profession, for some Ohio State decision makers, primarily those on its hospital board, hospital advertising was inappropriate. But the large community hospital, Riverside, not only advertised heavily in all media, it had pioneered and gone national with its own weekly television program. It even advertised in Ohio State's own football programs, angering one prominent faculty physician, doubtlessly speaking for others as well, who wrote Gee that he felt "undermined" by the athletic department for allowing it.

And what about customer preference? In a 1992 *physician* survey, Riverside Methodist and Mount Carmel, which advertised, were mentioned more often than Ohio State as the hospitals of their patients' preference. Ohio State was cited most often as the place *not* to be. In a *community* survey, Riverside was preferred over Ohio State 3-to-1 for "quality" health care and nearly 2-to-1 for an inpatient stay. Riverside's marketing had been so effective it was acknowledged as having "a better heart transplant unit than Ohio State" though that was hardly possible. Ohio State had the only unit in central Ohio.

It was not long, then, before the James, University Hospitals, and the College of Medicine became the Ohio State University Medical Center. Soon, Fraley's marketing chief, Sue Jablonski, was interviewing advertising agencies. Soon new signage, which had been terribly inadequate, was routing visitors off State Rt. 315 and smoothly to specific parking areas, buildings, and health care services. Soon, the Medical Center instituted what became an extremely popular "Ask-a-Nurse" program, putting Ohio State expertise only a phone call away. Soon, Franklin County residents were recognizing The Ohio State University Medical Center's smart new positioning statement, "Intensive Caring," and soon Ohio State was catching up in the surveys.

Also, for the purpose of administrative reorganization and letterhead, the Medical Center and all of the health care colleges and schools became The Ohio State University Health Sciences Center; and Manuel Tzagournis, the vice president charged with it all.

## *Prime Care*

By 1994, health care costs were increasing by 18 to 20 percent annually in most colleges and universities, but by "only" 10 to 14 percent at Ohio State because the university had introduced "Prime Care" in 1993. Prime Care was the exclusive provider plan for its own faculty, staff, and families, its own HMO; and its exclusive provider was, of course, Ohio State's preferred hospital—its own medical center.

University employees who joined the health plan named a primary care gatekeeper physician from the Medical Center, and all procedures and surgeries stayed within the center. Engineered on the university end by Human Resources Associate Vice President Larry Lewellen, the plan was phased in for fear that oversubscription the first year would flood the system. Meanwhile, the Medical Center built up its clinical faculty to handle the patient load.

Would faculty and staff have a choice of plans? When at a University Senate meeting in 1993 the president suggested they might not, a letter from one faculty member spoke for many others. Through his traditional plan, he wrote the president, he had formed a professional relationship with a non-Ohio State physician that "would be painful to surrender. Coming on the heels of a year without salary increases, the prospect of being forced into an HMO is very demoralizing."

While no one ever was forced, Prime Care became much the preferred system as the gap widened between the employee's portion of the premium in Prime Care and in two other offered plans. While guaranteeing The Ohio State University Medical Center thousands of new patients, the university had struck such a hard bargain with its own hospitals that it could pick up 85 percent of the premiums. A new type of employee health insurance, keeping both money and patients circulating inside Ohio State, was now the rule.

## *Efficiencies*

A 1994 OSU Medical Center report, *Imperatives for Change,* pulled no punches. "To remain competitive in the provision of health care while supporting the dramatically changing scope of teaching and research, University Hospitals must decrease expenses by $30 million by 1996." To do that, they would have to make many more changes than just adding Prime Care. "To do so," the report continued, "we will have to streamline processes, decrease bed capacity, shrink or eliminate some programs and services, and decrease the number of staff," as they did.

Bed capacity shrank from 600 to 541, some for rehabilitation instead of medical/surgical care, with allied in-hospital staff reductions. A compensation program separate from the university's was approved, to include monetary incentives; the hospitals themselves were given more independence in negotiating union contracts, and authority was delegated directly to Fraley in such areas as finance, materials management, and personnel.

Meanwhile, as inpatient care shrank, outpatient care expanded and new affiliations were made. One was the Health Care Consortium of Ohio, linking eleven smaller central Ohio hospitals with Ohio State. Another combined the university's emergency medical helicopter service with Grant Medical Center. The Rardin Family Practice Center opened north of campus, for clinical care as well as medical education. Extending into the community, MedOhio Health established a home-care company. It already had purchased nine former

Humana physician care centers in Columbus and Newark and staffed them under the name MedOHIO. The James opened a Comprehensive Breast Health Service in Dublin and opened a second mobile mammography unit. And other ambulatory procedures once limited to the main campus hospitals, in areas including gastroenterology, radiology, obstetrics, and gynecology, moved into Stoneridge Medical Center in northwest Columbus.

By the turn of the century, the OSU Medical Center would staff stand-alone primary care centers in family medicine, sports medicine, internal medicine, and occupational medicine, as well as some ten family practice centers throughout metropolitan Columbus.

## Mental Health Care

As *Imperatives for Change* had predicted in 1994, the following years certainly did bring medicine many challenges that required "a willingness to grow and change" at Ohio State.

With Ohio State's old inpatient psychiatry facility, Upham Hall, needing prohibitively expensive upgrades, including insulation and the electrical system, it was torn down and replaced with a new neuropsychiatric facility. However, tremendous breakthroughs were occurring in the development of psychotropic drugs, with drastic reductions in insurance coverage, limiting inpatients from stays of up to 120 days to approximately ten. Meanwhile, at least four weeks' psychiatric experience was required of every Ohio State medical student.

During this period, then, Ohio State affiliated in a joint venture with Columbus's other major residential treatment center, the campus-like Harding Hospital, where, eventually, all Ohio State inpatients were moved. In the university's new neuropsychiatric building, the focus became research, in such areas as neurobehavioral aspects of neurological disorders, Alzheimer's and other neurodegenerative diseases, and the anatomical basis of schizophrenia. As Paulson wrote in his history of the college, the times continued to be threatening for psychiatry, with inadequate national support for the care of the psychiatrically ill.

## Healy and the Doctors

Well before the American public took notice of the problem, culminating in "Antibiotic Armageddon" (*The Journal of Clinical Infectious Diseases*, August

1997), Pomerene Professor of Medicine Calvin Kunin had been counseling his patients and publishing papers about the misuse and overuse of antibiotics. Kunin's research exemplified Dean Bernadine Healy's pronouncement at the merger of the School of Medicine and the new School of Public Health soon after she arrived in September 1995. Public health, she said, which focused traditionally on populations, and medicine, which focused traditionally on individuals, "must now share a common purpose."

Kunin's international reputation, skill as a physician and teacher, and ability to attract large research grants reflected the new dean's charge from President Gee and the trustees: "To take us from better to best."

However, the process of doing medical research itself was changing under the time and liability pressures of managed care. As Ronald "Ron" Ferguson wrote in the department's *Surgery Today* (February 1997), research was now "a team sport rather than an individual activity." The age of the "triple threat" clinician-teacher-researcher, like the soon-to-retire Kunin, was coming to a close. "Even to perform basic research and remain active as a clinician and teacher," Ferguson wrote, "is difficult."

In her first speech to the full college faculty in December 1995, Healy quoted Woody Allen: "We are at a crossroads; one path leads to hopelessness; the other to despair. How will we have the wisdom to choose the right way?" The right way, she said, was not the path of despair some medical schools were treading by being "gobbled up" by their hospitals, with teaching and research in decline, to compete for patients and patient revenue.

Nor was it the path of hopelessness other medical schools were taking by selling their hospitals to for-profit corporations, "hoping that without the burden they can pursue research and teaching in peace." The most recent had been the University of Minnesota, and Colorado and West Virginia, both under Gordon Gee's presidencies, had done so in the 1980s.

The charge for Ohio State and from Gordon Gee, she said, was to take the third path: the path "to the next level of excellence."

Nevertheless, a year later, rumors did begin to abound that Ohio State was about to take that path of despair by selling its hospitals to the new parent company of both Grant and Riverside, U.S. Health. But they were squelched quickly. Yes, Vice President Tzagournis was talking to William Wilkins of U.S. Health, but not about selling. Only about ways they might work together. Nothing happened then or in the following year, 1997, when the behemoth Columbia/HCA, the largest for-profit hospital chain in the United States, threatened to enter the Columbus market. Investigated for Medicare fraud,

## Chapter 28

Columbia paid an $840 million settlement, sold 300 of its 500 hospitals, and never came to town.

Meanwhile, Dean Healy and her administrative colleagues were doing their best, as she put it later, "to elevate the mean," hiring distinguished new faculty as well as "supporting the very good talent we had." Perhaps the most highly publicized talent around the world has been the team of Janice Kiecolt-Glaser and Research Associate Vice President Ron Glaser, whose definitive work in the effects of stress on immune function and health later attracted the NIH Center in Stress and Wound Healing and gained Kiecolt-Glaser election to the National Institute of Medicine. Healy's own work, including her book, *A New Prescription for Women's Health*, helped fund the medical center as one of only six National Centers for Excellence in Women's Health.

In molecular life sciences alone, Healy and David Schuller recruited three internationally acclaimed cancer researchers. One was Clara Bloomfield, division of medicine chair at New York State's Roswell Park Cancer Center, considered the world's expert on how chromosomal changes influence the treatment and outcome of adult acute leukemia. She came as codirector of the James and director of hematology/oncology and of the Comprehensive Cancer Center.

Her colleague, Michael Caligiuri, president of Roswell Park's medical staff, had developed promising immune therapies for patients with leukemia, lymphoma, and AIDS patients with cancer. He joined as codirector of hematology/oncology and research associate director in the Comprehensive Cancer Center. Albert de la Chapelle, the University of Helsinki's chair of medical genetics (and Bloomfield's husband), had mapped and identified four genes that make certain families susceptible to colon cancer. Considered the most prominent scientist in Finland, he came to direct the human cancer genetics program.

Pascal Goldschmidt, a specialist in the molecular origins of heart disease, left Johns Hopkins to head cardiology here, though he later left to head cardiology at Duke. Robert Michler came from New York's Columbia-Presbyterian Medical Center, where he directed cardiac transplantation, to lead the Ohio State transplantation unit.

Said Healy of her time at Ohio State once it was all over, "It was a wonderful experience for me. I hope I made some differences." She would go on to become the head of the American Red Cross and then leave it two years later. In 1997, Reed Fraley, still running the hospital, would be promoted to associate vice president under Manuel Tzagournis, who would later retire as vice president, have a medical research building named in his honor, and keep practicing medicine.

In 1999, the search would begin for a new head of all health science programs, to be filled by Johns Hopkins's Fred Sanfilippo, once again combining deanship with vice presidency and fulfilling the old adage that "what goes around comes around."

# 29
# *Research and Research Parks*

> While other nations have placed their funds and trust in government agencies or state-run laboratories, basic research in the United States has been primarily the charge of our research-intensive universities. . . . Laser eye surgery . . . the Pap smear . . . the pacemaker . . . the Social Security System . . . actuarial tables . . . discovery of the Dead Sea Scrolls . . . even the childproof safety cap and the test of stannous fluoride for tooth decay are the products of university research.
>
> —From "Knowledge Pours from Colleges,"
> a 1995 op-ed column by Gordon Gee

In 1990, Stanford University was accused of making mistakes in billing the federal government for "indirect costs" on research grants. The government pays indirect costs, or overhead, ranging from 15 to 88 percent on its projects with universities and private contractors. At most universities the rate was between 40 and 60 percent, individually negotiated with each institution, with most private universities on the high end.

Stanford, doing $250 million that year in federal scientific work, allegedly had improperly billed the government $184,000 for depreciation on an oceangoing yacht and $185,000 for administration of a profitable shopping center. Department of Justice auditors also were reviewing bills for "wine, expensive furnishings, flower arrangements, and a wedding reception at the president's residence" (*New York Times,* March 25, 1991).

MIT, which had some $233 million in federal R&D work that year, was also soon being audited, as was Michigan's $180 million, its most-publicized offense being some small public relations costs at the 1989 Rose Bowl. As the *Boston Globe* commented in retrospect the following fall (September 11, 1991), "critics seized on the [Michigan] report as further evidence major universities have been bilking the government." One university that certainly wasn't was Ohio State; its low indirect reimbursements never had covered actual costs.

In the interim, when the House Committee on Oversight and Investigations, chaired by Michigan's John Dingell, requested audit information from all universities doing federal research, the national organization of the largest ones, public and private, the Association of American Universities (AAU), got moving. Soon presidents and lobbyists were working the agencies and halls of Congress to preserve their institutions' reputations as much as their overhead rates. Ohio State was being represented in one form by the seven-institution Midwestern University Alliance—Ohio State, Indiana, Iowa State, Minnesota, Missouri, Purdue, and Wisconsin—directed by savvy Washington lobbyist Newton Cattell.

The two cochairs of an ad hoc legislative committee representing higher education were William "Bill" Richardson, president of the private Johns Hopkins University, the number 1 institution in federal R&D funding at nearly $600 million, and, for the public side, Ohio State's Gordon Gee. With staff help from Federal Relations Director Dick Stoddard, Gee's role was to bring private and public presidents together. With much less to lose than the private university CEOs and, in some cases, nothing to lose at all, the public presidents were less than excited about marshaling forces. Harvard University's Medical School had the highest rate, 77 percent, and the top 27 rates all were at private universities or their medical schools.

Externally, in the media, Gee always was ready with a quotable quote about research as the engine of the economy and had a record at the University of Colorado to demonstrate his point. In the years of his presidency there, federal science and engineering funding had grown by $47 million or more than two-thirds, from $69 million in 1985 to $116 million in 1990, helping build a thriving Boulder economy.

In contrast, at Ohio State it had risen less than half in that time, from $53 million to $78 million. But increasing science and engineering grants already was high on Gee's radar screen, and in the next year alone they would rise by another $20 million under the new Research vice president, Edward Hayes (Sources for all federal figures: National Science Foundation data, as reported annually in the *Chronicle of Higher Education*).

Through his work with the AAU surrounding the indirect costs investigation, Gordon Gee would work closely again with Dr. Bernadine Healy, who

CHAPTER 29

had left the Research Institute of the Cleveland Clinic Foundation just that January to accept President Bush's appointment to direct the National Institutes of Health. She had formed a committee to advise her on indirect cost rate recommendations she was to send to the House Subcommittee on Labor and Health and Human Services Appropriations, which funded the NIH. On that committee was Ohio State President Gordon Gee, with whom she had negotiated an academic partnership with the Cleveland Clinic only months before. While most rates went down, others, mostly public, were too low and went up.

Five years and one Democratic administration later, Gee would lure Dr. Healy away from the Cleveland Clinic to which she had returned and make perhaps the most influential hire of his presidency.

## *The Rap on Researchers*

Though the 1980s had not been particularly kind to the "Rust Belt," as *Business Week* (May 20, 1991) noted, they still had been "heady" for most research universities. Headiness, however, was on the decline by the spring of 1991. According to a study by the Council on Competitiveness, a coalition of CEOs and university presidents to which Gee belonged, the U.S. standard of living had fallen for the first time in ten years. With layoffs mounting, university tuitions rising faster than the cost of living index, and a college education becoming more necessary than ever to land a good job, public opinion was beginning to harden against universities.

According to the American Council on Education, by survey margins of seven or eight to one, Americans were saying college was too expensive, was not a good value, and was rapidly pricing itself beyond the reach of all but the rich. This, of course, was not the case at most public institutions, where tuition remained in the low four figures and financial aid often rose with it. But the lumping prevailed, with national stories about high-five-figure private university tuitions rubbing off on the nation's underfunded state universities, tarring publics with the same brush.

When it tried to explain costs, all higher education found itself whistling in the wind about its own cost-of-living index, more dependent than the consumers' upon utility rates, paper (i.e., library books and journals), computers, and, of course, salaries. To the public, it was as if each university were using the machine in a cartoon that Jim Garland, then chair of Ohio State's physics department, facetiously sent to Gee that May: On the "World Famous Ohio State

Physics Department Budget Machine" were thirty buttons, eleven dials, seven levers, and two switches. All worked only in one direction, and that direction was "more." Garland offered Gee the machine, but he had to promise to give it back.

Now, the public had an entire class of culprits in its line of fire: research university faculty, they who had deserted the classroom for the lab and deserted "our" children for "their" tinkering. Through the spate of books and articles beginning to "diss" universities, Americans other than college students and their parents now knew about "teachers" who didn't teach undergraduates or didn't like to if they did.

And not all such teachers, they discovered, were senior professors who already might have done their time in the classroom. As documented by the NSF, the share of new doctoral degree recipients whose main duty was teaching had plummeted from 57 percent in 1976 to 30 percent in 1990. While many of these new Ph.D.s may have been most valuable to the nation when developing new medicines, new technologies, or new businesses, aggravating things further were those rich universities like Stanford and MIT, apparently milking the Feds of dollars. It was time, *Business Week* editorialized (May 20, 1991) "for universities to enter the real world" by ceasing to lionize faculty who attracted big grants, and to return to their primary mission—education.

It was also time for university presidents, trustees, and advocates to explain better to the nation the Dark Ages in which it otherwise would be living "if not for university research."

The early 1990s, then, began the period in which pressure mounted outside universities to enhance undergraduate teaching as it increased inside to attract more research revenue. This tension continued on university campuses through the decade. With the federal government cutting spending on some basic research, in part because of the Gulf War, one early side effect was the indirect cost scandal, which eventually caused audits of seventeen universities. Stanford, whose rate had risen between 1980 and 1990 from 58 to 74 percent, was capped at 61 percent.

Ohio State, one of those publics whose overhead rate was never high to begin with, dropped by only one percent, from 47 to 46. But it was revealed years later in the university's 1997 report of Gee's research commission that federal grant-getting never had broken even at Ohio State. Actual overhead was closer to 51 percent, the difference carried by other university funds. Paradoxically, the commission had been chaired by Dean Healy, who had helped set the rate when with the NIH.

The state of Ohio, meanwhile, was in the first stage of its budget crisis,

CHAPTER 29

which would take nearly $80 million from the university's general fund through the 1994–1995 academic year.

## *Economic Impact*

A case that Gordon Gee and his administration would make throughout the toughest budget years was of Ohio State's special virtues as Ohio's higher education flagship. Chief among them was its capacity to attract, and therefore spend in Ohio, hundreds of millions of out-of-state dollars generated through research. Ohio State generated hundreds of millions in state taxes through the salaries it paid. And it created tens of thousands of Ohio jobs even beyond its campuses through faculty research, hospital services, and extension offices.

Using *An Investment in Ohio's Economic Recovery and Future Growth*, an Ohio State economic impact report done by the School of Public Policy and Management, Gee would explain personally how the university was a $1.25 billion enterprise. Not only that, much more money—over $100 million more a year—already was generated through philanthropy, investments, its hospitals, and the federal government than came from the state of Ohio.

The report was released by Gee in Columbus at a January 1993 meeting of the Ohio Society of Professional Journalists and then carried by him personally to meetings with the state's major editorial boards. It proved so media-worthy that, when another one was produced three years later, it became the template for *Ohio's Education Portfolio 1996*, a system-wide study done by the Inter-University Council of Ohio. Ohio's public universities, the Council reported, were attracting $618 million in public and private sector grants and contracts alone to Ohio and were generating new opportunities for the state by creating new ideas, altered processes, and innovative technologies and products.

## *Investment Opportunities*

But where were the Ohio financiers ready to invest in start-up high-tech companies, as there were, for instance, in California and Texas?

Where was a massive state government-backed investment program to create and bring scientific industry and jobs to the Buckeye State?

And where were all the innovative technologies and products that were to have come from Ohio State's research park?

What indeed had happened to the research park Ohio State had been planning for its West Campus since 1984? For some people, visions of the Research Triangle Park spawned by Duke, North Carolina, and North Carolina State, and Silicon Valley, spawned by Stanford and Cal-Berkeley, had danced in their heads. Though a survey by the Enarson administration back in 1981 had found no more than a half-dozen such parks thriving, Ohio State still had done a feasibility study in 1983, established a Research Park Council in 1984, and placed tenants in three modest Kinnear Road buildings by 1989.

With little corporate or local government cooperation by 1991, and a community in which retail and fast food dominated entrepreneurialism, would the Gee administration try to reenergize such an initiative under a new vice president for research? At least Ohio State's patent policy was not as onerous as it had been. Until May 1989, faculty who developed patents received nothing. All royalty revenue went to the university, so entrepreneurial faculty just left. President Jennings finally changed that before he retired. Half of the first $75,000 in royalties now went to the inventor, as would a third of additional income.

In 1990, Jennings had also appointed a task force on interdisciplinary research and graduate study, whose work carried into the Gee administration, reporting in April 1991, Gee's first spring at Ohio State. To no one's surprise, *Fostering Interdisciplinary Research and Graduate Education* would report that interdisciplinary work at Ohio State was viewed unfavorably in large segments of the university. Some faculty thought it weak research. Communication barriers existed among programs and departments. And there was little recognition or reward.

Nevertheless, globally, scholarship was increasingly crossing departmental boundaries, and so was U.S. government funding. Ohio State would not be able to compete with its peer institutions, the report warned, without strong interdisciplinary activities; and for that to happen, disincentives had to be overcome. It was no coincidence that, from the very first, Gee talked about ending Ohio State's "silo mentality." Such was the environment that greeted Ed Hayes of Rice, the new vice president for Research, in his first month on the job, which also was April 1991.

## *Rice's Edward Hayes*

Terry Miller, the university's Eminent Scholar in experimental physical chemistry, chaired the search committee for Ohio State's new vice president for Research. Miller had joined the Ohio State faculty from Bell Laboratories in 1984, was an internationally respected research scientist in spectroscopy, and had

## Chapter 29

become one of the faculty's most active and respected leaders. Per the job description, with opportunity broadening in applied research, the vice presidency would demand an innovative leader who could build "increased cooperation with business and industry." Experience in attracting grants and contracts from both government agencies and industry was necessary.

One finalist whose credentials stood out was Edward F. Hayes, a highly respected physical chemist and administrator from Rice, who had top management experience in both the National Science Foundation and U.S. Office of Management and Budget. His bachelor's was from the University of Rochester, and his master's and Ph.D. degrees were from The Johns Hopkins University in his native Baltimore. Ed Hayes had joined Rice as assistant provost and vice president for information technologies. One Ohio State interviewer pointed out that his knowledge of the NSF had brought one of the first federal Scientific and Technology Centers to Rice.

In his interviews, Hayes greatly impressed many members of the search committee, including a number of deans. When asked why he was interested in leaving one of the finest private universities in the country, it was clear, one dean wrote Gee, that Hayes was seeking "a larger institution in which he could apply [his] assets and skills. This is a case where 'big' is indeed better."

After his first few weeks at Ohio State, the new vice president announced he would retain the existing management team. Special assistant Dick Stoddard would give increased attention to federal matters—so much so that he would be reassigned to the president in 1995. Acting Associate Vice President Mary Ellen Sheridan would continue handling administrative matters. Thomas "Tom" Sweeney, who had been acting vice president for the eighteen months since the retirement of Jack Hollander, would continue as both associate vice president and executive director of the Research Foundation.

## *Customer Satisfaction*

Ohio State's Roger Blackwell noted in his *From the Edge of the World*, published in 1992 and read by Gee, that U.S. industry was not yet addressing the real issues, product quality, service, segmentation, and customer satisfaction, and was continuing to lose when competing with Japan. That situation, as we know, would reverse later in the decade, but in 1992 Gordon Gee was citing a higher education parallel: a better product and better service would translate into higher "customer" satisfaction, whether the customer was a student, parent, legislator, or governor.

## RESEARCH AND RESEARCH PARKS

A white paper he and Ed Hayes distributed on the future of research stressed the intense competition for external and internal funds. Better products of research would be the ones that fulfilled "an unprecedented public demand" for societal benefit: in particular, the "effective transfer of technology to industry to make our region and nation more competitive."

The president and vice president had no "plan and no agenda," they wrote in the white paper. Both, they believed, should emerge from "a shared view of our mission" to be determined "ultimately . . . by the faculty." However, there was no denying that a major component of the academic plan for the future of Ohio State had to be research and development, technology transfer, and faculty entrepreneurialism.

Thus, the specific subject of research entered the dialogue about the future of Ohio State, which had begun with campus forums the previous March. That June, two major figures in the research discussions would be appointed deans: Jose Cruz in Engineering and Jim Garland in Mathematical and Physical Sciences. Gee would not receive his first blueprint, *The Strategic Plan for Research*, until September 1994, when the budget still would permit only modest investment, mostly through the new academic enrichment program and the major strategic investments in molecular life sciences and advanced materials.

In January 1997, the president and Provost Sisson decided it was time for another blueprint, this time using the university's new benchmarking practice, which was beginning to compare Ohio State to the Top 20 public universities; in particular, its ten most serious competitors for quality graduate students and external funding—the Universities of Arizona, Illinois, Michigan, Minnesota, Texas, Washington, Wisconsin, Penn State, and UCLA.

The Research Commission Gee appointed was to be chaired by Dean Healy, who had doubled research revenue while heading the Cleveland Clinic Research Institute from 1985 to 1991. The commission's objective was to prepare goals and strategies to improve the university's research productivity so much, it would move into the Top 10 publics. Healy was particularly aware of the huge grant potential for the University Medical Center through the National Institutes of Health, which she had headed from 1991 to 1993. (As she noted years later, "because it's much easier for politicians to put a few billion dollars into NIH research even as they are taking billions out of the patient care pool," the NIH budget did not drop during Gee's seven years as president, even as funding for teaching hospitals did.) Staff support for the Research Commission would be provided by Vice President Hayes.

CHAPTER 29

## *The Ohio Science and Technology Council*

In 1992, following the dedication of the State of Ohio Computer Center on West Campus, Gee and Hayes started a dialogue with Governor Voinovich and his development director, Donald Jakeway. It was about generating more state, industrial, and university cooperation to attract sponsored research and create new industry in Ohio.

The governor had referred optimistically to Ohio as "one large research park," and things were beginning to happen cooperatively between President Gee and Mayor Lashutka on other fronts. But it would not be until 1995 and the end of the years of state budget cuts that the governor would officially reconstitute Ohio's dormant Science and Technology Council.

Its cochairs were Glen Hiner, chairman and CEO of Owens-Corning Fiberglass Corporation, and E. Gordon Gee. The workhorses, titled "key advisors" in the solicitation letters to other CEOs and university presidents, were Warren Wolf, Owens-Corning's brilliant director of research and development, and Ed Hayes of Ohio State. Their charge was to review the state's science and technology activities, coordinate Ohio's response to science and technology issues, and marshal support for initiatives that would bring economic development to Ohio. But little activity was generated.

Apparently, Ohio was still neither a state replete with entrepreneurs ready to invest in high-tech enterprise or one with a state government ready to invest in its future through science and technology. At the turn of the millennium, Wolf would say Ohio still saw itself as a manufacturing state and Columbus as a center of service industries, while Voinovich, now a U.S. senator, would declare the dearth of new business brought in by the Council one of his great disappointments.

## *Research Park Reprise*

Trustee Ted Celeste was the consummate trustee advocate of Ohio State's research enterprise and one of Columbus's first in its handful of high-technology entrepreneurs. In 1982, he became one of the pioneers of interactive video, running his own company, which did well for a decade until its largest client, Pharmor pharmacies, went into bankruptcy.

Though a Cleveland native, as a graduate of the College of Wooster he had come in contact with the work of Ohio State's Agricultural Research and Development Center (OARDC) in that city, one of the premier agricultural experiment stations in the nation. As husband to the daughter of a Washington Court House farm family, he had learned even more about one of Ohio's leading industries: agribusiness. Thus, when he joined the Board, Ted Celeste's interests included the restructuring of what in a few years would be renamed the College of Food, Agricultural, and Environmental Sciences and the moving along of Ohio State's research park.

In July 1993, the trustees authorized Columbus to annex 11.5 acres of university property in Clinton Township, part of it for what then was called the Business Technology Center (BTC). The BTC had sprung from the Thomas Edison Program created nine years earlier by Governor Dick Celeste to create Ohio jobs by linking universities and start-up businesses. The BTC would move from its house in the former Orton Memorial Laboratory on Summit Street to occupy part of a building the university now owned on Kinnear Road, the old Simmons mattress factory. This, OSU Business Vice President Janet Pichette said in the press release, "would provide a dimension to the [research] park."

What research park? Six months later, an impatient Gee memoed Sisson, Hayes, Pichette, and Shkurti, reminding them that, while "we continue to talk about the development of the research park," no consultants had been brought in, which he thought they had determined to do some time back. Soon, the university leased land to the Edison Welding Institute, one of the major Celeste initiatives, to build a new home for it on Lane Avenue that would double its size (it opened as the Edison Joining Technology Center in 1996).

Meanwhile, a year-long study was launched, which included many meetings with representatives of the city, state, and area Chamber of Commerce. As trustee Ted Celeste remembered it, at first fingers were pointed at Ohio State for noncooperation. In fact, there was some truth to this. Ohio State's park was not to be just a convenient site for unaffiliated technology companies. There had to be some connection to Ohio State entrepreneurship or continuing research.

## *Battelle*

One great big connection that never connected was the Rubik's cube of Ohio State and Battelle. In 1929, Gordon Battelle opened his nonprofit corporation off King Avenue in Columbus as a memorial to his family, who had been leaders in America's early steel industry. Its purpose was to develop technologies and products, and it certainly had. Xerography, the Universal Product Code,

CHAPTER 29

the sandwiched coin, the crack-proof golf ball, the compact disc, polarized sunglasses, advanced sonar, even the Sensonic toothbrush owed their existence to Battelle.

In 1994, as Gordon Gee began to push his administration hard to both restart the nascent research park program and buy up peripheral property, Battelle officials were thinking about a move, possibly rebuilding on Ohio State's West Campus. As Robert Haverkamp, Ohio State's chief property attorney remembered it, "We weren't sure what to do with all the buildings, but we started having discussions," and they signed a confidentiality agreement that expired in 2000.

Until early 1996, they considered the options, Ohio State doing space studies and Battelle looking at property off Ackerman Road. One conundrum for Gee was the length of the "decommissioning," or decontamination, process of buildings licensed for nuclear work. Some could not be available until 1997 or 1998. Another was price: $40 million had been discussed. Another was whether to sell Ohio State land or lease it. In June 1995, as trustee George Skestos was stepping down as chair of the university's long-range planning committee, he wrote Gee, saying that he believed $40 million "excessive and burdensome," that no purchase should be made unless subleasing covered the interest on borrowing, and that the university should lease, never sell, West Campus land.

In the end, Ohio State leased one Battelle building for some of its medical administrative units, and Battelle stayed where it was.

## *The Research Park Corporation*

Finally, in January 1996, a month before the creation of the Research Commission, a new nonprofit corporation was announced, The Ohio State University Research Park Corporation (RPC), with a nine-member board. The three official Ohio State members were Gordon Gee, Ed Hayes, and Ted Celeste. Agriculture Vice President Bobby Moser also was on the board as a community representative, along with a banker, a marketer, a state representative, and two attorneys. One of the attorneys, Scott Whitlock, would soon become its first director. The city, university, and state each would fund $50,000 for the first three months as startup money. Celeste, who had visited parks at the universities of North Carolina, Texas, and Wisconsin, said later, "it should have been $50 million early in."

In September 1997, a few months after Gee accepted the Brown presidency, he memoed the Research Park Board, noting its approval of what would be called Science Village. By that time, Hayes had reorganized his office for the park, with David Allen, director of the Office of Technology Transfer, and Paul McSweeney, director of Industrial Outreach. Consultant Don Van Meter, who had advised the Ohio Science and Technology Council, was handling marketing and promotion, and Hayes and General Counsel Ginny Trethewey were the departing president's key leaders.

Soon, the research park had a new name: Science and Technology Campus. The RPC board became the Science and Technology Corporation (STC) board; and Science Village was building Phase 1 under the corporation's new president, engineer, and attorney, Ora Smith, with degrees from MIT and Harvard and twenty-plus years' experience in commercializing technology. The STC had $40.3 million in capital and operating funds, and the current chair of The Ohio State University Board of Trustees was Ted Celeste.

## *The Three Appointments*

By the time the report of Healy's Research Commission was published in July 1998, it was a recommendation for the administration of Brit Kirwan. But, in its development, the report was expected to be implemented by three of Gordon Gee's most significant appointees: Ed Hayes, Healy herself, and Dick Sisson.

As stairways to a Top 10 ranking among all public universities, the commission developed recommendations in five specific areas. "First and foremost, this report is about our faculty. The quality of the faculty will have the greatest impact of any single factor." The second area was the need for a more competitive research infrastructure, including facilities and equipment. "This will be a major challenge for the university . . . as we have fallen behind our peers and, on all measures, are overworking the existing facilities even for current lines of research."

Third was the need to continue to build multidisciplinary and interdisciplinary centers. "Team efforts across the university have not been as frequent or as effective as they should be." Not much headway had been made since the 1990 report that had greeted Ed Hayes. The fourth issue involved promotion and institutional confidence: "the extent to which OSU thinks, acts and promotes itself internally and externally as one of the top research universities in the country."

The recommendations that cut across all others, of course, were about

CHAPTER 29

money and resources. Continue forward in the capital campaign. Press the state for differential funding. Expand technology transfer. Improve the economics of sponsored research. "Investment and entrepreneurship, not entitlement and pleading, will bring the kind of major transformation to the university that the Research Commission believes is possible."

One point strongly made—and given the NRC rankings in 1995, there no longer could be an argument against it—was that Ohio State was indeed "Ohio's flagship university" and needed to position itself as such to "achieve the kind of state investment that has enabled our peer institutions to succeed."

But how far did Ohio State have to go to achieve the objectives of the commission? In the benchmark data of the report's appendixes were some indications of others' most significant successes. In ranking public universities in federal R&D spending, The University of Washington was ranked number 1. Number 10 was Arizona. Ohio State was number 18. In NIH research at medical schools, Washington was number 2, Michigan number 3, and Texas at Dallas number 10. Ohio State was not in the top 20. In members elected to the National Academies in the sciences, engineering, and medicine, Cal-Berkeley led with 173 members. North Carolina at Chapel Hill was number 10 with 34. Ohio State had 10.

There surely was a distance to go, but as the report's preface concluded, "The Research Commission has come to believe that the lofty goal of being counted among the top ten research universities in the nation is achievable."

Then, one evening in 1998—some time after Gee had left for Brown—Ed Hayes, who kept himself in good shape, came home from a run in his Upper Arlington neighborhood and suffered a fatal heart attack. He was only fifty-six.

## *Years of Service*

In Ed Hayes's seven years as the university's chief research officer, Ohio State's sponsored research support increased by more than 40 percent, from $145 million to more than $245 million a year. In championing undergraduate research, he attracted many of the state's finest new scholars to a growing Honors Program. In particular, the philanthropy of alumni Rick and Marte Denman today sustains the annual Undergraduate Research Forum that Hayes created. He taught chemistry and was an active researcher whose funding supported undergraduate, graduate, and postdoctoral students. Only at his funeral did many of his colleagues discover the breadth and depth of his charity to others.

# RESEARCH AND RESEARCH PARKS

At the time of Ed Hayes's death, Gordon Gee was at Brown and Hayes's friend and colleague Richard Sisson was presiding over the university as interim president. "A scholar in the truest sense," Sisson eulogized, "a man of deep thoughtfulness, great intellectual acuity, and kindly strength. Teaching was a passionate commitment, as was his exemplary regard for students. I am proud to have called him my friend." Brit Kirwan, of course, would take over for Interim President Sisson, who had accepted that appointment on December 15, 1997 and withdrawn as a finalist for the presidency of the University of Texas to do so. Sisson would return to the faculty and his research.

Having recovered from surgery on a brain tumor and returned full-time to work, Bernadine Healy, M.D.—who through her media prominence as a CBS television correspondent had become perhaps the best-known physician in the country—responded in 1999 to a call she could not turn down. While she had consistently rejected offers that would have taken her from Ohio State, here she knew she could really "make a difference" to society and could not say no. The American Red Cross wanted her to become its president and chief executive officer. "It was a wonderful experience," she said later of her four years at Ohio State, and she hoped she had made a difference to the university while she was dean. She never had "seen anything like the support" given the university by the city and its leaders. She still felt part of Ohio State and "would always treasure" her time there.

Yes, she had been urged by a number of people to seek the presidency of the university at Gordon Gee's announcement of his departure for Brown in 1997, "but never in any way" did she want it. As a member of the presidential search committee, when asked of her interest, her response had been consistent: "Let's see if we can get Brit Kirwan." And it was she, among others, who later joined trustee Alex Shumate in visiting Kirwan at the University of Maryland. Shumate, who chaired the search committee, would surmise years later that her presence that day most convinced Brit Kirwan to look at Ohio State. If the former head of the National Institutes of Health was there, it must be a place worth considering!

# 30

## *The High Street Legacy*

Few people in the Ohio State community could remember a time in which the University District was its own college town, where faculty, staff, and graduate students lived side by side. But it had been that way.

In the 1940s, 50 percent of district homes were owned by the residents who lived in them, and faculty, staff, and graduate and undergraduate students lived side by side. By 1996, home ownership was down to 11 percent, and not only had owners sold to absentee landlords, but the university, like virtually all of higher education, had abdicated responsibility beyond the campus. But times had changed and were changing again.

At Ohio State, from 1967 until the end of the Vietnam War, there had been peace marches, antiwar demonstrations, and eventual confrontations with the Columbus police and Ohio National Guard. The university had closed down from May 6 to May 18, 1970, following the notorious killings of four students at Kent State University. Ironically, but understandably, the generation of students whose activism had created the hands-off attitude had become the generation of parents now criticizing the performance of higher education and who, by and large, wanted those hands back on.

Asked in his exit interview to talk about the accomplishments in which he took most pride, intervention in the district was near the top of the president's list. "The rehabilitation of our campus area (through Campus Partners); the creation of opportunities for faculty and staff to move back in; the relationship of the Campus Collaborative to schools and social services may be one of the great experiments of any university."

Campus Partners, in fact, embodied Gee's rejection of the administrative credo his own student generation had created. Gee himself had said that the

## THE HIGH STREET LEGACY

first time he sat in a university president's chair was during an antiwar demonstration at Columbia in the early 1970s. Since that time, university administrations had constricted their responsibility, he would say, to "only what is the university's." They "threw up their arms" and confined their accountability to what would "get [students] in the classroom and get them out" (*Dispatch*, December 17, 1996).

By the 1990s the notion of *in loco parentis*, the university as parent, did seem to be edging back into public favor, while the university as urban landlord was becoming an issue peculiar to campuses like Ohio State. To Gee's mind, the two concepts meshed nicely.

When three students were arrested in a street melee after Ohio State's 1995 victory over Notre Dame, Gee had had them suspended from school. "What is the relationship of the university to its students, and does it extend beyond the classroom? Well, my answer is 'yes.' Does it extend beyond the campus? The answer is 'yes.'" The suspensions were overturned under Ohio State's student code of conduct, which did not extend off campus. But the story was covered and Gee's actions were generally applauded.

Gee also deplored the student living conditions he had seen in his walks through the East of High areas and blamed the absentee landlords. While without the $100 million investment that Les Wexner had suggested, Campus Partners could not afford to purchase much rental housing, it could and would work with the city to strengthen code enforcement as it bought up business acreage. In a November 19, 1997, talk to the Providence Preservation Society, Gee portrayed the living conditions around the university he was leaving this way:

> During my presidency, we faced a situation that threatened both the architectural integrity and the sense of community in a neighborhood bordering campus. Absentee landlords were building additions into their already crowded apartment buildings, often called "people packers". . . . They were crowded, unsightly, and turning the surrounding neighborhood into a true "student ghetto" [with] bad plumbing, broken screens, flimsy balconies. We saw the quality of student housing deteriorating around us.

Thus, the university had stepped in and created Campus Partners for Community Urban Redevelopment.

CHAPTER 30

A new friend helps Gordon lead a "High on Pride" university area cleanup, a Gee initiative, 1994.

## *South Campus*

Though a nondrinker and a weight watcher, his many ventures out to meet and talk with students had given Gordon Gee expert knowledge of the local bars and pizza joints. When in April 1996, Papa Joe's burned down—the place

## THE HIGH STREET LEGACY

*Columbus Monthly* (November 1997) called "the symbol—for good or ill... of what South Campus was"—some students sardonically asked whether anybody knew where Gordon Gee was last night? Papa Joe's, Waterbed's 'n Stuff—a vestige of the 1970s—and the bar known as Off Campus all were consumed, and all were prime purchase material in Campus Partners' design to redevelop the heart of the South Campus bar area.

"I was home with my wife," Gee had jested with mock guilt at the April trustees meeting, which happened to be the day following the fire. And he would gain a second laugh later, when he produced her "affidavit."

Soon, for $2.75 million, Campus Partners purchased the charred site of the Papa Joe's strip as well as the large, old, and empty Big Bear Bakery across the street. By this time, as they came up for sale some small properties also were being bought if the price was right, which it not always was. Unlike the Walt Disney Company, which had been able to conceal its plans for Walt Disney World while buying up much of central Florida, Campus Partners' appetite for land was hardly a secret. As *Columbus Monthly* reported, "a cat and mouse game" was under way. Campus Partners wanted uninflated prices. Owners hoped for top dollar. A leveling influence was the prospect of the Columbus City Council declaring their property "blighted," which would justify its being taken by eminent domain.

Was Ohio State killing the South Campus bar area that held so many memories for so many alumni? No, it was not, said *Columbus Monthly.* Ten years before, in threatening to withhold highway money from any state that did not change its drinking age from 18 to 21, "the federal government did." Saturday night bar crowds were half of what they had been before 1987, while at the same time the age change had created a proliferation of "keg parties" and the beer-fueled street revelries that sometimes followed. In response to Gee's initiatives against binging and with Mayor Greg Lashutka's support, Columbus police were cracking down hard on underaged drinkers and the bars that served them, as well as in the streets to which they fled.

In 1997, with funding from the city and Ohio State through Campus Partners, a forty-person advisory steering committee began working with the Boston urban planning firm Good, Clancy, and Associates to create what was hoped would be the final iteration of the plan for the High Street campus area. At the core of the plan was to be the University Gateway Center, which would include the properties that were once the Big Bear Bakery and Papa Joe's. It would be the year 2000 before *A Plan for High Street: Creating a 21st Century Main Street* would finally be published. It would be 2002 before Gateway Center construction would begin.

CHAPTER 30

## *The Lennox Center*

In the interim, to the west of what had been University Hospitals and was now called the University Medical Center, a completely new shopping entertainment destination had sprung up on Olentangy River Road. The Lennox Center, formerly the site of the manufacturing and distribution of air conditioners, was now home to an eighteen-screen movie theater, three restaurants, a Barnes and Noble bookstore, Staples, an Old Navy, and a variety of other shopping venues that catered to a university crowd. It had taken some of the heat off High Street as an outlet for off-campus activity, though, less high in profile, Gordon Gee and his staff, in particular Treasurer Jim Nichols, had facilitated the transformation. While the university itself had had the opportunity to buy the Lennox property, it had chosen not to pursue it.

In addition, on property owned by the university, a Cooker Restaurant had opened on Lane Avenue across from St. John Arena, and the old Jai alai restaurant on Olentangy River Road had been replaced by what immediately became a new institution, the Buckeye Hall of Fame Cafe, the first such facility licensed by the university.

All the while, Gee himself had viewed housing as *the* essential issue in the redevelopment of the High Street area. "With high quality housing, you get families, you get students, you get people who have a broader commitment to the community" (*Dispatch,* December 16, 1996). At his instigation, Campus Partners now offered Ohio State employees a $3,000 incentive grant to buy property, or to renovate what they already owned, in the district. He even suggested he might move there himself. Of course, he didn't. He went to Brown. But, when he returned full-time to the faculty in 2000, Provost and Interim President Richard Sisson and his wife, Willa, did.

# 31

## *Public Records*

> First, I want to report I did run and did finish the Columbus Marathon. I refuse to report the time and am doing everything I can to have it protected from the seemingly unimpeded reach of the Ohio Public Records Law.
> —Provost Richard Sisson, to a
> colleague in March 1995

Two months earlier, the Ohio Supreme Court had ruled work addresses and telephone numbers of public employees "public records," to be released upon request. The specific culprits were Ohio State University faculty doing animal research.

An attorney for the animal rights activist group Protect Our Earth's Treasures (POET) had asked for university records about such research. The university had released them, but blacked out the names of researchers in connection with specific research, along with their addresses and phone numbers, and POET went to court. The university argued for academic freedom and the constitutional right of privacy. At least two faculty, it submitted in affidavits, had received death threats. So had a university spokesperson, challenged by telephone to come out on his front porch, but no longer living in the home with the front porch, as listed in the last white pages.

In a case that began and ended in the Ohio Supreme Court, the university lost. While the court acknowledged an increase in "threats, harassment, and violence against animal research scientists" nationally, it found that fact to be irrelevant to the construction of the public records statute. The court did note, however, that it was dealing only with work addresses and telephone numbers, leaving the question of home addresses and phone numbers for another day.

In the spring of 1995, when Sisson wrote his sarcastic note, Ohio State was taking its public records fight to the Ohio General Assembly. Lobbyist Herb Asher and Gee were working the halls of power, as were their counterparts from the other state universities, their umbrella group the Inter-University Council, and the Ohio Board of Regents.

Protecting faculty animal researchers from potential harassment was just the tip of this iceberg. At its base was the protection of ideas, "intellectual property" such as research grant proposals and draft manuscripts. Its bulk consisted of all types of records: donor profiles, which might contain highly personal background information; student "education records," already protected by the federal Family Educational Rights and Privacy Act (FERPA); records of faculty and staff searches; and personnel records, including information about spouses and children, home addresses, and telephone numbers; even library circulation records.

Of particular concern to Sisson had been a 1994 State Supreme Court ruling that had opened faculty promotion and tenure files to public scrutiny. Would letters of recommendation or censure still say what they would have said now that anyone could make a public records request and read the file?

In the public sector, there was very little that could be guaranteed to be "private."

## *The Immediate Past*

In 1991, the *Toledo Blade* had gone after the files of the fund-raising arm of the University of Toledo, a separate foundation. While agreeing to share most of its records, the foundation had drawn the line at donor files. The foundation was private, chartered separately from the university, and could, its lawyers argued, shield its records from the public if it wanted. Not so, argued the *Blade:* the foundation exercises a function of the university and, therefore, is subject to the Ohio Public Records Statute.

To develop leadership of its first major capital campaign in 1984, Ohio State itself had created a foundation (OSUF). Before that, it didn't need one. But since the university board of voting trustees was appointed by the governor and limited to nine people, the university now needed a separate, larger board to lead the campaign and acknowledge its major donors. As the *Dispatch* wrote eight years later, by May 2, 1992, the board of the Ohio State Foundation was "stocked with prominent business and community leaders" who had given more than $50 million themselves and secured "the lion's share" of the $460 million raised between 1985 and 1990.

OSUF had not been the repository of donations in that first big campaign. It had been only a leadership organization. But in May 1992, the university board ok'd the administration's recommendation that the foundation become the university's primary fund-raising and gift-receipt organization as well. It also created the position of foundation president, who would be the same person as the yet to be hired new vice president for university development.

Was the university going to use its foundation to shield its donor files from public record requests? Said Gee, "This is simply a way for some people to be more comfortable about giving money to the university." Whether "comfort" ever would have been equated with "total privacy" became moot three months later when the Ohio Supreme Court held the University of Toledo Foundation to be a gift-receiving arm of the university, and thus subject to the Ohio Public Records Act, and that it could not withhold the names of its donors.

The majority decision was written by Chief Justice Thomas J. Moyer (who later also would chair the board of directors of the Ohio State Alumni Association). The vote was 6–1.

Wrote Ohio State's legal counsel Bob Duncan to that new foundation president and development chief, Jerry May: after thorough review of the opinion, briefs and memoranda of record in the case, and case law of other jurisdictions, "the Office of Legal Affairs is constrained to report that upon appropriate request the names of OSUF donors must be revealed."

While donor anonymity had been lost, the court had not specifically discussed whether other information—financial statements, estate plans, family data, written staff comments—also had to be disclosed. A development officer's background note, for instance, perhaps explaining why Louis or Louise was written out of a will and a university might be written into it, arguably did not yet have to be made public. But such types of information also had not been enumerated as specific exceptions by the Ohio General Assembly.

While the Toledo ruling appeared to be bad news for foundations, it could have been worse. To preclude much worse, "perhaps," Duncan had added in his memo to May, "the next resort is to go to the General Assembly to amend the statute." In the meantime, the Ohio Public Records Act had been used by many organizations and individuals for many reasons other than to seek donor names or faculty addresses and telephone numbers.

In September 1994, the State Supreme Court had found for an Ohio State faculty member denied tenure who wanted to read not only his own file, including letters pro and con, but other files within his department. Each time the university rebuffed him, he requested more files until he was up to 600 (*Dispatch,* September 2, 1994). In a unanimous decision, Justice Craig Wright wrote, "Promotion and tenure records maintained by a state-supported institution of higher education are 'public records.'"

The court had not been convinced that the integrity of the promotion and tenure system would be diminished by disclosure. Perhaps not diminished, but in some cases defrocked. In one particularly public situation the following spring, three Ohio State faculty, two of whom had received tenure, found out detailed information about their own reviews by reading *The Chronicle of Higher Education.* When one complained to Gee, he wrote back that it was nearly impossible to protect the privacy of faculty and staff with respect to institutional processes and suggested that state legislators and the local chapter of the AAUP might appreciate a call.

The latest case appeared to validate a credo of the late Dick Jackson, Ohio State's vice president for Business and Finance through March 1990, who sometimes cautioned his colleagues to put nothing in writing they would not want to read in the next day's newspaper.

Soon, in May 1995, the Ohio Supreme Court handed down another decision that affected the university. A Cincinnati television station wanted information on the current class of recruits in that city's police department. The department denied the request and the station sued. The court found for the station, even including access to reports of psychological exams made in the employment screening process, and strictly speaking not for purposes of medical treatment—and, thus, not protected as medical records. "For our purposes," Ohio State attorney Steve McDonald wrote to the new general counsel, Ginny Trethewey, "the most important part of the decision is its strong reaffirmation that personnel files are almost always public records . . . and that promises of confidentiality are completely ineffective without a specific statute to back them up."

The court also had reiterated that policy arguments had to be made to the General Assembly and not to the judges.

## *A Partial Victory*

"University research papers and profiles of people who give money to Ohio's public universities and colleges will become secret with recent passage of a new state law" (*Dispatch,* June 9, 1996). Eugene Watts, the state senator from Galloway and history professor at Ohio State, had included the two new exemptions to the Public Records Statute as an amendment to an unrelated bill on trademark counterfeiting.

While arguing to protect donor files and profiles, Gee and his colleagues had lobbied hardest to protect "intellectual property." They had argued that open access to research at public universities put their faculty at a disadvantage with respect to corporate and private university researchers, and they had been listened to. But on closing promotion and tenure review files, records of searches for top-level administrators, library circulation records, and personnel files, they had not found enough supporters to change the law.

In the last month of Gordon Gee's presidency, the U.S. Supreme Court declined to hear an appeal of an Ohio Supreme Court ruling in favor of the *Miami Student,* a student newspaper that had sued its university for student disciplinary records (as opposed to university police records, which were public). Soon *The Chronicle of Higher Education* asked both Miami and Ohio State for tens of thousands of pages of such records. And soon Ohio State was being sued again. This time, the U.S. Department of Education, which protected the privacy of student records through FERPA, was suing the two universities in federal court to block the records' release, which Ohio State's administration did not want to release in the first place.

In 1999, two years after Gee's departure from Ohio State, Miami, along with Ashland University and the University of Dayton, agreed to disclose the names of students disciplined through their judicial systems. Ohio State did not. On Monday, March 23, 2000, in U.S. District Court in Columbus, Judge George C. Smith ruled that student disciplinary records were protected by the federal Family Rights and Privacy Act and were not subject to the Ohio Public Records Law.

David Williams, vice president for Student Affairs and a lawyer, not yet on his way to work for Gordon Gee at Vanderbilt, told the *Dispatch* that day that Ohio State historically protected the rights of individuals. The ruling was, he said, "consistent with the benchmarks of jurisprudence in the United States." The ruling allowed for some exceptions, giving universities the discretion to release information in certain cases, including rape and other violent crime. The ruling was upheld by the 6th U.S. Circuit Court of Appeals in June 2002.

# 32
## *Trustee Retreat 1996*

> People believe that higher education is an essential public good today. They also believe they cannot afford the costs, and the services are overpriced and not a good value for the money. . . . Ample evidence already exists that opinion leaders are profoundly troubled about higher education.
> —From *Goodwill and Growing Worry: Public Perceptions of American Higher Education, A Report for the American Council on Education,* 1995

Had it been anger at the costs of higher education or just an attempt to keep jobs in Ohio? Perhaps it was a veiled attempt to rid Ohio of oft-maligned "foreign TAs," or to stop them from taking "our" knowledge back to their native countries. Whatever the reasons, a wrong-headed amendment proposed in spring 1995 for the next Ohio budget would have eliminated the state subsidy for out-of-state and international graduate students, transferring it instead to the subsidy for Ohio undergraduates.

While campuses with few graduate programs may have benefited, virtually no one in Ohio higher education supported the legislation. Ohio State and the University of Cincinnati would have been badly hurt, as would research-intensive programs such as the University of Akron's world-class polymer center. It was time once more for Gordon Gee to do a round of editorial boards.

The *Akron Beacon Journal* explained the situation well (March 31). International students graduate in the sciences, engineering, and mathematics, where there are drastic domestic shortages. Ohio and the nation needs them, it editorialized and, contradicting a misassumption, explained that they "stay in this country becoming top research scientists for U.S. companies as well as tax-paying citizens." With the help of such editorials, Gee again led the higher education charge, and the amendment was defeated in committee. It was one of the president's most important behind-the-scenes achievements and came just before his encounter with California.

Assisting Gee, as always, was lobbyist Herb Asher, who would retire on July 1, 1996, as state relations director and professor of political science, but remain a volunteer counselor to Gee and, later, guide the new John Glenn Institute through its startup year. Alumna Colleen O'Brien would resign as deputy director of the Ohio Office of Budget and Management to become Ohio State's new director of State Relations.

## *Retreat 1996*

As usual, he had risen at 5 A.M. and exercised for ninety minutes, half of it aerobic. Six months had passed since California, and on this day in January 1996 the president was addressing his own trustees at their annual planning retreat.

Having completed what he called his "own *Pilgrim's Progress*," he said he now felt "a great deal of pressure" to produce at Ohio State at "an even higher level." The pressure was not from them, he explained. It was self-imposed. "A malaise" Gee believed, had penetrated "the American spirit," and it was higher education's "enormous responsibility" to recharge the national will.

The malaise was not being helped by the news of the day. At home, national unemployment was edging up toward 6 percent; the national debt ceiling was up to nearly $5 trillion; House Speaker Newt Gingrich was slugging it out with the Clinton White House over the budget, shutting the federal government down for a month; and a grand jury was investigating what soon became known as "Whitewater" as a woman named Paula Jones sued the President of the United States for alleged sexual harassment. Abroad, Israeli Prime Minister Yitzhak Rabin was assassinated; U.S. troops had been sent to Bosnia; and American soldiers were killed by terrorists in a bombing in Saudi Arabia.

"Leadership" was the subject of the day's trustee retreat, and Gee was the lead-off speaker. It was, he said, up to the leaders of the nation's universities such as they and such as he "to create a responsible citizenry who can

## Chapter 32

effectively face the challenges of the 21st century." Though by January 1996 the U.S. trade deficit was shrinking, and the Dow Jones Industrial Average had closed at a record 5,200, Gee saw a three-part "unresolved and unrecognized revolution" still confronting the nation.

He used Japan's still-expanding steel industry as an example of the first revolution, discussing how a nation with virtually no native natural resources could convert them into marketable products. Using the example of "an individual in Bangkok" able today to borrow money "as easily as someone in New York," he discussed how computers and telecommunications were affecting world capital markets. There was no need to name such brand names as Samsung, Sharp, Goldstar, Toyota, Mitsubishi, Hyundai, and Honda to illustrate the revolution he called "reverse engineering . . . in which the United States no longer is master of the technologies we create."

Though Prime Minister Tomichi Murayama had resigned earlier in the month because of his country's recently slowed economic growth, had Gee predicted the economic crisis that lay just ahead for Japan, his message to the trustees would have been the same: The quality of its universities—particularly its large public universities—were the key to the nation's ability once again "to control our destiny and compete in the global market place"; Ohio State must be up to the task.

Call it disinterest. Call it self-interest. Call it Generation X. Whatever the causes, over the thirty years that Provost Dick Sisson's former institution UCLA had been surveying the nation's new freshmen, interest in things civic and political had reached an all-time low.

*The American Freshman: National Norms for Fall 1995* had found that less than 29 percent of freshmen cared enough about politics to answer, yes, they would "keep up to date with political issues as a life-time goal." In 1966, during the Vietnam War, the figure had been double that. The percentage who "discussed politics frequently" also was at an all-time low: 15 percent compared with a high of 30 percent in 1968, the year of the infamous Chicago Democratic convention. Following a small 1990–1992 blip in an otherwise downward drift, the trend line was heading down again in anything civic or political.

Having an interest in "influencing the political structure" was down from 20 to 17 percent; an interest in "influencing social values," down from 43 to 38 percent; in "cleaning up the environment," down from 33 to 22 percent; and in "participating in community action programs," down from 26 to 23 percent. Even something worthy as "promoting racial understanding" also was down, from 42 to 33 percent.

## *A Culture of Complaint*

A "culture of complaint and cynicism," endemic "not only on campus" but throughout society, Gee called it. He accused neither family nor religion nor education for abdicating responsibility, but said Ohio State must do more to see that "civic values and virtues are both developed and reaffirmed."

The country, he said, needed heroes, as did the university. Soon, he and Senator John Glenn, a true hero, would begin to discuss what would evolve into Ohio State's John Glenn Institute, designed to introduce students to public policy and motivate them to public service. Gee also would invite alumnus and B. F. Goodrich Chairman John Ong to speak at the December 1996 commencement, where Ong would deliver a clarion call for civility, which Gee would publish and distribute widely. Ong, who had transformed Goodrich, manufacturer of tires, rubber products, and plastics, into a profitable provider of specialty chemicals and aircraft systems and services, exemplified the effective American leader who had adjusted to the international economy.

Who could foresee that within five years the Japanese economy would overextend and tank; dotcoms would generate a U.S. boom only to bust in a blizzard of bankruptcies taking the Dow and Nasdaq with it; and the concept of patriotism would reenter the American psyche as flags flew from millions of homes following the tragedy of September 11, 2001?

What Gee had meant by university "heroes," though, were not the astronauts or the corporate giants. In calling for "heroes" he was using a new concept in the language of employee motivation, one that would virtually disappear once the country again had real heroes: the police and firefighters who died saving lives in the World Trade Center; the passengers who died stopping the takeover of American Air Lines Flight 93 over Pennsylvania; the mail carriers dealing with the potential of anthrax poisoning; the members of the Armed Forces called upon to fight and die against Al Qaeda in Afghanistan.

In 1996, the faculty member, staff member, or student accomplishing something extraordinary or doing the superlative could be considered a "hero," to be sought out, heralded, and rewarded. To create new heroes, no notion would be more pivotal, Gee said, than the basic "power of encouragement." While he did not say he exemplified such "power," he did not need to. Once when asked how he found so much time to write supportive notes that acknowledged the good work of so many people, he had said he knew how good he felt when he received them himself.

Chapter 32

## *The Customer Revolution*

"What does the customer want?" In addressing the question to the trustees, Gee did not have to remind them that the notion of eighteen-year-old "customers" might make some faculty retch. Public universities always had to be sensitive to their "citizens," but "customer" was different. "Citizens" could be dealt with by brochures or letters from the president. But now the president was talking about the other side of the desk or down the registration line. "Customer" was personal.

Was the old maxim applicable: Was the student as customer "always right"? Certainly not. But the student as customer should be treated with the respect you would expect for yourself. Would treating students like customers lower academic standards? To the contrary, academic standards would continue to rise, as would the quality of the student body. Would the curriculum be diluted to suit the "customer"? No.

Were other employees also customers? Definitely. Ohio State's version of the employee-driven Total Quality Management concept—something developed in the United States but carried to its best practice in Japan—already was enhancing effectiveness and morale among staff.

If treating virtually everyone like a customer needed further explanation, the president might have quoted leadership guru Warren Bennis, many times a faculty member, but only once a president, of the University of Cincinnati. If courtesy and efficiency were not reasons enough, in his 1989 *Why Leaders Can't Lead,* Bennis explained why no institution is more dependent on external forces, and thus more vulnerable, than the American university.

## *Four Agenda Items*

No place, the president knew from the first, could be more inhospitable to incoming students than a campus as formidable as Ohio State in Columbus. As early as his first day on campus, he had countered the "small is best" arguments of liberal arts colleges by coining and living a maxim of his own: "You can always make a large university small, but you can't make a small university large."

Of the more than 50,000 students on campus, even before arriving for freshman orientation, what student had not already heard of Gordon Gee? It was to a great extent his personal approach to the presidency that had made him chair of the Kellogg Commission, a national task force created to assess the weaknesses and recommend repairs for all of public higher education.

The Kellogg Commission issues were essentially those being pursued by Ohio State; and the group providing the most input to the Commission was the National Association of State Universities and Land-Grant Colleges (NASULGC) provosts, chaired by Dick Sisson. The Commission's first report, soon to be published, was titled *The Student Experience*. Gee had already created the Red Tape Task Force to find such and fix it at Ohio State. He had created Ohio State's Committee on the Undergraduate Experience (CUE), reviewing virtually everything in undergraduate life. He had handpicked the activist David Williams as vice president for Student Affairs and combined the Offices of Financial Aid and Admissions under the steady hand of Jim Mager. He had worked long and hard already to better "the student experience" at Ohio State, and he told the trustees that day that continuing to work at that was his first personal agenda item for 1996.

The second item, he said, would be "access"—soon to be the Kellogg Commission's second national focus, as well. The debate about access would endure at Ohio State, he said, because increasingly stringent entrance requirements would continue to be viewed by some people as barriers to access. But Ohio State had data to demonstrate just the opposite. Actual numbers from the Office of Enrollment Management would show that the number of new freshmen who were African American rose from 491 to 575 between autumn 1995 and 1997, with figures for Hispanic, Asian American, and Native American freshmen all also up.

The real issue, he said, was retention, not access.

His and the Kellogg Commission's third agenda item was "engagement" with the public. "The days of isolation and arrogance are over—not only because we need to have public support—but because the future of our universities must increasingly be one of engagement in public issues and public dialogue." Of course, he had already led the dialogue for six years and was, by this time, one of the most recognized public figures in Ohio—having visited every county in the state.

As with "public" vs. "customer," his and the Kellogg Commission's fourth item, some might say, was another question of semantics. University presidents now were differentiating between a "teaching" and a "learning" institution. "That means," he told the Board, that as a society, "we must encourage learning from kindergarten through life and make the universities' role central to that effort." At Ohio State, as with virtually all research universities, the relatively low value the public believed the professorate placed on teaching was a burr in its saddle.

"We must now focus on the culture of the campus," Gee said. "That means

# Chapter 32

we must ask very difficult questions about how we are organized, how we reward people within the institution, how we encourage high standards and develop high expectations." What was needed, he said, was nothing less than a higher education "Cultural Revolution." As for Ohio State specifically, the goal must be to "reach our potential and then move beyond," the guiding concepts being "outward looking, benchmarking, *and* world class."

In that context, he then issued a set of "aggressive challenges" over "the next five to ten years," urging the trustees to "commit to the concept of change. Set high expectations. Relentlessly and continuously measure progress against goals. And hold people accountable for results." With their support as might be necessary, he told the Board he would be "willing to confront and expel people and programs" who were "throwing up roadblocks to change."

Finally, as he often chided his staff to do, Gee "lightened up," closing his remarks with a few personal observations and metaphors, including: "It is very hard to steer a parked car." "In God we trust; but the rest of us need data." "The antidote to pessimism is innovation," and "Dreams can be fulfilled only when they are defined." Saying that, he opened a meeting that would last until the end of the following day.

Along the way, he had said, almost as an aside, "I have every intent of being here the next three to five years."

Some six months later, he hired Vice Chancellor Bill Napier from the Ohio Board of Regents to become his executive assistant and secretary of the Board of Trustees. Napier found Gee "one of the hardest working people I ever worked with. He never seemed to get tired. He never seemed to eat. His energy level was legendary. I sat in the office right across from his and I think that for the first six weeks I never saw him sit at his desk." But the president stayed at Ohio State only another year before succumbing to the siren call of the Ivy League by announcing he would leave for Brown in the winter.

Meanwhile, the trustees entered into an examination of their own role in governing the university, bringing in a Harvard business professor to facilitate their discussion and a consultant to help shape their future, and setting a precedent for other university boards to follow.

# 33

## More Short Subjects

This chapter serves as a continuation of important or just plain interesting Ohio State happenings that do not fit into other chapters.

### 1995
#### Naming and Pouring

A precept of major gift fund-raising is the "naming opportunity." On a 1993 trade mission to Israel with Governor Voinovich, Gordon Gee had seen it elevated to the finest art. At the University of Haifa, even bookshelves and chairs bore donor nameplates. "We had something still to learn," he said upon returning, about naming opportunities.

Naming "rights" were different yet from "opportunities." For the right to exclusivity on campus, a company might pay a lot of money. In 1995, AD Andy Geiger signed such a contract with Nike for $9.2 million in products and cash over five years. The Nike "Swoosh" soon appeared on footwear, apparel, and equipment of more than 800 athletes and coaches in thirty-four sports. No one seemed to mind, as most of the cash helped increase the number of varsity women's teams and scholarships, where federal parity requirements were forcing the elimination of men's teams at many places.

Then along came Coke and "pouring rights." Early in his presidency, Gee himself had begun conversations with Coca-Cola about the Critical Difference for Women, a college reentry program he and his first wife, Elizabeth, were championing, and Coke soon supported with half a million dollars. But toward the end of the Gee presidency, Student Affairs VP David Williams began investigating "pouring rights." Pepsi had knocked heads with Coke and won

CHAPTER 33

such exclusivity at the Ohio State Fair. It had then opened the collegiate door, signing a $14 million five-year deal with Penn State. Coke had then doubled that figure over ten years at the University of Minnesota.

While it took until 1999 and the Kirwan administration to press out all the wrinkles, before Williams left to join Gee at Vanderbilt he had signed a $30 million deal making Coke "the thing" and Ohio State "Pepsi-free" for the next ten years.

## Mel and Mel, a Chemical Stew

As Professor Matthew Platz wrote to his dean, Jim Garland, in May 1995, his distinguished department, chemistry, was "built on the shoulders of a number of chemical giants." The most distinguished were Melville Wolfrom and Melvin Newman, two of the few Ohio State professors yet elected to the National Academy of Sciences. But the university's newest chemistry building, built with state money nine years before and simply called the "New Chemistry Building," now was to be named for a former governor. More than a few people got mad. One of the nastiest e-mails to Gee asked, "Why not name it after Barney Rubble?"

Richard Celeste deserved the honor. Gordon Gee had said that Celeste's decisions had had the most positive impact on science in Ohio in twenty years. As governor from 1983 to 1991, Dick Celeste had established the Ohio Supercomputer Center and the Edison Joining Technology Center, the most advanced in the world, both on Ohio State's campus. He had funded the many competitive programs known as "Selective Excellence," including "Eminent Scholars," which, until curtailed in the 1990s, had been dominated by Ohio State in attracting distinguished research faculty to Ohio. In the first of his two administrations, what would become the Celeste Laboratory of Chemistry itself was funded.

Hadn't the chemistry faculty been consulted before the building was named? Yes, it had. With the benefit of hindsight, some faculty realized the department never had made a naming request. It would now. An addition was being built onto Evans Laboratory. In honor of the two giants of chemistry who had spent their entire careers at Ohio State, the addition was to be named the Newman and Wolfrom Laboratory of Chemistry.

## The Clinton Summit and Eddie George

On October 20, President Bill Clinton addressed 20,000 Buckeyes on the Oval in a drenching rain following a Midwest Economic Conference staged in the Fawcett Center with his entire Cabinet. In a panel discussion on educational

Like others who go pro, former basketball star, now television commentator, Clark Kellogg returns and gets his degree, 1996.

funding, Gee praised the President's national direct student loan program, which, by bypassing the banks, President Clinton said, had already "saved the taxpayers about $7 billion."

Overnight, the university had 10,000 rain ponchos flown up from Florida and distributed them all for the Oval speech that morning. For the two events, more than 3000 credentials were made, as well as 71,000 tickets, 500 table tents, and 280 signs. On his cavalcade ride to the airport, the President stopped to greet the number 1–ranked football team by the practice field on the berm of Olentangy River Road. The next time he and Gee met, he said, "I can't believe you lost to Michigan." The President wasn't the only one. This was the team with Heisman Trophy winner (best player) Eddie George, Beletnikoff Award winner (best receiver) Terry Glenn, Lombardi Award winner (best lineman) Orlando Pace, and Draddy Prize winner (best scholar) quarterback Bobby Hoying.

## Flat Stanley

He arrived in a letter from a second grader in Parkersburg, West Virginia, and his name was Flat Stanley. The story of Flat Stanley by Jeff Brown was a vehicle the child's teachers used to engage the class in the world around them. Once a month, a paper doll Stanley was mailed to a different special person, who returned him after a week and wrote the class about it.

Gordon packed Stanley in his suitcase and took him first to Miami. There, Stanley heard a speech about Ohio State from within the black leather briefcase at the foot of the head table, and the president wrote that Stanley was "certainly a good listener." Then Stanley went to Tucson, where he met other presidents and business leaders, and the president showed him a cactus but was "careful he didn't get stuck." Then they went all the way to Dresden, Germany, Columbus's sister city, along with the mayor of Columbus, and a bank president. After he returned, Stanley spent the rest of the week in the president's office "getting some much-needed rest." Flat Stanley had had quite a week, and was glad to get home. He had many adventures to tell.

## Testimony

When, in February, Vice President Al Gore declassified more than 800,000 U.S. spy satellite photos taken between 1960 and 1972, he was heeding a briefing by Ohio State landscape architecture professor Douglas Way on their peacetime value for the environmental sciences. The declassification was a milestone in the decline of Cold War secrecy.

Another milestone in declassification was the four million pages eventually made public through the work of the five-person John F. Kennedy Assassination Records Review Board, charged by Congress to find and make public information about the shooting of November 22, 1963. As one of its members, legal historian Kermit Hall, also dean of Humanities, began his work in 1994 and continued with it until the investigation closed. The board found no evidence of a conspiracy or second gunman.

## Ombuds-ending

The ombudsperson, an independent arbiter between institution and individual, was the creation of the social forces in the late 1960s. Autonomy was implicit. So was confidentiality. Ohio State's Office of Ombudservices was the last left in the Big Ten, and only four remained in comparable universities nationwide. Few records were kept by the Ohio State ombuds office, lest they be subpoenaed. While a review committee appointed by President Gee and chaired by Joan Huber reported the office "free from influence," it also reported it devoid of "guidance or control."

Since the 1960s, some sixteen conflict resolution procedures had been created at Ohio State, blanketing the university. Federal law now required Employee Relations to deal with sexual harassment; Academic Affairs had promotion, tenure, and salary grievance procedures; there was a Student Advocacy office, minority constituency offices, and a grade grievance procedure. Did Ohio State still need an ombuds office? And who guarded the guardians?

The Huber committee's report resulted in phasing out Ombudservices. "The overlap between Ombudservices and other offices is too high to justify the cost," the report concluded. Though it would be "a labor of Sisyphus," the committee urged the president to appoint someone "experienced in university governance" to handle the phase-out, assess advocacy programs throughout the university, and recommend any improvements. That person would be lawyer and Special Assistant to the President Rich Hollingsworth, also once dean of students. "It is good," Huber wrote, "that pushing a rock up a hill also brings the cholesterol down."

## The BCS

It was early November 1995. The Buckeye football team was undefeated and was projected to go 13-0, but had no chance for the national championship. The champion would be selected from the recently formed Fiesta-Orange-Sugar Bowl Alliance, which included neither the West Coast's Pacific Ten nor the Midwest's Big Ten, because they had their own Rose Bowl Alliance. Something, Gordon Gee said, would have to change, and *USA Today* (November 2) quoted him as a member of the NCAA Presidents Commission, ready to propose the NCAA's own poll to supersede the media and coaches' polls.

What Gordon wanted was to combine the alliances, and he was on the Big Ten presidents committee that could help make it happen. Soon he, Indiana's Myles Brand, and Penn State's Graham Spanier began talks with their Pac Ten counterparts, including Arizona State's Lattie Coor, whom Gee credited later with "making it happen." The alliances did combine in 1996, resulting in the BCS (Bowl Championship Series) rankings and inclusion of the Rose Bowl in the cycle of sites for the national championship game. The year 1996 also ended the historic football frustration, the tie game, with the NCAA creating "the tie-breaker" for the following season.

## *Quest* Was Best

In 1995, again it was number 1: the best external newspaper in higher education, as judged by editors of *The Chronicle of Higher Education*. Though it was

CHAPTER 33

the fourth time in its sixteen-year history that the research-oriented *Quest* had won the "Grand Gold Medal" of the Council for Advancement and Support of Education (CASE), awards do not a budget make. By 1995, though at its peak in journalistic quality, *Quest* was in the pits financially. Once distributed free to more than 300,000 alumni, too many budget cuts finally put *Quest* out of business in autumn 1997. Its final issue included a special section bidding farewell to Gordon Gee.

## *1996*
### Time Capsule

As part of the university's 125th year celebration, a time capsule went into a pillar next to the Thompson Library circulation desk. Its contents included a Gee bow tie, a student book pack, various pins and patches, university ID cards, musical CDs, and a fiber optic telephone receiver. The selection committee rejected many more items than it accepted, including T-shirts bearing carnal epithets and indelicacies about other universities.

Why a time capsule in a pillar and not underground? Explained University Archivist Raimund Goerler, there was no chance a sidewalk some day would be built over a pillar. The plaque on the pillar reminds its readers to open me up on the university's 200th anniversary. The committee was fairly sure that in 2070 there would be a library.

### "Keep the Stations"

While state budget cuts had been squeezing Ohio State through the decade, federal funding for public broadcasting did its biggest national squeeze between 1991 and 1996, dropping from $318 to $275 million. Were the Ohio State University radio and television stations now too expensive to keep? Or were the goodwill and publicity generated still worth the cost?

In the context of public broadcasting nationwide, emeritus provost Joan Huber researched the issue for Dean "Rip" Ripley, to whom the WOSU stations reported. Most stations in the Top 50 markets were community licensed. Only seven were affiliated with universities, and market size drove their private support. In Houston, 100 percent came from beyond the university; in Athens, Ohio, only 30 percent.

Alumnus Frank Stanton, the retired president of CBS and a good friend of Huber, read her report and wrote her back. While the year before, to memorialize his mentor, Stanton and his wife, Ruth, had funded The Harold E. Burtt Chair in Psychology, his response to the report may have as lasting an impact.

It had six quick points. The first was, "Keep the stations." The last was, "Keep the stations." The university kept the stations.

## Gee as Scholar

In November 1996, *Law and Public Education* came out with its first new edition since 1982. Given the changing nature of the law, this was a new book of a staggering 1,500 pages. Ohio State co-authors E. Gordon Gee and Professor T. K. Daniel had been working on it for four years. The research was also expected to create a number of articles and a second book.

Gee's first book, co-authored in 1978 while associate dean at Brigham Young, was *Education Law and the Public Schools,* named one of the ten best education books of the year by the National School Boards Association. *Information Literacy: Revolution in the Library* won the G. K. Hall Prize of the American Library Association in 1990, the year Gee came to Ohio State. In the early 1980s, while president of West Virginia, he co-authored one book on fair employment practices and another on violence, values, and justice in the schools.

Through all his years as an administrator, Gee continued to publish, keeping the books, articles, and monographs coming.

## Jesse

Sixty years after he became a world hero, his home town finally paid tribute to one of its greatest sons, James Cleveland "Jesse" Owens. At Ohio State, Owens had won eight Big Ten and eight NCAA track championships and had set three world records and tied a fourth within one hour in 1935. A year later, of course, he became the Allied hero of Hitler's Berlin Olympics.

On Saturday, June 29, ground was broken for the Jesse Owens Memorial Park and Museum in Oakville, Alabama. Just as Owens had overcome racism and bigotry, the man who spoke for Ohio State and Gordon Gee that day also had "overcome." Reginald "Reggie" Anglen, a communications specialist for the university, had been blind since birth and was the only one of seven children to graduate from college.

"As we look back on the life and accomplishments of Jesse Owens," Anglen said at the dedication, "we recognize his greatest legacy—the inspiration he provides even today for young people around the world who face challenges as

# Chapter 33

they dream of the better future." Certainly, Anglen might just as well have been talking about himself.

## SSejjengo

Of all his awards and acknowledgments, Gordon Gee is no prouder of any than of his honorary membership in the Hippo Clan of Uganda. There, at a ceremonial outdoor dinner, he was given the Lagunda name Ssejjengo, which, he sometimes reminded his staff humorously, means "Big Wave."

Uganda was the second part of a long African trip that began in Capetown, South Africa. Upon his return, the Big Wave wrote in one of his "Friends" letters, by which he communicated frequently, "when the oppressive policies of apartheid finally ended, Ohio State was one of the first universities to extend its hand to South Africa. And our graduates and programs have been helping redevelop Uganda since its ruthless dictator Edi Amin fled."

He told them about meeting Edwin Ngidi, an Ohio State Ph.D. in poultry science. In one of the poorest parts of rural South Africa, Ngidi was teaching local farmers "new ways to raise not only chickens, but the quality of their lives." And he wrote about Joseph Kibalama, whose Ph.D. was in agricultural engineering. Wearing his "Woody Hayes" hat, Kibalama "gave me a big hug, proclaiming 'I love Ohio State!' Then, with a smile, he cheered 'O-H-I-O,' complete with appropriate hand gestures. I could see in his eyes how moved he was by our visit and how much the university means to him."

The Big Wave was equally as moved by that experience and many others: the men's basketball team, the first to visit South Africa, teaching fundamentals in the townships of Soweto and Gugulethu to youngsters who had never played the game but knew of Michael Jordan; the enthusiastic greeting Nelson Mandela gave to Lupenga Mphande, once a freedom fighter to end apartheid, now the Ohio State languages professor coordinating this trip; treks in rural Uganda, where Ohio State alumni were experimenting with talapia fish farming and the development of hardier plantain; a dinner with some sixty Buckeyes, all working to make the agricultural economy self-sustaining in Uganda, and that night forming Ohio State's newest alumni club.

"Despite hardships," he wrote, "there is tremendous promise for the future." A little more of that promise would come from the new agreements he, Humanities Dean Kermit Hall, Agriculture Vice President Bobby Moser, and others would make. For one, by the following year, Professor Mphande was taking some twenty Ohio State students to the University of Natal to learn the Zulu language.

# MORE SHORT SUBJECTS

A rare honor: Constance and Gordon Dot the "I," 1995.

CHAPTER 33

## TBDBITL Goes Hollywood (Almost)

*My Fellow Americans* would star Dan Aykroyd, James Garner, Lauren Bacall, and Jack Lemmon as a former president from Ohio. In one scene, Lemmon was to be supported by a small brass band. And what better than some from "The Best in the Land"? Cincinnati's Jack Schiff, Sr., who occasionally brought his entire favorite all-brass band down south for Bengal halftime shows, thought this a great idea, as did trustee chair Les Wexner and two past chairs, Jack Kessler and Ambassador Milton Wolf. Thus, seventeen squad leaders winged off to Hollywood to perform for a "president," thanks to some quick donations. But when the movie aired, the scene was gone. TBDBITL had learned about the "cutting room floor," though a good time was had by all!

## Legends

Upon hearing complaints arising about potential traffic jams, Gordon Gee leaped at the opportunity to move the alumnus's projected museum to campus—where he thought it belonged in the first place. Ground had even been broken in Dublin when the traffic furor arose. On September 16, the president received an acceptance letter thanking him for "all your efforts in creating this opportunity." Yes, Jack Nicklaus believed his museum would "be a great fit" at Ohio State.

It would be sited near what would soon be the new William C. Davis Baseball Stadium and the new Jerome Schottenstein Center, built within the same large land area off Lane Avenue and Olentangy River Road that housed the Woody Hayes Athletic Center and, in another five years, would include the Jesse Owens Memorial Stadium.

A year later, the trustees would authorize naming the road to traverse the athletic complex north to south Fred Taylor Drive, after the coach whose team had won the Buckeye's last national men's basketball championship back in 1960.

## Write a Politician

It was "a rather disturbing report," State Senator Dennis Kucinich wrote Gordon Gee, the one about Ohio State's intent to "eliminate its Slavic and East European Languages and Literatures program." As one University of Chicago faculty member suggested in a letter to Governor Voinovich, with Yeltsin now in power, Ohio State was acting on a classic "peace scare. When things go well,

Russian and other [Slavic] languages are cut; when another threat arises, politicians and administrators rush to avoid blame." From the Bulgarian Academy of Sciences came an "appeal" to "keep the prestige of your university" by keeping the department.

For doing a restructuring review of the department, Humanities Dean Hall was also so pummeled; he warned Gee and Provost Sisson of the "virus at large." Gee had already answered Kucinich, explaining the review process and that "the university does not have plans to eliminate the program." The six-month review, headed by Brian Joseph, chair of Linguistics, did criticize the department's focus and management, recommended actions, and put it on three-year probation. The ten-person committee also told the department to neutralize damage done to the university's reputation by "misleading and occasionally reckless reports about administrative actions, past and present."

Earlier in the restructuring process, a pleasant letter had arrived on Gee's desk from Bob Taft, then Ohio Secretary of State. Taft, who has a master's degree from Princeton's School of International and Public Affairs, had learned of a proposal to eliminate or sharply cut back the School of Public Policy and Management within the College of Business. If anything, he said, it "should be expanded." The question, the president responded, is about location, not worth. Conversations already had begun with the College of Social and Behavioral Sciences, and the school that had graduated Cleveland Mayor Mike White, U.S. Representative Sherrod Brown, and Ohio State's own Bill Shkurti did land there.

## The Admiral's Diary

On May 9, 1926, Admiral Richard E. Byrd and pilot Floyd Bennett flew north from Spitzbergen, Norway in a Fokker trimotor, planning to be the first explorers to reach the North Pole. The hundreds of small American flags they planned to drop as they passed over the Pole would verify to Norwegian explorer Roald Amundsen that his dirigible, to take off three days later, came in second. The trouble was, one of the trimotor's motors sprung a leak twenty miles south of the Pole, though the plane continued on before returning. The admiral claimed he reached the Pole, but never dropped the flags.

Seventy years later to the day, Ohio State's chief archivist, Raimund Goerler, announced a discovery. Among the 523 cubic feet of family and polar artifacts and papers in Ohio State's Byrd Polar Research Institute, Goerler had found the admiral's diary, which included notes Byrd had passed to Bennett because the engines were too noisy for speech. To inspect the book and analyze the

# Chapter 33

evidence Goerler called in independent researcher Dennis Rawlins, who had questioned Byrd's claim. Did he or didn't he? Rawlins concluded that any suggestion Byrd had tried to deceive the public "now appears most likely to be false." The admiral, it appeared, had not simply taken off and flown around long enough to fake reaching the Pole.

## The Buckeye State Poll

What are Ohioans' biggest concerns? How will they vote in the next election? Would they pay higher taxes for schools? The *Columbus Dispatch* and WBNS-TV wanted regular polling data, and survey research professor Paul Lavrakas, fresh from Northwestern, wanted to provide it. So began the monthly Buckeye State Poll, which, Lavrakas wrote Gee, he believed to be "the only monthly large-scale survey of its state's population . . . getting regular high profile news coverage of its findings."

While the poll became the central project of what in time became The Ohio State University Center for Survey Research, Lavrakas would leave academe for the celebrated polling firm Nielson Media Research.

## *1997*
### Rankings

As Gordon Gee well knew, alumni resonate to positive rankings of their alma maters. So he was very pleased when *U.S. News* broke down in its eleventh annual issue and finally ranked America's "Top 25 *Public* Universities" apart from the dominating private ones. Ohio State tied for twenty-second place with Vermont and Colorado. Virginia was number 1. Gee and his administration had been lobbying the editors for such a separation for years.

He was not pleased when *Money* magazine did not rank Ohio State among its "Best Buys." Though its tuition was near the bottom of the state system, where was OSU? Ohio State was not a best buy because *Money*'s method used only out-of-state tuition, three times tuition for Ohioans. But who knew? While a letter to the editor explained it for some *Dispatch* readers, the *Money* confusion fueled the position of citizens and legislators who wanted to maintain a tuition cap at Ohio State. The cap was not lifted until Ohio once again faced a drastic tax revenue shortfall in fiscal 2002.

# MORE SHORT SUBJECTS

## Rain

The night before June commencement, Bob Greene, author and syndicated columnist for the *Chicago Tribune,* entered Ohio Stadium through an open gate and marveled at his good fortune. The Bexley kid who had grown up with the Buckeyes, to whom Ohio Stadium was every bit as splendid and historic as the Roman Coliseum, would be tomorrow's speaker. He would be introduced by Gordon Gee, the president he had promised to take to his high school hangout, Rubino's, for the best pizza in the world. And he would deliver a speech for two generations: to motivate the graduates and to honor his parents, seventy-eight-year-old Phyllis and eighty-two-year-old Robert Greene Sr.

But in the morning the monsoon came.

No commencement had been rained out since June 1941, which the alumni magazine described then as "heavy, driving rain [which] held off mischievously [but] broke suddenly just as the commencement procession started." The same can be written about June 1997. The ceremony began with a brave academic procession making its drenched way from the ramp to a canopied midfield, as all sat down to the cheers of soaked students, families and friends in the stands. Lord willin' an' the creek don't rise, the show would go on. But the creek did rise and, when the sound system blew, the president turned to Greene, invited him back for next year, and brought the curtain down.

Under the stands, as he wrote in his column, Bob Greene found his parents "soaked to the bone. Broke my heart. Made me want to cry." A year later, however, Greene was back as speaker again. This time, under the presidency of Brit Kirwan, the sun was out. Greene acknowledged his parents who, for fifty years, had gone together to Ohio Stadium every football Saturday, and he asked the crowd to give them a standing ovation. Which it did. "The roar," he wrote, "filled Ohio Stadium. It will sound in my heart forever."

## Roads Scholars

Penn State did it, and Gordon Gee thought it was a good idea: introducing new faculty to Ohio beyond Columbus and introducing Ohio to them. And so Ohio State's "Roads Scholars" program was born. With recently appointed State Relations Director Colleen O'Brien aboard, and University Communications' Sue Jones doing the detail work, four busloads of new faculty pioneered the program in September. Roads Scholars was only one of the

CHAPTER 33

outreach programs promoted by the president, even after his announcement for Brown.

Bringing more reporters to campus from Ohio's small towns, he thought, was also a good thing to do. And so began brunch briefings before every home football game by faculty luminaries such as gang criminologist Ron Huff and Mary Schiavo, once Inspector General of the U.S. Department of Transportation and author of *Flying Blind, Flying Safe*. With the briefing came the meal and two game tickets, and from it came coverage of Ohio State faculty research.

## A Tale of Two Ramps

In 1979, the university completed a twenty-year traffic plan for its medical center, priority one being direct access to and from State Rt. 315. In 1985, one ramp made the Ohio Department of Transportation (ODOT) long-range program, which, by 1989, became two ramps, both listed "fully funded." What Ohio State had to do first was expand and realign Cannon and Herrick Drives, which it did for $13 million. Then came Ohio's economic downturn, whereupon ODOT unfunded the project.

Enter Ohio State's Jean Hansford, the late senior campus planner, arguing the life-and-death need for access to the only level 1 trauma center in Columbus, whereupon ODOT listened. In 1996, with a stronger economy and under a new 50 percent rule, ODOT agreed to fund half the $7 million interchange, with Ohio State already having spent that $13 million and going federal for the difference.

While, with the help of Representative Deborah Pryce, the university got its $3.5 million, by the turn of the century Ohio State still had no interchange.

## Gordy, Dicky, and Jerry

When they played off each other, Ohio State President Gordon Gee and alumnus actor-comedian Richard Lewis could be nearly as funny as, well, two Richard Lewises. In 1997, when Lewis announced a new fall show, Gee wrote back in mock despair that he "was hoping for something more along the line of 'Gordy and Dicky.'"

Celebrated for his neuroses-laden television specials and an earlier series opposite Jamie Lee Curtis, the self-proclaimed "Prince of Pain," while watching a nationally televised Buckeye football game, spotted Gee on a university-produced public service announcement (PSA) and volunteered his services.

Two quick wits, Richard Lewis and Gordon Gee, cut a TV spot in Hollywood promoting the Citrus Bowl, 1992.

The two soon met on a Hollywood set, doing a PSA together to promote the 1992 Citrus Bowl game against Georgia. This led to many Lewis game visits, where Gordy and Dicky would parade together at halftime, pumping their fists and pumping up fans.

In 1995, Lewis agreed to commit his personal archives ("thousands of articles, missives, performances, scripts and, most precious, my comedy diaries") to the university. The Richard Lewis Archive was to become part of the Jerome Lawrence and Robert E. Lee Theatre Research Institute, its potential diminished tragically when Lawrence's California home and contents burned to the ground. Over time, Lewis promoted Ohio State on many visits to the late-night talk shows, did the voice-over for the College of Business campaign video, an on-camera student recruiting video, and a number of television spots for the university.

When one older alum complained about representation "by a graduate comedian" and background music akin to "Ding-Dong School," Gee's public relations office explained target audiences and younger consumer taste. The music had been arranged and produced as a gift to the university by another alum in show business, John Tatgenhorst. Tatgenhorst still often visited on Alumni Band Day to lead his signature arrangement of "Hang On, Sloopy," by now a part of Buckeye culture.

## Technology Enhancement

Although the university had not moved as fast as trustee David Brennan, in particular, would have liked, by fall 1997 Provost Sisson could report that Ohio State had twenty-five interactive and on-line courses, more than double that of 1995, and more than 250 classes using computer laboratories, twice that of the year before. More than 375 classes were using the World Wide Web, four times the year before, and technology-enhanced classroom seats had doubled to 8,000. E-mail accounts were up 150 percent, to 69,000, with 10,000 messages a month flowing across the university net, doubling in just six months.

In addition, the trouble-plagued $45 million Academic Resource Management System (ARMS), involving Human Relations and the Medical Center, was finally up and running. "We have," Sisson wrote Gee with his proverbial fingers crossed, "every reason to believe the project will meet our expectations."

## Ohio Who?

Chip Bok, The *Akron Beacon Journal*'s celebrated cartoonist, sent one of his pieces to Gordon Gee as a going-away present. It pictured a "Script Ohio" being completed in Ohio Stadium, as the sousaphone player dotting the "I" was being arrested for copyright violation. The joke was no joke to some people. It was about a trademark dispute over the name "Ohio."

In 1994, 190 years after its founding, Ohio University trademarked "Ohio" for sports and entertainment events and for athletic apparel. When Anne Chasser, Ohio State's licensing director, went to register "Ohio Stadium" in 1997, before its renovation began, she found she couldn't. So, too, with the simple "Ohio," once borne on track uniforms worn by Jesse Owens and still worn on some uniforms of the cheerleaders.

Argued Virginia "Ginny" Trethewey, Ohio State's general counsel, trademark registration laws are made to protect established territory, not to create it. Ohio State just wanted to keep "Ohio" for its historical and existing uses.

The dispute went past the Gee administration and into 1999. It was awaiting a hearing before the U.S. Trademark Trial and Appeal Board when what the

*Dispatch* termed "two old pals" decided to work it out. Ohio's Robert Glidden and Ohio State's Brit Kirwan knew each other well as former presidents of two Atlantic Coast Conference schools, Florida State and Maryland, respectively. They agreed that Ohio State would drop its trademark challenge and, in return, keep its current and historical uses of "Ohio."

Chasser, meanwhile, made quite an impression in Washington, for she soon was named Commissioner for Trademarks in the U.S. Patent and Trademark Office.

## Cradle of Presidents

On September 19, Gordon Gee spoke at the inauguration of the new president of Miami University, his friend and former Ohio State executive dean of the Arts and Sciences, Jim Garland. Garland was hardly the first recent Ohio State administrator to take a presidency. In the Jennings administration, provosts Diether Haenicke went off to Western Michigan and Myles Brand to Oregon and then Indiana, and Agriculture Dean Max Lennon left for Clemson.

The Gee administration more than maintained the training ground: with Garland to Miami; Provost Fred Hutchinson to Maine; Education Dean Nancy Zimpher to Wisconsin at Milwaukee; after an interim stop, Executive Dean Kermit Hall to Utah State; and psychologist and Senate Steering Committee Chair Judy Genshaft to South Florida.

## The Last Degree

"The lengths people will go to avoid listening to me talk," was the president's quip as he awarded his last degree at Ohio State. It was in a living room. The length Karen Reilly had gone to was to have Connor, her first child, on commencement day, December 12, while her university's departing president was delivering the address and accepting his own degree, an honorary doctorate in education.

On Christmas Eve morning, Karen was awake and Connor was in the crib when Ohio State attorney John Reilly answered a knock at the door. It was the president, alone, with Karen's doctorate in nutritional biochemistry in hand. He had posed with graduates and their families for a long time following commencement itself, a surprise the first time, a tradition by his departure. This, the last degree-handing photo was taken at home by a proud papa and husband in front of the Christmas tree.

# Chapter 33

At commencement itself, the president had finished his talk as follows:

On graduation day, each of you expects to hear some advice. I will not disappoint you. Always carry a safety pin. Buy a good alarm clock. Never answer e-mail from www.troubledloner. Help with the dishes. Don't use your MasterCard to pay your Visa bill. Stand for something, even if you stand alone. Never give up. Laugh often. And always, always remember your alma mater. We will not forget you. I offer you my personal congratulations, my affection, my love, my gratitude for the opportunities I have had as president, and my very best wishes. Godspeed on your remarkable journey.

# 34

# *The Philanthropists*

When Gordon Gee left Ohio State for Brown on December 31, 1997, more than $664 million had been raised for the "Affirm Thy Friendship" capital campaign, which would continue into 2000 and eventually top $1.2 billion. In the seven and a half years of Gee's presidency nearly $1 billion was raised and the amount per year more than doubled: $85 million in fiscal 1991; $176 million in fiscal 1997.

While more than 250,000 people made more than a million gifts from the beginning to the end of the campaign, and while there were more than 14,000 volunteers, some few people were particularly generous during Gee's presidency. Philanthropists cited elsewhere in this book include Larry and Isabel Barnett; David and Ann Brennan; John Berry, Sr.; Dorothy Davis and Bill Wells; Rick and Marte Denman; John Deaver Drinko; Daniel Galbreath; Dorothy Klotz and Marion Rowley; Austin "Dutch" Knowlton; Roy Lichtenstein; Richard and Elizabeth Ross; Thekla "Teckie" Shackelford and Gib Reese, and their father, Everett Reese; and the Jerome Schottenstein family.

Two others, who gave more than $5 million through their estate, were the late Ralph and Helen Kurtz, including Helen's gift of a half-million dollars in Ralph's name in Gee's first year. John and Jeanne McCoy kick-started Gee's National Merit Scholar initiative with gifts of more than $1.6 million just before the campaign kickoff in 1995. Twenty-eight Ohio State pathologists gave their privately owned $3 million-plus laboratory to the University Medical Center. In 1990, Zuheir Sofia established the M. S. Sofia Scholarship and Lecture Memorial Fund in Arabic; and in 1991 made a major gift commitment to bring the fund to the level necessary for a chair, when its name was changed to the "The M. S. Sofia Chair in Arabic Studies Fund." Peter Franklin, syndicated columnist of "Cookbook Nook" and once *Dispatch* business editor, donated

CHAPTER 34

his collection of 5,000 cookbooks, one of the world's largest. Cheryl Krueger, known for "Cheryl's Cookies," later Cheryl and Co., made and sold bow-tie cookies in the president's honor with profits to the campaign—and so on.

And so on. Here are some significant stories.

## Long-Term Trust: Moritz, Solove, and the Wolfe Family

One truism in university fund-raising is that, regardless of the number of donors, some 10 percent make or break a capital campaign and a handful lead the way. Another is that in philanthropy, as in other relationships, long-term friendships build trust. This formula could not have been demonstrated better than by three major gifts cultivated while Gee was president but donated after Gee had gone.

As Development Vice President Jerry May said about Gee and the process: "You develop long-term relationships. He was an incredible fund-raiser."

---

It was not until 2001, and after the "Affirm Thy Friendship" campaign had officially closed, that the largest gift in university history was made: $30 million that renamed the College of Law the Michael E. Moritz College of Law and included thirty full scholarships and four endowed chairs. Alumnus Mike Moritz had graduated at the top of his law class in 1961 after receiving a business administration degree three years before. He had joined the foundation board at the beginning of Gee's tenure, in 1990, and served all through the Gee administration. Sadly, in 2002 he would be killed in an automobile accident while returning from an Ohio State event in Naples, Florida.

---

In 1953, when his father was diagnosed with cancer, Richard Solove first heard Dr. Arthur James, his father's physician, speak of his dream for a stand-alone cancer hospital and research center. As a 1948 Ohio State pharmacy graduate, Solove had interned at an "always full" tuberculosis hospital and soon had seen the disease virtually eradicated through research. He knew then that similar answers for cancer could come only in the same way:

through vigorous, well-funded research. And, given proper resources, he believed it could be done.

Nearly fifty years later, during the Gee administration, Dick Solove chaired the James Hospital's campaign to raise $50 million for human cancer genetic research and helped lobby the legislature for state support. Then, in 1999, after Gee had left for Brown, he donated $20 million to what would now be named, in his honor, the James Cancer Hospital and *Solove* Research Institute. He thanked God he had been given the opportunity "to do something for humanity. This is not just for the James, or Ohio State, or Columbus, or Ohio—it's for the world."

---

When invited to Gordon Gee's box for a Buckeye football game, *Columbus Dispatch* publisher John W. Wolfe wrote back with appreciation, but declined. He did "not do football." But he did "do" philanthropy and he did "do" Ohio State. During the Gee years campaign, in honor of the late Harry Preston Wolfe, through Wolfe Associates, Inc., he created one of the university's best-funded chaired professorships, in accounting. Moreover, "J. W." was a preeminent advocate and fund-raiser for the James and, with community leaders Len Immke, Dean Jeffers, Dave Thomas, and Solove, had led its predecessor, the Ohio Cancer Foundation.

Thus it was fitting that, after John W.'s death in 1994, his cousin John F. Wolfe, a cochair of the campaign, would announce The John W. Wolfe Chair in Cancer Research and note in a university publication that only the private sector could give Ohio State the "extra edge."

Five years later, the Wolfe family gave more of that "extra edge": $6.5 million. It was from the Robert F. Wolfe and Edgar T. Wolfe Foundation. Most would create The John W. Wolfe Cancer Genetics Research Laboratories. The rest would augment the existing cancer research chair.

As John F. said in the announcement, John W. would be pleased.

## *The First Million*

The couple who handed the first million-dollar check to Gordon Gee had met at Ohio State the first day of freshman year 1935. They were prim and proper Betty Frank of Dayton and rough and ready Alex "Big Boy" Schoenbaum of Charleston, West Virginia. Alex would become a football All-American three

## CHAPTER 34

years running and graduate in business from Ohio State. Betty, an education major, would transfer to the University of Dayton, and they would marry in 1940. Then came Pearl Harbor and, though Alex volunteered, football had made him 4-F. At the war's end, he borrowed to open a drive-in restaurant in Charleston for the GIs he believed would be buying cars and traveling. He named the feature hamburger "Big Boy," after himself; and "Big Boy" and "Shoney's" soon entered postwar American history.

In 1981, an E. Gordon Gee, the new president of West Virginia University, came calling on the Schoenbaums. Sorry, they were giving to Ohio State, Alex told Gee. And they certainly would, donating the "lead" $1 million to build the Woody Hayes Athletic Center and millions more for scholarships in her college, Education, and his, Business. Then, nine years later, as Ohio State's president, Gee came calling again—and left with his first $1 million.

On November 26, 1996, Ohio State lost its only football game of the year, to Michigan, 13–9. All-American Alex Schoenbaum suffered a heart attack soon after watching it and passed away ten days later. In 2001, four years after Gordon Gee had left Ohio State and five after the death of her husband, Betty Schoenbaum was awarded an Ohio State honorary doctorate.

"To think," she said, "thousands of students will come through those doors and get their education and that we helped do it." She had just addressed faculty and friends in Schoenbaum Hall, the new undergraduate building named after Betty and Alex Schoenbaum of West Virginia in the magnificent new Business College named after another Buckeye who had given back: Max M. Fisher.

## *Two Good Friends*

Business school alumni Max Fisher and Les Wexner were good friends with mutual philanthropic interests who often talked to each other once a week by phone. In those conversations, Fisher sometimes warmly recalled his days at Ohio State, which he had entered on a football scholarship and from which he had graduated in 1930 to embark upon a hugely successful career. But Max lived in Michigan and had maintained his higher education philanthropy in that state, while Les's $25 million gift had created the Wexner Center for the Arts and led Ohio State's first capital campaign.

Max should consider a major gift to his alma mater, Les suggested. "I think you will enjoy it." His gift of the arts center had been "a joy. I'm engaged. I

# THE PHILANTHROPISTS

Fisher College Phase I, 1997.

worry about it. I can think about it, and tinker with it." Les was right, Max acknowledged. Send someone up to talk to me.

On October 4, 1990, Ohio State's new president, Gordon Gee, and development officer Dan Grafner made that visit. First, show him both quality and a commitment to eminence, Fisher told them. Only then could he be committed. Two months later, in his job offer letter as business dean, Gee pledged his own commitment to Joe Alutto. He was "fully prepared to work on a College of Business capital campaign," Gee wrote. "The stage is set to make tremendous progress."

For nearly three years, Alutto and his faculty worked at strengthening the college—increasing corporate partnerships, raising new endowments, hiring distinguished faculty, raising standards for entrance in all programs, and preparing the way to restructure both the MBA and the Ph.D. And it was nearly three years to the day from Gee's first visit to Max that Les dropped the president a note: Max and Les were still talking and the $20 million proposal was going to be fine.

On June 2, 1995, the shovels struck the turf for the ceremonial groundbreaking to mark a new campus of six buildings along Tuttle Park Place between Woodruff and Lane Avenues. This would become the site of the first of

CHAPTER 34

Ohio State's colleges to carry a name: The Max M. Fisher College of Business. By that time, *U.S. News and World Report* had already moved the college's MBA program into the Top 25; its program in real estate to fifth, and its graduate program in public policy and management into the Top 20.

"I've always thought that the school should be improved," Max Fisher said at the ceremony. "But a college is more than just a building. It's what's inside. It's the kind of teachers and students you have and how they prepare you for society."

"That," he concluded, "is what motivated me."

## *Father Figure*

If there was one wise old owl serving Ohio State philanthropically, it was John B. "Bernie" Gerlach. The son of an accountant, Gerlach left Ohio State one quarter short of his own accounting degree after marrying Ohio University home economics major Dareth Axene and going to work for dad. Later he completed his degree at Ohio University. Not one to sit behind a desk, he visited many of the factories and companies he and his father represented during World War II; and together they bought one, Lancaster Lens, when the war ended. Lancaster Lens began an enterprise that eventually became Lancaster Colony.

Feeling so fortunate to have done well, but shunning recognition, by the late 1960s Bernie Gerlach had become a fund-raising adviser to presidents and development officers and a quiet philanthropic force at Ohio State. By the 1990s, he not only was one of the largest donors in the history of the university, but perhaps its most effective volunteer. He had chaired the Columbus regional portion of the Jennings-era campaign, which raised $178 million locally. He then cochaired the Gee era campaign and chaired its Business component. As development officer and friend Linda Bowers once explained, "If Bernie asked them to do it, they couldn't say no."

In 1994, Bernie Gerlach finally received his Ohio State degree, an honorary Doctorate in Business Administration. In 1995, the president awarded him the Everett D. Reese Medal, Ohio State's highest recognition for fund-raising volunteerism. It had been Reese himself Gerlach had advised about fund-raising nearly thirty years before.

At age seventy in 1997, Bernie was hailed by Gordon Gee as "as close to a father figure as anybody this university has." He spoke of the man's generosity and firm commitment, his quiet service, and the fact he gave vast sums of money in other people's names. "Every university," he concluded, "should have a Bernie Gerlach." Soon the Foundation Board voted to name a new award for development volunteerism in his name. And when the first two halls of the Max M. Fisher business complex opened in 1998, the one for undergraduates was named Schoenbaum. The graduate school building was named Gerlach.

## Dresden's Dave Longaberger

Dave Longaberger was the small-town boy building his basket company on old-fashioned values and his conviction America still appreciated craftsmanship. Gordon Gee was the small-town boy now running an urban university who loved his visits to rural America and, as his late wife, Elizabeth, once wrote, its "down to earth practical folk." When Dave Longaberger and Gordon Gee met, you almost could hear the click. It was July 14, 1992, and the gathering that day in Dresden, Ohio, was a thank-you to Dave for a major gift funding the kind of university–industry partnership Gee was fostering: a scientific analysis of the effects of vision requirements in the workplace.

A few days later, he wrote Dave he had been "fascinated" by his business sense, "awed" by his accomplishments, and "appreciative" of his "wonderful family," daughters Tami and Rachel, already in their father's business. He was hooked and had not expected to be. The company Dave was building was born of a vision most friends thought crazy: reinventing the U.S. hand-made basket business, the product his father once crafted to carry decorative Ohio pottery. Dave was so right: the Longaberger Company would become a billion-dollar business.

Although Dave's life would end at age sixty-four on St. Patrick's Day 1999, his legacy at Ohio State already was in place. The year before, Rachel, now president of the Longaberger Foundation, had presented a basket to Ohio State's new president, Brit Kirwan, commemorating a $5 million gift, which included the The Dave Longaberger Endowed Chair in Urology at the University Medical Center. It also funded scholarships for women wishing to finish a degree otherwise interrupted, and support of the Hale Black Cultural Center, both born of Tami's chairing the Board of Trustees' Student Affairs Committee. Tami, an Ohio State marketing alumna, was now company president and CEO.

Finally, $2 million went toward building the new Alumni Association home

# Chapter 34

on the west bank of the Olentangy. At the announcement, Rachel recalled that even "during the lean years ... it never stopped Dad from his commitment to give back." Consistent with this, the family preferred the name be left off "their" building. By campaign standards, however, the gift was at the "naming" level and, as naming would benefit the university, they accepted, naming it the Longaberger Alumni House.

Thus, the Longaberger Alumni House was built next to the Annette and Richard Bloch Cancer Survivors Plaza. A survivor since 1978, Richard Bloch had been diagnosed with terminal lung cancer and given three months to live. He and his wife had dedicated their lives thereafter to helping cancer patients conquer the disease, and built inspirational plazas in large cities across the country and Canada. Ohio State's plaza includes eight life-size statues of people and a "Positive Mental Attitude Walk." Few people ever had a more positive mental attitude than Dave Longaberger. His belief in himself started the business, and his belief in others built it.

## *Erie, the Brushcutter*

"We took our academic robes and flew up to northern Ohio to confer the honorary degree. It clearly was enormously important to him, and then he passed away." Trustee Ted Celeste recalled how he and Gordon Gee were in the Heritage Inn in the Mennonite community of Archbold, Ohio, there to present an honorary Doctor of Humane Letters to a ninety-two-year-old, deeply spiritual man too weak to make the trip to Columbus.

"My father sent me into the woods to cut brush. So I kept on cutting brush and cutting brush and cutting brush." In that way, Erie Sauder had explained his success. He had rebuilt the interior of a burned-down church, which grew into a church pew business, which grew in the computer age to Sauder Woodworking, the company synonymous with ready-to-assemble furniture.

He had founded the Mennonite Economic Development Association, reestablishing German and Russian refugees of World War II in Paraguay, making eighteen hands-on visits himself, developing a wasteland into habitable and profitable land. In Archbold, he had built his own pioneer village to preserve the lifestyle of the settlers of northwest Ohio's Great Black Swamp. At Ohio State, because he so believed in peaceful alternatives to conflict, he had endowed the Peace Chair program in the Mershon Center. And because he so believed in the rural work ethic, he had funded a values-based 4-H training program for youngsters through the Agriculture College.

Erie Sauder never went to college, never went to high school, never went beyond the eighth grade. But he was an engineering genius and an advocate of higher education, and his son, Myrl, the company's vice president of engineering, was an Ohio State industrial engineer.

For Celeste, who attended every graduation ceremony during his nine-year appointment as an Ohio State trustee, the spirit of every degree crystallized that day when Erie Sauder expressed his humility at becoming Dr. Erie Sauder, *honoris causa*, before his loving family and by authority of the Board of Trustees of The Ohio State University.

## *A Detective's Son*

Milton Wolf's father, Sam, a Cleveland police detective, and his mother, Sylvia, kept a little blue box in their house for the Jewish National Fund, to which family members were expected to contribute, even during the Depression. That, he said later, was where he realized the importance of charity. During World War II, the Army Air Corps sent him to meteorology school and that, he said later, was where he realized the importance of learning. Few Ohio State alumni ever combined the two in so distinguished a way. A graduate of the university in 1954, where he met his late wife, Roslyn, Wolf became the U.S. Ambassador to Austria under President Jimmy Carter from 1977 to 1980, hosting SALT II, the second Strategic Arms Limitation Talks, with the Soviet Union. He later became president of the American Jewish Joint Distribution Committee, the foreign aid arm of the American Jewish Community, and, at the same time, served as an Ohio State trustee. While doing both, he also earned his Ph.D. at Case Western Reserve.

When finishing his term in 1996, and after committing more than $1 million to the campaign, he sent a thank-you letter to Gee and the trustees for "the most rewarding nine years of my life." At his retirement, the new chair, Leslie Wexner, called his work for the university "as close to perfect as mortals can get."

## *Two Kids from New Concord*

What could be even more valuable than money? Three hundred and fifty cubic feet of boxed documents and memorabilia from perhaps the most fulfilled life and career of anyone in the twentieth century. "God Speed, John Glenn."

# Chapter 34

As youngsters from small-town Ohio, Depression kids John Glenn and Annie Castor considered the world beyond New Concord to be the 75-mile National Road to Columbus. In 1941, when World War II broke out, it became the South Pacific, where he would fight fifty-nine combat missions. In 1943, they would marry, and, like millions of other war wives, Annie would wait it out at home. Later, there was the Korean Conflict and ninety-five missions; and, in 1957, Los Angeles to New York and the speed record for transcontinental flight. Then, in February 1962, in *Friendship 7,* John Glenn became history's most famous space traveler: the first person to orbit the earth.

Between 1974 and 1996, there were four terms in the U.S. Senate, a first for Ohio. He was one of the principal advocates of social reform in the spirit of Franklin Roosevelt, whose federal Work Projects Administration (WPA), through the Rural Electric Project, had given his World War I veteran father work and helped the family survive the Great Depression. Then there was a bid, though unsuccessful, for the presidency itself. And in 1998, in the Shuttle *Discovery,* John Glenn became the poster elder of space flight, testing experiments in aging through 134 orbits and nearly 214 hours.

The year before, in 1997, he had announced he would donate his personal papers and artifacts to Ohio State, and he, Gordon Gee, and Herb Asher had begun talking about creating an Ohio State public service institute to stimulate research and participation in public life. The nation, Senator Glenn had written Gee, needed to dispel the "looming danger" of our youth's "apathy, mistrust, and outright cynicism" about public service and rekindle its spirit "as a responsibility of good citizenship." The Midwest, he said, should have a center of excellence akin to Harvard's Kennedy School and Stanford's Hoover Institute, and he could think of no more appropriate institution than Ohio State.

A year later and less than two months before his Shuttle Mission STS-95, John Glenn, with Ohio State's new president Brit Kirwan, announced the John Glenn Institute for Public Service and Public Policy at The Ohio State University. Its initial location would be in a remodeled Stillman Hall. And it would be framed, appropriately, by three restored murals painted by Columbus's Emerson Burkhart, as commissioned in 1938 through the Federal Arts Project, part of that same WPA that had stimulated Glenn himself to serve in public office.

Senator John Glenn announces his papers and memorabilia are going to Ohio State, 1997.

## A Marion Man

If regional campuses could be named for philanthropists, Marion would be George H. Alber University, after a modest man who lived frugally and gave gigantically to his home town.

George Alber graduated from Ohio State in 1929 with three football letters, the presidency of his junior class, a Phi Delta Theta pin, and a degree in business. In 1937, thirty miles north of Columbus, in Marion, Ohio, he founded what became the largest privately owned granular fertilizer business in the United States. First, he and his wife, Dorothy, established a large scholarship fund. Then they contributed the naming gift for the campus's identifying structure, its bell tower. Soon, the campus's Enterprise Center for economic development was named in his honor, and later The George H. Alber Student Center.

On November 27, 1997, only weeks before the end of the Gee administration, George Alber passed away. Through the Columbus Foundation, he left a

CHAPTER 34

trust of more than $28 million for education and community service programs in Marion. Some third of it was for Ohio State Marion; a separate $4 million was also from his estate.

The Columbus Foundation gift, said its President Jim Luck, was the largest made in the United States for a community the size of Marion. The combined amount also was one of the largest gifts ever given to the university.

## *The General*

As it had in World War I for the Student Army Training Corps (SATC), the Ohio State Oval became a parade ground again during World War II for aspiring military officers. One of the seniors in the class of 1941 was business major and Reserve Officer Training Corps (ROTC) student Ray Mason. He would serve in an armored artillery battalion in Europe in 1944 and 1945 and be awarded the Silver Star for gallantry. And he would remain active in the U.S. Army Reserve until his retirement after thirty years as Major General Raymond E. Mason, Jr.

As the study of military history and the logistics of transportation had melded in his military career, so they have in his philanthropy. He and his wife, Margaret, established professorships in military history and transportation and logistics and scholarships for ROTC students and gave to the building campaign of Fisher College. With his business degree and his logistics expertise, Ray had also become highly successful in the truck and equipment business.

The same day that Schoenbaum and Gerlach Halls opened in 1999, so did the Fisher College's new business resource center, housing two state-of-the-art computer laboratories and the new business library. A large gathering space in the building was named after Margaret Mason's father, Daniel Everett Edwards. The building itself was Raymond E. Mason Hall, named after the World War II veteran who had become a general and whose gifts to the university now totaled some $5 million.

## *The Spirit of Giving*

During the Gee years, nearly $55 million was raised for scholarships and student support, $46 million for endowed chairs and professorships, $98 million for academic buildings and other construction projects, $59 million to be used by individual colleges, and $125 million in new money for the university endowment. The 1985–1990 $460 million university campaign had been, in a sense, a learning experience, with most of the giving going to donor priorities, not necessarily the institution's. This time the money not only flowed where needed; by campaign's end, all priorities had achieved their dollar goals.

The spirit of giving to Ohio State could not be exemplified better than by one event at the campaign kickoff in September 1995. As Development Vice President Jerry May recalled, "It was one of those nights you hope something special would happen because you were announcing an $850 million campaign." Jack Schiff, Sr., of Cincinnati, Business Class of 1938, walked over to Gordon Gee's table. The two had spoken about the campaign, but Schiff had made no commitment. Then, "without ever indicating he was going to do anything, he handed Gordon $1 million. Cash. Cash! It made Gordon's night and it was a very special moment. Gordon went on to tell the story again and again and again. Of course, years after that, Jack Schiff loved to host Gordon and host the band and host fund-raising events for Ohio State. He took the whole band to dinner! The whole band! He was a wonderful human being."

# 35

## *Crises and Condolences*

> Thank you for taking the time out of your busy schedule to send a letter and give me a call. You'll never know what that meant to me.
> —From a mother's letter to Gordon Gee

"The victory bell rang in Ohio Stadium yesterday for Jennifer Burdick, John Galyk and 5,408 undergraduates," the *Dispatch*'s Alan Miller wrote on June 11, 1994. "Great shouts of joy went up from the 5,408. Tears were shed for the two." Both had died recently in an apartment fire. President Gee and several faculty left the podium to award the parents of Jennifer and John their children's degrees. "Then the victory bell pealed throughout the stadium."

Grief, condolences, memorial services, funerals, candlelight vigils. Only a review of presidential archives reveals the dimension death plays in the life of the president of a huge university. Too many people, mostly young people, are taken before their time by illness, accident, suicide, or, as was Stephanie Hummer, even murder. There are too many fatal accidents, as that of twenty-year-old Nickole Danielle Nardo, who was a Miss Ohio finalist in 1993, the same year she died. A few led to public bereavements, such as the Mershon Auditorium funeral of another twenty-year-old, football star Jayson Gwinn, killed in a crash at Olentangy River Road and Lane Avenue during football season, also in 1993.

But most went unnoticed by all but the grieving friends and families, the Student Advocacy Center, and the president's office.

## Student Advocacy

In 1993, the president created two significant administrative offices that supported students and families in crisis: the Student Advocacy Office and the Parents Association. As the link created between parents of undergraduates and the university, the association sometimes became the conduit for its director, Bill Wahl, to hear of the problems of individual students, which then could be handled in the advocacy office. The advocacy office itself, recommended by Gee's ad hoc CUE (Committee on the Undergraduate Experience) committee, became the place students or parents would learn to go for crises small to monumental.

Through letters from grieving or irate parents, Gee had learned the administration needed such a place. A family whose child had a critical illness and missed final exams, whose apartment was gutted by fire, or whose child had died—such stories were coming in by mail to the president's office. Mary Basinger, the president's executive secretary, who screened the president's mail, wanted to help and became the first director of the new office. Certain coordination had not taken place before: such as making sure the family of a deceased student was not imposed upon by fund-raising letters or routine mail from the university. While the office handled any problem brought to its attention, none were more significant than the loss of a life and, often, its aftermath. One tragic event was the disappearance of Stacy Kolbert, a young alumna who went for a walk in the campus area in 1997 and never returned.

Following two suicides in their population in 1994–1995, an international student suicide prevention task force also was formed, this by the counseling and international education offices. The university's international student population had grown from 72 in 1945 to 3,827 and, though a Big Ten survey found the suicide number "not statistically significant," an Ohio State survey had found these students particularly vulnerable to problems of money, language, and the lack of American friends.

Two years later, a different kind of international tragedy took place on the other side of the world.

## International Tragedy

Renowned glaciologist Lonnie Thompson of the university's Byrd Polar Research Center had led high-altitude expeditions worldwide, drilling ice cores in the study of prehistoric climate patterns, joined by students and other scientists. In the fall of 1997, Ohio State graduate student Shawn Wight of Ashtabula was overcome by altitude sickness on an expedition in the Himalayas and was brought down from 23,000 feet. When an infection and blood clot developed in one leg, he was evacuated through Tibet, China, and Hong Kong to a hospital in Cleveland. He did not live.

An Ohio State review led by Research Vice President Ed Hayes determined the evacuation was handled properly. It also recommended new safeguards, which led to medical screenings and better communications procedures among research teams, campus officials, and families when students travel to remote areas. Later, a wrongful death suit filed by Shawn Wight's father was decided in favor of the university. There was evidence, said the attorney representing Ohio State, that Thompson and his team had "acted heroically" (*Dispatch*, March 22, 2001). In 2002, Professors Lonnie Thompson and Ellen Mosley-Thompson received the International Commonwealth Award for Distinguished Service in Science for their pioneering work demonstrating evidence of global warming.

## *Officer Blankenship*

On February 10, 1997, Ohio State lost its first police officer ever in the line of duty. Michael Blankenship had just finished leading a student seminar on self-protection when he and Officer Sandra Niciu responded together to a call from the Wexner Center. There had been a disagreement in the lobby between a Wexner guard and a distraught Mark Edgerton, an alumnus and Wexner Center member. Edgerton had left the building, but was on his way back. The next day's *Dispatch* reported Officer Blankenship "trying to search the man, who refused to take his hands out of his pockets [and] suddenly pulled a pistol," killing Michael Blankenship, firing at Sandra Niciu, and fleeing. Two days later, Edgerton was found dead in his apartment by his own hand.

Nearly 1000 police officers came from around the country for Michael Blankenship's funeral in Mershon Auditorium. The mountain bike he had used to patrol campus was onstage near his casket. The procession of vehicles to the gravesite at Sunset Cemetery was two miles long. The evening before there had been a candlelight vigil on campus, and among those speaking was Police Chief Ron Michalec and, of course, the president, who, as he did with so many people, had gotten to know Mike Blankenship well. At the funeral, Gee quoted a rarely sung verse of Ohio State's alma mater, Fred Cornell's *Carmen, Ohio*:

Though age may dim our mem'ry's store,
We'll think of happy days of yore.
True to friend and frank to foe,
A sturdy son of Ohio.

"Mike would want each of us to be brave, to be successful, to be free," he concluded. "Today, we take inspiration from his life and his example. We celebrate the values by which he lived and for which he died. He made the ultimate sacrifice for all of us. And for that, we are forever grateful. God bless you, Mike Blankenship."

In May, students began to raise funds for a memorial to be placed in front of a new building under construction. The building was the new police headquarters going up on West Campus: the newly named Michael Blankenship Hall.

## *My Father, My Hero*

"My father lost his battle with cancer," read a letter to the president. "[He] loved Ohio State football and basketball and on Saturday wore OSU sweatshirts with his 'Woody Hayes' black ball cap. Could you fax a note I can put with him in his coffin? I feel very lucky. My father was my hero." The president faxed a note.

Some people who figured large in the university were taken after they had lived long and active lives—many noted elsewhere in this book. Others included U.S. Representative Chalmers Wylie; Nobel Prize winner William Fowler; Basketball All-American Jimmy Hull; retired Athletic Director Hugh Hindman; and former trustees Len Immke, John Berry, and John Barone. For some, such as Dave Griner, stalwart of the university's bicycle safety program and the Special Olympics, and legendary athletic trainer Billy Hill, their hearts give out early. Cancer took all too many, including Human Ecology Dean Lena Bailey and distinguished History Professor Marilyn Waldman.

Consoling the families of all is part of the job of a president.

## 36

## *Gordon for Governor*

> The Governorship is the path to travel. . . . It is a natural evolution in his career.
>
> —From an April 1997 analysis of
> Gordon Gee's chances of running
> and winning in Ohio

One of the letters Gordon Gee received after rejecting the California presidency was on the letterhead of a Columbus real estate research, design, and development firm. The writer praised Gee for "cultivating the best in higher education in Ohio" and said he was delighted Gee had stayed on. At its close, former Ohio Governor James A. Rhodes suggested that Gee "had the makings of an extremely forceful political figure, if you should ever choose to follow such a path."

Curt Steiner, one of the key operatives in the Voinovich administration, who became a close friend of Gordon Gee, gave three reasons Gee could have won had he run for office in Ohio. And none had to do with the electorate. He delegated authority; he trusted those around him; and he allowed them to know him personally. "Allowing others [at the university] in on the inner process . . . They felt they were part of the excitement." A campaign team would have felt that way, too. "It's a very charismatic way to lead . . . [and] it's just the way he is."

Mike Curtin recognized "a very talented politician" as soon as he met Gee in 1990. Aide Herb Asher was ushering Gee about on one of his first days at Ohio

State. They had just visited Governor Celeste and legislative leaders at the Ohio State House when they ran into Curtin. Curtin would become president of the Dispatch Printing Company and associate publisher of the newspaper, but was then its political editor. Curtin recalls that as Asher made introductions Gee said "something like, 'Oh, you're such a fine journalist for such a fine newspaper.' He was complimenting me before he even knew me. You can't fool a good reporter." And Curtin was the best.

But you can charm him or her, as Gee consistently did. As its higher education reporter, before he was promoted to an editor's chair, the *Dispatch*'s Alan Miller watched Gee closely for four years. He was "probably the best PR practitioner I have met"—unequalled in "working the room . . . in working the politicians, in working the media . . . in working any constituency." Did Miller realize he was being "worked"? "Of course! And he knew that we knew. That was part of the game."

David Milenthal knew what it took to be elected. Milenthal created advertising campaigns that twice helped Dick Celeste become governor of Ohio. He also knew Gee well enough to be in the same box at the 1997 Rose Bowl. Gee, he said, "had passion" and was both "instinctively a wonderful marketer" and a man with "backroom skills." He also, Milenthal said, could communicate with virtually anyone about anything, exactly the facility that most had fascinated the *Plain Dealer*'s Ben Marrison as he covered Gee morning through evening on a 1996 football game day.

That Gee genuinely liked people not only showed. It glowed, and virtually nothing a politician might be asked to do could embarrass him. A dunk tank at a student fair to raise money for student government—he loved it. A sumo wrestling match in padded gear at Lima—he fell over laughing. A Santa Claus beard and suit for the cover of *Columbus Monthly*—he posed when "real" politicians declined. A solitary wade in the water to open the Olentangy Wetlands Research Park—grinning, he planted the flag. To promote fitness on campus, along with Columbus City Council President Cindy Lazarus, he vaulted onto a Velcro wall and stuck to it, then joked for the *Dispatch* (October 1, 1993) that he was "the Velcro president. Everything sticks to me." "Everything, it seems," wrote Brent LaLonde, "but public humiliation."

Said Milenthal, "I was always of the opinion he could pick his party. If you ask me whether he could have been governor, my answer would be 'yes.'"

The combination of qualities that made Gordon Gee so popular as Ohio State's president might, in fact, have won him an election—if there had been one in which he might have chosen to run. "There was very strong support for me in a couple of private polls," he acknowledged years later. "So the answer is

## Chapter 36

At a health fair, "The Velcro President" stuck to the Velcro wall, 1993.

Anything for student fund-raising: sumo wrestling at Lima, 1994.

Good sport Gordon wade-icates the first campus wetland, 1995.

'yes,' I could have been tempted." His answer also was, "I felt being president of Ohio State was the most important job in Ohio."

But some would suggest that, if the Republican Party had had more "room at the inn," temptation would have led to a candidacy. Was Gee a Republican, the only party he knew as a youngster in Utah and perhaps that of the majority of his colleagues on corporate boards—ASARCO, Bank One, the Limited? Or a Democrat, usually considered the party of the minorities he championed? While he called himself a fiscal conservative and a social liberal, in his line of

## Chapter 36

business it paid to be a registered Independent—which is what he was and how he lobbied.

To bring higher education issues to their attention, he had met with many legislators in their home towns. In the winter of 1996–1997 alone, he dined at the university residence or the Faculty Club with the Senate Finance Committee, the House majority leadership, the Senate Democratic Caucus, the House Finance Committee, and all of the governor's department directors. He, of course, became quite a good friend of Senate President Stan Aronoff, a Republican, and House Speaker Verne Riffe, a Democrat, as well as Riffe's successor, Jo Ann Davidson, a Republican—who in 2001, retired from government, would be named an Ohio State trustee.

If the truth were known, yes, Gordon Gee would have been comfortable running as a Republican. But as Steiner—who in 1996 would become Governor Voinovich's chief of staff—would point out, during the 1990s the Republicans "had gone from the party of no candidates to the party of an oversupply of candidates." At the same time, Democrats were in undersupply. Would Gee be their answer for governor?

On May 5, 1997, Marrison and *Plain Dealer* education writer John Funk revealed that both Riffe and Celeste had approached Gee to take on former Attorney General Lee Fisher for the nomination, quoting Riffe that Gee would "make a strong candidate." However, they also reported that Ohio Democratic Party Chairman David Leland would not offer Gee "a ticket to the governor's race," but did suggest he might make a fine U.S. senator or Ohio secretary of state. In answer to the latter, Gee would never have run as a second fiddle. For the former, his opponent would have been George Voinovich. Though Gee and Voinovich had had those high-profile public disagreements about budget cuts in the early 1990s, behind the scenes they had worked together, with Voinovich later saying Gee went "out of his way to accommodate me, work with me, and keep our dialogue going." In fact, they had become good friends and mutual admirers, as had their wives. Voinovich also was so popular that even Gee might not have been expected to win.

Not optimistic at all was *Plain Dealer* editorial page director Brent Larkin. Larkin, whom Gee had come to like and respect through many editorial board visits, wrote (May 11, 1997) that the Ohio State president "would be crazy to challenge Fisher—and crazy is one thing he is not." Larkin compared Gee to Bernadine Healy, by then Ohio State's dean of Medicine, an attractive Republican outsider "slaughtered" by Mike DeWine in the 1994 U.S. Senate primary. Gee, he wrote, "would lose to Fisher and probably lose big."

However, an unpublished analysis of Gee's electoral potential by political consultant Jerry Austin suggested that Gee's best bet indeed would be to run for governor. Though Gee would have faced an uphill battle against Fisher or any of three other Democrats considering running, Austin believed Ohio was ready for a nonconventional gubernatorial candidate and that Gee was the best politician in the state. Provided no huge skeletons were in the closet, which a first political race often can bare, and provided Gee could demonstrate the old-fashioned way—such as at county chicken dinners—that he indeed was a Democrat, Gee just might win the primary and the election. Not only might Gee win, the analysis said, he already knew how to govern.

When interviewed for this book, trustee Ted Celeste agreed completely with Austin. Celeste had run the Ohio campaign that put Jimmy Carter over the top as President in 1976 and was an experienced campaigner for his brother, the former governor. Healy, he said, may have had a national reputation as a medical scientist and an advocate for women's health. But, when she ran, she was little known in the state. Gee, on the other hand, was recognized everywhere in Ohio, which his Ohio State polls had verified.

And trustee Alex Shumate agreed. "Gordon Gee was to Ohio State what Woody Hayes was to Ohio State football. His name recognition was huge."

The problem was neither incumbents nor aspirants. The problem was party. Gee, said Ted Celeste, "was a Republican at heart. He couldn't run as a Democrat."

As it turned out, Gee soon announced for Providence, Rhode Island, rather than the Ohio State House or Washington, DC. By that time, Curtin had long since acknowledged more substantive aspects of Gee's political skill than buttering up journalists. Like most people who got to know him, Curtin had found part of the president's effectiveness to be "his ability to punctuate almost every discussion with some kind of humor, usually self-deprecating." But, more importantly, he remembered Gee as "always in command of the facts" and "always serious when he had to be serious about serious university issues."

Toward the end of 1997, Curtin warmly roasted Gee at a going-away dinner sponsored by the Columbus Society of Professional Journalists and later that evening told Gee personally that he "had more BS than any politician I had met." After twenty years of covering politics, that was saying something.

Did Gee have political aspirations? Or was he only an educator whose skills and talents made him a natural politician? Some people said later that Governor Voinovich kept "looking over his shoulder" until Gee decided not to campaign for the U.S. Senate. And Bill Napier, with years of lobbying experience at both Ohio State and the Ohio Board of Regents, believed that if Gee had

## Chapter 36

stayed at Ohio State, both parties eventually would have tried to recruit him for statewide office. Years earlier, after swapping gag lines on television with comedian Jay Leno, Gee told a staffer he would have loved to become a late-night host and standup comic such as Leno or Dave Letterman. But a personal letter from a friend, found in the Ohio State Archives, reminded Gee he once had talked about becoming "the first Mormon president."

Perhaps the talents for the two jobs are often similar, and consistent with the tough but good-humored style with which he presided over Ohio State. As Curtin would recall, Gee "understood his strengths," used them to sell his agenda, and "just engendered good feelings." The same has been said of another president, a man named Ronald Reagan.

## 37

## *Les Wexner*

Best known in Columbus as founder of the Limited, mastermind of the new New Albany, and philanthropist behind the Wexner Center for the Arts, as an Ohio State trustee Leslie H. Wexner was a vigorous force for academic progress. A source of support for the president during his first wife's battle with cancer, and of friendship that continued on, few knew that Wexner was also Gee's sounding board on many weighty university matters. The two met privately once a month.

From his interview with candidate Gee in 1990, in what he later called a presidential "shoot-off," Wexner found a man he believed met the criteria he wanted as Ohio State's president. "I thought the university really needed an energetic leader to the degree that highly influenced my vote. I thought Gordon could lead and could be a change agent for the university. It really needed shaping up and I wasn't disappointed." Similarly, Gee so projected Wexner's importance to his presidency that he would have rejected the offer had Wexner not agreed privately to remain on the Board the seven years left of his full term. Wexner, in turn, received a quid pro quo from Gee, though softened later by Gee's remarriage and the opportunity offered by California for the couple's new life together in a new place.

In 1990, Wexner had been explicit with Gee and the other candidates that "what the university needed was a CEO not an English chairman" and not a president "who would let the provost run the university." Wexner wanted leadership, not management, and saw in Gee both a strategist and a man who would run things hands-on. "And that," he said, "did happen." It also was Wexner, with his long letter of support sent to Gee in Hong Kong and his warning to Gee to consider "the devil you know versus the devil you don't," who helped the president choose against California. Though they never

# Chapter 37

discussed it, Wexner surmised, and Gee later concurred, that the decision to stay was in part "his commitment to me and my commitment to him" made five years earlier.

Though Wexner had just left the Board, he also urged Gee to think again before he accepted the offer of the Brown presidency in 1997. "I could see the challenge of going to an Ivy. I could see that in many ways it was an easier job. It's private. It has nothing to do with the Legislature. 'So, if that's what you want,' I said, 'I don't know who people want to be when they grow up.'" Gee told Wexner he believed he would stay, but changed his mind two days later. "I think," said Wexner years later, "he was just fascinated by the prestige of an Ivy," which, after he left Brown to head Vanderbilt in 2000, Gee admitted was correct and that Brown "was never the right fit."

## *Master Planning*

It also was Wexner who initiated the process that led to a new master plan for the university. No such thing had been done since 1962. "The university architect may or may not be competent," Wexner said later, "but that's really tactical. When you're planning an institution of this scale, you want to bring in world-class talent." By October 1995, with the help of the Sasaki and Michael Dennis consulting firms, a long-range concept plan was completed for the Columbus campus. Building off that, by February 1996 the trustees had approved two specific plans.

One was for the "Academic Core North District . . . a compact, walkable, central campus where the academic and living environment of the university is centered"; the other, a set of siting studies—for the Knowlton School of Architecture, College of the Arts, and new buildings for the lab-dependent departments of mechanical engineering and physics.

By September 1996, the "West Campus District" had an approved plan, including incremental development of 321 acres and 362 acres of green reserve. And by the end of Gordon Gee's presidency a plan for the "South Campus District," including the Medical Center, had been completed, with commitments made to complete master plans for parking, completed in 1998; landscaping, completed in 1999; the Olentangy River Corridor, completed in 1998; and the College of Food, Agricultural, and Environmental Sciences and all regional campuses.

Coincidentally, Campus Partners was continuing to buy up property in executing its program to revitalize the High Street area.

## Assets and Benchmarks

It had been Wexner who first urged the trustees to have the administration inventory and assess value on all its nonproperty assets, including patents and copyrights, trademark and licensing, collections, deferred gifts, and affiliated entities. Wexner's piercing questioning at trustee meetings was very much the initial impetus behind institutional benchmarking, peer group ranking, and the development of national standards. Trustee Alex Shumate emphasized later that from then on not only did Ohio data alone not satisfy the trustees, the Board became more critical of its own earlier analyses and demanded more of itself.

It was late 1992 when Wexner first pressed his benchmarking questions, which soon generated a memo from Provost Joan Huber and Vice President Bill Shkurti to Trustee Secretary Madison Scott. Big Ten enrollment, minority enrollment, tuition and fees, and freshman entrance data were attached, with a comparative summary. In addition, they were working on a comparison group of peer institutions outside of the Big Ten, which they would share with the Board as soon as it was completed.

He continued his probing over the years, stimulating both the administration and the trustees to inquiry and action, and prompting Gee to write him in 1994 that "I do believe your strategies are starting to work." "I remember saying to Gordon," Wexner said years later, that 'If you really care about the university, you need to figure out what our job is and how to do it.'"

Said presidential staffer Chip Elam years later, "It was as if Les pulled the trigger on the starting gun that began Ohio State's marathon toward the Top Ten."

"It was Les, who also always believed in best practices, who wanted the best and wanted to know what the best practices were," Shumate recalled, as well. Wexner said he used as his model for the university a large multidivision corporation, in which the deans were the divisional presidents, all making different products. "If you really want to know how to run Ohio State, look at GE." Over time, he had raised such questions as: How far are we in arrears in capital expenditures? How much maintenance has been deferred? How has our endowment performance been against other university endowments? Uncomfortable hearing what he later termed "blithering generalities" about the colleges instead of strategies and outcomes, he promoted bringing deans themselves into meetings to talk about their colleges and to answer questions directly from the board.

CHAPTER 37

## *The McKinsey Report*

Following a trustee retreat facilitated by Harvard Business School's Len Schlesinger, Gee wrote Wexner in late 1996 that "the past 24 hours have been among the most significant in my time at Ohio State, perhaps in my time as a university president." The retreat, which included only the trustees, Gee, and Dick Sisson, had been opened by Wexner as chair, who urged a review of virtually everything the trustees did, which, at the end of the day, all agreed to do. The result was what later was called the *McKinsey Report*.

As Shumate later expressed it, "We first took a critical look at ourselves. We asked ourselves are we providing the maximum value to the university. Are we engaged in activities that take advantage of our highest and best use? The candid answer was 'no.'" The trustees had taken small steps in governance before, under chairs Shirley Dunlap Bowser and Joel Teaford, by beginning to reassess and adjust their role; by holding annual retreats with university leadership; and by bringing in such strategic discussion catalysts as Robert Zemsky of the University of Pennsylvania's Institute of Research on Higher Education and Harvard economist Henry Rosovsky.

But they had not taken the giant step—the audit to be done by the international consulting firm McKinsey & Company. Done over six months, the review found the Board had many strengths on which to build, perhaps most importantly a "robust" value system in which dedication to the university superseded any political agendas. It analyzed five historical primary roles that defined the Board's purpose: ensuring self-governance, proper institutional direction, fiduciary responsibility, key relationships with external constituencies, and superior long-term institutional well-being. A sixth goal was new: governance of entrepreneurial research and health care "affiliated entities" created by the necessities of the 1990s. Presented to Shumate, who by this time was Board chair, the *McKinsey Report* held forty-six individual recommendations and became a blueprint for a three-year plan.

An immediate need, however, unexpected when the review began, was to find a new president.

So rare in higher education was this kind of consult that Shumate soon discovered he was the nation's expert trustee on university governance and began speaking to national higher education leadership audiences. The National Association of State Universities and Land-Grant Colleges adopted the Ohio State model as one of its strategic initiatives.

"Being a trustee is like driving in a snowstorm at 100 miles per hour, with issues flying at you," Wexner told *onCampus* at his departure from the Board, which was in spring 1997 as the McKinsey team was doing its study. "The Board meets regularly, and spends a lot of time doing things that are very important—examining capital and operating budgets, evaluating deans and the administration," he said, adding sardonically, and "setting the price of football tickets."

Following McKinsey's review, the trustees no longer would vote on every small issue such as the price of tickets, but would publish a list of items to be handled in one vote as a consensus agenda.

Les Wexner took the job of trustee very seriously and, as did all trustees during the Gee years, expended tremendous amounts of time and energy on it and never played politics. The politics of the entire Board, as the *McKinsey Report* attested, was always scarlet and gray.

If he could make one change, he said, he would increase the number of trustees to twenty, "so there would be enough trustees to do the work." He felt strongly that the Board makeup itself—only nine voting members, all required to be Ohio residents, all gubernatorial appointments—did not reflect the global research university Ohio State had become. He hoped that, in time, there would be national seats, international seats, and representatives of specific professions—medicine, law, education—a larger group, "racially diverse, geographically diverse, diverse by occupation." The national average experience of university presidencies is less than five years. "The continuity of leadership and success has to come from the Board."

In his years supporting the university as philanthropist and trustee, Wexner had been the first chair of The Ohio State University Foundation, chaired the Wexner Center's Foundation Board and instituted the annual Wexner Prize in the arts, was lead donor to the first university-wide fund-raising campaign in 1985–1990, funded the new Wexner Jewish Student Center and the Wexner Institute for Pediatric Research at Children's Hospital, where Ohio State's pediatricians are trained, and been instrumental in raising large sums for the university from others.

After receiving his degree in business administration in 1959, he entered the law school, but left to work at his father's clothing store, named Leslie's. With a $5000 loan from his aunt, he struck out on his own in 1963, opening the first Limited at the Kingsdale Shopping Center in Upper Arlington; his life's ambition was to own three stores. The rest of the story is legendary; much of it includes his sense of community responsibility, where "community" includes his alma mater. "Whether it's volunteering time for Columbus Reads or giving $25 million," he said in an interview for this book, what matters is "how you address those responsibilities, how you apply the skills God has given you for

## Chapter 37

Baryshnikov, Gee, and Les Wexner at the Wexner Center first anniversary, 1990.

community good. If there's some purpose in life, perhaps we have the responsibility to enrich others."

"I never decided to be a great man," he told *onCampus* upon his retirement from the Board in 1997. "But I did make a conscious decision that it was important to have a life that was balanced. How you feel about yourself is important. I want to be proud of myself and do the right things. Nobody remembers who sold the most togas in Rome."

# 38

## *Brown*

> In my family room there are four pictures. Three are high school graduation pictures of my three children. The fourth is of you, my daughter, and her friend. . . . [My daughter] met you in her freshman year. Wondering if your open door was an actual policy, she ventured in. You were not in the office, but she was thrilled when she later received an invitation to breakfast in your office. It was your birthday, and she was touched to be asked. That is what you have done so well—touched the lives of many students. Kids have built-in radar. They detect honesty, thoughtfulness, intelligence and good humor. They rest easier when they know the person in charge is someone they can trust. [My daughter] called today with the news of your new job. She feels as if she is losing a friend. We are all sorry that you are moving on. We hope this will bring you and your wife peace and joy. We can only wish the best for you, and remember to thank you for the years you have been at the helm.
> 
> —Excerpts from a parent's letter to the president

Gordon and Constance Gee rarely stayed up until 4 A.M. But this night was unlike all others. It was zero hour in the decision for him to become the seventeenth president of Brown or remain the eleventh president of Ohio State. The couple were on the back porch of the house on Commonwealth Drive, finally deciding.

The Ivy League had been hiring presidents out of the Big Ten: Princeton's Harold Shapiro had been president of Michigan; MIT's Jim Vest had been

# Chapter 38

Michigan's provost. Dartmouth's Jim Friedman and Cornell's Hunter Rawlings both had been presidents of Iowa. How often, if ever, would such an opportunity come along? Columbia, Gordon's graduate alma mater, a logical possibility, had filled its presidency with Rice's George Rupp less than four years before. But Vartan Gregorian, Brown's president for eight years, was leaving to head the Carnegie Corporation in New York City, and Gee had been offered the job. If Ivy were to be in his future, the future was probably now.

Gordon had told only a few people when he was being considered for the job, and they had understood the need to maintain confidentiality. Some understood that an opportunity to preside over *la crème de la crème* of academe might never come again.

Others suggested it made no difference. No place ever would be more suited to his skills and personality than Ohio State, they said, and they urged him to look more closely at what really made him happy. There would be no huge stadium at Brown in which to be energized by 100,000 fans and talk to the nation on television; Brown not only gave no football scholarships, its team was at the league bottom. And no eighty-eight counties to welcome him in their extension offices, alumni clubs, and high schools; Rhode Island was a very small state. And no seven major cities, each with media eager for interviews; there was only Providence. And no political arena in which to wage combat for the university and all public higher education. "Gordon," they would say, "you'll be bored."

But how could anyone be bored by the adventure of making one of the world's great universities even greater? Brown was primarily an undergraduate institution, and Gee could see a challenge ahead in strengthening some of its graduate programs. Like all other universities, Brown had its "silos" and Gee could see more interdisciplinary centers. Though large by most standards, Brown's $800 million endowment was modest for the Ivy League; so huge opportunities existed there.

If there were no eighty-eight counties, there was Boston and New York, London, and Paris. If the football Bears were in the league cellar, he could personally recruit scholars who thought big and hit hard, and help take them to the top.

And if there were no state halls of government to work, if the truth were known, Gee was weary of the strife.

## *Pigging Out at the Trough*

Again, he had dueled that winter and spring with Governor Voinovich over adequate funding for public higher education. The Ohio economy had rebounded and public higher education had requested a 7 percent catch-up increase for each year of the next biennium. Governor Voinovich had called the request "an attempt to 'pig out' at the state trough" (*Cincinnati Enquirer,* January 19, 1997), and Gee was more than just upset.

No sector of state government, he wrote the governor, had reformed more aggressively than public higher education. At the state level, it had restricted doctoral programs and created a new funding formula that recognized performance and the uniqueness of institutional missions. All institutions had taken large cuts and adjusted. Ohio State alone, he pointed out, had downsized by nearly 2,000 jobs, eliminated or consolidated nearly 25 percent of its academic departments, and, he wrote, "engaged in the most massive repositioning and reengineering program of any major public university in the country."

The Higher Education Funding Commission, created through the last appropriations bill, had spent eight months studying higher education, he noted, including its relationship to the state of the Ohio economy; and, he pointed out, the Higher Education Funding Commission itself had recommended those 7 percent increases.

Would higher education performance be rewarded, or would "pigging out" lose the day and add another reason for Gee to consider leaving? At a special meeting of all state university trustees on March 7, Governor Voinovich explained his position. Ironically, Ohio's economic comeback was blocking the 7 percent increase: Because of the state's prosperity relative to the immediate past, the federal government was increasing Ohio's portion of shared Medicaid costs by $160 million.

That $160 million, Voinovich explained to the trustees, "would largely have enabled the state to meet the Board of Regents' funding request."

## *DeRolph*

Not only was Gee weary of such disappointments, on the horizon he saw the threat of higher education's worst economic disaster yet. It was called *DeRolph v. the State of Ohio.*

The DeRolph case was filed in 1991 by a coalition of 500 Ohio school districts and had already been in litigation six years. As a *Dispatch* editorial (March 25, 1997) again explained, those 500 districts "shared the opinion that the Ohio general assembly and local taxpayers have been too miserly in providing money for primary and secondary schools."

CHAPTER 38

Total support of Ohio's public schools was one *DeRolph* issue; equalization among school districts was another. Reliance upon local property taxes made some Ohio school districts much richer than others, while the existing state-mandated minimum was only $3,663. The Ohio Supreme Court just had voted 4–3 in favor of DeRolph, overturning an appeals court ruling from 1995; the Supreme Court had given the legislature one more year to overhaul the system and reduce its reliance on property taxes.

As a parent and citizen, the president agreed that primary and secondary education needed better and more nearly equalized support, but would the legislature itself raise new taxes? Gee thought not. Could turnips give blood? The legislature might take the issue to the voters, and would the citizens of Ohio then approve higher taxes? Gee thought not and was proved right a year later, when already at Brown, when a penny-a-dollar sales tax increase, half for schools, half for property tax relief, was defeated.

Eventually, Gee believed, the legislature would rob Peter to pay Paul, Peter being Ohio's public colleges and universities.

## *Yes*

On June 27, 1997, Gordon and Constance Gee were in the Madison Alumni Center on the campus of Brown University in Providence, Rhode Island. Ohio State Board of Trustees Chair Alex Shumate was in the Grand Lounge of the Faculty Club on the campus of The Ohio State University in Columbus, Ohio. Facing Shumate was a phalanx of media and a group of trustees, faculty, and staff. Arrangements had been made for Shumate to broadcast live to the people of Ohio the news that Gordon Gee had resigned as president of Ohio State. A large screen was set up so that those in the room could also watch Gee's announcement, which was being televised from Brown.

The Gees had visited Brown that Tuesday and returned to Columbus to think things over. His offer included an appointment as professor of public policy and education, with tenure. Her offer was a tenure-track assistant professorship in the same department. At 6 A.M., there had been a knock at the door. A group of Ohio State students were there, begging the president to stay. At 7:30 A.M., he pulled into a parking space at Bricker Hall and was met by the president of Student Government, John Carney, and more students with a similar appeal. They wore T-shirts reading, "55,000 Students Need You." They linked arms, sang *Carmen Ohio*, and pulled hard on the president's heartstrings.

The new president of Brown University returns to talk to the Ohio press, 1997.

## Chapter 38

Once in the building, he went straight to his office where his staff assembled. He teared up. He needed tissues. So did some of his staff. But he was leaving. Then his vice presidents came in. The Gees soon boarded a plane for Providence and the news conference there.

In the Faculty Club, Shumate began to speak. "In a decade in which many universities have lost ground," he said, Gordon Gee "helped make Ohio State a leader among leaders. He has brought out the best in all of us." The trustees' plan, he said, was for the president to stay through the calendar year. Seven years before, Gee had left for Ohio State too rapidly for the good of the University of Colorado, and neither Gee nor Shumate wanted to make that mistake again. The trustees, Shumate said, would immediately start a search process "that will find us a president whose leadership will continue our momentum . . . a man or woman who will again be the right person for this great university at the right time."

Before Shumate spoke in Columbus, in Providence the former "right person," E. Gordon Gee, had finished his news conference. He had been selected from among more than 165 candidates and had been elected unanimously by a special meeting of the Brown Corporation to assume his duties on January 1. University Chancellor Artemis A. W. Joukowsky said Gee had been selected because of his "extraordinary record of leadership at one of the nation's premier public research universities."

As the *Providence Journal* reported, Gordon had "bounded up to the podium, leading his wife . . . by the hand, pronouncing that 'You have been one of the great assets at Ohio State and you can stay right here.'" "Once I have made up my mind," *Dispatch* writers Tim Doulin and Doug Caruso reported Gee explaining, "I get on about it joyfully." Not so with Constance. On that podium, when her husband, who had removed the Brown baseball cap just given him, talked about Ohio State, she had left hers on so she could pull its beak down over her eyes to hide her tears at leaving Columbus.

Later that day, the Gees flew home and the president met with reporters in the Faculty Club. Early the next day, he took out one of his blue felt-tip pens and began writing his personal notes of thanks. The first was to Les Wexner. Gee thanked Les for his "sound advice" and explained that he did "listen carefully and wrestled mightily." Yet, he wrote, "in this decision, I do feel that it is once in a lifetime and that I should seize the opportunity."

Only time would tell if the opportunity seized would be right for Gordon and Constance Gee.

## *A Collective Commitment*

As part of the process that led to Ohio State's reaccreditation later in 1997, less than two months before Gordon Gee accepted the Brown presidency, Purdue President Steve Beering had led a twenty-member team on an Ohio State site review. One of the members was Brown Classics Professor David Konstan. Konstan was also a member of Brown's presidential search advisory committee and could not have but helped Gee's candidacy there with his report. As he told the *Brown Daily Herald* upon Gee's appointment, he had formed "a very good opinion" of Gee on the accreditation visit, finding "optimism, and confidence in Gee's leadership . . . everywhere."

Given the public passion to keep Gee when he had dallied with California, there was some surprise off campus when such optimism not only remained after June 27, but when such confidence transferred easily to the transitional leadership. Dick Sisson called it a "collective commitment" to continue "the accomplishment of things that flourished" under Gee, and Kermit Hall offered that Gee had "effected . . . the kind of change that makes it entirely possible for someone to replace him" (*Dispatch*, June 28, 1997).

While Sisson, Hall, and Agriculture's Bobby Moser already were being written up as capable candidates for the next presidency, the most significant vehicle for such optimism and confidence may well have been the new chairman of the trustees. At the news conference, televised throughout central Ohio, Alex Shumate spoke with such eloquence and bearing about Gordon Gee's legacy and the brightness of the university's future, he created a murmur in those assembled about his own presidential qualities. His presence was warm but commanding; his grasp of institutional nuances, evident.

"Certainly, we wanted Dr. Gee to stay on as president," he told the *Plain Dealer* following his comments. Though, as he said later, "You think of Ohio State, you think of Gordon Gee," this time the trustees had given Gee no counteroffer. Shumate and trustees George Skestos and Tami Longaberger had met with Gee at Shumate's house, after which, as Longaberger said later, "it was clear Gordon was ready to move on." As former trustee Jack Kessler, who had become one of the president's closest friends, explained, "If we thought we could have changed his mind we would have tried."

What the trustees and a few close friends also knew was how close they had come to losing their president only weeks before, when Gee had become one of three finalists for the chancellorship of the University of North Carolina system, a job similar to the one in California. As Constance was a graduate of one of its sixteen campuses, and the state remained home to her family, the pull of

CHAPTER 38

the North Carolina job on the recently married couple had been particularly powerful. A few former and current trustees, expecting Gee to receive an offer, were preparing a counteroffer when Gee dropped out of the North Carolina search. If he were to move again, he said later, he had decided against a system. He wanted the vibrancy of a campus. That decision, in turn, led to Brown.

As Shumate said at the Faculty Club news conference, Gee had "led Ohio State on a path toward academic excellence" and was departing with it "poised to reach a new level." His departure, the *Dispatch* editorialized, "should not come as a total surprise." He had said, "there will be a time . . . when the university needs new leadership and I need a new challenge." There would also be a time when the trustees would finally give up trying to hold him. Only a few days after the editorial, North Carolina named Molly Corbett Broad its new president.

As arranged by Shumate, who wanted a smooth transition to the next president, the Ohio State transition period of six months did create a somewhat lame departing duck. Though Gee never lessened his schedule, he spent much time saying good-byes to local constituencies and circuiting the state on last visits to donors, legislators, alumni clubs, and media. He went off the Ohio State payroll in New Orleans when the clock struck midnight, ushering in 1998, and watched the Buckeyes lose the Sugar Bowl game to Tennessee on January 1 as a former president of Ohio State.

Though Shumate would acknowledge later that some people thought the president stayed too long, he disagreed. "Gordon kept us balanced. We exceeded our fund-raising campaign. We kept the planning strategy going. We didn't miss a beat." That being the case, in Dick Sisson and Alex Shumate, the university had a concertmaster and first violinist, though there could be argument as to which was which.

## *Shumate*

Over nearly two decades, first under Ed Jennings, then under Gordon Gee, Ohio State had rallied around a charismatic leader. At the June 27 news conference, if there was such a vacuum to fill, Alex Shumate filled it. He had experienced the university and its people even before day one of the Gee administration, having served on the search committee that hired him. He was in his ninth and final year as a trustee and had counseled the president on many, if not most, of the issues that made headlines. Besides the monthly one-on-one the president had had with Wexner, there was also a foursome: Gee,

Wexner, Milt Wolf, and Shumate, who had met regularly to talk institutional strategy, direction, and leadership.

As the lone African American trustee, Shumate sometimes had also been a man in the middle, pressed by African American leaders to explain or defend institutional actions or policies, or looked to by others, unreasonably if not unfairly, as a spokesperson for Black Columbus. Throughout the years, he had handled everything with dignity, grace, and strength of character and had become one of Columbus's citizen giants. If verification was necessary, in 1996 he had joined Wexner, Gee, and Jack Kessler in *Columbus Monthly*'s list of the city's ten most powerful people.

From childhood, Alex Shumate had been a leader. In high school, he had headed student government. As an undergrad at Ohio Wesleyan, he had captained the tennis team. He had been a leader in his church, where he had learned well the art of oration. In the Ohio Attorney General's Office, as chief of consumer fraud, he gave many public speeches, television interviews, and legislative testimonies. He had then become chief counsel and deputy chief of staff for Governor Richard Celeste. He was a member of the U.S. Supreme Court bar, as well as the federal and Ohio bars. He had been a member of the Ohio Wesleyan board of trustees.

Since 1991, he had been managing partner of his law firm, the Columbus office of Squire, Sanders & Dempsey, and, without the flexibility the home office gave him, he could not have worked as he did for Ohio State in that final year. His work was so thorough and presence so assuring, there was once a brief discussion and some encouragement within the search committee itself for him to become a candidate. He had no interest and thought it inappropriate. "But," one committee member emphasized years later, "that indicated the level of support Alex Shumate had."

That afternoon at the Faculty Club, he said later he had "felt the magic. The support that came from the university." He named some names. "Sisson. Asher. Shkurti. Moser. Tzagournis. Healy. Geiger," his fellow trustees. "People were saying, 'By God, we're not going to lose the momentum,' so they rallied. I mean, the support was unbelievable. But," he said, "we should give Gordon much of the credit. You know how a real test of parenting is when your children do what they're told when no parent is there? That's when you find out whether you've helped them grow, develop, and mature into people who can sustain themselves. Gordon did that for the university."

# 39

## *Over and Out*

"The eyes of Texas" certainly were upon Dick and Willa Sisson in early winter 1997. Ohio State's senior vice president and provost was a finalist for the presidency of the oil-rich, land-grant University of Texas, whose endowment was third only to those of Harvard and Yale. Texas had advanced its academic reputation in the second half of the twentieth century and, along with Washington, Arizona, and UCLA, was one of only four institutions outside the Big Ten that Ohio State was using for its own benchmarking. Austin, too, had become one of the nation's most cosmopolitan cities. It was the state capital; home to seven universities, Dell computer, and hundreds of high tech companies; a Columbus with rolling hills that had achieved its technology aspirations and where the Sissons agreed it would not be a chore to live.

After coming to Ohio State from UCLA as vice president and provost in 1993, Sisson had been queried by a few presidential search committees, which, he said later, "did not believe I would stay the course" as a second in command. "But I said I would when I accepted the job" and he did. Given his reputation as both a scholar and architect of what might be academe's smoothest and most far-reaching restructuring, by 1997 he was even more prime presidential timber, rejecting inquiries even in his wife's native California, where they had met, married, and lived. Turning sixty, he not only did not know if he really wanted a presidency, but, before Gee announced for Brown, he had broached with Gee stepping down as provost and returning full-time to the faculty.

The University of Texas, however, was a search Sisson was prepared to follow to its end. If Texas wanted him he would go and complete his career as a flagship president. This Ohio State's trustees knew and found the loss of his steady hand an unhappy prospect. On November 4, Texas announced five finalists. One, Shirley Strum of the State University of New York, already was a president. The others were provosts: Stanley Chodorow of the Ivy League's University of Pennsylvania; Wisconsin's John Wiley; the eventual appointee, Illinois's Larry Faulkner; and Sisson, all of the Big Ten.

Sisson had been the first into Austin for two days of interviews. According to the *Houston Chronicle* (November 12, 1997), many questions put to him were about minority issues and his views on affirmative action. The famous Hopwood court decision ruling out ethnicity as an admissions factor at UT's College of Law had been applied campus-wide and then was ruled applicable statewide by the Texas attorney general. Minority applications at Texas–Austin were down 20 percent already, with some state legislators threatening to gut state support from campuses whose minority enrollments were in drastic decline.

Sisson reportedly was impressive in the interview. He had issued his own report on Ohio State's affirmative action programs in December 1996; its first section, "Diversity, A Matter of Principle," reflected his philosophy. In the report, he had pointed to growth in minority admissions across the board, even as Ohio State policy stayed within the guidelines of California's earlier *Bakke* decision. Female students at Ohio State were up to 50 percent, from 47 percent a decade before. The 7,074 minority students represented 13 percent of the total student population, up from 7 percent. Though he was not satisfied with the results, in 1993 the last year of available Big Ten data, only Michigan and Michigan State exceeded Ohio State in their proportion of African American faculty. He had the support of Gee, who told the *Austin American Statesman*, "very few people in the country are better trained to take the role of university president," but, Gee added, Ohio State would "do everything it can" to keep him.

Assuming he would not yet have his new president when Gee left on January 1, Trustee Chair Shumate expected the Board to appoint an interim president then. But the Texas situation moved up the decision. Sisson was offered Ohio State's interim presidency with the same salary as Gee, $231,000. If D stood for "decision," the Sissons made one the day before D-day: on December 6, he agreed to withdraw his candidacy at Texas. Meanwhile, it was rumored the decision in Texas had narrowed to Faulkner and Sisson.

## *The Interim President*

When Gee had announced for Brown, few Ohio State people would have favored a same-day desk cleaning, the corporate model for departure. Yet, for

## CHAPTER 39

Willa and Dick Sisson, the interim "first family."

many faculty Sisson already was an interim president by December 6, and making it official was greeted warmly. The faculty chair of the University Senate's Faculty Council and now a member of the presidential search committee, Alan Randall, told *onCampus* (December 11), was "delighted in the selection."

Sisson's first official presidential workday was December 15, 1997; Gee's last official act was his commencement address two days earlier. Associate Provost Ed Ray, the inside candidate for provost five years earlier—a job he would earn in the next administration—became acting senior vice president and provost. Ray, in turn, would rely heavily upon historian Martha McMackin Garland, who had been named vice provost for undergraduate studies only in July, upon Robert Arnold's return to the art faculty; mathematician Alayne Parson, vice provost for program evaluation, with general responsibility for all academic

Constance, Gordon, a tear, and Trustee Chair Alex Shumate at the university's farewell, 1997.

programs; and geographer Randy Smith, who wrote the university's reaccreditation report and would become a vice provost in the next administration.

Over the months since Gee's announcement, Sisson had headed a transition team that included Ray, Bill Shkurti, David Williams, trustees Ted Celeste and Shumate, with Garland, Herb Asher, and a few others in the wings. Sometimes they had worked with Gee, but often on their own. From the first, Sisson and Gee had had a chemistry that operated on trust. "We didn't have to check everything with each other. Increasingly over time, Gordon and I could anticipate how the other was going to respond. Trust in the goodwill and good judgment of one another enabled each of us to devote all of our energies to the university." By December 15, 1997, Gee already was devoting a good deal of his energy to his transition to Brown.

The trustees held his farewell dinner on December 4, with speechwriter Barbie Tootle penning on his first note card, "Why the hell are you going to Brown?" By that time, Dick Sisson and Alex Shumate were running Ohio State.

When he announced the Sisson appointment, Shumate said the "entire community owes Dick a deep sense of gratitude" for dropping out of the Texas

CHAPTER 39

race and accepting the offer. It was "a sign," he said, "of Dick's commitment and love of Ohio State that he made this choice at this time." As provost, Sisson had skillfully guided university restructuring. Significant developments under his academic leadership had included across-the-board givebacks for "academic enrichment" and the competitive "selective investment" programs. Both were lauded in *The Chronicle of Higher Education* years later (June 1, 2001) as singular examples in higher education of not "avoiding tough decisions" and finding a way to support the university's best programs "if it wanted to keep the whole ship from sinking." There also were new faculty recognition programs to acknowledge the highest levels of excellence in research, teaching, and service; and new promotion and tenure guidelines that particularized individual department missions and aspirations.

The farm boy from near Porter, Ohio, who had enrolled as an undergraduate music major at Ohio State, switched to international studies; been president of the International House, the Men's Glee Club, the Symphonic Chair, and the John D. Mershon Honorary Society; received his Ohio State master's degree in political science and then followed through with his Ph.D. at UC-Berkeley; and had come home to his alma mater in 1993 as provost was now his university's president, if only in the interim.

As interim president, Sisson told *onCampus* he would continue "the relentless pursuit of academic excellence." He would also continue the fight to retain higher education funding against the threat of the *DeRolph* case. "A solution," he said, that would try to address the K–12 problem by depriving higher education of funds "is short-sighted and detrimental to the people and businesses of this great state." And, in a struggle as old as the 1907 Carnegie Foundation report on Ohio higher education, he would attend to "institutional positioning," the continuing campaign to see Ohio State uniquely funded as Ohio's flagship university.

## *Another Search*

Shumate had said in the fall he expected Ohio State to name its new president by the end of March. But for some trustees, David Brennan in particular, March was not soon enough. Six months was transition enough. Another factor in moving ahead more quickly was that the Ohio Board of Regents had named a new and nontraditional chancellor. Roderick Chu had replaced the retired Elaine Hairston. Chu had spent twenty years with Anderson Consulting, once was New York State's tax commissioner, and, as a trustee of the State

University of New York, had chaired the system's Committee on Vision and Mission. New York state, dominated by private universities, had one of the few state systems with no true flagship university. It was imperative Ohio State lose no ground there.

On the Sunday following Gee's Brown announcement, Shumate had visited Gee at the university residence, where the president had offered to do anything he could to help recruit his successor. It is unusual to find the chairman of the Board also chairing the search committee, but Shumate was an unusual leader. "Do you want my opinion?" Gee asked, and Shumate said he did.

"There are four or five people in the country who can do this job," Gee told Shumate. "It's a tough one and you need the right person to build on what we have done." Presidents of large American universities get to know each other quite well, often through the Association of American Universities (AAU) or the President's Commission of the National Collegiate Athletic Association (NCAA). A particular few had been prominent in both. Two had been Gordon Gee of Ohio State and the Big Ten and Brit Kirwan of the University of Maryland and the Atlantic Coast Conference.

It was the first time Shumate ever heard the name "Kirwan."

Soon the trustees were hosting a campus forum so that the university community could discuss qualities the next president should possess. As reported in *onCampus* (October 9), Terry Miller, the university's Eminent Scholar in chemistry, called for "a person intent on our goals, someone who has the ability and determination to reach them." Willa Young, coordinator of gender services for Student Affairs, called for a president who would encourage a curriculum incorporating studies of women, people of color, and gays and lesbians. Larry Cline, a Marion campus trustee, pointed out that diversity includes differences in age. Eric Reeves, a law student, argued that in light of the erosion of affirmative action the land-grant ideal of access was more important than ever.

The trustees listened and incorporated many suggestions into a messianic presidential profile. It called for "a highly respected academic leader and tough-minded managerial leader who would be expected to carry a strong record of implementation and strategic capability and must have a demonstrated ability to energize and attract highly talented people." Intrinsic personality qualities sought included "outstanding intellectual breadth and depth, strong interpersonal traits, genuine concern for students, a high level of energy informed by perseverance, excellent communications skills, and exemplary integrity, trustworthiness and wisdom."

The search committee had been appointed back in early September. On it

## Chapter 39

were four trustees—Shumate, Tami Longaberger, Jim Patterson, and George Skestos; five faculty—Chemistry's Bruce Bursten, English's David Frantz, Engineering's Jane Fraser, Environmental Sciences' Alan Randall, and Allied Medicine and Pathology's Sally Rudmann; three campus administrators, Development's Jerry May, the Humanities' Kermit Hall, and Medicine's Bernadine Healy; two staff members, Development Officer Jeri Kozobarich and the Registrar's Office's Jack Miner; two students, Student Government President John Carney and doctoral candidate Clara Cuellar; and Dan Heinlen, president and CEO of the Alumni Association. Board Secretary Bill Napier would coordinate the search. Bill Funk of Korn/Ferry International would do the head-hunting and initial screening.

Prior to the creation of the search committee, there had been speculation within the university about six possible internal candidates: Hall, Healy, Sisson, Bobby Moser, Nancy Zimpher, and David Williams. At the outset, Sisson informed Shumate that he would not be a candidate, given that rumor of an inside candidate would make a vigorous national search more difficult than it already would be.

Though he was a scientist and though his college had pioneered restructuring and now was Food, Agricultural, and Environmental Sciences, as good an administrator as Moser was, it would be tough, some said, for an Aggie to become president.

Ditto for Zimpher, a popular dean of Education, with an Ohio State Ph.D., a strong administrator, great in the community, executive dean of the professional colleges, and national president of the Holmes Partnership, which was revolutionizing teacher training. People with education doctorates, however, rarely commanded flagship presidencies, at least as their first presidency. Gordon Gee, who had started at West Virginia University, was an exception, but he also had a law degree from Columbia. As the search committee was being formed, Gee was writing Korn/Ferry's Funk, suggesting he meet Zimpher: "truly a talented individual who ought to be on your radar screen" for other presidencies. Zimpher would become chancellor of the University of Wisconsin–Milwaukee in 1998.

Student Affairs Vice President and Law Professor Williams, a good friend of Gee and strongest advocate of students, was a powerful administrator but had chafed some people with his direct ways. He would leave in 2000 to become Gee's vice chancellor and general counsel at Vanderbilt.

Hall, dean of Humanities and executive dean of Arts and Sciences, was certainly presidential material, but he would have to leapfrog Sisson. Hall would become provost at North Carolina State in 1999 and president of Utah State two years later.

Following a miraculous recovery from a brain tumor surgery, Healy would become president of the American Red Cross; its search committee was chaired by Dimon McFerson, CEO of Nationwide, and later an Ohio State trustee. Healy would resign from the Red Cross in a policy controversy over the disposition of funds received after the tragedy of September 11, 2001. She would acknowledge then (*New York Times,* December 23, 2001) that she had been given only three months to live when her tumor was diagnosed while she was at Ohio State. When the diagnosis proved wonderfully wrong, she had left for "the chance 'to do good'" through the American Red Cross.

The odds were terrible, in any case, for an internal candidate to become Ohio State's president. In Ohio State history, only President William Rightmire (1926–1938), first the Law dean, then acting president, had been selected from within.

## *Brit Kirwan*

"The overwhelming challenge was to try not to replace Gordon, but to find the right person for this time. The challenge in following Gordon for anyone," trustee Tami Longaberger said later, "no matter how wonderful and well prepared he or she might be for the position, was enormous. People were prepared 'to jump off the cliff' for Gordon and that's what we were looking for." While publicly it looked as if Sisson would have at least until March as Ohio State's only president, by December the committee had settled on the person it wished to recommend as Gee's successor. The trick was to get him to agree.

All but one of the finalists were sitting presidents, and all but one of the finalists had been virtually smuggled into central Ohio, their privacy protected; the interview site was a building down an old gravel road on rural property owned by the Longabergers. The one finalist who was met elsewhere, Longaberger said later, "was never a candidate." He had been visited at his home university by Shumate, Healy, and Trustees Patterson and Celeste under the pretence of discussing the Kellogg Commission. Ten minutes into the conversation, Shumate said, "You know we really don't want to talk to you about the Kellogg Commission, we want to talk to you about becoming president of The Ohio State University."

His interest was solicited again at a meeting in Crystal City, Virginia. Finally, on Thanksgiving weekend, his interest now piqued, he had agreed to and

## CHAPTER 39

did fly into a private airport in central Ohio to visit the campus and lunch with the trustees at the home of committee member and trustee George Skestos. He was also shown the campus and met with the governor.

It was now Sugar Bowl week, and most of the trustees, some of the university executive committee, and others were staying in the Hilton Hotel in New Orleans. During the days, former President Gee was planning his first weeks at Brown while saying farewells, including an emotional goodbye to the alumni where thousands gathered at the traditional pre-bowl "Buckeye Bash." Interim President Sisson was representing the university at official Sugar Bowl functions and leading an Ohio State group in an admirable new element of such a bowl visit: daily community service projects in the poorer sections of New Orleans.

Meanwhile, Alex Shumate, who took part in the community service projects, as did Ted Celeste, was reeling in his president.

While still in New Orleans, on New Years Eve day, Communications Director Baroway and consultant Don Van Meter were readying a press release just in case the story broke prematurely out of Maryland. Pending official trustee approval, Shumate believed Ohio State had its president. He told Sisson it was Brit Kirwan.

On Saturday, January 3, a story copyrighted by Michael F. Curtin, editor of the *Columbus Dispatch,* announced William E. Kirwan, president of the University of Maryland at College Park, as the "leading candidate to become the new president of Ohio State University. Kirwan, 59, has been offered the position and is expected to give OSU officials an answer by Monday. . . ." Kirwan had been at Maryland for thirty-three years, having moved through the ranks of the mathematics professorate; he had become a dean, vice chancellor, and finally president of this flagship campus in a system headed by a higher official, the system chancellor.

Known as "Brit," a play on his middle name, which was "English," he was married to the former Patricia Harper and had two grown children. He had been Maryland's president more than eight years, had recruited Gary Williams away from Ohio State as his basketball coach, and lost Andy Geiger to Ohio State as athletic director. He was no restructuring neophyte: His own state's budget problems had led him to streamline College Park, eliminating thirty-two degree programs, seven departments, and one college.

Alex Shumate said he could not comment on any candidate.

The next morning, the *Washington Post* copyrighted its own story. The chairman of Maryland's Board of Regents told the *Post* that Kirwan had telephoned him and was "definitely taking" the job. Just as the Colorado campus and the state's politicians had been shocked eight years before by Gee's departure to Ohio State, so it was in College Park and throughout the Maryland State House. While the governor, Parris Glendening, had planned to announce a major increase in state funding for higher education, investment banker Edwin S. Crawford, the finance chairman of the regents, surmised that it had not come fast enough.

One day later, Ohio State's Board of Trustees appointed William E. Kirwan the twelfth president of the university. Brit and Patty Kirwan flew in and were there for the special session and news conference. Kirwan had been the unanimous choice of the search committee, and his appointment was confirmed unanimously. "We set high standards in the search," Shumate said, "so high that some people questioned whether or not we could reach them. My fellow trustees and I are very pleased to say that we have found, in William Kirwan, a person who has all the qualities of leadership, scholarship, vision, innovation, and integrity we sought."

As had Gee, Kirwan would stay put through a six-month transition to give Maryland time to find the right person to replace him. Over the transition, the university press release said, Richard Sisson would "continue to manage the operations of the university as interim president." In early May, Sisson informed both Ted Celeste, the new board chair, and Brit Kirwan that he did not want to return to the provostship, but rather wished to return to the faculty of the department where he got his first two academic degrees. He would continue, however, for a year as senior advisor to the president, maintaining his role through the next phase of the presidential transition from E. Gordon Gee to Brit Kirwan. On June 18, Brit Kirwan, who would begin his presidency on July 1, accepted "with great regret" Dick Sisson's decision to step down as provost, effective the last day in August.

Sisson had been the second longest-serving provost in Ohio State history. From the time of Gee's announcement to the first day of the Kirwan presidency, he served as chief steward of the university for more than a year. He would continue to serve as a senior advisor to the new president and would return to the faculty as Board of Trustees Chair in Comparative Politics. He would resume, he said, his scholarly work on political and economic change in South Asia and "the challenges to international strategy occasioned by recent events" in an area few Americans were paying attention to in early 1998: India and Pakistan. Both had nuclear weapons. He also would begin work as one of two general editors of the first *Encyclopedia of the Midwest.*

Meanwhile, at Brown, Gee would begin reorganizing the administration and reviewing all academic programs. Later, he would announce a new program in

# Chapter 39

brain science and his plan to raise bonds for a $78 million life sciences building. All four decisions, the *Times* reported on February 8, "ruffled faculty feathers." He also raised $100 million. For what it was worth, his football Bears won the Ivy League title in 1999, whereupon Gee told *The Chronicle of Higher Education* (January 11, 2000), "we tore down the goal posts. I had to show them how to do it." It was, he joked, "the peak of my academic achievement."

It should be so simple. On February 7, 2000, Gordon Gee stunned many people by accepting the chancellorship of Vanderbilt University. Joe B. Wyatt had retired at Vanderbilt and an old friendship had kindled interest in Gee: Gee and Vanderbilt trustee John R. Hall, then chairman and CEO of Ashland Oil, had first met in West Virginia and then again in Columbus. Each had lost a spouse to cancer, and mutual grief formed a singular bond. When the Vanderbilt job opened, Hall had urged his board to seek Gee out, and thus had the wooing begun. Even as he and Constance returned to Ohio State for the presentation of his official portrait in October 1999, a Vanderbilt trustee had been in Columbus pressing him to consider an offer.

While Vanderbilt was already one of the nation's most respected private universities, Gee had aspirations for it to become even better. "I do not intend on being a chancellor of a university that has high aspirations," Gordon Gee said at the announcement of his appointment. "I intend on being the chancellor of a university that has met its aspirations, has exceeded its aspirations and then has set the bar even higher." For many people at Ohio State, this had a familiar ring. They wished him well and knew he could do it. He had at Ohio State.

In March 2002, Edward H. Jennings, Ohio State's president from 1981–1990, retired from the Business faculty. On spring break, Ohio State's Brit Kirwan announced he had accepted the chancellorship of the University System of Maryland, and the process of seeking a president for Ohio State began once again. In May, Rebekah Gee became a doctor, and prepared to enter the Harvard Residency Program in Obstetrics and Gynecology. In May, ground finally was broken for the "Gateway" project, Campus Partners' key project to resurrect High Street.

On June 7, the wheel came full circle when Jim Patterson, the new chair of The Ohio State University Board of Trustees, named Edward H. Jennings interim president. Jennings still looked like he could block the plate to transgressors and homer with the bases loaded.

# Appendix

## Trustees Who Served During the Gee Administration

**TRUSTEE (term)***

Shirley Dunlap Bowser (1982–1991)
Hamilton J. Teaford (1983–1992)
John J. Barone (1984–1993)
Deborah E. Casto (1985–1994)
John W. Kessler (1986–1995)
Milton A. Wolf (1987–1996)
Leslie H. Wexner (1988–1997)
Alex Shumate (1989–1998)
Theodore S. Celeste (1990–1999)
Michael F. Colley (1991–2000)
George A. Skestos (1992–2001)
David L. Brennan (1993–2002)
James F. Patterson (1994–2003)
Zuheir Sofia (1995–2004)
Tami Longaberger (1996–2005)
Daniel M. Slane (1997–2006)

*All trustees chair the Board in the final year of their appointment.

**STUDENT TRUSTEE (term)**

Sophia L. Paige (1989–1991)
David A. Tonnies (1990–1992)
Kristen Cusack (1991–1993)
Hiawatha N. Francisco, Jr. (1992–1994)
Amira N. Ailabouni (1993–1995)
Thomas C. Smith (1994–1996)
Holly A. Smith (1995–1997)
Mark E. Berkman (1996–1998)
Soraya Rofagha (1997–1999)

## Private Support (in Millions) During the Gee Administration

| Fiscal Year | Total Gift Activity |
| --- | --- |
| 1990 | $85.4 |
| 1991 | $84.7 |
| 1992 | $87.4 |
| 1993 | $101.1 |
| 1994 | $127.8 |
| 1995 | $128.0 |
| 1996 | $170.4 |
| 1997 | $175.9 |
| 1998 | $184.8 |

APPENDIX

## Commencement Speakers

| | |
|---|---|
| December 7, 1990 | Stanley J. Aronoff, President, The Ohio Senate |
| March 22, 1991 | D. Allan Bromley, Director, U.S. Office of Science and Technology Policy |
| June 14, 1991 | E. Gordon Gee, President, The Ohio State University |
| August 30, 1991 | Manuel T. Pacheco, President, University of Arizona |
| December 13, 1991 | Lena Bailey, Dean, Human Ecology |
| March 20, 1992 | His Excellency Arpad Goncz, President, Hungarian Republic |
| June 12, 1992 | Bernadine Healy, Director, National Institutes of Health |
| September 3, 1992 | Frank H. T. Rhodes, President, Cornell University |
| December 11, 1992 | Samuel DuBois Cook, President, Dillard University |
| March 19, 1993 | Nancy E. Betz, Professor of Psychology |
| June 11, 1993 | Leonard Downie, Jr., Executive Editor, the *Washington Post* |
| September 2, 1993 | John B. McCoy, Chairman, Banc One Corporation |
| December 10, 1993 | Damon J. Keith, Judge, U.S. Court of Appeals for the 6th Circuit |
| March 18, 1994 | Martha McMackin Garland, Associate Dean, Humanities |
| June 10, 1994 | Mark R. Goldston, President and CEO, L.A. Gear |
| September 1, 1994 | Dimon Richard McFerson, President and CEO, Nationwide Insurance |
| December 9, 1994 | Charles J. Ping, President Emeritus, Ohio University |
| March 17, 1995 | General John R. Galvin, U.S. Army Ret., Ohio State visiting faculty |
| June 9, 1995 | Shimon Peres, Minister of Foreign Affairs, Government of Israel |
| August 31, 1995 | Peter L. Scott, Retired Chairman, Black & Decker Corporation |
| December 8, 1995 | Thomas J. Dougherty, Roswell Park Cancer Institute; Sullivant Medal recipient |
| March 15, 1996 | Herb Asher, Counselor to the President; Professor Emeritus, Political Science |
| June 7, 1996 | John Jakes, author |
| August 29, 1996 | Barbara A. Reynolds, *USA Today* columnist; President, Reynolds News Service |

APPENDIX

December 13, 1996   John D. Ong, Chairman of the Board, the B. F. Goodrich Company
March 21, 1997   Kathryn D. Sullivan, astronaut; President and CEO, Center of Science and Industry (COSI)
June 13, 1997   Ceremony canceled by rain (Bob Greene, author, rescheduled)
August 29, 1997   Edward E. Hagenlocker, Vice Chairman, Ford Motor Company
December 12, 1997   E. Gordon Gee, President, The Ohio State University

## The Wexner Prize Recipients

1992   Peter Brook, film and theater director
1993   Merce Cunningham, composer
        John Cage, choreographer
1994   Bruce Nauman, artist
1995   Yvonne Rainer, filmmaker and choreographer
1996/97   Martin Scorsese, filmmaker

## Honorary Degree Recipients (conferred)

December 7, 1990   Stanley J. Aronoff, Doctor of Laws
March 22, 1991   Nyle C. Brady, Doctor of Humane Letters
        D. Allan Bromley, Doctor of Science
        Robert L. Metcalf, Doctor of Science
June 14, 1991   William N. Lipscomb, Jr., Doctor of Science
August 30, 1991   Martin Meyerson, Doctor of Humane Letters
        Peter Taylor, Doctor of Letters
March 20, 1992   Arpad Goncz, Doctor of Humane Letters
        Helmut Moritz, Doctor of Science
        Harold A. Sorgenti, Doctor of Humane Letters
May 1992   Warren E. Burger, Doctor of Laws (received at Hooding Ceremony at the College of Law)
September 3, 1992   Frank H. T. Rhodes, Doctor of Education
        Kenneth E. Boulding, Doctor of Science
December 11, 1992   Ralph W. Cummings, Doctor of Education
March 19, 1993   Roald Hoffmann, Doctor of Science
June 11, 1993   Leonard Downie, Jr., Doctor of Humane Letters
        Frank Ellis, Doctor of Science
        Hideo Sasaki, Doctor of Fine Arts
        William H. Sweet, Doctor of Science

APPENDIX

| | |
|---|---|
| September 2, 1993 | John B. McCoy, Doctor of Business Administration |
| December 10, 1993 | Don Kirkham, Doctor of Science |
| | Howard M. Metzenbaum, Doctor of Laws |
| | Thomas J. Moyer, Doctor of Laws |
| March 18, 1994 | Virginia Hamilton, Doctor of Humane Letters |
| | Torsten N. Wiesel, Doctor of Science |
| June 10, 1994 | John B. Gerlach, Sr., Doctor of Business Administration |
| | Damon J. Keith, Doctor of Laws |
| September 1, 1994 | Willy Burgdorfer, Doctor of Science |
| December 9, 1994 | Rajammal P. Devadas, Doctor of Humane Letters |
| June 9, 1995 | Shimon Peres, Doctor of Diplomacy |
| | Alberto P. Calderon, Doctor of Science |
| | David H. Hubel, Doctor of Science |
| | James Thurber, Doctor of Humane Letters (awarded posthumously) |
| August 31, 1995 | Peter L. Scott, Doctor of Business Administration |
| | John Price Hirth, Doctor of Science |
| | Austin E. Knowlton, Doctor of Architecture |
| | Howard T. Odum, Doctor of Science |
| December 8, 1995 | Daniel Hillel, Doctor of Science |
| | Jeanne Bonnet McCoy, Doctor of Humane Letters |
| March 15, 1996 | Leon H. Sullivan, Doctor of Humane Letters |
| June 7, 1996 | John Jakes, Doctor of Humanities |
| | Neal Lane, Doctor of Science |
| | Chang-Lin Tien, Doctor of Engineering |
| August 29, 1996 | Barbara A. Reynolds, Doctor of Humane Letters |
| | George H. Alber, Doctor of Business Administration |
| | Robert F. Furchgott, Doctor of Science |
| December 13, 1996 | John D. Ong, Doctor of Humanities |
| | Lawrence R. Barnett, Doctor of Fine Arts |
| | E. Travis York, Doctor of Science |
| March 21, 1997 | Ada E. Deer, Doctor of Humanities |
| | Daniel E. Koshland, Jr., Doctor of Science |
| | Clifton R. Wharton, Jr., Doctor of Humane Letters |
| June 13, 1997 | Ceremony canceled by rain; Bob Greene, Doctor of Journalism (received at Spring 1998 Commencement) |

APPENDIX

|  |  |
|---|---|
|  | Walter Mischel, Doctor of Science (received at Autumn 1997 Commencement) |
|  | Eugene P. Odum, Doctor of Science (received at Winter 1999 Commencement) |
|  | Erie Sauder, Doctor of Humane Letters (received in absentia) |
| August 29, 1997 | Edward E. Hagenlocker, Doctor of Science |
|  | Sir James Black, Doctor of Science |
|  | Viktor E. Frankl, Doctor of Humane Letters |
|  | Pancras John Mukasa Ssebuwufu, Doctor of Education |
|  | David Thomas, Doctor of Business Administration |
| December 12, 1997 | E. Gordon Gee, Doctor of Education |
|  | John W. Berry, Sr., Doctor of Business Administration |
|  | Willard Miller, Doctor of Science |
|  | Milton A. Wolf, Doctor of Diplomacy |

## Buildings Constructed During the Gee Administration
### 1990
James Cancer Hospital & Research Institute, Arthur G., 300 W. 10th Avenue, Columbus
Tobacco Curing Bldg-Southern Substation, OARDC-7283 Gardner, Ripley
ATI Swine Nursery Barn (Apple Creek), Agricultural Technical Institute, Wooster
Mansfield Storage Building #2, OSU Mansfield, Mansfield
Coffey Road Sports Center, 1966 Coffey Road, Columbus

### 1991
Hay Storage Building-Wagner Farm, OARDC-Wooster, Wooster
Piketon Research/Extension Center Office Lab/HDHSE, 1864 Shyville Road, Piketon
Farm Equipment Stg Building-Wagner Farm, OARDC-Wooster, Wooster
Piketon Research/Extension Center Farm Ops/Shop, 1864 Shyville Road, Piketon
Piketon Research/Extension Center Aqua Cult Res, 1864 Shyville Road, Piketon
Snow Removal Equipment Storage Building (FAA), 1892 W. Case Road, Columbus
Laboratory Animal Center Building 5, 6089 Godown Road, Columbus

Biocontainment Facility, 670 Tharp Street, Columbus
Classroom Building No. 2 (Lima), 4240 Campus Drive, Lima
Columbus Fire Station 11, City of, 2200 W. Case Road, Columbus
Classroom Building No. 1 (Lima), 4240 Campus Drive, Lima

**1992**
Mansfield Bookstore (N), OSU Mansfield, Mansfield
ATI Land Lab Barn (Apple Creek), Agricultural Technical Institute, Wooster
Finley Equine Stall Barn, State Rt. 142, West Jefferson

**1993**
Dairy Maternity & Calf Barn, OARDC-Wooster, Wooster
ATI Aquaculture Building (Apple Creek), Agricultural Technical Institute, Wooster
Science and Engineering Library, 175 W. 18th Avenue, Columbus
Traffic Control Booth No. 3, 1931 Tuttle Park Place, Columbus
ATI Farm Machine Storage-Shop (Apple Creek), Agricultural Technical Institute, Wooster
Math Annex, 209 W. 18th Avenue, Columbus
Mathematics Tower, 231 W. 18th Avenue, Columbus
Early Childhood Lab-Marion, 1339 Mt. Vernon Avenue, Marion
Office-Northwestern Substation, OARDC-4240 Rangeline, Custar
Public Service Building (Lima), 4240 Campus Drive, Lima
Biotechnology Support Facility, 1096 Carmack Road, Columbus
Biological Sciences Greenhouses, 332 W. 12th Avenue, Columbus
LeFevre Hall-Newark (N), 1179 University Drive, Newark
Traffic Control Booth No. 1, 102 W. 19th Avenue, Columbus

**1994**
Radiation Dosimetry Calibration Facility, 1296 Kinnear Road, Columbus
Tzagournis Medical Research Facility, 420 W. 12th Avenue, Columbus
Neuropsychiatric Facility, 1670 Upham Drive, Columbus
Piketon Research/Extension Center Farm Equipment Storage, 1864 Shyville Road, Piketon
Health Sciences Center (NCTC)-Mansfield, NCTC (N. Central Technical College), Mansfield
Child Development Center (NCTC)-Mansfield, NCTC (N. Central Technical College), Mansfield
Riffe, Vernal G., Jr. Building, 496 W. 12th Avenue, Columbus

# APPENDIX

## 1995

Marion Prairie Storage Facility, OSU Marion, Marion
Turfgrass Foundation Research & Educational Facility, 2710 North Star Road, Columbus
Pesticide Storage & Handling-Veg Crops Br, OARDC-1165 County Road 43, Fremont
Northwood-High Building, 2231 N. High Street, Columbus
Library Book Depository, 2700 Kenny Road, Columbus
WOSE-FM Transmitter Building, 26653 State Rt. 60 N, Warsaw
Newman and Wolfrom Laboratory of Chemistry, 100 W. 18th Avenue, Columbus
Poultry Research Facility, OARDC-Wooster, Wooster

## 1996

Pesticide Stg/Disp-NW Substation, 4240 Rangeline, Custar
Lima Engineering & Indust. Tech. Building, 4240 Campus Drive, Lima
Marion Library/Classroom Building, 1469 Mt. Vernon Avenue, Marion
Pesticide Handling Facility, 2530 Carmack Road, Columbus
Galbreath Equine Center, Daniel M., 685 Tharp Street, Columbus
Edison Joining Technology Center, 1248 Adams Drive, Columbus
Farm Science Review Restroom 1, 132 N. State Rt. 38, London
Laboratory Animal Center Building 6, 6089 Godown Road, Columbus
Pesticide Storage/Disposal-South Substation, 7283 Gardner, Ripley

## 1997

Recreation Field Support/Utility Building, West Campus, Columbus
Compost/Biomass Utility Research Building, OARDC-Wooster, Wooster
Pesticide Storage/Disposal-Western Substation, 7639 S. Charleston Pike, South Charleston
Pesticide Storage/Disposal Building, OARDC-Wooster, Wooster
OARDC Poultry Science Research Facility, OARDC-Wooster, Wooster
Lima Agriculture Building, 4240 Campus Drive, Lima
ATI/OARDC Apartment Village, 1901 Apple Orchard Drive, Wooster
Davis Baseball Stadium, William C., 650 Arena Drive, Columbus

# Chronologies

## 1989–1990

### JULY 1989
Trustees announce $1.08 billion budget including $305 million in state support.
Randy Ayers promoted from assistant to head basketball coach.
Alex Shumate appointed to the Board.

### SEPTEMBER
Third year of selective admissions attracts continuously stronger entering class: only 18 percent with academic deficiencies (excluding arts) compared with 66 percent in 1982 and 40 percent in 1985; 27 percent in top 10 percent of class.

### OCTOBER
Frank W. Hale Black Cultural Center opens.
Trustees reinstate five-year retirement buyout plan up to 5 percent each of faculty and staff for two years.
Transfer articulation agreement signed with Columbus State.
Campaign passes $400 million, $50 million past goal.

### NOVEMBER
Wexner Center opens with national media attention.

### DECEMBER
Ed Jennings announces retirement effective September 1.
Joe Russell of Indiana named vice provost for Minority Affairs.
The James, not yet opened, floods from burst pipe.

## JANUARY 1990

Trustee chair John Berry appoints Jack Kessler to chair presidential search committee.
Football team plays first bowl in three years; loses to Auburn in Hall of Fame.

## FEBRUARY

Freshman selective admissions extended to summer and winter quarters. Spring still open admissions.
Airport master plan adopted.

## APRIL

Citizens' Crime Patrol formed.

## MAY

Jennings forms Committee on Racism. Gay, Lesbian and Bisexual Office opened in Student Life.
Master's degree in Women's Studies approved.
Elaine Hairston named fifth chancellor of the Ohio Board of Regents.

## JUNE

The James opens.
Trustees approve $1.167 billion budget.
Bill Shkurti named VP for Finance.
Penn State joins the Big Ten.
On June 26, the trustees appoint E. Gordon Gee the university's eleventh president effective September 1.

## 1990–1991

## JULY 1990

Trustees authorize faculty legislation providing one-year terminal appointments, shortening tenure-granting period by one year, and reducing probationary appointments for untenured associate professors.
Bernadine P. Healy, chair of Cleveland Clinic Research Institute, appointed to the University Hospitals Board.
Gee brings "Auburn Report" team in to review central administration.
Croswell Road president's home authorized for sale. Ohio State Foundation buys $600,000 Bexley residence.

## AUGUST

Anne Hayes donates forty years of Woody memorabilia.
Men's Glee Club named "Choir of the World" over 132 groups from 32 countries.

## SEPTEMBER

Peter Coors hosts luncheon introducing Gordon Gee to the Columbus business community.
Capital Campaign closes at $460.2 million.
New General Education Curriculum (GEC) in effect for freshmen: to include a foreign language for all undergrads and more structured requirements elsewhere.
Wexner Center is site for Jodie Foster's movie *Little Man Tate*.
Ohio Stadium Astroturf replaced by $900,000 grass field.
Alcohol and drug policy written in response to Drug-Free Schools and Communities Act. Federal funding would stop at institutions that do not comply.
"Chip" Elam named Gee special assistant.
*Reservists are activated for the Gulf War. Ohio State jobs are protected.*

## OCTOBER

Office of Technology Transfer established.
Law School breaks ground on new addition.
Final report and plan of the Task Force on Undergraduate Recruiting: "Ohio State is far behind virtually all private and public universities."
Gee's first University Senate speech outlines initiatives: develop a greater sense of community, improve the undergraduate experience, continue addressing issues of diversity, and reduce the bureaucracy university wide.
Lighting master plan announced.
Lima faculty organizers withdraw petition to unionize.

## NOVEMBER

Ohio State links with North Carolina A&T and Hampton University in U.S. Department of Education Research consortium linking fourteen traditionally Black and seven Midwest universities.
54,094 at Columbus is largest student body since 1980; 60,165 total.
Gee named to Bank One board.
Cigarette vending machines removed from campus.

Fred Hutchinson named senior vice president and provost.
B.S. degree approved in Materials Science and Engineering.
$7 million awarded for national Center for Science Teaching and Learning.
Wexner Prize announced.
Football team loses to Michigan, 16–13.
Governor Celeste projects $262 million state deficit; Shkurti projects 4 percent budget cut.
Student escort service begins van rides to off-campus destinations.
Bike riding Fred Hutchinson passes out, strikes head and heart stops. Will recover.

**DECEMBER**

Assistant U.S. Secretary of Education Michael Williams says race-exclusive scholarships are illegal.
Ohio Senate President Stanley Aronoff is Gee era's first commencement speaker.
Wexner Center for the Visual Arts eliminates "Visual" from name.
Mansfield campus celebrates twenty-fifth anniversary.
Trustees: OK adding temporary south end seating at stadium and an Alumni Association addition to the Fawcett Center.
Baryshnikov here for Wexner Center first anniversary.
Buckeyes lose Liberty Bowl to Air Force Academy.

**JANUARY 1991**

Gee freezes all but essential jobs; faculty is essential.
*U.S. News* rates Ohio State number 31 in academic reputation among national universities; but 143 in student selectivity and 138 in graduation rates.
Professor Susan Fisher develops inexpensive way to control zebra mussels.
Retired VP Richard Jackson dies at fifty-six.

**FEBRUARY**

Trustees approve academic partnership with Cleveland Clinic; three appointments for Elizabeth Gee; Joe Alutto hired from SUNY Buffalo as Business dean.
Gee establishes Commission on Women, Faculty Salary Equity Review Committee, and Athletic Salary Review committee.
Shooting incident in Ohio Union shuts down student dances.

Ohio State vets urge affirmative action plan with preference in hiring and promotion for Vietnam veterans.

*USA Today* features Ohio State and Gee in positive story on control of campus crime.

Gee fires Jim Countryman as Lima dean.

Hutchinson forms Commission on Dependent Care.

Cancer Hospital loses $8 million in first six months.

**MARCH**

William Havener, former chair of Ophthalmology, dies after long battle with cancer. Havener Eye Clinic named in November.

Trustees authorize upgrade of Morrill and Lincoln Towers; remodeling Dodd Hall; relocating Byrd Polar Institute; improving airport runway, taxiway, and ramp.

Open forums begin on the future direction of the university.

First Gee state tour is to southwest Ohio, but he returns to campus following call that Elizabeth's cancer has recurred.

State budget crisis curtails Ohio Eminent Scholar, Academic Challenge, and Program Excellence competitions begun in 1983.

First Ohio State academic scholarship competition for high school seniors is a success.

Gee establishes Red Tape Reduction task force and begins to discuss students as "customers."

Men's basketball team loses to St. John's in third round of NCAA.

*Gulf War ends as some still serve.*

**APRIL**

Personnel Services and Human Relations offices combined as Human Resources and Relations.

Edward Hayes is new vice president for Research.

Gee testifies before Ohio House: "Higher education already is doing more with less."

Gee honors Distinguished Scholars and Teachers with apples.

WOSU-TV ends long history of football replay broadcasts.

**MAY**

Trustees approve Hospitals managed care plan for university employees.

Nine faculty named Presidential Young Investigators; only MIT and Wisconsin have more.

Strike averted as Communications Workers of America (CWA) settle.
Gee appointed to board of the Limited.
Hispanic Action Plan released.
Academic Computing reports $800 million projected costs.
Ohio State announces 103 National Merit and Achievement Scholars in fall class.

## JUNE
Gee institutes University Staff Advisory Council.
Henry Fields is new Dentistry dean.
Gee delivers Commencement address. *Dispatch:* "Gee makes doubters eat words."

## 1991–1992
### JULY 1991
Ohio State endowment breaks into Top 10 among publics: $351 million; by January, $410 million.
Gee reorganizes administration.
Cancer Hospital Board oversight committee created by trustees.

### AUGUST
Gee on alumni tour to Eastern Europe, in USSR when coup fails.
Robert Smith quits football team amid national publicity.

### SEPTEMBER
William M. Mercer Inc. hired to conduct review of staff classification system.
Ohio State withdraws from Mt. Graham telescope because of $60 million projected cost.
Law School Centennial observed.
Elizabeth Gee begins "additional therapies" for recurrence of cancer.
Gee addresses Senate with "Fenceposts and Fulcrums" speech.
U.S. Labor Department reviews Ohio State policies on veterans. Veterans Affairs Office instituted after report shows OSU spent only $400 to support veterans.
$11 million of $14.6 million budget cuts come from eliminating 365 staff positions.

## OCTOBER

Bobby Moser promoted to Agriculture dean as Bob Warmbrod returns to faculty.

Mayoral candidates Ben Espy and Greg Lashutka, both Ohio State football alumni, speak on campus.

With four vice presidencies open, Women's Grass Roots Network petitions Gee to hire women.

Staff survey recommends new and increased benefits, including expanding maternity leave to fathers.

Mac Stewart promoted to dean of University College.

Nancy Zimpher committee reports Ohio State staff has increased by 67 percent since 1981, much in the hospitals.

Hispanic Action Plan issued.

*U.S. News* ranks Ohio State number 29 in academic reputation.

*Lantern* editors resign over policy to call in legal counsel when editor and adviser disagree.

## NOVEMBER

Gee attends Logan Elm Press relocation reception, lauds it, but later must close it.

New first quarter freshmen down 10 percent at Columbus, on target as Gee begins to decrease size of undergraduate student body.

Gee appoints Managing for the Future task force following Voinovich mandate.

Gee and Attorney General Lee Fisher announce that Bob Duncan will head a new Office of Legal Affairs as Jim Meeks returns to College of Law.

Michigan beats Ohio State 31–3, after Gee announces Cooper contract extension.

## DECEMBER

U.S. Secretary of Education Lamar Alexander releases document explaining how colleges can give scholarships to minority students without violating antidiscrimination laws.

Trustees authorize $15.2 million neuropsychiatric building.

Commonwealth Park presidential home leased from the Foundation for $1 a year.

Lead Balloon luncheon—EGG gets Diogenes Award for "self-inflicted wounds."

$15 million added to Ohio State capital budget for "International Garden of Knowledge" Ameriflora building, razed when Ameriflora ends.

Elizabeth Gee passes away on December 17 at age forty-six.

At Hall of Fame Bowl events, Rebekah Gee makes first public appearance with her father. Ohio State loses to Syracuse, 24–17.

**JANUARY 1992**

Trustees report feasibility study to take place on a remodeled Student Union.

Reprint of Jane Ware's *Ohio State Profile* adds Gee chapter.

Gee announces staff hiring freeze to help combat $14 million cut.

*Lantern* editors reject revisionist Holocaust ad, then print it as news copy. Gee chastises staff but defends their right to publish as national media weigh in.

Gee announces Ohio State will begin long-range budget planning.

Computer art pioneer Chuck Csuri retires with forty-three years of service.

**FEBRUARY**

Gee monthly op-ed series begins for Ohio newspapers, continues through 1997.

Trustees approve sick and bereavement leave for domestic partners, early retirees returning part time. Also double competitive bidding minimums, and commit Ohio Stadium for a World Cup bid.

Gee chairs governmental relations' council of National Association of State Universities and Land-Grant Colleges (NASULGC), giving him national platform.

OhioLink links all Ohio and Ohio State University Libraries.

Early buyout incentive ends: 170 faculty and 330 staff take it.

Francis Hazard retires as dean of Marion.

**MARCH**

Rebekah Gee accepts YWCA Women of Achievement Award for her mother.

Joan Huber appointed senior vice president and provost as Fred Hutchinson leaves to become University of Maine president. Trustees also approve Shkurti, Pichette, and Tom vice presidencies; add magna cum laude abolishing "with University Honors"; abolish Department of Photography and Cinema and the Labor Education and Research Service.

Gee reports Ohio State has reduced costs by $45 million in eighteen months. Begins statewide campaign to dispel five myths: plenty of fat in the budget; faculty are unproductive and faculty research is irrelevant; all Ohio State cares about is athletics; we don't reach beyond campus; universities should be run more like a business.

Karl Rubin awarded Cole Prize, highest honor for numbers theory.

*onCampus* reports on sixty consensus-building town meetings.

Arpad Goncz, president of Hungary, is commencement speaker.

Senate mandates that appropriate OSU publications must state that ROTC violates the university's nondiscrimination policy.

Jim Jackson-led men's basketball team loses to Michigan in NCAA fourth round.

**APRIL**

Trustees lift mandatory retirement at age seventy.

Students march to Ohio Statehouse to protest budget cuts.

*Lantern* feature on Gee meeting with students bares "damn dummy" quote.

Rodney King verdict generates riots in south central Los Angeles with impact on Ohio State.

**MAY**

ACTION makes demands on the administration.

Gee reports it is the seventy-fifth year of the quarter system: "I have just one word for that: semester."

New York City dinner kicks off the National Council of Women.

Gee receives standing ovation as Bowling Green commencement speaker.

Gee resumes state tours—North Central/Northwest. Meets with Hispanic leaders in Lucas County.

Mercer Report urges compensation system changes.

**JUNE**

Trustees approve Ed Ray, Don Dell, and Nancy Rudd as associate provosts. Jerelyn Schultz named Human Ecology dean.

Groundbreaking for Bio-Sci rooftop greenhouse and 12th Avenue parking garage.

Bradford Commons renamed Frank W. Hale, Jr., Hall. African American living learning center recommended.

## 1992–1993

**JULY 1992**

Gee state tour to southwest and southern Ohio includes Xenia, Ironton, Piketon, Gallipolis, and Athens.

Trustees raise tuition 5 percent; emphasize $1.5 million will increase high demand courses by 16,000 seats. No pay raises, 5–7 percent unit cuts, 120–185 layoffs ahead.
*Code of Student Conduct* extended off campus.
Violet Meek named Lima dean; Nancy Zimpher, Education acting dean.
Bernadine Healy is commencement speaker.
State tour to northeast Ohio includes first meeting with the Longabergers.
Ohio Agricultural Research and Development Center (OARDC) celebrates its centennial year.
Ohio Managing for the Future task force reports out. Major recommendations are: consolidate branch campuses and tech schools; develop faculty workload with performance evaluations (per institution); redefine tenure as commitment to academic freedom but not employment guarantee; recognize Ohio State and Cincinnati as "comprehensive research institutions." President's Commission on Women makes recommendations to change inequities.

## AUGUST

Ohio State's own Emergency and Fire Prevention Services shut down as a budget cut.
David Williams becomes vice provost for Minority Affairs.
Gee signs cooperative agreement with Arthur E. Thomas, president of Central State.
Gee key fundraising visits include Raymond Firestone and John Drinko.

## SEPTEMBER

Trustees appoint Jose Cruz as Engineering dean; Jim Garland, Mathematical and Physical Sciences dean; Jerry May, vice president for Development and president of the Foundation.
Gee reports more than 80 percent of students got courses they requested for autumn quarter.
Robert Leone fills first Berry Chair.
A new Gee tradition: the first welcoming convocation for new students.
To survive budget cuts, *onCampus* accepts advertising.
*U.S. News* ranks Ohio State number 31 again in academic reputation.
Gee Washington trip generates interviews in *USA Today* and *U.S. News*.

## OCTOBER

Gee address to Senate calls for improved resource management, enhanced learning environment, strengthened research support, enriched campus life.

Presidential task force on the university's communications criticizes decentralization. Of many recommendations, reducing university printing costs by 25 percent and combining video units are implemented.

Jill Morelli hired as university architect.

Mal Whitfield, gold medalist in the 1950 Olympics, is Alumni Association Medalist winner.

Distinguished marketing professor Arthur Cullman dies.

Eisenhower Clearinghouse for Math and Science Education to come to Ohio State.

Insensitivity in hospitals to campus rape victim prompts immediate changes. Rape education added to the University Course for all freshmen.

## NOVEMBER

*Term Limits approved in Ohio as Bill Clinton is elected President.*

University's Managing for the Future task force reports: redefine institutional missions, streamline organization and governance, improve information management, document academic achievement, improve academic support services, have State of Ohio change subsidy formula so as not to penalize stable enrollments. Trustee George Skestos heads steering committee to implement recommendations.

Gee addresses annual meeting of rejuvenated Alumni Advocates.

Gee addresses NASULGC presidents meeting, calling for President Clinton to halt unfunded federal mandates.

Freshman class of 5,411 includes 102 National Merit and seven National Achievement finalists. All minority figures are up.

Underdog Buckeyes tie Michigan 13–13 at home.

## DECEMBER

Dedication of the Museum of Biological Diversity.

Trustees vote to change name of Cooperative Extension Service to Ohio State University Extension; approve Ohio State mission-vision statement.

Regents announce plan in response to Ohio Managing for the Future report: will set new standards for efficiency and accountability, and focus on duplication of doctoral programs.

Gee cuts Citrus Bowl video psa with Richard Lewis on Los Angeles set.

Randy Ayers gets five-year contract extension through 1998–99 season.

Ohio General Assembly approves $195 million in tax increases proposed by Governor Voinovich; saves public universities from further spending cuts.

Inquiry into Citrus Bowl events with Ohio legislators ends Ohio State expense coverage.

**JANUARY 1993**

Buckeyes lose to Georgia, 21–14.

Gee releases economic impact study at Society of Professional Journalists luncheon. Ohio State impact is $3 billion, seven times greater than the state's investment.

Governor Voinovich signs executive order to phase in the smoke-free workplace in state buildings.

*Science* article ranks Ohio State fifth in graduating African American Ph.D.s. Rebekah Gee will attend Columbia University.

Gee meets with 250 in Bricker Hall opposing elimination of Child Care Center subsidy; only small cut results.

**FEBRUARY**

As Gee turns forty-nine, John Cooper gives him "another tie." Staff provides Gourmet Budget Crunch Bars, weighing "a little less than it should be," made of "50 percent less than other budget bars."

Trustees name Zimpher Education dean. Financial Aid and Admissions combined under Jim Mager. Continuing Education moves to University College; Young Scholars to Minority Affairs; Center for Teaching Excellence to Academic Computing. Approve $500,000 for second phase of campus lighting.

IBM gives $3.2 million processor to consolidate administrative and academic computing. Students utilize new e-mail system.

Gee testifies before Ohio Education Subcommittee that state support per student in Ohio has fallen from $5204 to $4040 per student since 1988.

New HIV/AIDS information and policy published.

Washington University polls national reporters on use of campus news services: top five in order are Stanford, Ohio State, Harvard, Johns Hopkins, and Cornell.

**MARCH**

Marjorie (Mrs. Novice) Fawcett passes away.

Trustees create speech and hearing science department; appoint Ron Ferguson surgery chair.

*U.S. News* ranks Medicine second in new category: "comprehensive medical schools."
Gee state tour to southwest Ohio includes Dayton and Cincinnati.
Eleven colleges and units owe $44 million; payback plan published in *onCampus*.
Katie Smith leads women's basketball team to NCAA Finals, 84–82 loss to Texas Tech.
Formal induction ceremony of the new Academy of Teaching.

**APRIL**

Trustees name Dominic Dottavio Marion dean; Randall Ripley, dean of Social and Behavioral Sciences; purchase Northwood property for Family Practice center.
Newark opens LeFevre Hall.
*Dispatch* reports Gee not interested in Michigan State presidency.
Gee sends letter to community on race relations during Rodney King trial deliberations.
"Grand Illusions" Cancer Research black tie "sautés" Gordon Gee.

**MAY**

Law Building addition and renovation dedicated as Drinko Hall.
Gee testifies for increased National Science Foundation funding before U.S. House Appropriations Subcommittee.
Trustees appoint Dick Sisson of UCLA vice president and provost; Gregory Williams of Iowa, Law dean; Ed Ray, senior vice-provost.
Maya Lin in residence, working on Wexner Center environmental sculpture.
1991 recruiting violations involving high school player Damon Flint generates NCAA investigation.
Gee announces deficit may be $25 million next year; positions and budgets frozen for ninety days; top administrative salaries frozen for next year; no multiyear commitments; targeted reductions.
Prime Care rolled out as low premium HMO.

**JUNE**

Alber Bell Tower dedicated at Marion.
News conference announces Ohio State will offer 500 annual scholarships.
Ric Wanetik named "cultural consultant" to Gee.
Gee plants flag in marsh at Wetland Research Park groundbreaking.

Rebekah graduates as her father delivers address at Columbus School for Girls.

Journalism School alumnus Leonard Downie Jr., *Washington Post* executive editor, is commencement speaker.

Gee state tour of northeast Ohio.

David Williams is new VP for Student Affairs; Sherri Geldin new Wexner Center director.

## 1993–94

### JULY 1993

Gee keynotes Mansfield's "Poised for Advancement" Campaign—$2 million goal for a Learning Center; faculty development, scholarships.

Trustees authorize $5.5 million for building at Northwood and High; design on Heart-Lung Institute; to annex 11.5 acres in Clinton Township to Columbus for Business Technology Center; $1.25M to bring Mershon Auditorium into compliance with Americans with Disabilities Act.

Ohio State police arrest two in "pot plane" at Don Scott field.

*onCampus* chart shows Ohio State had a 4.4 percent budget decrease between 1990 and 1993, worst in the Big Ten. Wisconsin led with a 10.9 percent increase.

1995–2000 capital plan lists thirty-one "physically or functionally obsolete buildings," including Brown, Cunz, Hagerty, Hopkins, Jesse Owens Centers, Larkins, Neil, Page, Pomerene, Starling-Loving.

Nancy Sherlock (Currie), '80, is mission specialist on Shuttle *Endeavor*.

Hospitals "Ask A Nurse" program marks five years, 800,000 telephone calls.

### AUGUST

Hugh O'Brian Youth Foundation (HOBY) 1993 international seminar—Ohio State hosts 190 students from U.S. and twenty-five other countries.

Family and medical leave policy allows up to twelve weeks for every twelve months' service to care for ill family member, child in the first year, or one's own health. Prompted by new federal act.

### SEPTEMBER

Bob Duncan named Board secretary and vice president for Legal Affairs/general counsel.

Fund-raising totals $89.2 million, 25 percent above last year.

Gee announces loan application turnaround down from thirteen weeks to one week.

"Third phase of restructuring" officially under way.

Madison Scott retires.

Law Professor LeRoy Pernell appointed interim head of Minority Affairs.

Gee removes administration recommendation to permit gay couples in Buckeye Village from Board consideration.

Mel Schottenstein passes away.

Graduate student orientation instituted.

Billy Graham and Gee meet as *Dispatch* reports Graham's conversion to a Buckeye.

New faculty reception guests include Constance Bumgarner of Art Education.

Gee and City Council president Cindy Lazarus leap on Velcro wall at Health and Fitness Fair. "I'm the Velcro president. Everything sticks to me." *Dispatch* comments "everything, it seems, but public humiliation."

**OCTOBER**

Trustees appoint Glen Hoffsis as Veterinary Medicine interim dean; E. Chistopher Ellison to Robert M. Zollinger chair and chief of General Surgery.

Overlook Farm sold for $233,000.

Sisson recommends each dean redirect 7 percent of general fund budget in fiscal 1995, identify another 7 percent over three years, and look for ways to merge, relocate, or eliminate programs.

Steve Loebs's Ohio Health Care Study finds 13,000 excess beds, too many specialists and not enough general practitioners.

*U.S. News* ranks Ohio State thirty-first in academic reputation again, tied for thirteenth among publics.

Sue Mayer retires from the president's office after thirty-four years of service.

University Hospitals develops volunteer advocate program for sexual assault and domestic violence survivors.

The new technology "Voice Mail" is explained in *onCampus*.

Kiplinger Program in journalism celebrates twentieth anniversary.

Jerry Lucas is Homecoming grand marshal.

*Dispatch* reports statewide public college enrollment down 2.6 percent; Ohio State, down 3.2 percent.

Unity Day Celebration on campus offered as preferred option to confronting Klan rally at State House.

Barry Serafin interviews Gee for ABC special on unfunded mandates. Bob Villa interviews Gee for *Home Again*.

Horticultural garden behind Main Library replanted, originally planted in 1929.

Science and Engineering Library dedicated.

Gee reports to Foundation Board that next capital campaign is being readied.

Renovated Derby Hall rededicated.

**NOVEMBER**

Nation of Islam participates in rally on Bricker steps calling for Gee to address more African American issues.

Fraternities and sororities "adopt" Indianola Alternative Elementary School.

Trustees adopt sexual harassment policy and appoint first James Hospital Board.

EGG letter urges students to stay in football seats after scores are injured in Wisconsin win over Michigan.

Max M. Fisher donates $20 million as naming gift for the College of Business.

Sisson holds open meeting on restructuring in University Hall.

**DECEMBER**

Gee and Dave Thomas make television psa acknowledging the James's Thomas Ambulatory Chemotherapy Center.

Oversight Committee for University Restructuring is Sisson, Williams, Alayne Parson, Gerry Reagan, Ted Allen, Tom York, Susan Huntington, and Bob Warmbrod.

AAU names Gee to executive committee; Sisson chairs Council on Academic Affairs of NASULGC.

Student referendum to fund $54 million Ohio Union remodeling and expansion fails, 3:1.

Funeral for football star Jayson Gwinn, killed in automobile accident, is held in Mershon Auditorium.

Gee delivers Kent State commencement address.

Gee *Dispatch* interview introduces subjects of stadium expansion and "luxury boxes, a new arena-ice rink complex and a baseball stadium." "I do believe a university arena should be on campus."

**JANUARY 1994**

Gee wins "Lead Balloon Award" again.

-22 degree temperature and deep snow cancels classes on the 19th.

Gee signs "articulation" transfer agreements with Lorain, Cuyahoga, and Lakeland Colleges.

History department contracts "electronic bookshelf" for on-demand publishing.

**FEBRUARY**

Off-campus housing report shows 3 percent student decline in 43201 zip code and 18 percent in the "red zone"—High to Conrail tracks, 5th to 12th.

Gee hosts Constance M. Bumgarner at a faculty dinner day before 50th Gee birthday which, as always, is February 2, Groundhog Day.

Ron Michalec becomes chief of police.

Trustees approve early retirement buyout for faculty, open one year; Athletic Director Jim Jones and Associate AD Phyllis Bailey among takers.

University Area Improvement Task Force created to address problems of crime, trash, and deteriorating conditions.

Regents gives each university responsibility to follow through on House Bill 152: "a minimum 10 percent increase of statewide undergraduate teaching ... to restore reductions experienced over the past decade."

Gee receives Distinguished Alumnus Awards from both University of Utah and Columbia University Teachers College.

Revised Sunshine Law takes affect, requires research protocols to be discussed in open sessions.

Ruth Gresham to direct new Off-Campus Housing Office.

**MARCH**

Functional mission statement published.

Student Stephanie Hummer is murdered.

New Math Tower dedicated.

Most administrative offices will stay open until 7 P.M.

BRUTUS computerized registration system wait lists students for closed classes.

**APRIL**

National "Names Project" AIDS memorial quilt visits Ohio State.

Rafael Cortada named Newark dean as Newark trustee board is established.

Sisson recommends folding Social Work into College of Education. Later retracts.

On the 15th, 200 Black law students protest acts of racism.

Andy Geiger named Ohio State's seventh athletic director.
City announces plans to install hundreds of new streetlights in University District.

**MAY**

First graduating class of Central Ohio Young Scholars inducts twenty new scholars. Statewide, 101 of 113 graduates will attend Ohio State.
Board authorizes Business School computer fee.
*U.S. News* sends Paul Glastris to Ohio State to do story on Gee and restructuring. Story appears in following fall's *College Guidebook,* but not the magazine.
Gee presents Distinguished Service Award personally to Roy Kottman, who passes away in June.
Verne Riffe confirms $15 million for an Ohio State arena will be in capital bill.
Coca-Cola announces $500,000 Critical Difference gift to honor Elizabeth Gee.
Kermit Hall of University of Tulsa hired as Humanities dean.
Thomas Taylor joins Ken Wilson and Leo Paquette in the National Academy of Sciences.
Stephanie Hummer Recreation Park announced as a memorial.
Two-tier (West/East Campus) parking rates announced, will include bus passes. Lighted campus maps placed in twelve locations, first maps in ten years.
Pink Floyd packs Ohio Stadium.

**JUNE**

University Area Task Force recommends a not-for-profit "improvement/redevelopment" corporation.
Trustees authorize budget of $1.43 billion; $556 million in general funds. Approve restructuring of Agriculture, Engineering, and Veterinary Medicine. Promote Tzagournis to vice president for Health Sciences, Zimpher and Garland to executive deans.
Early retirement plan extended through June 1995—350 faculty expected to participate, saving up to $11.7 million a year.
Gee addresses Cleveland Fifty Club on the 50th anniversary of D-Day.
Parents of two seniors who died in an April 9 fire, John Galyk and Jennifer Burdick, accept their degrees at commencement.

Nuclear Regulatory Commission cites Ohio State for thirty-two minor violations, levies small fine.
NCAA sanctions are announced, placing men's basketball team on probation.
Julius Greenstein retires as dean of Newark and Central Ohio Technical College.

## 1994–1995
### JULY 1994
Mansfield, Marion, and Lima get their own trustees.
1929 Kenny Road and its five acres purchased for $3.4 million.
Medical Center and Harding Hospital merge psychiatry residency programs.
Gee east Ohio state tour.
Quality Improvement partnership links Ford Motor and Ohio State.
Buck ID accounts instituted to replace cash.

### AUGUST
Ohio State Catalog for Automated Retrieval (OSCAR) goes online.
Trustees appoint Pernell to head Minority Affairs. Endowed chairs named: Jay Barney of Texas A&M, Bank One chair, Frederick Davidorf, Martha G. and Milton Staub chair, Jacques Zakin, Helen C. Kurtz chair; and Gilbert and Kathryn Mitchell chair, M. Ronald Glaser named associate dean. Retired professors honored include Phyllis Bailey, Henry Hunker, Arne Sletteback, and John Kessel.

### SEPTEMBER
Gee and Columbus Mayor Lashutka hold joint press conference to announce separate arenas.
Ron Pizzuti announces he will seek a National Hockey League team. OSU arena estimated at $75 million.
Equine Trauma Center groundbreaking.
New assistant men's basketball coach Ken Turner collapses of heart attack and never recovers.
Regents propose new funding formula with three funding elements: foundation, enrollment-based, and performance.
Fifth member of Randy Ayers's 1992 recruiting class dismissed for disciplinary reasons. Transfers include Derek Anderson to Kentucky.
Lashutka and Gee announce $20 million fund from AFL-CIO Investment Trust for neighborhood redevelopment.

Ground broken for addition to Child Care Center for medically fragile children.
Administrative Resource Management System (ARMS) announced to replace general ledger accounting and Human Resources information system.
Park near Dodd Hall named after Ernest Johnson.

**OCTOBER**

Gee urges tenure and promotion standards review.
Miechelle Willis comes to Ohio State from Temple to oversee sixteen varsity sports, including men's and women's basketball, as associate director of Athletics.
Gee leads "High on Pride" as 30 tons of garbage is picked up in a 55-block area.
Helicopter Service merged with Grant Hospital's.
Barry Humphries to head Campus Partners. Tony Tripodi of Florida International is new Social Work dean.
Agriculture's "Project Reinvent" kicks off with Kellogg Symposium on future of the land-grant university.
Emeritus Athletic Director Hugh Hindman dies at sixty-seven.
Governor Voinovich and Gee fight one-cent pop tax repeal. Lose.
Cleveland Mayor Mike White is Homecoming grand marshal.
Eisenhower National Clearinghouse celebrates new online math/science curriculum information service for K–12 teachers.
Dedications of Business Technology Center and Radiation Dosimeter Calibration Facility.
Hispanic students protest for a Hispanic Affairs unit in Minority Affairs, more Hispanic administrators.
Dedication of Dreese Lab Addition for computer and information science.

**NOVEMBER**

Trustees approve renaming School of Architecture after Austin Knowlton following $10 million gift; hire arena architects Sink Combs Dethlefs of Denver and Moody/Nolan; resume investing in companies that do business in South Africa, revoked in 1985.
Margaret Thatcher visits Kuhn Honors Center. Regents mandate review of all state doctoral programs.
Liza Minnelli featured at Wexner Center fifth anniversary Gala.
E. Gordon Gee and Constance Bumgarner are married November 26.
Ohio State 22, Michigan 6.
James Thurber's 100th birthday is November 8.

## DECEMBER

Nationwide donates $2.5M to Fisher College campaign.

Trustees accept late Raymond Firestone's offer to buy property for $5 million appraised at $8 million in 1987. David Brennan to head committee.

Park south of 19th Avenue named after Neal and Faye Smith.

Four faculty are Presidential Young Investigators.

Vernal G. Riffe, Jr., Building for interdisciplinary research in biological sciences and pharmacy is dedicated.

Decline in state college-going rate results in $23 million state surplus. Ohio State gets $4.5 million.

## JANUARY 1995

Buckeyes lose to Alabama, 24–17, in Citrus Bowl.

Public records ruling gives Protect Our Earth's Treasures (POET) access to 20,000 pages of documents on OSU animal research.

Academic Affairs announces fourteen enrichment projects, establishes faculty-wide salary appeal process.

National Cancer Institute re-funds Ohio State as a Comprehensive Cancer Center.

Articulation agreements signed with Sinclair and Clark State Community Colleges.

## FEBRUARY

Twenty-fifth annual United Black World Month.

Trustees appoint Ginny Trethewey vice president and general counsel.
Appoint Campus Partners' Board (Duncan, Nichols, Pichette, Ray, Shkurti, Skestos, Williams, and Zimpher) and authorize $600,00 one-time funds for comprehensive plan and $500,000 per year operating. Authorize agreement with MedOhio Health Inc. to provide home health care.

Geiger announces revenue from August's Kickoff Classic football game will fund two new women's varsity sports: crew and lacrosse, will make male-female ratio 60:40, thirty-seven varsity teams.

Law Dean Gregory Williams's book, *Life on the Color Line: The True Story of a White Boy Who Discovered He Was Black*, is *New York Times* best seller.

Kermit Hall appointed to JFK Assassination Records Review Board.

Gees and others visit Dresden, Germany, representing Columbus in ceremony commemorating fiftieth anniversary of terrible firebombing.

Billy Hill, head athletic trainer, dies at forty-seven.

Ohio State lobbies for changes in public records law to protect intellectual property after losing two cases: making tenure and promotion records open; naming animal research scientists and divulging documents about their research.

Chuck Csuri's computer artwork is cover story of *Smithsonian*.

Human Ecology restructures from five to three departments.

## MARCH

Gee is cover in *Columbus Monthly*.

Roy Lichtenstein Retrospective opens at Wexner Center.

Trustees amend Medical Practice Plan, including changing payments to Teaching and Research Fund from fixed dollars to 3 percent of gross income; announce $1.4 million gift from Frank and Ruth Stanton to establish chair honoring Harold E. Burtt.

Presidential and Medalist competition now has 700 competitors.

Campus Campaign enters second decade with $27 million so far.

*Lantern* reports EGG salary number 8 among Big Ten presidents at $168,504. Michigan's Duderstadt is number 1 at $232,421.

Gee lobbies for federal support of academic medicine, keynotes Association of Academic Health Centers.

*U.S. News* survey of graduate programs ranks College of Education number 9; Fisher College, 25; Law School, 38; graduate engineering, 18; political science, 17; psychology, 24; sociology, 25; counseling psychology, 2; industrial and organizational psychology, 4.

## APRIL

Nobel Peace Prize recipient Elie Wiesel helps dedicate new Wexner Jewish Student Center and Hillel Foundation.

"A lifetime of service to Ohio, a tribute to speaker Vern Riffe" raises $800,000 for the Riffe Chair in government and politics.

Two hospitals affiliate with University Medical Center and the Health Care Consortium of Ohio: Ohio Regional in Martin's Ferry and Greenfield Area in Greenfield.

Gee state tour includes VanWert, Kalida, Findlay, and Toledo.

Five-year Evaluation of President Gee submitted to Board of Trustees. Trustees appoint Greta Russell as university controller; Thomas N. Hansen, new medical director of Children's Hospital, chair and professor of pediatrics.

Groundbreaking for the Richard and Annette Bloch Cancer Survivors Center.

Thirty-fifth anniversary reunion dinner of 1960 national champion basketball team.
Remodeled Fawcett Center opens.
Marcel Marceau does workshops and master classes.
Bernie Gerlach receives the Reese Medal.
College of Medicine proposes a School of Public Health.

**MAY**

Trustees approve Master of Arts in arts policy. New trustee Sofia establishes professorship in Arabic Studies with $500,000 gift commitment.
Drew Durbin wins NCAA title in pommel horse.
Orton Hall Centennial.
Mendenhall Hall, built in 1904, rededicated after major renovation. Room named for Charles H. Summerson, emeritus geology professor, who coordinated this and Orton renovations.
King Gordon and Queen Constance reign at Renaissance Festival.
Charles Kleibacker retirees as curator of the Historic Costume and Textiles Collection.
Gee addresses commencement at North Carolina State.
Board of Regents study finds universities overbuilt; urges universities pay construction debt from operating budgets instead of bonds.
First Mobile Mapping Symposium hosted by Center for Mapping.
WBNS-TV airs special on Wexners and Gees. Angela Pace interviews Wexners; Dave Kaylor, Gees.
Queen Sylvia of Sweden visits the James to dedicate Patients Resource Center donated by the Swedish pharmaceutical firm, Pharmacia.
Everett Reese, class of 1919, passes away.

**JUNE**

Trustees appoint Susan Huntington acting dean of the Graduate School as Roy Koenigschnecht returns to speech and hearing faculty. Dick Morrow chair and King George III professorships established.
Fisher College groundbreaking.
Edison Joining Technology Center groundbreaking includes Ohio State welding institute.
Nobel Peace Prize recipient Israeli Minister of Foreign Affairs Shimon Peres is commencement speaker.
University Hospitals reduces prices by 3.6 percent to compete; eliminates 165 jobs.

Gordon Gee is California Board of Regents selection to head its university system. Full-court press keeps Gee at Ohio State.

## 1995–1996
### JULY 1995

Trustees approve merging Journalism and Communication, University Systems and Academic Technology Services. Bernadine Healy named Medicine dean; Glen Hoffsis, Veterinary Medicine dean; John P. Schoessler, Optometry acting dean; Richard Hall, Biological Sciences acting dean.

Faculty rules broadened to extend probationary period for factors beyond faculty members' control—as time to set up lab, or departmental restructuring.

Grades now available to students on Web through University Technology Services, with password given.

Trustees raise Gee salary by 31 percent to $220,000.

$105,000 approved for 125th anniversary celebration, "A Past with a Presence."

Gee state tour of Toledo and northwest Ohio, also Detroit. California development trip follows.

### AUGUST

Big Ten celebrates centennial year.

Mershon Center's Joe Kruzel, on leave as Deputy Assistant Secretary of Defense for European and NATO affairs, killed in accident outside Sarajevo at age fifty.

Ohio State defeats Boston College, 38–6, in Kickoff Classic at Meadowlands.

### SEPTEMBER

Trustees approve five-year contract for John Cooper. Ed Jennings appointed to William H. Davis chair: John Fellingham, H. P. Wolfe chair; Peter D. Easton, John J. Gerlach chair; David R. Rudy, Pomerene chair.

*U.S. News* ranks Fisher College number 16 for undergraduate education; Engineering, number 17. Ohio State number 15 among public universities in academic reputation; number 36 among all universities.

Dorothy Klotz and Marion Rowley gave $9 million to the James.

Daniel M. Galbreath Equine Trauma Intensive Care and Research Center named following his death at sixty-seven.

National Research Council releases graduate education rankings, reporting on

3,634 Ph.D. programs in 41 fields and 274 universities. Top 25—geography, 5; linguistics, 8; industrial and systems engineering, 12; political science, German, 17; materials engineering, psychology, 21; chemistry, electrical engineering, classics, 22; astronomy, 23; physics, philosophy, aeronautical engineering, 24; mechanical engineering, sociology, 25.

Gordon and Constance Gee dot the "I."

"Scarlet Fever": Gee institutes large-scale pep rally followed by dance to open school. Also, first transfer student orientation.

"Affirm Thy Friendship" kicked off for $850 million. Honorary chairs: John Berry and Max Fisher; cochairs, Larry Barnett, Bernie Gerlach, Teckie Shackelford, and Milt Wolf.

Wendy's opens in the Ohio Union.

**OCTOBER**

Pharmacy in Clinics Building run by Pharmacy College replaces one closed by University Hospitals.

Gee state tour close to home includes Coshocton, Crooksville, and Zanesville.

Trustees appoint Jim Mager assistant VP for Enrollment Management; Eric Kunz, assistant VP for Resource Planning; Sarah Blouch, traffic, parking and transportation director. William L. Berry named to Ross Chair.

Homecoming begins 125th anniversary celebration with birthday party on the Oval. Richard Lewis is parade grand marshal.

Bill Davis Stadium groundbreaking.

On the 20th, President Clinton addresses 20,000 rain-soaked Buckeyes on the Oval, then leads Midwest Regional Economic Conference in Fawcett Center. All U.S. Cabinet attend: Henry Cisneros (HUD); John Gibbons (Science and Technology); Dan Glickman (Agriculture); Roger Johnson (General Services); Phil Lader (Small Business); Frederico Penya (Transportation); Robert Reich (Labor); Richard Riley (Education); Alice Rivlin (OMB); Donna Shalala (HHS); Joseph Stiglitz (Chair, Economic Advisors); Laura D'Andrea Tyson (Assistant for Economic Policy).

Dedication of Law Building as John Deaver Drinko Hall.

Ohio State and Columbus police sign mutual aid compact, but services to be furnished, even in an emergency, only "upon request . . . in so far as such services are available."

Varsity O Women Sports Hall of Fame inducts diver Kelly McCormick, Olympic silver, 1984; bronze, 1988 medalist.

California regents eliminate race-based admissions and hiring. Million Man March takes place in Washington.

## NOVEMBER

Press conference with Gee supports a ten-year levy for COTA, which fails.

Trustees approve $28 million investment in Campus Partners as Campus Partners drafts plan to include eminent domain. Department of Women's Studies approved.

Black Greek Council joins National Panhellenic Council.

Memorial service at the Wexner Jewish Student Center for assassinated Prime Minister of Israel Yitzhak Rabin.

Gee participates in ROTC "rock ceremony" honoring Ohio State alumni killed in action, commemorates fiftieth anniversary of the end of World War II.

Press conference announces a $12.5 million gift from Schottenstein Stores Corporation and Value City Stores. Name of the facility: Schottenstein Center. Main basketball/hockey arena, Value City Arena.

Forty-seven members of university-area Short North Posse arrested.

Autumn quarter enrollment is 54,781, down 1006 students. Columbus enrollments is 48,676, down 866, but still the largest single campus in the nation. On target.

Restructuring eliminates Office of International Affairs and Logan Elm Press. Four vice provost positions cut through reorganization in Academic Affairs.

Michigan 31, Ohio State 23. Football All-American Alex Schoenbaum has fatal heart attack at home following game. Heisman Trophy Winner Les Horvath also dies this month.

## DECEMBER

Trustees approve joint venture for inpatient and outpatient mental health with Harding Hospital.

Susan Huntington appointed acting vice provost for graduate studies.

Chemistry building replacing "old Sawtooth" named the Richard F. Celeste Laboratory of Chemistry.

Faculty and staff can take payroll deductions for Schottenstein Center seat licenses.

Merit scholarships increased to 100 from forty: ten full "Presidential," thirty resident tuition "Medalist," sixty half-resident tuition "Traditional."

Sisson tells University Senate "financial equilibrium" has been reached, first since 1990.

*Modern Health Care* lists University Hospitals among the top 100.

Cleveland campaign celebration guests include former governor Richard Celeste and new wife, Jacqueline Lundquist.

Eddie George wins Heisman Trophy and Doak Walker Award as top running back, Maxwell Award and Walter Camp Award as top collegiate football player. Other awards for team are: Greg Bellisari, Academic All American; Terry Glenn, Beletnikoff Award as nation's top receiver; Orlando Pace, Lombardi Award as top lineman; Bobby Hoying, Draddy Prize from National Football Foundation as nation's top football scholar.

Jim Smith of World Wrestling Federation named athletics marketing director.

Andy Geiger signs $9.25 million five-year contract with Nike: $1.85 million per year includes supplements in pay of all coaches.

Dance ranked number 1 in survey by *Dance Teacher Now*.

## JANUARY 1996

Board of Regents will fund only Ohio State and Ohio University history doctoral programs as Miami and Akron discontinue. Cincinnati funds internally.

Time capsule, to be opened in 2070, sealed in Thompson Library wall.

Governor Voinovich reorganizes Ohio Science and Technology Council as Gee chairs with Owens Corning's Glen Hiner. Gee also chairs national Kellogg Commission.

New York City Campaign kickoff. Gee annual February Florida trip includes Naples, Sarasota, and Boca Raton kickoffs.

Campus Collaborative introduced, chaired by Nancy Zimpher.

## FEBRUARY

Gee again wins Lead Balloon Award from Downtown Athletic Club.

Trustees authorize $9 million to pay ARMS off in three years; approve third phase of Campus Master Plan—Academic Core North. Joseph Rich appointed to the Ralph Kurtz chair; Rene Stulz, the Everett Reese chair.

Randall Harris is interim director of the new School of Public Health.

Ohio State Health Network established to plan and develop a regional healthcare and delivery system. Trustees authorize loan to MedOhio Health to develop an HMO.

Book depository opens at archives on Kenny Road with capacity of 2 million volumes.

Lease not renewed on SETI "Big Ear" telescope as Ohio State to leave property at end of 1997.

Ohio Retirement Study Commission withdraws recommendation to raise retirement age to sixty-seven after public outcry.

## MARCH

Trustees appoint Colleen O'Brien State Relations director; Sally Kitch chairs new Department of Women's Studies.

Katie Smith finishes basketball career as highest scorer in Ohio State history, men and women.

Annual media reception at university residence is first hosted by Gordon and Constance Gee.

Human Resources announces "flextime" and "flexplace."

"Echoes across the Oval," WOSU-TV's 125th anniversary documentary, premieres.

Ad hoc committee to evaluate top administrators.

Distinguished Service Award to Anne Hayes.

Gee state tour of southern Ohio.

New 330 area code affects OARDC and ATI.

Broadbanding melds fifty pay ranges into five.

*U.S. News* reports on some doctoral programs: education, 6th; chemistry, 20th; physics, 23rd; engineering, 20th; business, 28th; law, 48th.

Jim Garland named president of Miami University.

## APRIL

Schottenstein Center groundbreaking.

Analysis shows Ohio State salaries below market in administration and professional; paraprofessional and technical.

Enarson Hall reopens as Ohio State Admissions Visitors' Center.

State tour of southeast Ohio.

Notices of appointment document eliminated as unnecessary paperwork.

First Young Scholars Academic Awards dinner funded by $100,000 gift from the late Lt. Col. Lovell Tipton.

Slavic and East European Languages and Literature to remain independent unit in Humanities. Council for the Advancement and Support of Education (CASE) cites Ohio State's *Quest* as the best external newspaper in higher education.

## MAY

Campbell Hall addition dedication includes Geraldine Schottenstein Wing of the Historic Costume and Textiles Collection.

Trustees refinance Ramada Inn debt.
Archivist Raimund Goerler announces he has discovered Admiral Byrd's North Pole diary, seventy years after the flight.
Dedication of new South Campus outdoor recreation facilities.
Law hooding ceremony honors speaker, Attorney General Janet Reno.
Fiftieth anniversary reunion is last class (1946) not swelled by GI Bill.
Dedication of Richard and Annette Bloch Cancer Survivors Plaza.
Outpatient Psychiatry opens center for addiction treatment and research.
Regents tell Ohio State to combine undergrad biochemistry and medical biochemistry.
Ohio attitude survey shows four of ten Ohio voters can identify Gordon Gee as the president of Ohio State.
National Public Radio's Nina Totenberg keynotes Humanities baccalaureate.
First Undergraduate Research Forum is a new program of Ed Hayes.
Edison Welding Institute receives $36 million federal contract to operate the U.S. Navy Joining Center.

## JUNE

Trustees video-conference "town meeting" with regional campus boards to demonstrate interactive distance learning; authorize College of Education reorganization into three schools: physical activity and educational services, teaching and learning and educational policy and leadership. Approve new major in soil science. Bob Gold is acting dean of Mathematical and Physical Sciences. Yale historian Geoffrey Parker appointed Andreas Dorpalen Designated Professor in European History
Madison Scott passes away.
Hospitals new pay plan shifts to raises on anniversary dates.
Don Dell takes two-year appointment to head merged journalism and communications.
116-year-old statue of Ohio's first psychiatrist, Samuel Smith, placed outside new neuropsychiatric building.
Gees lead Ohio State contingent to South African and Ugandan universities to build ties with their programs as men's basketball tours South Africa.

# 1996–1997

## JULY 1996

State tour of western Ohio includes Urbana, Dayton, Troy, and Piqua.

Trustees authorize a diversity committee reporting to the Senate combining Senate committee on women and minorities with the president's committee on diversity. Barbara Hanrahan from North Carolina to direct University Press; Richard Lebow from Pitt, Mershon Center; Alan Goodridge of Iowa is Biological Sciences dean; William Napier, Regents' vice chancellor for external affairs, named secretary of the Board and executive assistant to Gee. Karen Bell promoted to chair of Dance; Kermit Hall is new executive dean of Arts and Sciences.

Buckeyes in Summer Olympics are Butch Reynolds and Rich Jones, 400 meters; Joe Greene, long jump; Mark Croghan and Robert Gary, steeplechase; Patrick Jeffrey, David Pichler, Mary Ellen Clark, diving—coach is Vince Panzano; Marco Strahija, backstroke; Blaine Wilson, gymnastics—coach is Peter Kormann; Roger Smith, tennis; Nancy Darsch, women's basketball assistant coach.

Gee testifies to Congress that public university tuition is less than half of what the public thinks it is and $5,000 below public estimates for private universities.

U.S. Supreme Court refuses to examine Circuit Court decision (University of Texas vs. Hopwood) that race cannot be considered in admissions decisions.

## AUGUST

"Merry Makers" celebrate seventeen years of partnership with Ohio State with an award to Gee. Gee keynotes Akron Zip football dinner feting new coach Ohio State's Lee Owens.

Simon Dinitz receives distinguished service award.

## SEPTEMBER

Eagle Scout Gee presents distinguished Eagle Scout award to Mayor Lashutka; Gee received similar award at Colorado.

Regents approve Dayton collaborative doctoral program in Engineering at Wright State. Cincinnati and Ohio State involved, including electronic delivery system of classes from Ohio State.

Trustees approve Susan Huntington as Graduate School dean; John Schoessler, Optometry dean; Terry Foegler, Dublin assistant city manager, new president of Campus Partners; Stephen J. Schwartz, Carl Haas chair; Stephen Sebo, Neal Smith chair; Philip Tetlock, Harold Burtt chair. Research Park preliminary report recommends Business Technology Center and "Science Village."

*U.S. News:* Ohio State is number 37 in academic reputation; 63 overall; 14 among public universities.

Dedication of the Newman-Wolfrom Chemistry Laboratory, five-story addition to Evans.

Dedication of Galbreath Equine Trauma Intensive Care and Research Center.

$400,000 federal grant to Campus Collaborative to improve Weinland Park area.

Riotous parties along 12th Avenue and High Street follow Ohio State victory over Notre Dame. Gee suspends three students following their arrests.

**OCTOBER**

Campaign marks first year with celebration dinner at Columbus Museum.

Henry Kissinger speaks at Independence Hall.

Dedication of Max Kade German House.

Homecoming grand marshals are Erin Moriarty and Butch Reynolds.

Dean Lena Bailey passes away.

Gee participates in AAU discussion on tenure precipitated by University of Minnesota regents proposal to allow release of tenured faculty.

Supercomputer center one of thirteen to connect to National Science Foundation high-speed network expected to lead to Internet 2.

**NOVEMBER**

Trustees authorize construction bids for Knowlton School, Life Science Research Building, Food Science and Technology Building; $9.5 million to continue ARMS.

Ruth Mount receives Dan Heinlen Award for thirty years of service and leadership.

Gee delivers eulogy at funeral of Dorothy Davis.

First University Distinguished Lecture: will be three per year, each receives $5,000.

Ohio State loses to Michigan, 13–9, but shares Big Ten title. President Clinton speaks at St. John Arena. Clinton to Gee: "I can't believe you lost to Michigan."

## DECEMBER

Ohio Senate President Stan Aronoff retires. Gee: "the first honorary degree I presented as president."

Linda Tom retires. New student financial aid director is Natala "Tally" Hart from IU-Purdue; new undergraduate admissions director, Scott Healy of Oklahoma.

Ohio Global Trade Conference 1996 cosponsored by the office of Senator Mike DeWine and Fisher College.

David Williams chairs NCAA panel on sports counseling for transition after college.

"Gordo the great: OSU president E. Gordon Gee is loved by all," cover story of *Plain Dealer* Sunday magazine.

## JANUARY 1997

Rose Bowl: Ohio State 20, Arizona State 17.

Mary Schiavo, former U.S. Department of Transportation Inspector General, named Anderson professor in public policy. Pascal Goldschmidt of Johns Hopkins to direct Heart and Lung Institute; ground to be broken in 1998 after Upham Hall is razed.

Articulation agreement signed with Columbus State at ceremony with President Valeriana "Val" Moeller and Regents Chancellor Elaine Hairston.

John B. Gerlach dies at seventy at his Upper Arlington home.

## FEBRUARY

Gee chairs meeting of the University Research Association, Inc. of the National Academy of Sciences; initiates Ohio State Research Commission chaired by Bernadine Healy.

Trustees authorize Campus Partners to buy High Street site of burned-down Papa Joe's, Waterbeds, and Off Campus Bar for $425,000; approve student referendum authorizing $9-per-quarter fee to ride COTA.

Three major cancer researchers named: Albert de la Chapelle of University of Helsinki, Immke Chair; Clara Bloomfield of Roswell Park, Pace Chair and director of Comprehensive Cancer Center; Michael Caligiuri of Roswell Park to Nationwide Chair.

Ohio State officer Michael Blankenship murdered in Wexner Center lobby. Suspect Mark Edgerton commits suicide. Trustees vote in March to name new police headquarters Michael Blankenship Hall.

Gee narrates "A Lincoln Portrait" at Cleveland's Severance Hall with OSU concert band and Men's Glee Club.

## MARCH

*U.S. News* graduate school rankings have colleges of Education, 7; Pharmacy, 7; Veterinary Medicine, 8; Medicine, 15 in primary care; Fisher MBA, 22 (up from 28); Engineering, 22; Law, 47.

Randy Ayers and Nancy Darsch both have contracts bought out.

Gee northern Ohio state tour.

## APRIL

Trustees approve Xen Riggs as director of the Schottenstein Center. Three acres are purchased adjacent to Marion campus. Beth Burns is new women's basketball coach at salary parity with Jim O'Brien, new men's basketball coach: $150,000 and five-year contracts.

Kellogg Commission releases Gee-led *Returning to Our Roots: The Student Experience*. Gee keynotes American Assembly of Collegiate Schools of Business. Joe Alutto is president.

Football team honored at State House.

## MAY

Ground broken for 40-acre West Campus intramural sports fields.

Bill Davis Stadium dedicated.

Trustees approve University Neighborhoods Revitalization Plan of Campus Partners; authorize purchase of Columbus bakery for $1.39 million. Honor Bernie Gerlach by naming John B. Gerlach Graduate Programs Building in Fisher College. Jose Cruz named to Howard Winbigler Designated Chair. Student trustee Mark Berkman first dental student named Howard Hughes scholar and will work at NIH.

Blaine Wilson named U.S.'s top male gymnast.

Forensics Team wins two individual national championships. College Bowl Team eighth at nationals.

Ellen Goodman lectures as part of celebration of twenty-fifth anniversary of Women's Studies at Ohio State.

Threat to state subsidies for international students floated in legislature as Gee and other presidents successfully defend the need. Gee also testifies to Ohio House Education Committee in favor of House bill to give voting privileges to student trustees. Bill fails.

Media report some Democrats have approached Gee to run for governor.

Tax levy for downtown arena fails.

Gee inducted into Motor Board; also returns to West Virginia University as commencement speaker, receives honorary degree.

Alumni House groundbreaking on new site following discovery of toxic waste under original site.

Community Charitable drive increased beyond United Way.

Provost's office announces it will establish benchmarks to meet strategic objectives, comparing with publics in the top 20.

Reception for alumni in the 122nd General Assembly: Senators Ben Espy, Merle Kearns, Dick Schafrath, Doug White, Representatives Bill Batchelder, Otto Beatty, Ed Core, Joe Haines, Ron Hood, Joan Lawrence, Priscilla Mead, Ron Mottl, Amy Salerno, Frank Sawyer, E. J. Thomas, William Thompson, Pat Tiberi, Bill Taylor.

"Scholars Grove" inaugurated with tree planting ceremony at Honors House honoring Marshall Scholars Dean Allemang, Gerard Willinger, Dianne Ulrich, and Garth Robins and prior Rhodes Scholars.

## JUNE

Arts Dean Donald Harris retires.

Humanities baccalaureate keynoted by Julian Bond. *Goosebumps* author alumnus R. L. Stine honored.

Trustees OK Firestone land sale for $12 million.

Trustee chair Alex Shumate initiates monthly chairperson's report. James Davis named associate provost and director of University Technology Services; Denis Medeiros is interim Human Ecology dean.

Erie Sauder, 92, receives Doctor of Humane Letters from Gee at Archbold Heritage Inn.

Groundbreaking for the John K. Pfahl Executive Education Building in Fisher College.

Commencement halted by torrential downpour.

On the 27th, Gordon Gee accepts the presidency of Brown University: to leave Ohio State at end of year.

## 1997–1998

### JULY 1997

Trustees name Berkeley's David Ashley as Engineering dean; Bob Gold, acting dean since 1996, named Mathematical and Physical Sciences dean. Judith Koroscik, associate dean since 1990, named Arts dean.

Board chair Alex Shumate announces both transition team and presidential search committee.
Marvin Kuhn, 45, killed when crane topples from Schottenstein Center site.
Vernal G. Riffe, Jr. passes away.
Endowment reaches $813.5 million as the Dow Jones industrial average reaches 8,000.

## AUGUST

Trustees appoint Martha McMackin Garland vice provost for undergraduate studies; Barbara Rich, interim vice provost for Minority Affairs. School of Public Policy moves from Business to Social and Behavioral Sciences. Black Studies renamed Department of African American and African Studies. Institute for Ergonomics approved. Martin Feinberg of University of Rochester named to Richard Morrow chair.
Final Gee state tour includes Cleveland, Lorraine, Sandusky.
Athletic department extends Ohio Stadium lease for Columbus Crew a second year.
New Distinguished University Service Award to Harry Allen, Randy Smith, and Paul Young.
Ruth Weimer Mount is killed in an automobile accident.
U.S. Supreme Court strikes down part of the Communications Act that would have made it illegal to send "indecent" or "patently offensive" material over the Internet if it could be accessed by minors. Higher education issue was concern about scholarly information.
Albert de la Chapelle elected to the National Academy of Sciences.

## SEPTEMBER

Trustees approve first increase in nine years for supplies and equipment.
Lawrence Libby appointed to Swank chair. Portion of Fyffe Road near Schottenstein Center renamed Fred Taylor Drive. Rob Livesy is new Director of the Knowlton School of Architecture.
The Alumni Advocates hold twentieth annual meeting.
Gordon Gee keynotes 234th opening convocation at Brown University. Gives final fall address to the University Senate.
Rolling Stones perform concert in Stadium.
Roy Lichtenstein succumbs to pneumonia at seventy-three.
Nineteen projects receive total $1.5 million in Academic Enrichment grants from Academic Affairs, bringing total to more than $6 million.

## OCTOBER

U.S. Senator John Glenn announces he will donate his papers and artifacts to Ohio State; is genesis of the John Glenn Institute.
Trustees authorize hiring of architect to design Ohio Union renovation.
Gee delivers first Lena Bailey Memorial Lecture.
Freshman class data has average ACT score of 24, up from 23.5 last year and 22.8 in 1995.
Ohio Supreme Court ruling may require $1.2 billion for equitable primary-secondary school funding.
New Alumni Association Board Chair is Thomas Moyer, Ohio Supreme Court Chief Justice.
Rosa Smith is new Columbus Public Schools superintendent.
Alumni astronauts Nancy Currie and Ron Sega are grand marshals at Homecoming as Gee is honorary grand marshal.
Unique licensing agreement signed with Buckeye Hall of Fame Café.
Ohio State's Eisenhower National Clearinghouse to receive $23 million over next five years from U.S. Department of Education.

## NOVEMBER

Dancer Savion Glover in residence at Wexner Center.
Trustees approve taking bids for $150 million renovation of Ohio Stadium, to include moving track to a 10,000-seat stadium dedicated to Jesse Owens. Stadium dorm to relocate at Mack Hall. Approve Clinical Trial Management and Coordinating Center to conduct clinical trials on new drugs. Approve South District Plan.
Alumnus Jerry M. Hultin named U.S. Under-Secretary of the Navy.
Gee keynotes general session of 100th annual NASULGC meeting.
Dick Sisson named one of five finalists for presidency of the University of Texas.

## DECEMBER

Trustees approve new Doctor of Pharmacy program and B.S. in pharmaceutical sciences; merge registrar, admissions, financial aid into Office of Enrollment Services.
Provost Sisson accepts invitation by the Board to serve as interim president; withdraws candidacy at Texas.
At University Senate, Alex Shumate introduces trustee goal for Ohio to become recognized academically as one of the ten best public universities.

"Celebrating Seven Years of Achievement" dinner honors Gordon and Constance Gee.

Trustees establish Gee Presidential Scholarship Fund. Large seal at head of Bricker Hall installed in his honor.

Gee is Commencement speaker, receives honorary Doctor of Education; Ambassador Wolf receives honorary Doctor of Diplomacy; John W. Berry, honorary Doctor of Business Administration. David Scott receives posthumous Distinguished Service Award for his father, Madison Scott.

Roderick B. W. Chu named sixth chancellor of the Ohio Board of Regents.

On first official day as Brown president, January 1, 1998, Gee attends Sugar Bowl as last event at Ohio State. Buckeyes 14, Florida State 31.

# About the Author

Malcolm Baroway researched and wrote *The Gee Years* following sixteen years in Ohio State's central administration. From 1983 to 1999, he directed public relations for the university, serving under three presidents as executive director of university communications: Edward H. Jennings, E. Gordon Gee, and William E. Kirwan.

His career also includes the top public relations post at Jacksonville University, the University of Michigan, Ohio Wesleyan University, and Boston University, where he also was editor-in-chief of its award-winning magazine, *Bostonia*. He holds a B.A. in English and M.A. with honors in the Writing Seminars, both from The Johns Hopkins University.

Baroway's work has received the highest honors in his profession, including the "Silver Anvil" of the Public Relations Society of America and many "Grand Gold" awards from the Council for Advancement and Support of Education (CASE). During the 1980s, he became one of higher education's experts in grassroots lobbying, coordinating statewide programs that helped defeat tax rollbacks in Michigan and Ohio. His Michigan program won the Silver Anvil.

Baroway is married, with a blended family of eight adult children and seven grandchildren. His wife, Dee, is a psychotherapist in private practice with degrees from Ohio State and Michigan. They live in Columbus.

# Index

Abigail House, 210
Academic Core North District, 326
Academic Enrichment program, 239
Academic Resource Management System (ARMS), 298
Academy of Teaching, 134
accreditation, 239, 337
ACTION. *See* Afrikans Committed to Improve Our Nation (ACTION)
Action Plan for the Recruitment and Retention of Black Students, 114, 134
ACT scores, 42, 44, 46
Adams, David, 3
admissions: open, 91; and race, 184–85, 232; selective, 39, 41–42, 74–75, 76, 141
Admissions and Financial Aid offices, 103
admissions office, 44
affirmative action, 106–8, 114, 178, 229, 232–33, 341. *See also* diversity
"Affirm Thy Friendship" campaign, 126, 129, 141, 144–45, 301, 312–13
African Americans: on faculty, 185, 341; in Gee's administration, 67; student population, 134, 176, 185, 281. *See also* Afrikans Committed to Improve Our Nation (ACTION); JustUs
Afrikans Committed to Improve Our Nation (ACTION), 93, 111, 114–15, 181–84. *See also* JustUs
agriculture, 25, 236, 261, 290
AIDS, 47–49
AIDS Education and Research Committee, 39
Ailabouni, Amira, *232*
Akron, Ohio, 124

*Akron Beacon Journal,* 96
Alber, Dorothy, 311
Alber, George H., 311–12
Albino, Judith, 94
Alexander, Lamar, 110
Allen, David, 263
Alluto, Joseph, 305
Altschuld, James, 134
alumni club, African, 290
Alumni Teaching Award, 134
Alutto, Joseph, 30, 98–99
American Council on Education, 254
*The American Freshman: National Norms for Fall 1995,* 278
American Health Security Act (1993), 242
American Jewish Joint Distribution Committee, 309
American Red Cross, 347
Americans with Disabilities Act (1990), 106, 112
America Reads Steering Committee, 174
*America's Best Colleges Guide,* 46, 194
AmeriFlora, 61
Amundsen, Roald, 293
AMVETS, 115
Anderle, Fred, 167
Anderson, Carole, 207
Anderson, Derek, 159
Anderson, Donald P., 20
Anderson, Kenneth, 67
Anderson, Mark, 159
Anderson, Martin, 131
Anglen, Reginald "Reggie," 289–90
Annette and Richard Bloch Cancer Survivors Plaza, 63, 308

## Index

antibiotics, 248–49
Appalachian white, 176
Arcetri Astrophysical Observatory, 51
Archbold, Ohio, 308
arena issue, 212, 215–23
Arizona State University, 148
Arkin, Robert, 42–44, 47, 135
Arnold, Robert, 92, 342
Aronoff, Stanley, 24; at annual breakfast, 164; and arena, 217; on higher education cuts, 87; relationship with Gee, 322; and tax increase, 89, 133; on term limits, 163; and Tzagournis, 244
Arthur G. James Cancer Hospital and Research Institute: advertising, 245–46; budget problems, 30, 96; Comprehensive Breast Health Service, 248; directorship, 244, 250; Elizabeth's work with, 63; fund-raising campaign, 303; gifts to, 144, 223; online, 38; opening, 18, 49; ranking, 46
Ashe, Janet Pichette: background, 27; on Business Technology Center, 261; on Continuous Quality Improvement, 138–39; on Firestone land, 124, 127; hiring of, 118, 212–13; on Ohio Stadium, 227; on University Area Improvement Task Force, 31
Asher, Herb, 21; and arena, 217, 218; on budget cuts, 83; on expenditures, 165; on Gee's communication skills, 173; and media, 170; on public records, 272; on public service institute, 310; retirement, 277; and term limits, 163; on transition team, 343
Ashland University, 275
Asian Americans, 281
"Ask-a-Nurse" program, 246
Associated Press, 156
Association of American Universities (AAU), 253
astronomy department, 50–53, 130
athletics, 25–26, 146–61, 213–28. *See also* arena issue; basketball; football; stadia
*Atlanta Journal-Constitution,* 173

Atlanta Tip-off Club, 156
Auburn, Norman, 19
Auburn Report, 19–22, 25, 27, 40
Austin, Jerry, 323
Austin, Sarah, 27, 118
Axene, Dareth, 306
Ayers, Carol, 157
Ayers, Randy, 156–61

Bailey, Lena Charles, 61, 317
Bailey, Phyllis, 148
Baker, James, 58
Bakke case (U.S. Supreme Court), 106–7, 184–85, 341
Ballam, Deborah, 115
Bank One, 17
Baptist, Bob, 225
Barnebey Center, 203
Barnett, Isabel Bigley, 189–90
Barnett, Larry, 145, 189–90
Barone, John, 39, 317
Baroway, Malcolm: on announcement of Gee's departure, 348; and Constance, 191; on Gee's popularity, 197, 198; and hiring of Geiger, 213; marketing plan, 42; and private investigation, 21; on telescope project, 53; on University of California, 231
*Barron's Profiles of Colleges and Universities,* 42
bars, 33, 268–69
Baryshnikov, Mikhail, *330*
Basinger, Mary, 21, 67, 189, 315
basketball, 156–61, 223–25, 290. *See also* arena issue
Bath Township, 124, 127–29
Battelle, 261–62
Battelle, Gordon, 261
Bay, Rick, 25, 148, 225
BCS (Bowl Championship Series), 287
Beatty, Otto, 89
Beck, Paul, 77, 118
Beering, Steve, 337
Bennett, Bill, 243
Bennett, Floyd, 293

# INDEX

Bennis, Warren, 280
Berry, John, 145, 317
Betz, Nancy, 91
Bexley, Ohio, 16–17, 17
Beytagh, Francis X. "Frank," 20, 100, 108
Bianco, Catherine, 205
"Big Boy," 304
Big Ear, 54–55
Big Ten Conference, 19, 174, 220, 240
Bill Davis Baseball Stadium, 213, 216, 225–26
Bishop, Jim, 176–77
Bishop, "Munch," 173
Biskind Realty Company, 129, 130
Black United Fund of Central Ohio, 205
Blackwell, Roger, 142, 258
Blankenship, Michael, 316–17
Blanshan, Sue, 21, 26, 59, 109
Bloch, Annette, 63
Bloch, Richard, 63, 308
Block, John, 172
Bloomfield, Clara, 250
Blue Jackets (hockey team), 218, 222
Board of Trustees, 117, *232*, 276–82, 328–29
Boettcher, Richard, 101
Boggs, Bob, 89, 164
Bok, Chip, 298
Boren, David, 194
Bosley, Jami, 159
Boston, David, 149
Bowen, William, 5, 118–19
Bowers, Linda, 225, 306
bowl games, 164–65, 287
Bowser, Shirley Dunlap, 5-6, 20, 38, 135, 236, 328
Boyne, David, 55, 92
Brace, Ben, 29
Bradford Commons, 182, 183
branch campuses. *See* regional campuses
Brand, Myles, 37, 91, 287, 299
Branstool, Eugene "Gene," 208
Brazeau, Paul, 158
Brenlin Group, 126
Brennan, Ann, 129

Brennan, David, 32, 125, 126–30, *232*, 344
Bridgman, Ross, 135
Brigham Young University, 13
Broad, Molly Corbett, 338
Brodeur, Arthur, 124, 183
Brook, Peter, 61
Brown, Greg, 64
Brown, Larry, 160
Brown, Lenore, 173
Brown, Max, 173
Brown, Sherrod, 293
Brownell, Herbert, 12
Brown University, 331–39; announcement of presidency at, 193; decision to accept presidency of, 220, 222, 233–34; football program, 149–50, 350; reorganization at, 349–50; Wexner on, 326
*Brown v. Board of Education,* 106
Bruce, Earle, 25, 146, 147
Buckeye Hall of Fame Cafe, 270
Buckeye State Poll, 294
Buckeye Village, 108, 180
budget cuts, 82–89, 103–4; and appointments and resignations, 92–94; end of, 239; and hiring freeze, 156; and Managing for the Future Task Force, 135; and reallocations, 121–23, 151; and salaries and programs, 94–97
Bumgarner, Constance. *See* Gee, Constance Bumgarner
Bunge, Walter, 116
Burcover, Al, 173
Burdick, Jennifer, 314
Burger, Warren, 12
Burkhart, Emerson, 310
Burnett, Leo, 167
Burns, Beth, 160, 225
Bursten, Bruce, 346
Buser, Steve, 77
Bush, George, 57–58, 110, 177
Business Technology Center (BTC), 261
*Business Week,* 254, 255
bus service, campus, 103, 203

399

# Index

Byrd, Richard E., 293–94
Byrd Polar Research Institute, 293

Cachio, Debbie, 160
calendar committee, 39–40
California Board of Regents, 198
Caligiuri, Michael, 250
*Cambridge Daily Jeffersonian*, 164
Campbell Hall, 223
Campus Collaborative, 36, 266
Campus Partners for Community Urban Development, Inc., 20, 34–36, 266–70, 326, 350
*Canton Repository*, 97
Capital Improvements Bill, 212
Capriotti, Eugene, 53
*Carmen Ohio*, 316–17
Carnegie Foundation, 52, 76
Carney, John, 334, 346
Carr, Greg, 109, 183, 184
Carter, Jimmy, 309
Caruso, Doug, 173
Casto, Deborah, 102, *208*
Castor, Annie, 310
Cecutti, Dave, 159
Celeste, Richard, 15, 83; accomplishments of, 284; on Columbus Project, 52; staff of, 339; on state budget, 98; and Thomas Edison Program, 261; and Tzagournis, 244
Celeste, Ted, *232*; on agriculture advocacy, 236; appointment as trustee, 39; on domestic partners, 179–81; on Gee as politician, 323; in New Orleans, 348; and research, 260–63; on Sauder, 308–9; on transition team, 343
Celeste Laboratory of Chemistry, 284
Center for Socio-Legal Studies, 100
Central Michigan University, 159
Chafetz, Sidney, 117
"Chance to Grow Means Letting Go," 73
Chapelle, Albert de la, 250
Chapman, Jim, 125
charter schools, 126
Chasser, Anne, 175, 298–99
Cheblina, John, 129

Cheek, Steven, 135
chemistry program, 240
Cheryl's Cookies, 302
*Chicago Tribune*, 173
chief information officer (CIO), 136
Chodorow, Stanley, 341
Christie, John, 221
*The Chronicle of Higher Education*, 274
Chu, Roderick, 344–45
Cincinnati, 274
*Cincinnati Enquirer*, 96
*Cincinnati Post*, 96
Citrus Bowl, 164, 297
City University of New York, 107
Civil Rights Act, 106
Clark, Bunny, 5
classified employees, 60
Cleveland, Ohio, 125
Cleveland Clinic, 31, 38, 49–50, 134
Cleveland Clinic Foundation Health Sciences Center–The Ohio State University, 49
*Cleveland Plain Dealer*, 6, 86, 152, 164, 231–32
Cline, Larry, 345
Clinton, Bill, 88, 210, 242, 277, 284–85
Clinton, Hillary Rodham, 242
Clinton Township, 261
closed courses, 97, 103
Clovis, Albert, 100
Coca-Cola, 283–84
Coleman, Trevor, 173
College Fund/United Negro College Fund, 205
College of Agriculture, 37–38, 195, 261
College of Business, 98–99
College of Education, 237, 238
College of Food, Agricultural, and Environmental Sciences, 195, 201, 326
College of Humanities, 97–98
College of Law, 100, 126, 302
College of Mathematical and Physical Sciences, 97
College of Medicine, 50, 246
College of Social and Behavioral Sciences, 293

# Index

College of Social Work, 238
College of the Arts, 237, 326
College of Veterinary Medicine, 121, 129, 144
Colley, Michael, 55, 135, *232*
Columbia/HCA, 249–50
Columbia Teachers' College, Penn State, 187
Columbia University, 11–12, 31
Columbus and Franklin County Metropolitan Park District, 203
Columbus Area Chamber of Commerce, 36
*Columbus Call and Post*, 115, 172–73
*Columbus Dispatch*, 6–7, 97, 230–32, 348
Columbus Foundation, 311–12
Columbus Museum of Science and Industry, 219
Columbus Project telescope, 38, 50–54, 130, 134
Columbus Public Schools, 177
Columbus School for Girls (CSG), 16, 17, 69, 157
commencements, 299–30
commencement speakers, 199, 295, 300
Commission on Women, 210
Committee on Institutional Cooperation, 19
Committee on the Undergraduate Environment (CUE), 281
Common Cause Ohio, 162
communications, 166–75
Communications Workers of America, 29
Community Charitable Drive, 205
Community Crime Patrol, 29
Community Shares, 204–5
computer laboratories, 298
computer system, 103
Conley, Dean, 89
Conners, Bob, 173
Continuous Quality Improvement (CQI), 136, 138–39
Cook, Beano, 228
Cook, Herb, 173
cookbooks, 302
Cooper, John, *134, 149;* contract extension, 146–48, 150; on Gee, 151; staff of, 216
Coor, Lattie, 287
Coors, Peter, 171
Corbally, John E., 19
Corbato, Charles, 92
Corby, John, 173
Cordray, Richard, 89
Cornell, Fred, 316
Cornell University, 86, 245
*The Costs and Resources of Legal Education* (Council on Legal Education), 12
COTA (transportation system), 203
Council for Advancement and Support of Higher Education (CASE), 288
Council of Churches, 163
Council on Academic Affairs, 121
Council on Academic Excellence for Women, The (CAEW), 112
Council on Competitiveness, 254
Countryman, James, 61
CQI (Continuous Quality Improvement), 136, 138–39
Cramblett, Henry, 243
Craver, Wendy, 173
Crawford, Edwin S., 349
crime, 32–35
Critical Difference for Women Program, 63, 283
Crossley, Linda, 64
Crowell, Becki, 143
Cruz, Jose, 60, 92, 119, 139, 259
Csuri, Chuck, 61
Cuellar, Clara, 346
cultivation, 125
Cunningham, Bill, 172
Curtin, Michael F., 173, 230, 318–19, 323–24, 348
customer satisfaction, 258–59, 280

D'Angelo, Gene, 173
Daniel, T. K., 289
Darby Dan Farms, 6
Darsch, Nancy, 158, 160
database, on-demand, 205–6

INDEX

Davidson, Jo Ann, 89, 164, 322
Davidson, Justin, 20
David W. Longaberger Chair at the University Medical Center, 307
Davis, Dorothy Wells, 225, *226*
Davis, Jene, 159
Davis, Michael, *236*
Davis, Molly, 62
Davis, William H., 225
*Dayton Daily News*, 96
Dean, John, 12
Delaney, Paul, 173
Delaware, Ohio, 54–55
Dell, Don, 92
demonstrations, 114–15, 266
Denman, Rick and Marte, 264
Department of Athletics, 25, 214. *See also* athletics
Department of Communications, 237
*DeRolph v. the State of Ohio*, 333–34, 344
DeWine, Mike, 322
Diamond, Raylynn, 34
DiDonato, Greg, 164
Diemer, Tom, 167
Dilenschneider, Bob, 167
Dine, Jim, 61
Dingell, John, 253
distance learning, 126, 129–30
diversity, 67, 106–15, 119, 176–86. *See also* affirmative action
Dixon, Robert, 54
doctoral programs, 132
Dodson, John Jr., 173
domestic partners, 179–81. *See also* homosexuals
Dominic, Virgil, 167
Don Scott Field, 39
Doria, Vince, 173
Dottavio, Dominic, 92
Doulin, Tim, 2–3, 53, 80–81
Dove, Mona, 5
*Dover-New Philadelphia Times-Reporter*, 96
Downie, Len Jr., 173
Dresden, Germany, 286
Dresden, Ohio, 307

DRG (Diagnostic Related Groups), 242
drinking age, 269
Drinko, John, 100, 125–26
Drug-Free Schools and Communities Act, 29, 30
drug problems, 32, 34
Duke University, 150, 245
Duncan, Robert, *232*; on Cooper's contract, 146; on Gee's administrative team, 27, 61, 202; on Gee's schedule, 173; and Huber, 97; on public records, 273; report on diversity, 185–86; on David Williams, 214

Eaker, Gerald, 159
Early Retirement Incentive (ERI), 122–23
East Carolina University, 187
*Ebony* magazine, 100
economy, 256, 277–79, 333
Edgerton, Mark, 316
Edison Joining Technology Center, 261, 284
Edison Welding Institute, 219, 261
Education Amendments Act (1972), 106, 154
*Education Law and the Public Schools* (Gee), 289
Edwards, Daniel Everett, 312
Ehman, Jerry, 54
Eisenman, Peter, 205
Elam, John W. "Chip": appointment as special assistant to president, 26; and Constance, 191; on Elizabeth, 14; on Gee's humor, 228; on Gee's popularity, 197; on Kessler, 16; on search committee, 4–7; on University of California, 229, 230; on veterans' affairs, 59; on Wexner, 327
electrical engineering program, 240
Ellis, Mark, 173
e-mail system, 103, 298
Embrey, George, 167
Eminent Scholar Program, 39, 284
Enarson, Harold, 82, 243
Enarson Hall, 44
*Encyclopedia of the Midwest*, 349

402

## Index

endowed chairs, 98–99, 141
enrollment, 40–41, 136
entrance requirements, 74–75
Espy, Ben, 89
evaluations, five-year, 194–98, 237
Everett D. Reese Medal, 141, 306
extraterrestrial intelligence, search for, 54

faculty: diversity of, 185, 341; evaluation of, 95; fund raising for, 141–42; records, 272–75; tenure, 80, 133; and Total Quality Management, 139; workload, 84–85, 132–33, 136, 255
Faculty Hiring Assistance Program (FHAP), 185
Fairfield County, 203
Family Educational Rights and Privacy Act (FERPA), 272, 275
family leave benefits, 179–80
Family Rights and Privacy Act, 275
Faulkner, Larry, 341
Fawcett, Novice, 19, 141
Fechheimer, Nathan, 5
Federal Arts Project, 310
Federal Bureau of Investigation (FBI), 108
Ferguson, Dave, 143
Ferguson, Ronald "Ron," 249
Fiorelli, Mike, 173
fire, 268–69
Firestone, Jane, 124, 125
Firestone, Raymond, 124–29
Fisher, Lee, 202, 322
Fisher, Mark, 173
Fisher, Max M., 99, 144, 304–6
flag burning, 115
Flat Stanley, 285–86
Flint, Damon, 158
Foegler, Terry, 36
football, 146–56, 216, 228, 285, 287, 350
Ford Motor Company, 138
Form, Bill, 91
*Fostering Interdisciplinary Research and Graduate Education*, 257
Fowler, William, 317
Fox, Michael, 180

Fraley, Reed, 243, 244, 247, 250
Francis, Jerry, 159
Frank, Betty, 303–4
Frank Hale Jr. Black Cultural Center, 115, 182, 307
Frank Hale Jr. Hall, 183
Franklin, Peter, 301–2
Frantz, David, 98, 346
Fraser, Hamish, 38–39
Fraser, Jane, 346
Fred Taylor Drive, 292
Freeman, Mabel, 47
Freshman Foundation, 184
Friday, William E., 19, 25
Friedman, Jim, 332
*From the Edge of the World* (Blackwell), 258
fruit farm, 235
Fubara, Aya, 183–84
fund raising, 125–30, 140–45, 272–73, 283–84, 301–13. *See also* "Affirm Thy Friendship" campaign
Funk, Bill, 346
Funk, John, 132, 322

Gable, John, 45
Galbreath, Daniel M., 6, 129, 144
Galbreath Company, 129
Galloway, Joey, 216
Galyk, John, 314
gangs, 33–34
Gardner, Ralph III, *134*
Garland, James: on budget deficit, 97; on higher education costs, 254–55; hiring, 60; on Managing for the Future Task Force, 135; presidency of, 299; on provost search, 119; and research, 259; responsibilities of, 92, 238; on telescope project, 53; on Total Quality Management, 139
Garland, Martha McMackin, 205, 342, 343
Gauthier, Howard, 77, 92
Gay, Lesbian, and Bisexual Student Services Office, 180
Gay and Lesbian Alliance (GALA), 108

# INDEX

Gee, Cherie, 8
Gee, Constance Bumgarner, 187–93, *192, 210, 343;* on departure for Brown, 234, 336; dotting of "I," 145, 228, *291;* on flight from New York, 173; relationship with Rebekah, 70; at Rose Bowl, 149; trip to Uganda, 71
Gee, E. Gordon: childhood, 8–10; image, 1–3; marriage to Constance, 70, 191; marriage to Elizabeth, 11–12; personality, 3–5; relationship with daughter, 72–73, 189; resignation, 55; sumo wrestling, *320;* and Velcro wall, *320*
Gee, Elizabeth, 62–68, *63;* admiration for, 3; career, 11–13, 62–63, 188; and Critical Difference for Women Program, 283; death, 55, 61, 64–65, 68, 181; honor of, 192; illness, 18, 200; influence on Gordon, 14, 16–17; marriage, 11–12; relationship with daughter, 71; on religion, 65–68; on small towns, 10
Gee, Elwood A. "Gus," 2, 3, 8, 9
Gee, Rebekah, 69–73, *210;* career, 350; on mother, 64–65; and move to Columbus, 14, 16–18; relationship with father, 72–73, 189; in Russia, 200; on University of California offer, 229
Gee, Vera, 8, 9
Geiger, Andy, *215;* on arena size, 222; on basketball programs, 158; contract with Nike, 283; on Cooper, 148–49; on Dorothy Wells Davis, 225; hiring of, 212–14; marketing efforts, 175; on O'Brien, 223; on Ohio Stadium, 227; and pregame brunches, 152; problems inherited by, 215–16; release of Ayers, 159–60; and Title IX, 154; at University of Maryland, 348
Geldin, Sherri, 92
gender neutrality, 210–11
General Education Curriculum (GEC), 41, 97, 114
Genshaft, Judy, 20, 299

geography program, 240
George, Eddie, 171, 173, *174,* 228, 285
George Bush School of Government, 238
George H. Alber Student Center, 311
Gerlach, John B. "Bernie," 141, 145, *226,* 306–7
Germaine, Joe, 149
Gerstner, Ruth, 127
Gibson, Burr, 143
gifts, 144, 223. *See also* fund raising
Gill, Deborah, 183
Gillmor, Paul, 244
Gin Press, 205–6
Glaser, Ron, 250
Glastris, Paul, 194–96
Glendening, Parris, 349
Glenn, John, 279, 309–10, *311*
Glenn, Terry, 285
Glidden, Robert, 299
Glower, Donald E. Sr., 20, 44, 141
Goerler, Raimund, 288, 293–94
Goldschmidt, Pascal, 250
Goncz, Arped, 199
Good, Clancy, and Associates, 269
Goodman, N. Victor, 81
Gorbachev, Mikhail, 200
Gore, Al, 286
governorship, 318–24
Gradney, Scott, 159
graduate programs, 132
Grafner, Dan, 305
Graham, Scotty, 183
Grant Medical Center, 247
Gray, Ted, 89
Green, Maxine, 71
Greene, Bob, 173, 295
Greene, Phyllis, 295
Greene, Robert Sr., 295
Gregorian, Vartan, 332
Grendell, Tim, 128
Griffin, Archie, 154, 216, 225
Griner, Dave, 317
"Groundswell," *206*
Gugulethu, South Africa, 290

404

INDEX

*A Guide to Effective Searches,* 114
*Guide to Non-Sexist Language* (Association of American Colleges), 210–11
Guilmartin, John Jr., 59
Gunyula, Lisa, 30
Gwinn, Jayson, 314

Haenicke, Diether, 91, 299
Hagenlocker, Edward, 138
Haines, Joe, 64
Hairston, Elaine, 23, 39, 49–50, 184, 344
Hale, Frank Jr., 110–11, 114–15
Hale, George Ellery, 52
halftime reports, 168
Hall, David, 173
Hall, John R., 350
Hall, Kermit: candidacy for president, 346–47; as dean of College of Humanities, 98; on Gee's departure for Brown, 337; on Kennedy assassination, 286; presidency of, 299; on restructuring, 293; on search for Gee's successor, 346; on South Africa, 290
Hancock, Charles, 177
"Hang On, Sloopy," 298
Hansford, Jean, 29, 296
Harding Hospital, 248
Harold E. Burtt Chair in Psychology, 289
Harris, Don, 189, 209, 237
Harvard University, 142, 239, 253
Hastings Center for Ethics and Life Sciences in Briarcliff, New York, 63
hate speech, 116–17
Havener, William, 204
Haverkamp, Robert, 47, 124, 127, 262
Hayes, Anne, 154
Hayes, Edward: on Columbus Project, 52, 53; death, 264–65; on death of Shawn Wight, 316; hiring of, 61; on hospital costs, 243; and Ohio State University Research Park Corporation, 262–63; research grants under, 253; as vice president for research, 257–60
Hayes, Woody, 145, 154

Hayot, Pat, 16
Health Care Consortium of Ohio, 247
health care costs, 241–43
Healy, Bernadine, *245;* candidacy for president, 346, 347; career of, 265; and Cleveland Clinic, 30, 49–50; hiring of, 20, 254; on indirect research costs, 253–55; recruitment of doctors, 248–50; and Research Commission, 259, 263; on search for Gee's successor, 346; in Senate primary, 322–23
heart pump, motorized, 50
Heidrick & Struggles, 5, 6, 118–19
Heinemann, Sally, 173
Heinlen, Dan, 6, 346
helicopter service, medical, 247
Helms, Jesse, 188
The Henry Painting Company, 178
Hermann, Chuck, 238
Hermann, Richard, 57–58
heroes, 279
Hershey, Bill, 167, 173
Heward, William, *134*
Heyman, Ira Michael, 202
Higher Education Act (1972), 213
Higher Education Center for Alcohol and Drug Prevention, 174
Higher Education Funding Commission, 333
"High on Pride" day, 35, *268*
High Street, 266–70, 326, 350
Hilbert, John, 164
Hill, Billy, 317
Hill, Dick, 141
Hillel Society, 117
Hilliker, James, 135
Hindman, Hugh, 317
Hiner, Glen, 260
Hippo Clan of Uganda, 290
*The Hispanic Action Plan,* 111, 134
Hispanics, 111–12, 134, 176, 185, 281
Historic Costume Collection, 223
*History of the Ohio State University, The Story of its First 75 Years* (Pollard), 74–75

405

H.M.S., 166
Hocking County, 203
Hoffmeister, John, 46
Hoffsis, Glen, 121
Hogan, Michael, 205–6
Holland, Earl, 59–60
Holland, Earle, 50
Hollander, Jack, 20
Hollingsworth, Rich, 287
Holocaust advertisement, 11–117
homosexuals, 67, 93, 107–8. *See also* domestic partners
honorary degrees, 208–10
Honors Program, 264
Hood, Marshall, 1
Hooley, Bruce, 159, 173
Hopwood court decision, 341
Horton, Frank, 81
Hoskins, W. Lee, 135
Hospodar, Bill, 60
housing: and domestic partners, 180–81; presidential, 17, 70; student, 32–33; in University District, 267–70
Howard, Mark, 159
*How Professors Play the Cat Guarding the Cream* (Huber), 131–32
Hoying, Bobby, 285
Hoyt L. Sherman Studio Art Center, 209
Huber, Joan: background, 90–91; on benchmarking, 327; and budget cuts, 94–96, 103–4; and Columbus Project, 53; deanship, 91–92, 101–2; and fund raising, 143; interview by Auburn team, 20; on National Research Council ranking, 237; on ombuds office, 286–87; on public broadcasting, 288; recommendation of Gregory Williams, 100; as senior vice president and provost, 27, 61, 90–105
Huber, Richard, 131–32
Huff, Ron, 33, 296
Hull, Jimmy, 317
Human Relations and Minority Affairs, 109
Human Relations, 298
Human Resources, 136, 139

Hummer, Stephanie, 32–35
humor, 171–72
Humphries, Barry, 35–36
Hunt, Lamar, 222, 227–28
Huntington, Susan, 238, 239
Huntington Club, 220, 221
Hutchinson, Fred: accident, 30; on affiliation with Cleveland Clinic, 49–50; appointment to provost, 37–38; appointment to senior vice president and provost, 26; interview by Auburn team, 20–21; in Maine, 55, 299; relationship with Gee, 55–56; and student recruitment, 40–44; on telescopes, 52–54
Hymowitz, Carol, 173

Ihrig, Weldon, 20, 38
"I Know I Can," 177
Immke, Len, 303, 317
*Imperatives for Change*, 247–48
*Imposters in the Temple* (Anderson), 131
incentive-based budgeting, 239
Indiana University, 155, 239, 253
*Information Literacy: Revolution in the Library* (Gee), 289
insurance, 181
International Garden of Knowledge, 61
Inter-University Council, 256, 272
*An Investment in Ohio's Economic Recovery and Future Growth* (School of Public Policy and Management), 256
Iowa State University, 253
Iraq, 57–58
*Ironton Tribune*, 96
Issue 4, 162
Ives Hall, 144

J. Reuben Clark Law School, 13
Jablonski, Sue, 246
Jackson, Jesse, 229, 233
Jackson, Jim, 154, 156
Jackson, Keith, *168*
Jackson, Richard, 20, 30, 38, 274
Jai alai restaurant, 270
Jakeway, Donald, 260

# INDEX

James, Arthur, 61, 302
Japan, 278
Jeffers, Dean, 303
Jennings, Ed, 79; admissions policy, 75–76; and athletics department, 25; and Big Ear, 54; on excellence, 44–45; and Firestone land, 124, 129; and fund raising, 140–41, 143; Huber on, 91; on Hutchinson, 37–38; as interim president, 350; interview by Auburn team, 20; patent policy, 257; on presidential housing, 17; problems inherited by, 82; problems inherited from, 22–23; recruitment of, 6; reputation, 1; on tax repeals, 162; and Tzagournis, 243; and Woody Hayes memorabilia, 154; and Young Scholars Program, 176
Jent, Chris, 157
Jerome Lawrence and Robert E. Lee Theatre Research Institute, 297
Jerome Schottenstein Center, 213, 216, *217*, 221–23
Jesse Owens Memorial Park and Museum, 289
"Jimmy Jam," 172
job description, 10–11
John Deaver Drinko Hall, *101*, 126, 145
John F. Kennedy Assassination Records Review Board, 286
John Glenn Institute for Public Service and Public Policy, 277, 279, 310
Johns Hopkins University, 52, 239, 245
Johnson, Christina, 71
Johnson, Ed, 173
Johnson, Ernest, 202
Johnson, Tom, 164
John W. Berry Sr. Chair in Business, 99
John W. Wolfe Cancer Genetics Laboratory, 303
Jones, Jim, 25, 146–48, 157–58
Jones, Sue, 295
Joseph, Brian, 293
Joukowsky, Artemis A. W., 336
*Journal of Mormon History,* 65
JustUs, 26, 29, 108–10. *See also* Afrikans Committed to Improve Our Nation (ACTION)

Kansas State University, 159
Katchen, Alan, 117
Katz, Barry, 173
Katz, Mark, 173
Kaylor, Dave, 173
Kellogg, Clark, 161, *285*
Kellogg Commission, 174, 280–81
Kellogg Foundation, 201
Kent State University, 80, 266
Kern, C. William, 5, 20, 52, 53
Kerr, Clark, 193
Kessler, Jack, *232;* 15–17; on Cooper's contract, 146; and Firestone land, 125; on Gee's departure for Brown, 337; interview by Auburn team, 20; on Issue 4, 163; on presidential candidates, 14; reputation in Columbus, 339; on search committee, 5–7; on University of California interview, 230, 231
Kessler, Jane, 14, 16
Kibalama, Joseph, 290
Kiecolt-Glaser, Janice, 250
King, Rodney, 111, 114
Kingsdale Shopping Center, 329
Kinnison, William, 75–76; *Building Sullivant's Pyramid,* 75–76
Kirwan, Patricia Harper, 348
Kirwan, William English "Brit," 347–50; departure for University of Maryland, 350; Gee's recommendation of, 345; and Geiger, 213; hiring of, 265; and "pouring rights," 284; and Sisson, 105, 207; on trademark, 299
Kitsmiller, Gary, 143
Klarsfeldt, Bea, 117
Kleberg, John, 29
Klotz, Dorothy, 144
Knight Commission on Intercollegiate Athletics, 25
Knowlton, Austin E. "Dutch," 144
Knowlton School of Architecture, 144, 326
Koenigsknecht, Roy, 20, 238
Koffler, Henry, 52
Kolbert, Stacy, 315
Konstan, David, 337

Koroscik, Judith, 5, 77, 188, 193
"Kosher Karaoke," 172
Kottman, Roy, 37
Kozobarich, Jeri, 346
Kramer, John, 135
Kraus, John D., 54
Krauskopf, Joan, 112
Krebs, Paul, 204
Krueger, Cheryl, 302
Kruzel, Joe, 58
Kucinich, Dennis, 292–93
Kuhn, Albert, 135
Kuhn, Marvin, 220
Kunin, Calvin, 249
Kunz, Eric, 141
Kurtz, Ralph and Helen, 301
Kuwait, 57–58

labor, organized, 163
Labor Education and Research Service, 92
LaLonde, Brent, 319
Lancaster Colony, 306
Lancaster Lens, 306
land-grant movement, 75–76
landlords, absentee, 267
*The Lantern*, 6, 116–17, 167
Large Binocular Telescope (LBT), 50–54, 130, 134
Larkin, Brent, 173, 322
Lashutka, Greg, 30; and arena, 212, 217, 219–20; on underage drinking, 269; and University District, 31, 35, 36
Latinos. *See* Hispanics
Lauray Farms, 124–30
Lavrakas, Paul, 294
law degrees, 12
*Law in Public Education* (Gee and Daniel), 289
Lawrence, Robert E. Lee, 297
Lawson, Wayne, 193
Lazarus, Cindy, 319
League of Women Voters, 163
Lebow, Ned, 238
Leet, Dick, 141
LeFevre, Howard, 208

Leff, Myron, 79
legal counsel, chief, 201–2
Legislative Black Caucus, 179
Lehner, George, 173
Leitzel, Joan, 38
Leland, David, 322
Lemmon, Jack, 292
Leningrad, 200
Lennon, A. Max, 20, 38, 299
Lennox Center, 270
Leno, Jay, 324
Lenz, Donald, 28
Leonard, Lee, 88
Lessels, Doug, 173
Letterman, Doug, 173
Lewellen, Larry, 246
Lewis, David T., 12
Lewis, Richard, 296–97
Liberty Bowl, 146, 155
libraries, 209
Lichtenstein, Dorothy, 209
Lichtenstein, Roy, 205, 209–10
*Life on the Color Line* (Williams), 100
*The Light Around the Dark* (Gee), 10, 11, 64–65
Lima campus, 207
Limited, the, 17, 325, 329
Lincoln, Abraham, 75
Lincoln Tower, 44, 134
linguistics program, 240
Lin, Maya, 205, *206*
Loebs, Steve, 77, 203–4, 241–42
Logan Elm Press, 237
Longaberger, Dave, 307–8
Longaberger, Rachel, 307–8
Longaberger, Tami, 133–34, 307, 337, 346, 347
Longaberger Alumni House, 307–8
Longaberger Company, 307–8
Longaberger Foundation, 307
Lore, Dave, 54, 104–5
Luck, Jim, 312
Lunsford, Andrea, 77, 112
Luper, Carol, 145, 173
luxury boxes, 218, 220, 221
Lynch, Amos, 172

# INDEX

"The M. S. Sofia Chair in Arabic Studies Fund," 301
M. S. Sofia Scholarship and Lecture Memorial Fund, 301
Macon, Charles "Killer," 158–59
Magellan Project, 52
Mager, Jim, 35, 41–42, 44, 281
Magrath, Peter, 19–20, 196–97, 230–31, 233–34, 237
Maine, 55–56
Malloy, Father, 171
mammography unit, mobile, 248
managed health care, 241–44, 249
Managing for the Future Task Force, 79–81, 84, 132–37, 181
Mandalfino, Dominic, 30
Mandela, Nelson, 72, 290
Manila, 229–30
Mansfield campus, 207
Mapplethorpe, Robert, 187
marching band (TBDITL), 82, 145, 292
Marion campus, 207, 311–12
marketing, 42, 175
Marquette University, 31
Marrison, Ben, 66, 152–53, 173, 319, 322
Martin, Phil, 180
Mason, Margaret, 312
Mason, Raymond E. Jr., 312
mass transit, 202–3
Mathematical and Physical Sciences, 97
Max M. Fisher College of Business, 99, 144, 304–6, *305*, 312
May, Jerry, 142–44; and Bill Davis Stadium, 226; departure of, 92; on Firestone land, 126; on fund raising, 125–26, 302, 313; hiring of, 60, 98, 142–43; on public records, 273; on search for Gee's successor, 346
May, Troy, 173
Mayo, Gerald E., 134–35
McCartney, Bill, 25
McConnell, John H., 222
McCorkle, John, 202
McCoy, John and Jeanne, 301
McCue, Gerald, 125
McDonald, Steve, 274
McFerson, Dimon R., 222, 347
McKinsey & Company, 328–29
*McKinsey Report,* 328–30
McSweeney, Paul, 263
media, 169–70
Medical College of Ohio, 243
medical school, 49–50
Medicare, 242
MedOHIO, 248
MedOhio Health, 247
Meek, Violet, 61, 92
Meeks, Jim, 60, 61
Mekhjian, Hagop, 243, 244
Mennonite Economic Development Association, 308
Men's Glee Club, 120, *142,* 144, 145
mental health care, 248
Merget, Astrid, 20
Mermelstein, Mel, 117
Mershon Auditorium, 144–45
Mershon Center, 238, 308
Meshel, Harry, 244
Meyer, John, 143
*Miami Student,* 275
Miami University, 22, 74, 76, 275
Michael Blankenship Hall, 317
Michael Dennis consulting firm, 326
Michael E. Moritz College of Law, 302
Michalec, Ron, 316
Michler, Robert, 250
Midwest Anti-Defamation League, 117
Midwest Economic Conference, 284
Midwestern University Alliance, 253
Midwest University Consortium for International Affairs (MUCIA), 230
Milenthal, David, 166, 220–21, 319
military reservists, 30, 57–58, 156
Miller, Alan, 173, 314, 319
Miller, Ray, 89, 178
Miller, Terry, 257–58, 345
Millet, Alan, 58
Miner, Jack, 346
Minnesota Vikings, 156
Minority Affairs Office, 177
minority issues, 29–30; and administrative restructuring, 23–24,

26–27; budget for, 103; set-aside policy, 178–79; and student recruitment, 134; at University of Texas, 341. *See also* affirmative action; African Americans; Asian Americans; diversity; Hispanics; Native Americans; women
Minority Scholars, 184
Minton, John, 30
mission statement, 77–79, 81
MIT (Massachusetts Institute of Technology), 252–53
*Money* magazine, 294
Montgomery, Betty, 178
Moore, Penny, 173
Moore, William Jr., 5
Mora, Victor, 111
Moriarty, Erin, 144, 145, 167
Moritz, Mike, 302
Mormon faith, 65–68
Morrill, Justin, 75
Morris, Phillip, 173
Moser, Bobby: appointment as vice president and dean, 25, 61; candidacy for president, 337, 346; and College of Agriculture restructuring, 195; and Ohio State University Research Park Corporation, 262; and outreach, 201, 238–39; in South Africa, 71, 290
Mosic, Skip, 65, 66, 167, 173
Mosley-Thompson, Ellen, 316
Mount Carmel Hospital, 246
Mount Graham International Observatory, 50–53, 130, 134
Moyer, Thomas J., 273
Mphande, Lupenga, 290
Ms. Foundation for Women, 206–7
Mueller, Scott, 143
muggings, 33
Murayama, Tomichi, 278
Mussberger, Brent, 153
*My Fellow Americans*, 292

naming opportunities, 283–84, 308
Napier, Bill, 80-81, 243, 282, 323–24, 346
Nardo, Nickole Danielle, 314
National Academy of Engineering, 236

National Academy of Sciences, 236
National Achievement Scholars, 43, 46, 103, 151
National Assembly of the Council for Advancement and Support of Education (CASE), 170
National Association of State Universities and Land-Grant Colleges (NASULGC), 20, 88, 121, 174, 281, 328
National Campaign Executive Committee, 144
National Centers for Excellence in Women's Health, 250
National Comprehensive Cancer Network, 244
National Council for State Legislatures, 88
National Endowment of the Arts (NEA), 187–88
National Governors Association, 88
National Hockey League, 218, 222
National Institutes of Health, 250, 254, 255, 259
National Merit Scholars, 43, 46, 103, 151, 301
National Research Council (NRC), 236–40
National Science Foundation, 104–5, 175, 258
National Task Force on Health Care Reform, 242
Nation of Islam, 183
Nationwide Arena, 218, 222
Native Americans, 176, 185, 281
NBA franchise, 218
NCAA Presidents Commission, 287
NCAA Presidents' Council, 174
NCAA sanctions, 215–16
NCAA tournament games, 157, 217–18, 224–25
Nestor, Harold, 233
New Albany, Ohio, 325
Newark, Ohio, 248
Newark campus, 93, 207–8
Newman, Barbara, 92, 111, 181–82
Newman, Melvin, 284

# INDEX

Newman-Wolfrom Laboratory, 284
*A New Prescription for Women's Health* (Healy), 250
Newsom, Gerald, 53, 77
New York City, 11–12, 173
New York Liberty, 158
Ngidi, Edwin, 290
Nichols, James L., 20, 29, 31, 33, 127, 270
Niciu, Sandra, 316
Nicklaus, Jack, 292
Nike, 283
"The Ninth Woman," 64
Nixon, Corwin, 89
North Central Association of Colleges and Schools, 123, 136, 239
North Pole, 293–94
nurse practitioner program, 207

*Oakland Tribune*, 198
Oates, Jim, 167
O'Brien, Christine, 223
O'Brien, Colleen, 277, 295
O'Brien, Jim, 160, 223–25
Ocasek, Oliver, 244
Office of Business and Administration, 136, 138
Office of Human Resources, 60
Office of International Affairs, 238
Office of Minority Affairs, 185
Office of Student Affairs, 109
Ohio Agricultural and Mechanical College, 74
Ohio Agricultural Research and Development Center (OARDC), 96, 260
Ohio Board of Regents, 132, 136, 176, 272
Ohio Coalition for the Homeless, 204
Ohio Coalition on Sexual Assault, 204
Ohio Cooperative Extension, 201
Ohio Department of Transportation (ODOT), 296
Ohio Ethics Commission, 165
Ohio House Bill 442, 180
Ohio House Bill 492, 165
Ohio House Bill 642, 63
Ohio House Bill 790, 219

Ohio Northern University, 42
Ohio Office of Veterans' Affairs, 60
Ohio Public Records Statute, 272–75
Ohio Science and Technology Council, 260
*Ohio's Education Portfolio 1996* (Inter-University Council of Ohio), 256
Ohio Society of Professional Journalists, 256
Ohio Stadium: renovation, 213, 215, 216, 227–28; smoking ban, 204; soccer in, 219
Ohio State Extension, 201
*An Ohio State of Mind*, 167
Ohio State Radio Network, 153
*The Ohio State University American History Bookshelf*, 205–6
"The Ohio State University Campaign," 140–41
The Ohio State University Center for Survey Research, 294
*The Ohio State University College of Medicine* (Paulson), 202, 244
Ohio State University Foundation (OSUF), 125–26, 272–73, 329
Ohio State University Health Sciences Center, 246
Ohio State University Medical Center, 49, 246–48, 298, 301, 326. *See also* University Hospitals
*The Ohio State University Report to the North Central Association of Colleges and Schools*, 123
Ohio State University Research Park Corporation (RPC), 262
Ohio Supercomputer Center, 284
Ohio Supreme Court, 271–74
"Ohio" trademark dispute, 298–99
Ohio Union, 30
Ohio University, 42, 74, 76, 298
Ohio Wesleyan University, 54–55, 339
Olentangy River, 227
Olentangy River Corridor, 326
Olentangy Wetlands Research Park, *321*
ombudspersons, 286–87
Ong, John W., 125, 279

# Index

on-line courses, 298
Open Housing Coalition, 204
O'Reilly, Patrick, 135
Orr, Bob, 173
Orton, Edward, 74–75
*Other Paper*, 212
outdoor sculpture, 205
outreach, 201, 238–39, 295–96
Owens, James Cleveland "Jesse," 227, 289–90

Pace, Angela, 173
Pace, Orlando, 285
Pacheco, Manuel, 53–54
Papa Joe's Bar, 84, 268–69
Paprocki, Ray, 173
Paquette, Leo, 104–5
Para, Michael, 47, 48–49
Parents Association, 60, 315
Parker, Quinton, 155
Parson, Alayne, 342
patent policy, 257
Patterson, Bill, 169
Patterson, James F., *232*, 235–36, 346, 350
Patton, Joan, 5
Paulson, George, 202, 204, 244, 248
Paul Werth and Associates, 52
Peace Chair program, 308
Peltason, Jack, 198
Penn, Scoonie, 224
Pennsylvania State University, 154, 187, 188, 259, 284
Pepsi, 283–84
Perfect, Kim, 190–91
Perkins, Robert, 47
Perkins Observatory, 55
Persian Gulf War, 57–58, 156
Peterson, Bradley, 77
Peterson, C. A., 135
Petro, Jim, 160
Pew Foundation, 55
Philadelphia 76ers, 160
philanthropists, 301–13
Philbin, Regis, 171
Phillips, Jody, 135
Photography and Cinema, 92

physics program, 240
Pichette, Janet. *See* Ashe, Janet Pichette
Pizzuti, Ron, 219–20
placement tests, 184
plagiarism, 104–5
*A Plan for High Street: Creating a 21st Century Main Street*, 269
planning, 326
Platz, Matthew, 105, 284
Plummer, Jake, 148
Plunkett, Roy, 208
police, university, 113
political science program, 240
Pollard, James E., 74–75
polls, 44–47, 153, 197, 236–37, 294
Poole, Ron, 31
posters, 46–47
post-tenure review, 95
pouring rights. *See* naming opportunities
Powell, Colin, 199
Pratt, Richardson "Jerry," 187
Pratt Institute, 187
pregame brunches, 151–52, 296
Presidents Club, 141
President's Commission on Women, 112
President's Council, 170
Prime Care, 246–47
Pritchett, Henry, 76
*Progress and Priorities*, 103
"Project Reinvent," 201
*Proposals for Change*, 28–29
Protect Our Earth's Treasures (POET), 271
Providence Preservation Society, 267
provost search, 118–19
Pryce, Deborah, 296
psychology program, 240
psychotropic drugs, 248
publications, 289
public policy in the arts program, 188–90
public records, 271–75
public relations, 151–52, 166–67
public service announcement (PSA), 296–97
public universities, 294
Purdue University, 253

quarter system, 39–40
*Quest,* 47, 59, 287–88

racism. *See* diversity
radio station, 288–89
Randall, Alan, 342, 346
rankings, 44–47, 153, 294
Rardin Family Practice Center, 247
Rawlings, Hunter, 332
Rawlins, Dennis, 294
Ray, Edward J. "Ed," 77, 92, 119, 207, 342, 343
Raymond E. Mason Hall, 312
Reagan, Gerald, *134,* 209
Redd, Michael, 224
*Redevelopment Plan for the University Neighborhoods,* 35
"Red Tape Task Force," 133, 181
Reese, Everett, 141, 208, 306
Reese, J. Gilbert "Gib," 207–8
Reeves, Eric, 345
regional campuses, 80–81, 132–33, 207–8
Rehabilitation Act, 106
Reilly, John, 299
Reilly, Karen, 299
reinvestments, 122–23
remedial programs, 184
Renaissance Festival, *192*
reorganizations, 136
Reputation Management, 169
research, 80–81; biomedical, 243; and customer satisfaction, 258–59; federal, 252–55; interdisciplinary, 257; leadership for, 257–58; and managed health care, 249
Research Commission, 259, 263–64
Research Corporation, 53
researchers, 254–55, 271–72, 275
research park, 256–57, 260–63
Research Park Council, 257
Resource Management System (ARMS), 136
responsibility-centered management (RCM), 239
restructuring, 23–27, 195–96, 238–40, 293

retirement age, 93
Revere Land Conservancy, 128
Reynolds, Barbara, 173
Rhoden, William, 158
Rhodes, Frank, 86–87
Rhodes, James A., 82, 244, 318
Rice University, 258
Richard Lewis Archive, 297
Richardson, William "Bill," 253
Riemenschneider, Amy, 77
Ries, Carol, 21, 152
Riffe, Verne, *79*; and arena, 212, 217–20; name recognition, 197; relationship with Gee, 322; on tax increase, 88, 89, 133; on term limits, 163; and Tzagournis, 244
Rightmire, William, 347
Right to Life, 93
Riley, G. Michael, 20, 37, 93, 97–98
Rinehart, Dana, 28
Ripley, Randall "Rip," 92, 238, 288
Rivera, Rhonda, 47
Riverside Methodist Hospital, 245–46
Roads Scholars program, 295–96
Robert F. Wolfe and Edgar T. Wolfe Foundation, 303
Robert Shaw Institute, 237
Robinson, Gary, 173
Roche, Mark, 77
Ronald Reagan Award, 177
Rose Bowl, 148–50, 287
Rosenman, Martin, 216
Rosenthal, Elizabeth, 243
Rosovsky, Henry, 328
Ross, Charles, 101–2
Ross, Elizabeth, 144
Ross, Richard M., 144
Roswell Park Cancer Center, 250
Rotaru, Ronald, 219
ROTC, 108, 312
Roth, Randy, 160
Rowley, Marion, 144
Rudd, Nancy, 5, 92, 95, 135
Rudmann, Sally, 346
Ruffner, Fred, 141
*Rules of the University Faculty,* 102

Rupp, George, 332
Russell, Joe, 26, 38, 61, 109, 110
Russia, 200–201
Ruth, Robert, 34

salary structure, 94–96, 98
*Salem News,* 96
SALT II, 309
Salt Lake City, 191
Sample, Steve, 5
San Carlos Apaches, 51
Sanfilippo, Fred, 251
*San Francisco Chronicle,* 198
Sargas, Edmund, 34
Sasaki consulting firm, 326
SAT scores, 42, 44
Sauder, Erie, 308–9
Sauder, Myrl, 309
Sauder Woodworking, 308
Sawyer, Thomas, 197
Scanlan, Jim, 200
Scanlan, Marilyn, 200
Schiavo, Mary, 296
Schiff, Jack Sr., 292, 313
Schlesinger, Len, 195, 328
Schmidt, Benno, 194–95
Schoenbaum, Alex "Big Boy," 303–4
Schoenbaum Hall, 304
scholarships: and budget cuts, 103; and fund raising, 141; and race, 110, 184; and reallocation of funds, 151; and student recruitment, 43–44, 46–47; for underprivileged students, 176–77
Schooler, David, 6
School of Health, Physical Education and Recreation, 237
School of Journalism, 116, 237–38
School of Medicine, 249
School of Natural Resources, 203
School of Public Health, 249
School of Public Policy and Management, 293
Schottenstein, Geraldine, 223
Schottenstein, Jerome, 222–23
Schottenstein Center. *See* Jerome Schottenstein Center

Schuller, David, 244, 250
Schultz, Jerelyn, 92
Science and Technology Campus, 263
Science and Technology Corporation (STC), 263
Science Village, 263
Scioto Peninsula, 219
Scott, Madison, *24;* on deferred compensation, 94; duties in Gee administration, 26; and private investigation, 21; recommendation involving, 109; on spousal equivalency, 107–8; on veterans' affairs, 59
search committees, 5–7, 345–49
Sears, Susan, *134*
seat licenses, 220, 221
*Securing the Future of Higher Education in Ohio,* 132–33
Seifert, Walter, 118
Seitz, Linda, 143
"selective excellence" programs, 151, 284
semester system, 39–40
Serrano, Andres, 187
set-aside policy, 178–79
SETI (search for extraterrestrial intelligence), 54
"Sexual Assault Guarantee," 113
sexual harassment, 102, 113
Shackelford, Don, 243
Shackelford, Thekla (Teckie), 141, 145, 177
Shapiro, Harold, 331
Sharkey, Mary Ann, 86
Shaw, Robert, 237
Shea, Mary Ann, 71
Sheridan, Mary Ellen, 258
Sherman, Hoyt L., 209–10
Shkurti, William J.: appointment to vice president in finance, 212; on benchmarking, 327; on budget deficit, 97; deanship, 20, 27; education, 293; on Firestone land, 127; on fund raising, 140–41; and media relations, 170; on transition team, 343
Shoemaker, Pamela, 116, 238
Shoney's, 304

INDEX

Shore, Roy, 3
Short North, 33
Short North Posse, 34–35
Showalter, Vera. *See* Gee, Vera
Shumate, Alex, *343;* on admission policy, 41; on domestic partners, 179; on excellence, 45–46; on Gee as politician, 323; on Gee's departure for Brown, 334–39; on Huber, 103; on interim presidency, 341; on *McKinsey Report,* 328; and minority issues, 109, 183; on Mormon faith, 66; on search committee, 5, 6; on search for Gee's successor, 344–46, 348–49; on transition team, 343; on University District, 36; on University of California interview, 230; visit to Kirwan, 265; on Wexner, 327
Sierra Club Defense Fund, 51
Simpson, Greg, 158–59
Singleton, Bob, 173
Sisson, John Richard "Dick," *342;* background, 120; on benchmarks, 259; on budget, 103, 121–23; candidacy at University of Texas, 340–41; candidacy for president, 346–47; on closings and restructuring, 238–40; on Columbus Project, 53; on diversity, 185; on faculty, 349; and fund raising, 143; on Gee's departure for Brown, 337, 338; on Edward Hayes, 265; as interim president, 341–44, 348–49; on Kellogg Commission, 281; on Managing for the Future Task Force, 135–37; on mission statement, 81; as provost, 92, 102, 104–5, 118–20; on public records, 272; and Research Commission report, 263; in University District, 270
Sisson, Septimus, 121
Sisson, Willa, 104, 121, 270, *342*
Sisson Hall, 121
Skestos, George, *232;* on arena, 219–20; on Battelle, 262; on Gee's departure for Brown, 337; on search for Gee's successor, 346; on University District, 36; on University of California interview, 230
Skurow, Evyln, 59
skyboxes, 218, 220, 221
Slane, Dan, 36
Slavic and East European Languages and Literatures program, 292–93
Smith, Bob, 2, 173, *232*
Smith, Dennis, 244
Smith, George C., 275
Smith, George, 78
Smith, Jay, 173
Smith, Katie, 158
Smith, Keith, 65–68, 201
Smith, Ora, 263
Smith, Randy, 343
Smith, Robert, 146, 147, 154, 156
smoking bans, 203–4
Snapp, Steve, 153
soccer, 219, 220
Sofia, Zuheir, 301
Sojourner Truth–Frederick Douglass Society, 183
Solove, Richard, 302–3
Soter, Anna, *134*
South Africa, 71, 290
South Campus, 268–69
South Campus District, 326
Southern Theatre, 219
Soviet Union, 200–201
Soweto, South Africa, 290
Spanier, Graham, 7, 287
speaking skills, 169
Special Events unit, 152
speech writer, 199
Spencer, Gil, 1, 2
Spillman, Russell, 21, 25–27, 109, 110
Spinrad, Phoebe, 59
Spohn, Paul, 173
Spring, Tom, 57
Squire, Sanders & Dempsey, 339
squirrels, 51, 53
Ssejjengo, 290
St. John Arena, 218–19, 223
St. John's University, 156
St. Pierre, Ronald, 49

INDEX

stadia, 215, 216, 220–21, 225–28. *See also* Bill Davis Baseball Stadium; Ohio Stadium
Stanford University, 150, 252, 255
Stanton, Frank, 288–89
State of Ohio Computer Center, 260
state support, 76
Steiner, Curt, 318, 322
stewardship, 125
Stewart, Mac, 61
Stewart, Tom, 173
Stinziano, Mike, 89, 164
Stoddard, Richard, *18,* 21, 253, 258
Stoneridge Medical Center, 248
Stonewall Community Agency, 204
*The Strategic Plan for Research,* 259
Straub, David, 6
Strode, George, 150, 219
Strughold, Hubertus, 177–78
Strum, Shirley, 340
Student Advocacy Office, 315
Student Affairs, 139
*The Student Experience,* 281
Student Health Center, 113
Student Health Insurance Committee, 181
student recruitment: and athletics, 150–51; commitment to, 40–47; and condition of University District, 35; minority, 134; neglect of, 22–23, 31
students: advocacy office for, 315; apathy of, 278; diversity of, 185, 281; international, 276–77, 315; records, 275; treatment of, 133–34, 280–81; underprivileged, 176–77
Students for Domestic Partners, 179
Suddes, Tom, 173
Sugar Bowl, 172, 338, 348
Suhadolnik, Gary, 108
suicides, 315
Sullivan, Mike, 160, 218
Summit County Metro Parks Board, 127, 129
Sundaralingam, Muttaiya, 39
*Surgery Today,* 249
Sweasy, David, 6

Sweeney, Patrick, 220
Sweeney, Thomas L., 20, 258
Syracuse University, 147

Taft, Robert, 86, 293
"Take a Daughter to Work Day," 206–7
"Task Force for the Next Campaign," 141
Tatge, Mark, 32, 173
Tatgenhorst, John, 298
taxes, 85, 87–89, 133, 162–64, 220–21, 334
Taylor, Fred, 157, 292
Teaford, Hamilton "Joel," 5, 6, 51–53, 94, 328
technical colleges, 80–81
technology-enhanced classrooms, 298
Teflon, 208
telescope projects, 50–55
television station, 288–89
Temple University, 31
tenure, 80, 133, 272–75. *See also* post-tenure review
term limits, 163–64
Texas A&M University, 238
Texas Tech University, 155
"Things Done Right" award, 139
*This Week,* 191
Thomas, Dave, 244, 303
Thomas, E. J., 89
Thomas, Linda, 30
Thomas Edison Program, 261
Thompson, Lonnie, 315–16
Thompson, Stan, 77
Thompson, William Oxley, 76, 80
Thurber, James, 208–9
*The Thurber Carnival,* 209
time capsule, 288
Title IX, 106, 154
Tobin, Thomas, 20, 140
*Toledo Blade,* 97, 172, 272
Tom, Linda, 27, 60, 97, 118
Toomey, Beverly, 101–2
Tootle, Barbie, 21, 152, 191, 199–200, 343
Torry, Jack, 167

INDEX

Total Quality Management (TQM), 138–39, 280
track teams, 158
trademark counterfeiting, 275
trademark dispute, 298–99
traffic, 292, 296
Trethewey, Virginia "Ginny," 127, 160, 202, 263, 298
Troy, Dan, 164
tuition cap, 294
Turner, Ken, 159
two-tiered public university system, 80–81
Tzagournis, Manuel: career, 243–44; and Dorothy Wells Davis, 225; on hospital costs, 243; and interview by Auburn team, 20; popularity of, 24; responsibilities of, 238, 246; retirement, 250–51; and U.S. Health, 249

Uganda, 71, 290
Uintah High School, 11
unclassified jobs, 60
Undergraduate Research Forum, 264
United Negro College Fund, 205
United States Armed Forces, 108
United States Department of Education, 275
United States Supreme Court, 12, 106–7, 184–85, 341
United Way, 204–5
University Area Improvement Task Force, 31–32
University Communications Office, 152
University Community Business Association (UCBA), 29, 31
University District, 29, 31–36, 266–70
University Gateway Center, 269, 350
University Hospitals, 241–51; AIDS research at, 48–49; Continuous Quality Improvement in, 136, 139; ranking, 46; and rape victim, 113; smoking ban, 204. *See also* Ohio State University Medical Center
University of Akron, 80
University of Alabama, 148, 245

University of Arizona, 51–53, 130, 259, 264
University of California, 107, 145, 229–34, 325-26
University of California-Berkeley, 264
University of California Los Angeles (UCLA), 118–20, 259, 278
University of Chicago, 51
University of Cincinnati, 80–81, 137, 158, 243
University of Colorado, 2–3; Burns at, 225; deferred compensation at, 94; Elizabeth at, 63; football program, 151, 228; medical center, 244; medical school, 249; nurse practitioner program, 207; ranking, 294; research at, 253
University of Dayton, 275
University of Haifa, 283
University of Illinois, 91, 142, 155, 259
University of Iowa, 155
University of Kentucky, 159
University of Maryland, 94–95, 107, 348–49
University of Michigan: audit of, 253; budgeting at, 239; comparison to, 150; and external funding, 259, 264; faculty, 142; football, 146–49, 155; Huber on, 91; May at, 143; NCAA tournament loss to, 157; state funding of, 137
University of Minnesota, 249, 253, 259, 284
University of Missouri, 253
University of Natal, 290
University of North Carolina, 157, 264, 337–38
University of Notre Dame, 171
University of Oregon, 244
University of Pennsylvania, 31
University of Pittsburgh, 147
University of South Carolina, 159
University of Southern California, 155
University of Tennessee, 148, 172
University of Texas, 107, 244, 259, 264, 340–41
University of Toledo, 42, 272–73

University of Toledo Foundation, 273
University of Utah, 11, 12
University of Vermont, 294
University of Virginia, 294
University of Washington, 259, 264
University of Wisconsin, 91, 142, 253, 259
University Priorities Committee, 95
University Senate, 27, 195
University Technology Services (UNITS), 239
University Wives Club, 171–72
Updike, Phyllis, 71
Upham Hall, 248
U.S. Basketball Writers Association, 156
U.S. Department of Labor, 60
U.S. Fish and Wildlife Service, 51
U.S. Health, 249
*U.S. News and World Report*, 44–47, 153, 194, 294, 306
*U.S. Protectionism and the World Debt Crisis* (Ray), 119
*USA Today*, 173
Uzelak, Eliot, 156, 228

Value City Arena, 216, 220, 222–23
VanBuren, Gus, 29
Vanderbilt University, 153, 214, 234, 350
Van Meter, Don, 263, 348
Vernal, Utah, 4-5, 8–13
Vest, Jim, 331
veterans, 58–61
Veterans' Affairs Office, 59–60
Vickers, Don, 193
Victorian Village, 35
Vietnam Era Veterans' Issues Committee, 59
Vietnam Era Veterans Readjustment Act (1974), 59
Vietnam War, 58–61, 266
Visci, Chip, 173
Vocational Rehabilitation Act (1973), 48
Voinovich, George, *85;* on affirmative action, 178; appointment of Patterson, 235–36; and arena, 217; and Bowl invitations, 165; on education budget, 332–33; on Managing for the Future Task Force, 79, 81, 132; relationship with Gee, 229, 322; on repeal of pop tax, 163; on research, 260; and Tzagournis, 244; on university budget, 82–87, 89
voucher program, 126

Wade, Benjamin, 75
Wahl, Bill, 60, 315
Waldman, Marilyn, 317
Walker, Lee, 135
Wallace, William R., 20
Walton, Rob, 12
Walton, Tom, 173
Wanetik, Ric, 209
Ware, Jane, 173
Warmbrod, James R. "Bob," 20
Washington, D.C., 12–13
*Washington Post*, 173, 348–49
Washington University (St. Louis), 31
Watts, Eugene, 89, 108, 164, 274–75
Way, Douglas, 286
WBNS radio network, 167
Weaver, Leah, 21
Webster, Mary Carran, 116
Wells, Bill, 226
West Campus District, 326
West Virginia University, 13, 19, 151, 159, 228, 249
Wexner, Leslie H., *232,* 325–30; agreement with Gee, 14–15, 325; appointment as trustee, 39; on benchmarks, 91–92, 327; on excellence, 45; on marching band, 292; note to, 336; philanthropy of, 304–5, 329; relationship with Gee, 325, 338–39; on University District, 32, 36, 267; on University of California interview, 230, 231; on Milton Wolf, 309
Wexner Center for the Arts, 92, 205, 316, 325
Wexner Hillel Student Center, 172
Wexner Institute for Pediatric Research at Children's Hospital, 329
Wexner Jewish Student Center, 329

# INDEX

Wexner Prize, 61, 329
wheelchair access, 202
Whetstone River, 227
Whipple, Harry, 173
White, Mike, 293
Whitlock, Scott, 262
*Why Leaders Can't Lead* (Bennis), 280
Wight, Shawn, 315–16
Wilburn, Nate, 159
Wiley, John, 341
Wilkins, William, 249
William H. Davis Medical Research Center, 225
Williams, Catita, 6
Williams, David, 214, *215;* appointment as student affairs vice president, 26; candidacy for president, 346; and hiring of Geiger, 213; and Huber, 97; and Ohio Stadium, 227; on "pouring rights," 283–84; on public records, 275; on release of Ayers, 160; and Sojourner Truth–Frederick Douglass Society, 183; and student satisfaction, 281; on transition team, 343; on trip from New York, 173; on University District, 31, 34, 36
Williams, Gary, 154, 156, 348
Williams, Gregory H., 100
Williams, Michael, 29, 110
Willis, Miechelle, 154
Wilson, Ken, 104
Wilson, Pete, 229, 233
Wilson, Rostamon, 34
Winston, Deborah, 164
WJW-TV, 167
Wobst, Frank, 221
Wolf, Milton, *232;* and "Affirm Thy Friendship" campaign, 145; and Firestone land, 125, 128; on marching band, 292; philanthropy of, 309; relationship with Gee, 339; on University of California interview, 230
Wolf, Roslyn, 309
Wolf, Sam, 309
Wolf, Sylvia, 309
Wolf, Warren, 260

Wolfe, Ann, 72
Wolfe, Harry Preston, 303
Wolfe, John F., 173, 222, 230, 231, 303
Wolfe, John W., 303
Wolford, Kate, 229, 230, 231
Wolfrom, Melville, 284
women, 112–14; in administration, 118–19; attitude toward, 67; commitment to fair treatment of, 181; on faculty, 185; and gender neutral language, 210–11; students, 134, 341. *See also* Women's Grass Roots Network
*Women in Higher Education,* 119
Women's Grass Roots Network, 77, 93, 115, 118–20
Women's Place, 206–7
women's studies, 39
Woods, Jacqueline, 125
Woody Hayes Athletic Center, 304
Wooster, Ohio, 260–61
Works Projects Administration (WPA), 310
World Jewish Congress (WJC), 177–78
World Wide Web, 298
WOSU, 82
Wright, Craig, 274
Wright, Ronald A., 20
Wyatt, Joe B., 350
Wylie, Chalmers, 244, 317

*Xenia Gazette,* 96

*Yale Daily News's Insider's Guide to the Colleges,* 42
Yale University, 194–95
Yeltsin, Boris, 200–201
Young, Willa, 345
Young Scholars Program, 176–77
*Youngstown Vindicator,* 96

Zemsky, Robert, 328
"Zero Defects," 138
Zimmers, Neal, 164
Zimpher, Nancy, 92, 107, *134,* 238, 299, 346

www.ingramcontent.com/pod-product-compliance
Lightning Source LLC
Chambersburg PA
CBHW030125240426
43672CB00005B/24